GST and E-Commerce:
Planning and Risk Management

a Wolters Kluwer business

Brent Jay, B.Comm., LL.B.

CCH Canadian Limited
300-90 Sheppard Avenue East
Toronto Ontario
M2N 6X1
1 800 268 4522

Published by CCH Canadian Limited

Important Disclaimer: This publication is sold with the understanding that (1) the authors and editors are not responsible for the results of any actions taken on the basis of information in this work, nor for any errors or omissions; and (2) the publisher is not engaged in rendering legal, accounting or other professional services. The publisher, and the authors and editors, expressly disclaim all and any liability to any person, whether a purchaser of this publication or not, in respect of anything and of the consequences of anything done or omitted to be done by any such person in reliance, whether whole or partial, upon the whole or any part of the contents of this publication. If legal advice or other expert assistance is required, the services of a competent professional person should be sought.

Library and Archives Canada Cataloguing in Publication

Jay, Brent
    GST and e-commerce: planning and risk management / Brent Jay.

ISBN 1-55367-675-0

1. Goods and services tax — Canada. 2. Electronic commerce — Taxation — Canada. 3. Goods and services tax — Law and legislation — Canada. 4. Electronic commerce — Taxation — Law and legislation — Canada. I. CCH Canadian Limited II. Title

HJ5715.C2J39 2006   343.7105′52   C2006-904669-7

Typeset by CCH Canadian Limited.
Printed in the United States of America.

Acknowledgements

I would like to acknowledge a number of individuals without whom this book could not have been written. This truly has been a team effort.

First, I would like to acknowledge the many professionals at CCH who have been central to bringing this book forward. Robin Mackie, Natasha Menon, Ian More and Jerry D'Souza in particular have contributed immeasurably to this project. However, Natasha is deserving of special recognition for the countless hours which she has committed to quarterbacking every element of this process and for her considerable patience and fortitude throughout.

I would also like to thank my father, Tim Jay for the very significant contributions which he has made to this project. From the earliest days he has very actively and unselfishly lent his assistance on issues ranging from general conceptual and legal matters through to the application of linguistic and grammatical conventions.

Finally, and most importantly I would be remiss if I did not thank my wife Christina for her support and assistance throughout this complex process. Christina fully supported this project from its earliest days notwithstanding the time and resources required to see it through to fruition. This unwavering support has been absolutely invaluable.

Brent Jay

TABLE OF CONTENTS

Chapter 1

Overview of the Book and Evolution of E-Commerce GST Rules

A. OVERVIEW OF THE BOOK

The objective of this book is to provide a comprehensive description of the manner in which the Canadian goods and services tax applies to e-commerce activities.

Perhaps the best way to describe the scope of this book is to provide a definition of the term "e-commerce". The Canada Revenue Agency ("CRA"), in its initial e-commerce public discussion paper,[1] defined this broad, ethereal concept in the following manner:

> Electronic commerce can simply be defined as conducting business with the assistance of telecommunications and telecommunications-based tools. It includes transactions that take place by telephone, facsimile, automated banking machine, television shopping, secure private networks (electronic data interchange) and by Internet with payment made by credit card, debit card or similar means. For purposes of this paper, references made to "electronic commerce" are meant to include only supplies made over the Internet.

The CRA has, for the most part limited its consideration of e-commerce strictly to activities conducted through the Internet. This book, however, has adopted a much broader approach which includes discussions of a number of issues which are tangential to e-commerce. These discussions are intended to provide practical guidance for businesses which operate exclusively in the e-commerce environment, as well as for businesses which engage in e-commerce activities as a means of supporting, or enhancing, one or more other lines of business.

B. SPECIAL E-COMMERCE CHALLENGES

The GST has proven to be a tax which at times may be difficult to apply to more elaborate, or novel, business transactions. These complexities are evidenced in particular by the substantial body of jurisprudence[2] which has developed under the *Excise Tax Act* ("ETA"), and by the CRA's issuance of thousands of pages of interpretive reference materials. These materials include rulings, policy statements, memoranda, technical information bulletins, and other administrative documents.

Applying the GST to e-commerce activities presents a range of special challenges. This is because e-commerce activities by their very nature are typically very innovative and elaborate. The complications may also be exacerbated by the following:

---

[1] Discussion Paper: GST/HST and Electronic Commerce, dated November 2001.

[2] In excess of 1,000 court cases have now been decided under the GST portion of the *Excise Tax Act* (Canada).

(a) Bundled (or complex) supplies are very common in the e-commerce environment. For example, services are often supplied with intangible personal property.

(b) The place of supply rules which apply to e-commerce activities are very broad.

(c) Agents are very commonly used to deliver supplies in the e-commerce environment.

(d) E-commerce supplies will always involve a telecommunications element. Telecommunication services are subject to a number of special rules.

(e) Complex jurisdictional issues frequently arise in the e-commerce environment. The manner in which these items are resolved will, in part be a function of the risk of tax leakage. For example, suppliers located anywhere in the world may use the Internet to make sales in Canada in circumstances where the supplier may not be required to collect GST. This issue will typically arise where the supplier is not GST registered and has little or no presence in Canada.

The following examples are provided to illustrate the unique challenges associated with applying the GST to e-commerce activities. In the first of the two examples, the ETA place of supply rules are applied to a sale of ordinary consumer goods. The first example demonstrates that the application of the place of supply rules to ordinary goods is relatively straightforward. The second example describes how the place of supply rules apply to a transaction involving software. In the second example, a number of preliminary issues must be resolved before the place of supply rules may be applied. This latter example demonstrates the special complexities which are typically associated with resolving even the most fundamental e-commerce issues.

Example 1: Trade in Goods

A Canadian resident supplier sells home appliances to customers located both in Canada and in the United States.

Where the appliances are delivered or made available to a customer at a location in Canada, they will be deemed to be supplied in Canada and will be subject to Division II GST. The reference to "delivered or made available" is a reference to the location where possession of the goods is transferred to the recipient.

Where the appliances are delivered or made available to a customer at a location outside Canada, they will be deemed to be supplied outside Canada and will not be subject to Division II GST.

The "delivered or made available" test is the relevant test which will always be applied to the appliances because they are considered to be tangible personal property.

Example 2: Trade in E-Commerce

A Canadian resident supplies software to customers located both in Canada and in the United States.

The software may be considered to be a supply of a service, tangible personal property, or intangible personal property.

The characterization of the software will require that a number of factors be taken into account including the manner by which it is delivered to the customer and the nature of the rights provided to the customer.

It is only once the software has been characterized that the appropriate place of supply rules may be applied.

C. POLICY CONSIDERATIONS

Policy considerations are always central in resolving GST e-commerce issues. This has been openly acknowledged by the CRA. For example, in its original electronic commerce discussion paper, the CRA noted that the following taxation principles[3] will be very significant in determining the manner in which the GST will apply to both e-commerce and more traditional forms of commerce:

(a) Neutrality

(b) Efficiency

(c) Certainty and simplicity

(d) Effectiveness and fairness

(e) Flexibility

The principles of neutrality, effectiveness and fairness, are perhaps the most significant of these tax considerations in the e-commerce environment. With respect to neutrality, the CRA's discussion paper specifically noted that:

> Taxation should seek to be neutral and equitable between different forms of electronic commerce and between conventional and electronic forms of commerce. Business decisions should be motivated by economic rather than tax considerations. Taxpayers in similar situations carrying out similar transactions should be subject to similar levels of taxation.

---

[3] Agreed to by the CRA and a number of other taxation authorities at the OECD Ministerial Conference held in Ottawa in October 1998.

Similarly, with respect to effectiveness and fairness, the CRA noted that:

> Taxation should produce the right amount of tax at the right time. The potential for tax avoidance should be minimized, while keeping counter-acting measures proportionate to the risks involved.

References are made throughout this book to the CRA's leading GST policy objectives: minimizing opportunities for persons to engage in activities which may result in tax leakage and ensuring that suppliers (including non-resident suppliers) are subjected to a "level playing field" in connection with the application of the GST.

The activities which present the greatest challenge to these policy objectives typically involve non-resident persons or activities carried on only partially in Canada. It follows that the primary means by which the CRA minimizes these threats is through the application of the rules which "connect" non-resident persons to Canada. These connection rules include the "carrying on business in Canada" test, the "permanent establishment in Canada" test, and the non-resident registration requirements. Policy considerations will also commonly manifest in the manner in which supplies are characterized and in the circumstances in which the non-resident override and zero-rating relief is available.

These concerns should be carefully considered by any person (and in particular a non-resident person) who transacts business in a manner which might offend against these policy objectives. The CRA has provided the clearest of signals that the technical rules contained in the ETA should never be applied in a wooden or mechanical manner to e-commerce activities.

D. EVOLUTION OF E-COMMERCE GST RULES

1. Absence of Subject Matter-Specific Provisions

The subsequent chapters of this book describe the manner in which specific ETA provisions apply to e-commerce transactions. However, a full understanding of the manner in which the GST applies to e-commerce activities requires that the background to the current regime be considered.

When it was introduced in 1991, Part IX of the *Excise Tax Act* contained no provisions relating specifically to e-commerce products or services. This should not be surprising, given that at that time the Internet was obscure, largely undeveloped, and in no way resembled what is in use today.

However, even today, after years of exponential growth in e-commerce activities, the ETA and corresponding regulations still contain very few e-commerce specific provisions. To many, the absence of specific taxing provisions in relation to such an important area of commerce appears to be anomalous. In fact, this general approach is consistent with the overall manner in which the ETA has been developed from its earliest days. In developing the ETA, the federal Department of Finance made a conscious decision to create a regime which would avoid, where possible, the establishment of specific subject matter rules. Instead, the approach which has been adopted involves general provisions which are intended to apply to a wide range of existing and new property or service offerings. This general approach ensures that the tax applies to an extremely wide base of property and services without the requirement for frequent updates or amendments.

This flexible approach is evidenced, for example, in the manner in which the very important "carrying on business" test has been established. The ETA contains several critical provisions which turn on the issue of whether a person is carrying on business (and in some cases, whether it is carrying on business in Canada). The ETA, however, does not define the terms "carrying on business" or "carrying on business in Canada".[4] Accordingly, the meaning of these terms will be ascertained by reference to the common law. This approach allows the scope of the terms to evolve as new business methodologies develop.[5]

2. Comparison to Provincial Approach

The approach adopted by the federal government with respect to the taxation of e-commerce offerings stands in stark contrast to the approach adopted by many of the Canadian provinces. Provincial retail sales tax legislation is typically drafted in a manner which places far more emphasis on subject matter rules.[6] Given the considerable importance of subject matter rules under those provincial sales tax regimes, the application of tax to e-commerce transactions has typically required that specific legislative amendments be made.

The following example is intended to illustrate a typical difference between the federal and provincial approaches. The broad and inclusive definition of "service" contained in the ETA should be contrasted with the more specific and restrictive definition which is provided in the *Retail Sales Tax Act* (Ontario):

---

[4] However, in certain circumstances a person will be deemed to be carrying on business in Canada.

[5] The corresponding term "business" is defined, but in a manner which does not preclude the operation of the common law.

[6] The most prominent exception relates to the retail sales tax which is levied in Quebec under the *Act in Respect of the Quebec Sales Tax*. This legislation is similar in structure to the *Excise Tax Act*.

Excise Tax Act

"Service" means anything other than

(*a*) property

(*b*) money; and

(*c*) anything that is supplied to an employer by a person who is or agrees to become an employee ...

Retail Sales Tax Act (**Ontario**)

"taxable service" means

(*a*) telecommunications services ...

(*b*) transient accommodation

(*c*) labour provided to install, assemble, dismantle, adjust, repair or maintain tangible personal property other than a computer program

(*c*.1) labour provided to install, configure, modify or upgrade a computer program ...

(*d*) any contract for the service, maintenance or warranty of tangible personal property other than a computer program ...

E. ADEQUACY OF THE GENERAL APPROACH

Notwithstanding that the ETA had been specifically designed to accommodate the taxation of new products or services, the emergence of e-commerce offerings throughout the 1990s called the adequacy of the existing approach into question. Many wondered whether the ETA in its existing form would continue to be sufficient, given that the new e-commerce offerings were so fundamentally different than existing products or services, and given that the means by which the offerings were provided were also so radically different.

In particular, the Internet provided non-resident suppliers with a completely unprecedented (and perhaps unexpected) means by which revenues could be earned in Canada without any corresponding presence in Canada. The suggestion was that new taxing provisions might be required to be introduced in connection with e-commerce activities.

The federal Department of Finance and the Canada Revenue Agency[7] considered these issues in detail throughout the late 1990s as well as the various options. Ultimately, it was determined that the existing legislative framework would in fact be sufficient (subject to minor legislative and regulatory changes) for the purpose of taxing e-commerce products and services. It now appears safe to say that major legislative changes relating to e-commerce activities will not likely be introduced into the ETA.

However, notwithstanding that only minimal legislative changes were made, other major e-commerce changes did in fact occur, including the following:

(a) the CRA made a substantial commitment to more closely examine and better understand e-commerce businesses and transactions. These measures included forming an Advisory Committee on Electronic Commerce, and later the Electronic Commerce Technical Advisory Group on Consumption Taxes;

(b) the CRA committed to the development of a comprehensive GST e-commerce position paper. This culminated in the July 2002 release of Technical Information Bulletin B-090, "GST/HST and Electronic Commerce" ("TIB 090");

(c) formal headquarters rulings in relation to e-commerce activities began to be issued by a newly formed electronic commerce unit staffed by senior CRA employees with a high level of subject matter expertise;

(d) the CRA substantially revised two of its leading jurisdictional policy statements to include, among other things, new references to e-commerce activities. Policy Statement P-208R, "Meaning of Permanent Establishment in subsection 123(1) of the *Excise Tax Act* (the Act)" was released in revised format on March 23, 2005. Policy Statement P-051R2, "Carrying on Business in Canada" was released in revised format on April 29, 2005; and

(e) following the release of the revised "Permanent Establishment" and "Carrying on Business in Canada" policy statements, the CRA stepped up its monitoring and enforcement activities, particularly in relation to e-commerce jurisdictional issues.

The release of TIB 090 was particularly important because this document provided comprehensive guidance on a wide range of leading

---

[7] The federal Department of Finance and the Canada Revenue Agency are charged with corresponding responsibilities in connection with the GST. The federal Department of Finance is responsible for the development and evaluation of GST policies and legislation. The actual collection of taxes and interpretation of tax law are the responsibility of the Canada Revenue Agency.

e-commerce issues. Even today this document remains the CRA's leading position paper with respect to GST and e-commerce. However, notwithstanding the importance of TIB 090 its limitations became apparent immediately following its release. As a practical matter, no single document could possibly provide direction with respect to every conceivable GST e-commerce issue. As e-commerce methodologies continue to grow more elaborate, this particular limitation has become even more apparent.

However, in addition to providing important direction on a number of leading GST issues, TIB 090 also appears to have achieved another important objective: the bulletin raised awareness levels in the business community, both with respect to the need to engage in e-commerce GST planning and with respect to the many complexities associated with applying the GST to e-commerce activities.

This heightened awareness was evidenced by the massive proliferation in ruling and interpretation letter requests filed with the CRA following the release of TIB 090. In the six months following its release, more than 30 e-commerce related headquarters rulings and interpretation letters were issued.[8]

F. PRACTICAL IMPACT OF THE CURRENT APPROACH

1. General Issues

The practical impact of the general and flexible approach which has been adopted is that the GST will apply in a principled manner to a wide range of offerings, including new product and service offerings. This approach is particularly effective in ensuring that the tax base remains broad and consistent.

However, this general and flexible approach should also be expected to result in more interpretation difficulties for persons engaged in e-commerce activities. For example, to determine the manner in which the GST applies to a particular person or transaction will require that a number of general ETA provisions be identified and applied. The CRA's administrative policies and general principles of common law should be expected to impact very substantially upon the manner in which these general provisions are interpreted.

The following is a list of some of the issues which a non-resident person would typically be required to consider when making a simple e-commerce sale to a Canadian person:

---

[8] Presumably the regional tax services offices across Canada would also have been issuing additional ruling and interpretation letters in relation to e-commerce issues during this period.

1. What is the nature of the supply (i.e., intangible personal property, a general service or a telecommunication service)?

2. Is the supply a taxable supply (or is it exempt)?

3. Is the supply a taxable but zero-rated supply?

4. If the supply is a taxable supply, is it considered to be supplied in Canada?

5. If the taxable supply is made in Canada, what is the rate at which the tax will apply (this will call for a determination of the province of supply)?

6. If the supply is a taxable supply made in Canada, does the non-resident override apply to deem the supply to be made outside Canada?

7. Is the non-resident a person who is required to register for GST, in order to collect the tax (i.e., is the person deemed resident in Canada, or is it carrying on business in Canada)?

8. If the non-resident is a person who is not required to register for GST purposes, should the non-resident consider registering on a voluntary basis?

In addition to the difficulties associated with issue identification, the resolution of the issues can be daunting, particularly where more elaborate, unique, or complex offerings are provided, where multiple product or service lines are offered, or where agents are involved in the supply chain.

Another problem which is associated with the current regime relates to compounding of errors. Where errors are made with respect to threshold issues (including, for example, the registration requirement), it should be expected that corresponding errors will be made with respect to the resolution of secondary issues.

2. Exposure Risks

It is not uncommon for e-commerce suppliers to underestimate their GST exposure risks. For example, it is not uncommon for suppliers to assume that, given the "flow through" nature of GST, any GST discrepancies will be easily repaired once identified on audit. Unfortunately, this assumption is generally incorrect. The following two examples illustrate how typical e-commerce activities may lead to considerable exposure:

Example 1: Non-Resident Supplier

A non-resident corporation supplies users with the right to interact with online digitized products which are offered through its Web site.

The non-resident accepts payment from Canadian customers in Canada, maintains a bank account in Canada, and advertises in Canadian newspapers.

The non-resident is not registered and does not collect GST from any of its customers.

On audit, it is determined that the non-resident was in fact carrying on business in Canada and did not qualify as a small supplier.

The following GST results flow from the conclusion that the non-resident was carrying on business in Canada:

(a) The non-resident was required to have been registered for GST purposes;

(b) The non-resident was required to collect, report and remit the GST in respect of supplies provided to Canadian customers; and

(c) The non-resident was required to collect, report and remit the GST in respect of supplies provided to non-resident customers (except if the non-resident can prove that it specifically prohibited the customer from using the products from any location in Canada).[9]

On audit, the CRA would require that the non-resident supplier remit the GST which should have been collected (plus interest and penalties) in respect of any supplies deemed made in Canada. The supplier would be free to attempt to collect the GST from the customers. However, the supplier's obligation to remit this amount to the CRA would not be contingent upon its collection success.

Example 2: Canadian Supplier

A Canadian GST registered entity which operates from offices located in Nova Scotia provides a customer with the right to interact with its educational software while the customer is online.

The relevant contract does not restrict the location where the customer may access the software. However, it is assumed that the non-resident customer would likely interact with the software from a home computer.

Where the customer is a non-resident, the supplier neither charges nor collects GST.

The right to interact with software online is considered to be a supply of intangible personal property. The property is deemed to be supplied in any

---

[9] See Chapter 17, Internet Courses, Electronic Books, and Other Educational Offerings, for a detailed discussion of these issues.

location where it may be used (meaning "allowed to be used"). Given that there are no restrictions as to the place of use, the supply will be deemed to be made in Canada.

Further, given that the supply is deemed to be made in a participating province[10] and that zero-rating is not available in respect of this type of supply, the applicable rate of tax will be 14%.

On audit, the CRA would require that the Canadian GST-registered supplier remit the GST which should have been collected (plus interest and penalties) in respect of the supply made to the non-resident customer. The supplier would be free to attempt to collect the GST which was attributable to the supply from the customer. However, the supplier's obligation to remit this amount to the CRA would not be contingent upon its collection success.

G. APPROACH OF THIS BOOK

This book is divided into two general parts. Part One discusses the leading threshold issues which should be considered and resolved in any e-commerce situation. Many of these issues will relate to legislative provisions and principles of common law which are not at all e-commerce specific. The focus throughout the chapters in Part One is upon the structure and policy considerations which drive all GST decision making.

Part Two considers specific e-commerce issues from a subject matter perspective. Chapter 11 introduces the Part Two chapters. Chapters 12 through 17 discuss the tax implications of various groupings of offerings, with guidance and discussion in the form of headquarters rulings and interpretation letters. These chapters also discuss issues which have not yet been specifically contemplated in publicly available CRA documents. Chapter 18 focuses upon the unique GST issues associated with supplying e-commerce offerings to Indians, Indian Bands, and Band Empowered Entities.

In some of the Part Two chapters, a seemingly wide range of product and service offerings are discussed. This approach has been adopted to allow for comparisons and distinctions to be made between different types of offerings. This broad approach to grouping products and services is also intended to "draw out" and identify trends in the CRA's approach.

---

[10] This is because the place of negotiation is in a participating province and the supply may be used otherwise than exclusively outside the province.

H. LIMITATIONS OF THIS BOOK

Throughout this book, every effort has been made to describe the manner in which the GST relates to e-commerce activities by reference to specific legislative and regulatory provisions. However, as noted above, the legislative provisions contained in the ETA are for the most part not e-commerce specific. Accordingly, this book attempts to reconcile specific e-commerce factual situations to more general legislative provisions. Uncertain results are an inevitable product of this type of approach.

Generally, in attempting to interpret particular legislative tax provisions two of the more common means by which issues of ambiguity may be resolved are by reference to:

(a) explanatory notes issued by the Department of Finance; or

(b) the common law treatment of the particular provision.

Unfortunately, given that any potentially relevant legislative provisions were for the most part enacted long before e-commerce gained any prominence, and given that the provisions are not e-commerce specific, the explanatory notes will typically be of little value in resolving e-commerce ambiguity issues.

A substantial body of case law (jurisprudence) has developed in connection with issues relating to carrying on business in a particular jurisdiction, the location of permanent establishments, and the meaning and scope of agency. However, very little jurisprudence exists with respect to other more secondary issues.

Accordingly, by default the primary source of guidance in interpreting ambiguous provisions becomes administrative policies and guidelines issued by the CRA. This guidance comes in the form of interpretation letters, rulings, and more formalized policy papers (such as TIB 090). The limitations and dangers associated with relying extensively upon administrative policies and related documents are discussed in Chapter 11, Introduction to the Rulings Chapters.

Chapter 2

Overview of the GST

A. OVERVIEW

As discussed in Chapter 1, the ETA contains very few e-commerce specific provisions. Accordingly, the determination of the manner in which the GST applies to any given transaction will typically involve the application of a wide range of general ETA provisions. The effective resolution of GST e-commerce issues will also require that jurisprudence which has been decided under the ETA,[1] and administrative policies issued by the CRA (which may or may not be e-commerce specific), also be taken into account.

Given that the GST rules, which apply to a particular matter, may be located anywhere within the ETA or corresponding regulations,[2] the primary and most difficult challenge will be the identification of the legislative provisions which might potentially apply. With this challenge in mind, the focus of this chapter is upon providing an overview of the structure and operation of the ETA as a whole. Methodologies for resolving the leading e-commerce issues are discussed in subsequent chapters.

This chapter also discusses some of the primary policy considerations which underly the interpretation of the ETA. The development of an understanding of the policy considerations is important for interpreting and reconciling vague ETA (or regulatory) provisions. Further, understanding the policies behind the ETA will assist in confirming whether a potentially relevant provision has been "missed" in the course of the research process. For example, where research has been performed which appears to allow for a "windfall opportunity", policy considerations will suggest that the research is flawed.

B. FUNDAMENTAL GST POLICY CONSIDERATIONS

1. Overview of GST

The ETA was designed to result in the application of GST to the consumption in Canada of a wide range of property and services. Intangible personal property is among the types of property which is typically subject to GST when consumed. The GST was not intended to result in the taxation of consumption which occurs outside Canada.

Although most property and services consumed in Canada will be subject to GST, some supplies may not be subject to GST because they are

---

[1] Generally, the relevant jurisprudence will be in the form of decisions of the Tax Court of Canada.

[2] More than 40 separate sets of regulations have been promulgated under the ETA.

exempt or because they are zero-rated.[3] Some of the supplies which benefit from the special tax treatment described above are groceries, specified medical supplies and services, specified financial services, and certain offerings when supplied by public service bodies (such as registered charities).

Generally, e-commerce supplies are not eligible for any such special relief. Accordingly, this book does not discuss any supplies which may be made on an exempt basis. Similarly, the only form of zero-rating relief which is discussed in this book is in connection with exported supplies.

2. Leading Policy Considerations

The CRA's paramount GST policy consideration is the minimization of the risk of "tax leakage". Accordingly, where a particular method of conducting business might result in leakage, it should be expected that this activity will be closely scrutinized by the CRA.

The primary source of GST leakage has always related to inter-jurisdictional activities. The federal Department of Finance and the CRA regularly monitor cross-border transactions to ensure that the ETA adequately minimizes this tax leakage risk. To the extent that the existing regime may be insufficient to minimize this risk in connection with particular activities, legislative amendments are made and/or administrative policies are revised.

Among the most closely monitored activities are those of non-resident suppliers who sell property or services to Canadians through the Internet. This is because, apart from e-commerce, there are very few other opportunities for suppliers outside Canada to regularly make sales to Canadians without the establishment of some form of presence in Canada. This particular concern with tax leakage is apparent throughout the CRA's leading administrative position paper, Technical Information Bulletin B-090, GST/HST and Electronic Commerce ("TIB 090"). This concern is also apparent in the e-commerce rulings which have been issued to date.

A second leading policy consideration which is particularly important in the e-commerce setting, should also be noted. In administering tax laws the CRA is responsible for ensuring that taxes apply in a fair and consistent manner, particularly with respect to similarly situated persons. A serious discrepancy will have occurred where a non-resident person may make supplies in Canada which are not subject to GST but at the same time, a Canadian supplier (or a non-resident supplier who is registered) is required to collect GST in relation to similar supplies. The CRA actively monitors and takes steps to ensure that a "level playing field" is provided.

---

[3] Zero-rated supplies technically are subject to GST, but at the nominal rate of 0%.

Enforcement measures which are implemented in connection with the policy imperatives described above will, in some cases, result in unintended or undesirable consequences. Although the CRA makes every effort to ensure that its anti-avoidance measures are proportionate to the particular risk, it is inevitable that there will be circumstances when the anti-avoidance measures will have secondary consequences. For example, in order to prevent or minimize a particular form of leakage, provisions may be introduced (or policies administered) which would result in the tax applying in an overly aggressive manner to other transactions that are not in any way offensive or avoidance related. This issue arises quite frequently in the e-commerce context.

To illustrate this issue, consider the supply of intangible personal property to a non-resident. The ETA is not intended to apply to consumption which occurs outside Canada. Accordingly, the ETA contains a number of zero-rating provisions which allow for property or services to be supplied to non-residents without attracting any GST. However, the circumstances in which intangible personal property may be supplied to a non-resident on a zero-rated basis are relatively narrow. As a result of this narrow relief opportunity, many supplies of intangible personal property made by way of the Internet to non-resident persons will be fully subject to GST. This issue is discussed in detail in Chapter 6, Zero-rating.

Fortunately, anomalous situations like the one described above are the exception. Although a wide range of GST relief opportunities are available in respect of e-commerce supplies, in many cases some tax planning will be required in order to take advantage of the opportunities. Consider again the example set out above which relates to the limited circumstances in which zero-rating relief is available when intangible personal property is supplied to a non-resident. Notwithstanding the limited availability of zero-rating relief, the GST need not apply to this supply. This is because it is relatively simple to ensure that the supply is considered to be made outside Canada and thus not subject to GST. The manner in which this type of tax planning is to be accomplished is described in Chapter 5, Place of Supply.

C. STRUCTURE OF THE ETA

The ETA has been organized into the following 12 distinct divisions:

- Division I contains general provisions and definitions;

- Division II contains the provisions relating to the Division II GST levied on consumption in Canada;

- Division III contains the provisions relating to the Division III GST levied on goods imported into Canada;

- Division IV contains the provisions relating to the Division IV GST levied on certain imported taxable supplies;

- Division IV.1 contains the provisions relating to the Division IV.1 GST levied on property and services brought into a participating province;

- Division V contains the provisions which relate to the reporting, collection and remittance of the Division II GST;

- Division VI contains the rebate provisions;

- Division VII contains a number of miscellaneous provisions;

- Division VIII contains administrative and enforcement provisions;

- Divisions IX and X contain transitional provisions; and

- Division XI contains tax inclusive pricing provisions.

The ETA also contains a number of schedules. For the purposes of this book, the most important of those schedules are:

- Schedule V: Exempt Supplies;

- Schedule VI: Zero-rated Supplies; and

- Schedule IX: Province of Supply.

The ETA is unique in that it allows for the GST to be levied under any of Division II, Division III, Division IV or Division IV.1. Each of these divisions operates independently, and as a result, it is not uncommon for more than one type of GST to apply to the same transaction. This means that for any particular e-commerce event, the GST levied under each of the Divisions should be separately considered.

The following is an example of a common situation in which more than one form of GST will apply to a single transaction:

Example

A GST registered, non-resident supplier sells goods to a Canadian customer.

The goods will be delivered to the customer's facility in Canada.

The non-resident vendor will be required to collect the Division II GST from the Canadian customer. This is because the supply is considered to be made in Canada.

The person who imports the goods into Canada (either the supplier or the recipient) would in addition be required to pay Division III GST to the Canada Border Services Agency at the time of importation. The Division III GST will apply even if the goods qualify as originating under NAFTA.

Although on occasion more than one type of GST may apply to a particular sale, the divisions have been designed to dovetail with each other. This means that where the GST which is levied under a particular division does not apply to a transaction, the GST levied under a different division may apply to that same transaction. The following example illustrates this dovetailing effect:

Example

A non-resident vendor provides a taxable service to a Canadian individual customer. The customer will enjoy the benefit of the service in Canada.

If the non-resident vendor is GST registered and is considered to supply the service in Canada, the Division II GST will apply to the supply.

If the non-resident vendor is deemed to supply the service outside Canada, the Division II GST would not apply. However, this does not mean that GST would not apply to this transaction. The individual customer would be required to self-assess the GST owing in respect of the consumption of the service under Division IV.

The following is a summary overview of the operation of Divisions II, III, IV, and IV.1. The operation of these divisions in connection with e-commerce transactions will also be considered in the subsequent chapters. Given that most e-commerce transactions do not involve any shipments of goods, the focus throughout the remainder of this book will be upon describing the manner in which the GST applies to transactions involving intangible personal property or services.[4]

D. DIVISION II GST

1. General Issues

Most references to the GST are in fact a reference to the Division II GST. This is because it is the most commonly applied and most visible form of GST.

Division II GST applies to virtually every supply of property (including intangible personal property) or services considered to be made in Canada.

---

[4] The most notable exception to this general approach is contained in Chapter 17, Internet Courses, Electronic Books, and Other Educational Offerings, where issues relating to the sale of textbooks are considered.

The ETA contains specific rules for determining whether any given supply is considered to be made in Canada. These rules are commonly referred to as the "place of supply rules" and are described in detail in Chapter 5, Place of Supply. For example, services are typically considered to be supplied in Canada if the service is performed in whole or in part in Canada. Tangible personal property is considered to be supplied in Canada where the property is delivered or made available to the recipient of the supply in Canada.

Division II GST applies at every level of the supply chain including with respect to business-to-business transactions. This will include, for example, sales made by manufacturers and by wholesalers. Only those who are registered (and who make subsequent taxable supplies) will be entitled to claim input tax credits ("ITCs") to recover the GST expense which they have incurred.[5] The levying of GST at all levels of the supply chain encourages all businesses to become GST registered. This inclusive approach minimizes the potential for tax leakage.

In order to avoid tax cascading (i.e., the embedding of the GST in the price of a product or service over and above the GST which is specifically charged, most GST expenses incurred by purchasers, which are related to the making of a subsequent taxable supply, will be fully recoverable by way of ITC. ITCs are claimed from the CRA in the registrant's GST returns which are typically filed on a monthly or quarterly basis.

Those who are not GST registered, and who incur GST expenses to purchase goods or services, are not entitled to claim input tax credits in respect of the expenses incurred. Typically, it is the consumer who will not be entitled to recover any ITCs. However, non-residents who do not become GST registered may also incur GST expenses which are not eligible for recovery.

Where a GST registered supplier makes a supply which is subject to Division II GST, the supplier is responsible for collecting the tax from the purchaser (referred to in the ETA as the "recipient") of the supply. The amount of GST owing is calculated based upon the consideration which is attributable to the supply. It should be noted that the recipient will not necessarily be the person who enjoys the benefit of the supply. For example, if a service benefits Corporation A, but related Corporation B is invoiced for the service, Corporation B will be considered the recipient of the supply.

The applicable rate of tax for taxable supplies (i.e., supplies which are not exempt supplies) made in Canada is a function of the following:

---

[5] Technically, a person who is a "registrant" (i.e., a person who is required to be registered) is also entitled to claim ITCs. However, as a practical matter the person will need to be registered in order to file the claim.

(a) If the supply is zero-rated, the tax will apply at the rate of 0%. Generally, for the purposes of this book, supplies may be eligible to be zero-rated where the supply is provided to a non-resident of Canada. Zero-rating is discussed in detail in Chapter 6, Zero-rating.

(b) If the supply is not zero-rated, the supply will be taxable at 14% if provided in one of the participating provinces (Nova Scotia, New Brunswick, or Newfoundland and Labrador) or at the rate of 6% if supplied in any other Canadian province.

In order to determine the province of supply, of a supply made in Canada, the ETA contains a second set of deeming rules. The province of supply rules are contained in Schedule IX. These rules are analogous to the place of supply rules and are discussed in detail in Chapter 5, Place of Supply.

2. Example of Operation of Division II GST

The following is an example of the manner in which the Division II GST would apply to a series of property related transactions. The example is premised on the assumption that all entities are located in Ontario and apart from the final consumer, all entities are GST registered.

(a) Manufacturer A purchases rubber from Manufacturer B at a price of $10,000 to be used in the manufacture of automotive tires. Manufacturer B charges and collects the amount of $10,600 from Manufacturer A (that amount is comprised of $10,000 as the principal charge + $600 in GST).

(b) Manufacturer B remits the $600 collected from Manufacturer A to the CRA. The remittance is made in Manufacturer B's monthly GST return (other claims may be used to offset this amount).

(c) Manufacturer A manufactures 50 pairs of automotive tires which it then sells to Retailer C. Manufacturer A collects $31,800 from Retailer C on the sale of the tires ($30,000 + GST of $1,800).

(d) Retailer C then sells the 50 pairs of tires to various consumers at a price of $800/pair. Each consumer pays $848 for the tires ($800 + GST of $48). The 50 consumers (as a whole) pay $2,400 in GST.

Each of Manufacturer A, Retailer C, and the consumers account for the GST in the following manner:

	GST expense incurred	ITC which may be claimed	GST collected from customers	Net GST owing to CRA (to be reported in GST return)
Manufacturer A	$600	$600	$1,800	$1,200
Retailer C	$1,800	$1,800	$2,400	$600
Consumers (aggregate)	$2,400	None	None	No return required to be filed

The net effect is that Manufacturer A and Retailer C are each made whole by collecting GST from their respective customers and claiming ITCs in respect of GST expenses incurred in the course of acquiring and selling their products. The consumers are the only party in the supply chain who will incur non-recoverable GST expense. The GST expense, which the consumers incur, is a function of the full selling price of the goods.

While most GST expenses incurred by GST registrants are fully recoverable, there are certain limitations associated with the claiming of ITCs. The identification of these limitations, many of which do not relate to e-commerce, is beyond the scope of this book.

3. Registration Issues: Canadian Resident Businesses

As a practical note, virtually every Canadian business is GST registered. This includes incorporated businesses and also other forms of businesses, including sole proprietorships, partnerships, and trusts. There are two reasons why most of these Canadian businesses are registered:

(a) **Registration is required:** every Canadian resident person who makes taxable supplies in Canada in the course of an adventure or concern in the nature of trade or in the course of a business carried on in Canada is required to register for GST purposes unless the person qualifies as a small supplier. To qualify as a small supplier a person would typically be required to post gross annual sales of less than $30,000; or

(b) **Registration is not required but has been undertaken voluntarily:** Canadian persons who make taxable sales but who are not required to be registered (for example, if the person qualifies as a small supplier) may choose to voluntarily register. Registration will typically entitle the person to claim ITCs in respect of the GST expenses which they incur.

In the e-commerce context there are many circumstances where it will be important to determine whether a person is registered or is required to be registered. These very important registration issues are considered in detail in Chapter 7, GST Registration and the Non-resident Override.

4. Registration Issues: Non-resident Businesses

As with Canadian resident businesses, many non-resident businesses are GST registered. Although some of these businesses were required to be registered many have chosen to voluntarily register.

Conversely, a significant number of non-residents regularly conduct business with Canadians without ever being GST registered. In some cases, the particular manner in which their operations have been structured allows the non-resident to avoid the registration requirement. However, in many cases the decision to remain unregistered is attributable to a misunderstanding of the registration requirements. Unfortunately, this type of error is not typically revealed prior to a CRA audit.

The circumstances in which registration will be required will differ depending on the residency status of the business. It should also be noted that the determination of whether a non-resident person is required to be registered is far more complicated than the resolution of the corresponding issue for Canadian resident persons. These issues are discussed in detail in Chapter 7, GST Registration and the Non-resident Override.

E. DIVISION III GST

The GST which is levied under Division III of the ETA applies only to tangible personal property which is imported into Canada. The tax applies based on the value for duty of the goods.

The tax is paid by the importer of record of the goods (typically either the vendor or purchaser of the goods) and is paid at the time that the goods are imported. This form of GST shares many of the characteristics of a typical customs duty. An example of the operation of the Division III GST is as follows:

Example

Corporation A, a non-resident of Canada, sells 100 computers to Corporation B, a Canadian resident corporation, at a price of $1,000 each.

Under the terms of the agreement the computers are sold FOB plant and Corporation B is responsible for clearing the goods through customs.

Corporation B retains Customs Broker C to clear the goods through customs.

Customs broker C pays $6,000 in Division III GST to the Canada Border Services Agency to clear the goods through customs.

Corporation B (and not the customs broker) is considered to be the importer of record of the goods and to have paid the Division III GST (the customs broker acted as the agent of Corporation B in clearing the goods).

Corporation B will need to determine whether it is eligible for the recovery of the Division III GST.

The following example illustrates a typical interaction between Division II GST and Division III GST.

Example

Corporation A, a GST registered, non-resident of Canada, sells 100 computers to Corporation B, a Canadian resident corporation, at a price of $1,000 each.

Under the terms of the agreement, the computers are sold on a delivered basis to Corporation B's premises in Ontario. However, under the terms of the agreement Corporation B assumes responsibility for clearing the goods through customs.

Corporation B retains Customs Broker C to clear the goods through customs.

Customs Broker C pays $6,000 in Division III GST to the Canada Border Services Agency to clear the goods through customs.

Corporation A charges and collects $6,000 in Division II GST from Corporation B. This is because the goods are delivered to Corporation B in Canada.

Corporation B (and not the customs broker) is considered to be the importer of record of the goods and to have paid the Division III GST (the customs broker acted as the agent of Corporation B in clearing the goods).

Corporation B will need to determine whether it is eligible for the recovery of the Division III GST ($6,000) and the Division II GST ($6,000).

The person who acts as the importer of record (and who pays the Division III GST) is not required to be GST registered in order to make this payment. Notwithstanding this flexibility, careful consideration should be given to the issue of the person who acts as the importer of record of the goods. This is because the ETA contains a number of restrictions relating to the circumstances in which ITCs may be claimed and by whom. For example, in many situations the person who actually imported the goods (and paid the Division III GST) will not be entitled to claim the ITC notwithstanding that the person is GST registered. Conversely, there are a number of situations in which the person who incurred the Division III expense may "shift" the right to claim the ITC to another person in the supply chain. However, this "shifting" may only occur where it is specifically authorized by the ETA.

Given that Division III GST issues do not typically arise in connection with e-commerce transactions, these complex ITC restrictions are not discussed in the book. However, it is recommended that any person who imports goods into Canada consider these issues in more detail.

F. DIVISION IV GST

The Division IV GST typically applies where a person acquires taxable intangible property or services outside of Canada but for consumption or use within Canada. There is, however, one notable exception to this rule. Division IV tax will not apply where the person acquiring the supply is GST registered, and would to the extent that it incurs a GST expense be entitled to claim full ITCs. This is consistent with the anti-avoidance function served by the Division IV GST.

The Division IV GST turns on the concept of an "imported taxable supply". That term is basically defined in section 217 of the ETA as including:

(a) a taxable supply of a service made outside Canada to a person who is resident in Canada, other than a supply of a service that is

(i) acquired for consumption, use or supply in the course of a commercial activity,

(ii) consumed by an individual exclusively outside Canada,

(iii) in respect of real property situated outside Canada, or

(iv) a service in respect in respect of tangible personal property that is situated outside of Canada at the time the service is performed; and

(b) a taxable supply of intangible personal property made outside Canada to a person who is resident in Canada, other than a supply of property that;

(i) is acquired for consumption, use or supply in the course of commercial activities of the person or activities that are engaged in exclusively outside Canada by the person and that are not part of a business or adventure or concern in the nature of trade engaged in by the person in Canada,

(ii) may not be used in Canada, or

(iii) relates to real property situated outside Canada, to a service to be performed wholly outside Canada, or to tangible personal property situated outside Canada.

Persons acquiring imported taxable supplies from outside of Canada are required to report and pay the GST directly to the Minister of National Revenue. The manner in which the GST is reported depends on whether the person is, or is not, GST registered.

The rate of tax applicable to imported taxable supplies is typically 6% of the consideration paid for the supply. However, a number of special rules relate to purchases made by residents of the participating provinces. Under section 218.1 of the ETA, residents of the participating provinces who acquire taxable intangible personal property or services, must pay an additional 8% tax. Section 132.1 of the ETA sets out the rules for determining who is a person resident in a participating province.

The GST which is levied under Division IV very frequently applies in the e-commerce context most notably in connection with consumer transactions. Whenever supplies are acquired from vendors outside of Canada and the vendor has not charged the GST, the purchaser should be aware of the potential impact of Division IV. One very common e-commerce situation in which the Division IV GST will apply in connection with the non-resident override is as follows:

(a) a non-resident supplier makes a supply which is considered under the place of supply rules to be made in Canada;

(b) the supply is deemed to be made outside Canada because of the application of the non-resident override (i.e., the non-resident is not GST registered, does not carry on business in Canada and does not make supplies through a permanent establishment in Canada);

(c) a Canadian person who is either not registered (such as an individual purchasing for personal use) or who is engaged in exempt activities (such as a banking or insurance entity) is the purchaser of the supply; and

(d) the Canadian will be required to self-assess the GST owing under Division IV.

G. DIVISION IV.1 GST

Division IV.1 GST applies to property (including intangible personal property) and services which are brought into a participating province for consumption in a participating province. Collectively, these rules ensure that where property or services are supplied outside of the participating provinces, but are acquired for consumption, use or supply in the participating provinces, they are subject to the appropriate rate of tax.

Chapter 3

Characterization of Supply

A. OVERVIEW

It is critical that supplies be properly characterized for GST purposes. This is because the manner in which this issue is resolved will directly impact on the manner in which a number of other legislative provisions are interpreted. Where a particular supply is improperly characterized, it will typically follow that other provisions will be inappropriately applied.

The appropriate characterization of supplies will have a particularly substantial impact on the following critical issues:

(a) which place of supply rules will apply;

(b) which province of supply rules will apply; and

(c) whether zero-rating is available for a particular supply.

In the e-commerce setting, the particular supply in issue will invariably be either a service or intangible personal property.[1] However, a number of secondary characterization issues are also required to be considered. Where it has been determined that a service is being supplied, it must then be determined whether the service is a telecommunication service. Where the service is a telecommunication service, a determination must be made as to which type of telecommunication service is being supplied.

Where a service is other than a telecommunication service, the service may need to be further categorized. For example, advertising services, agency services, and consulting, advisory and professional services, are all subject to special rules.

A similar characterization analysis is required to be performed with respect to intangible personal property. For example, intangible personal property which is also intellectual property qualifies for special zero-rating concessions.

In resolving the issues described above, the distinction between single and multiple supplies, and the incidental supply rules, should be taken into account. These considerations are discussed in detail in Chapter 4, Single versus Multiple Supplies.

---

[1] The CRA has established that all e-commerce supplies will be either services or intangible personal property. This should be contrasted with some of the Canadian provincial sales tax regimes which deem software, including software delivered electronically, to be tangible personal property.

B. DISTINGUISHING BETWEEN SERVICES AND INTANGIBLE PERSONAL PROPERTY

Drawing the distinction between services and intangible personal property is anything but an intuitive process. In many of the rulings discussed in Part II of this book, applicants described their offerings to the CRA as being in the nature of either intangible personal property or a service, only to find that their characterization was incorrect. Given that the ordinary visceral approach to characterizing supplies often does not work, the following section focuses upon the first principles which should be considered.

1. The Default Rule

The starting point in any characterization analysis is the definition of a "supply". This term is very broadly defined as:

> ... the provision of property or a service in any manner including sale, transfer, barter, license, rental, lease, gift or disposition[2]

The terms "property" and "service" are also defined in a correspondingly broad manner:

> "Property" means any property, whether real or personal, moveable or immoveable, tangible or intangible, corporeal or incorporeal, and includes a right or interest of any kind, a share and a chose in action, but does not include money[3]

> "Service" means anything other than
>
> (a) property;
>
> (b) money; or
>
> (c) anything that is supplied to an employer by a person who is or agrees to become an employee of the employer in the course of or in relation to the office or employment of that person[4]

These broad definitions effectively preclude the advancement of the position that a particular offering is something which is neither property or a service. Where a particular supply does not appear to be property, and does not appear to be a service, then by default the supply will be deemed to be a service. This default rule is critical because it may result in a supply being deemed to be a service even where the supply does not have any of the traditional trappings of a service.

---

[2] Subsection 123(1) of the ETA.

[3] *Ibid.*

[4] *Ibid.*

2. Specific Rules for Identifying Intangible Personal Property

The default rule described above is not typically required to be applied to determine the nature of a particular supply. This is because the supply will usually possess the essential characteristics of either property or a service.[5]

In Technical Information Bulletin B-090, GST/HST and Electronic Commerce ("TIB 090"), the CRA established that, in its view, the presence of any of the following factors will suggest that intangible personal property is being supplied:

(a) a right in a product or a right to use a product for personal or commercial purposes is provided, such as:

— intellectual property or a right to use intellectual property (e.g., a copyright);

— rights of a temporary nature (right to view, access, or use a product while online);

(b) a product is provided that has already been created or developed, or is already in existence;

(c) a product is created or developed for a specific customer but the supplier retains ownership of the product; or

(d) a right to make a copy of a digitized product is provided.

These guidelines are referred to in this chapter as intangible personal property rules (a) through (d).

(a) Application of the Guidelines

The guidelines described above suggest that where a product has been created in advance of the identification of the customer, and rights are provided to the customer to use this existing product (including the right to make a copy of the product), then the supply will typically be considered to be intangible personal property.

---

[5] Where a bundled supply is provided, the supply will typically possess the essential characteristics of both a service and intangible personal property. The methodology for characterizing bundled supplies is discussed under heading 4, Characterization of Bundled Supplies.

Example

Corporation A provides its customers with the right to download specific reports from its Web site in return for a fee. The customers are granted a non-exclusive license to view and use the information contained in the reports in exchange for a monthly access fee.

The supply is considered to be a supply of intangible personal property. This is because the product in issue is already in existence.

The guidelines also suggest that where ownership of an existing product is transferred to a customer, generally this would be considered to be a supply of intangible personal property. However, where full ownership of a product is transferred to the customer and the product was created or developed specifically for that customer, the supply will likely be considered a service. This is consistent with the fundamental concept that a service typically involves specific work done for a specific person, including where property is supplied as an element of the service.

However, if a product is created specifically for a particular customer, but the supplier retains ownership in the product (presumably for the purpose of subsequently supplying rights in the product to other customers or for some other purpose), the supply will be considered to be intangible personal property. This seems to be because, notwithstanding that specific work has been done for a specific person, the supplier is retaining the right to make future supplies of the same product to other customers.

Example

A Web site designer develops a Web site specifically for a customer but retains the ownership of the Web site.

This would be a supply of intangible personal property because of the ownership rights retained by the supplier.

From a practical perspective this would never happen. Web sites are by their very nature intended to be unique, and so Web site designers typically provide full ownership rights to their customers. As a result, the supply of a Web site design is typically characterized as a service. This issue is covered in more detail in Chapter 16, Online Content, Services, and Other General Offerings.

(b) Specific Examples of Supplies Characterized as Intangible Personal Property

TIB 090 provides a number of examples to illustrate the manner in which it draws the distinction between services and intangible personal property. The following is a summary of the examples in which the CRA concluded that the supply was in the nature of intangible personal property.[6] It should be noted that each of the examples set out below relates to a simple supply comprised of a single element. The section below entitled "Characterization of Bundled Supplies" should be referred to where bundled supplies are provided.

Example 1: Electronic ordering and downloading of digitized products

A customer selects an item from an online catalogue of software or other digitized products and orders it electronically directly from a commercial supplier. There is no separate charge to the customer for using the catalogue. The product is downloaded onto the customer's computer. For a separate fee, the customer will receive updates and add-ons to the product, which are also downloaded directly to the customer's computer.

The supplies considered in this example (i.e., the software or other digitized products, updates, and add-ons) are products which are already in existence at the time of ordering (i.e., they are listed in a catalogue). The customer is provided with a copy of the product, as well as the right to use the product. Consequently, the supplies are characterized as intangible personal property.

Example 2: Limited duration software and other digitized information licences

A customer receives the right to use software or another digitized product for a period of time which is less than the useful life of the product. The product is downloaded to the customer's computer. Upon termination of the licence, all copies of the digitized product are deleted or become unusable.

This is a supply of intangible personal property. The characteristics of the supply are the same as in Example 1 (except with respect to the duration of use). Limiting the period of use does not affect the characterization of the supply as one of intangible personal property. This rationale applies even if the digitized product can be used only once.

Example 3: Subscription to a Web site that allows the downloading of digitized products

A supplier makes a Web site available to subscribers that features copyrighted digitized products (e.g., music). Subscribers pay a fixed periodic fee to access the site and to select and download digitized products.

---

[6] The example numbers correspond with the numbers established by the CRA in TIB 090.

This supply is one of intangible personal property. The subscribers are acquiring a right to use the digitized product and to copy it (by downloading) and the product is already in existence.

Example 14: Data retrieval

A supplier makes a vast repository of information available to customers for search and retrieval purposes. Customers pay a fee which enables them to access the data and to search and extract specific information from the repository. In some instances, the supplier adds significant value in terms of content (e.g., analysis of raw data), but the resulting product is not prepared for a specific customer and there is no obligation to keep the contents confidential. Such products might include special industry or investment reports, which are either sent electronically to subscribers, or are made available for purchase and download from an online catalogue or index.

The supply to the customers is a supply of intangible personal property. The supplier is providing customers with a right to access and use the repository of information (i.e., a product already in existence), as well as the software programs required to search and retrieve information from the repository. Although there may be human involvement in maintaining the repository of information (e.g., by adding content or raw data analysis), this is considered to be an input to the supply. There is no human involvement on the part of the supplier when a customer accesses and retrieves information.

Example 17: Undisclosed technical information

A customer is provided with undisclosed technical information concerning a product or process (e.g., narrative description and diagrams of a secret manufacturing process).

If the customer is provided with the right to use information by way of licence, the supply is one of intangible personal property. It will not matter whether the information is in existence or is developed specifically for the customer.

If the supply is one of developing information for a specific customer, and the customer is provided with ownership of the information, a service is being supplied.

Example 18: Information delivery

A supplier delivers data electronically on a periodic basis to subscribers (e.g., news clippings or stock market quotations), in accordance with their personal preferences. The principal value to the customers is the convenience of receiving information in a customized format tailored to their specific needs.

The supply is one of a right to receive customized information. There is no human involvement on the part of the supplier in the making of the supply. Consequently, the supply is characterized as one of intangible personal property.

3. Specific Rules for Identifying Services

The CRA has also established a corresponding list of factors in TIB 090 to assist in identifying when a service is being provided. The presence of any of the following factors will suggest that a service is being supplied:

(a) the supply does not include the provision of rights (e.g., technical knowhow), or if there is a provision of rights, the rights are incidental to the supply;

(b) the supply involves specific work that is performed by a person for a specific customer; or

(c) there is human involvement in making the supply.

These guidelines are referred to further in this chapter as services rules (a) through (c).

The reconciliation of services rule (a) above, and the intangible personal property rules is relatively straightforward. Where no rights are provided to the customer, or the rights which are provided are incidental to the provision of a service, it stands to reason that a service is being provided.

However, the reconciliation of the remaining services rules against the intangible personal property rules is far more difficult. For example, where a supplier designs a digital product specifically for a customer (and retains ownership) services rule (b) suggests that this is a service. However, intangible personal property rule (c) suggests that this would be a supply of property.

There are many other situations where the rules appear to conflict, and unfortunately, there does not appear to be any clear methodology in place to resolve these issues. Where ambiguity arises, the drawing of analogies to existing rulings may prove helpful.

(a) Specific Examples of Supplies Characterized as Services

As noted above, TIB 090 provides a number of examples which are intended to illustrate the manner in which the CRA draws the distinction between services and intangible personal property. The following are summaries of examples where the CRA concluded that a service was being supplied in connection with the offering of an other than bundled supply:

Example 6: Application hosting — separate licence

A customer with a perpetual licence to use a software product enters into a contract with a host entity, whereby the host entity loads a copy of the software on servers owned and operated by the host and provides technical support to protect against system failures. The customer can access, execute and operate the software application remotely. The application is executed either at the customer's computer after it is downloaded, or remotely on the host's server. This type of arrangement could apply, for example, to financial management, inventory control, human resource management or other enterprise resource management software applications. The customer has no control over the equipment used by the host entity.

The agreement between the host entity and the customer is to host software on a server maintained by the host entity. Since the software licence is held by the customer, there is no provision of rights in the software or for the use of the software between the host entity and the customer. The host entity is essentially providing the space to store and run the software application on its equipment, as well as technical support. Consequently, this is characterized as a supply of a service.

Example 9: Web site hosting

An Internet Service Provider (ISP) hosts its customers' commercial Web sites on its servers. The ISP does not obtain any rights in the copyrighted material on the site. Customers can remotely manipulate the site, including modifying its content, but do not possess or have direct control of the server(s) used to host the site. The customer pays a fee based on the passage of time.

The agreement between the supplier and the customer is to host the customer's Web site on a server maintained by the supplier, and the customer maintains all rights in the site. There is no supply of rights or of property between the supplier and the customer, and therefore the supply is characterized as a supply of a service.

Example 10: Data warehousing

A customer stores its computer data on servers owned and operated by a supplier. The customer can access, upload, retrieve and manipulate data remotely. No software is licensed, or rights transferred, to the customer in this transaction. The customer does not have control over or possession of any specific equipment used by the supplier in the data storage. For example, a retailer may store its inventory records on the supplier's hardware, and the retailer's employees may remotely access this information to allow them to determine whether orders can be filled from current stock.

This is similar to Example 9. The agreement between the supplier and customer is to store the customer's computer data on a server maintained by the supplier. Since there is no provision of rights or property, the supply is characterized as a supply of a service.

Example 11: Advertising

Companies pay a fee to Web site operators to place advertisements on their Web sites. Advertising rates may be determined in a number of ways, including the cost per thousand "impressions" (i.e., the number of times the advertisement is displayed to a user), or the number of "click-throughs" (i.e., the number of times the advertisement is clicked by a user). For example, "banner ads," which are small graphic images embedded in a Web page, allow a company's Web page to be loaded to a user's computer when clicked by the user.

An advertising service is a service of creating a message and a service directly related to the communication of such a message. The message must be oriented towards soliciting business, attracting donations, or calling public attention in the form of an information notice, political announcement, or other similar communication.

By publicizing companies' messages on the Internet (i.e., placing advertisements on Web sites), the Web site operators are supplying an advertising service to the companies.

Example 12: On-line shopping portals

A Web site operator hosts electronic catalogues of various merchants on its servers. Shoppers can select products from these catalogues and place orders online. The Web site operator has no contractual relationship with the shoppers, and merely transmits orders to the merchants, who are responsible for accepting and filling them. The merchants pay the Web site operator a commission based on a percentage of the value of orders placed through the site.

By hosting the catalogues, the Web site operator is communicating a message intended to solicit business for the merchants. This is a supply of an advertising service.

Example 13: On-line auctions

A Web site operator displays a vendor's items for purchase by auction. On-line shoppers purchase items directly from the owner of the items, rather than from the operator. The vendor compensates the Web site operator with a percentage of the sale price or a flat fee. The vendor and online shoppers have only the incidental use of the software to perform certain tasks in respect of the transactions (e.g., payment processing), but are not provided any rights to use the software.

The supply by the Web site operator to the vendor is considered to be a supply of a service. No rights in property or for the use of property are supplied between the operator and the vendor.

Example 16: Electronic access to professional advice (e.g., consulting)

A consultant, lawyer, doctor or other professional service provider advises clients through e-mail, video conferencing, or other remote means of communication.

The supply of the advice to clients, delivered by electronic means, is a supply of a service, as it involves specific work that is performed for a specific client, and does not involve a supply of rights to an existing product.

(b) Guidance Provided by the Examples

To many people it may seem intuitive that for a service to be provided, there must be a high degree of interaction between individuals. However, the examples demonstrate that a service may be provided in circumstances where the customer does not interact with any individual (i.e., an employee of the supplier) in order to obtain the benefit of the service. In examples 9 (Web site hosting) and 10 (data warehousing) there typically would not be any (or very little) human interaction associated with the supply because the services would be performed by computers and computer programs. In examples 11, 12, and 13 (advertising, shopping portal, and third party sales, respectively) there may be some human interaction, but this interaction should be expected to be quite minimal in nature.

Only examples 6 (application hosting with technical support) and 16 (online professional consulting) describe traditional service offerings where human interaction is at the core of the supply. This even further emphasizes how a formalized approach is required to be followed in order to determine whether a service or property is being supplied.

4. Characterization of Bundled Supplies

Reconciliation of the services and intangible personal property tests will be particularly difficult where packages (or bundled supplies) are offered to customers. It is very common in the e-commerce environment for a particular bundle to be provided which contains elements which are in the nature of services and other elements which are in the nature of intangible personal property.

For example, where a supplier provides a customer with the right to use an existing product, but supports the customer's use of the product with technical support (but for no additional charge), intangible personal property rule (a) suggests that property is being supplied, while services rule (c) suggests that a service is being provided. The complexity of this issue is compounded by the fact that services rule (a) suggests that where property rights are supplied which are incidental to a service, the supply will be a service. However, there is no corresponding rule for situations where the services are incidental to the property.

Where the various competing elements may be carved off from each other, the resolution of the characterization issues will be relatively straightforward. Each one of the distinct supplies will be characterized separately in accordance with the guidelines described above. However, where the competing elements are considered to form part of a single supply (including as a result of the application of the incidental supply rule), the approach which is adopted by the CRA to characterize the supply is described below. A full discussion of the issues relating to distinguishing between single and multiple supplies is contained in Chapter 4, Single versus Multiple Supplies.

(a) The Principal Object Test

To resolve difficult characterization issues relating to single supplies comprised of multiple elements, the CRA typically employs a "principal object" test. This test is also referred to in TIB 090 as "an essential nature of the transaction" test. Although TIB 090 provides a number of examples of the manner in which the CRA applies the test, there is no corresponding description of this test. The test seems to call for the identification of the core (or most significant) offering which is a component of the particular supply. It would appear that this determination will be made from the perspective of the recipient of the supply (i.e., what is the one element of the supply which the recipient most requires).

Where a single supply is considered to be made as a result of the application of the incidental supply rule, the principal object should be expected to be the particular element to which the incidental supply is considered incidental. However, where a complex single supply is made other than as a result of the application of the incidental supply rule, the principal object test will be more difficult to apply.

(b) Specific Examples of Application of "Principal Object" Test

The following are summaries of examples provided in TIB 090 where the "principal object" test, or the similar "essential nature of the transaction" test, was applied to determine the nature of the particular complex supply.

Example 4: Software maintenance

A supplier and customer enter into a software maintenance contract, which typically bundles software updates with technical support. The customer is given the right to copy and use the product for personal or commercial purposes and is charged a single annual fee for the software updates and the technical support. The principal object of the contract is the software updates.

As the principal object of the supply is the provision of a software update delivered electronically, the supply is characterized as one of intangible personal property.

Example 5: Customer support over a computer network

A software supplier provides a customer with online technical support, including installation advice and trouble-shooting information. This support is in the form of online technical documentation, a trouble-shooting database, and, as a last resort, communication with a technician by e-mail.

If the technical support is essentially the supply of a right to use existing technical information in the form of online documentation and access to a trouble-shooting database, and the interaction with the technician is incidental, the supply would be characterized as one of intangible personal property.

If technical support is provided through interaction with technicians, and the provision of any rights to documentation or databases is incidental, the supply would be characterized as a supply of a service, since it is of specific work performed for a specific customer.

Example 7: Application hosting

For a single fee, a user enters into a contract whereby a host entity, which is also the copyright holder, allows access to one or more software applications, hosts the applications on a server owned and operated by the host, and provides technical support for the hardware and software. The user can access, execute and operate the software application remotely. The contract is renewable annually for an additional fee. The principal object of the contract is the provision of software applications.

This is similar to the supply in Example 6. However, as the host entity (rather than the customer) is the copyright holder for the software, the customer is being provided with the right to use the software. Although the supplier is also hosting the software application(s) on its server(s), and providing technical support for the hardware and the software, the supply is essentially the provision of a right to use software. Consequently, it is characterized as a supply of intangible personal property.

Example 8: Service provider

A supplier has a licence to use a software application in the course of its business. It hosts the software on a server that it owns, operates and maintains. The supplier enters into an agreement with a customer to manage a particular back-office function (e.g., the customer's payment processing), and provides the customer with access to the software application, enabling the customer to perform specific tasks when required (e.g., data entry, addition of tombstone data for new suppliers and clients). However, the supplier is responsible for the major aspects of the payment processing, such as cheque issuance and bank verification, and uses the software application to automate these tasks. The customer has no right to copy the software or use it other than for the specific functions assigned by the supplier, and at no time does the customer have possession or control of the software (since it resides on the supplier's server).

The supply in this instance is for the management of a particular business function, such as payment processing. In making the supply, the supplier has the licence for the necessary software, equipment and personnel necessary to process payments. The customer is provided with access to the software for specific tasks, such as entering data. The provision of the right to use the software for these specific tasks is incidental to the overall supply being made by the supplier (e.g., processing payments on behalf of a customer). Since the supply does not involve the provision of rights (other than incidentally) or other property, it is characterized as a supply of a service.

Example 15: Access to an interactive Web site

A supplier makes a Web site featuring digitized content available to subscribers, including information, music, video, games, and activities, whether or not developed or owned by the supplier. The subscribers pay a fixed periodic fee for access to the site. The principal value of the site to subscribers is interacting with the site while online, as opposed to getting a product or services from the site. The supplier also charges companies a fee for placing their banner or pop-up ads on the site.

In this example there are two separate supplies: the provision of the right to access the content on the Web site, and the placement of banner or pop-up ads.

The subscribers' right to access the content on the Web site is a supply of intangible personal property. In essence it is a supply of a right to use software, and the right to access other digitized content on the Web site. Although a copy of a digitized product is not provided, there is a supply of a right to view, access or use a product while the customer is online. As in Example 14, any human involvement occurs behind the scenes in establishing and maintaining the Web site, but there is no human involvement on the part of the supplier when subscribers access the site and its digitized content.

The placement by the supplier of the banner or pop-up ads on its site is a supply of an advertising service.

Example 19: Content acquisition transactions

A Web site operator pays various content providers for news stories, information, and other online content to attract users to a site. Alternatively, the Web site operator might hire a content provider to create new content specifically for the Web site.

This could be characterized as either a supply of a service or intangible personal property, depending upon the facts.

Where the supply made by the content provider is of the right to use copyrighted content, it is considered to be a supply of intangible personal property, regardless of whether the content is already in existence (e.g., it has already been published), or it is developed specifically for the customer. Where the content provider develops content specifically for the Web site operator, and the Web site operator owns the content, the supply is characterized as a supply of a service.

(c) Guidance Provided by the Examples

All of the examples described above, when considered as a whole, suggest that the following guiding principles should be taken into account in characterizing supplies:

(a) Where a supplier provides consulting for the individual client which is delivered by electronic means, and no rights are provided in any products, a service will be provided. See Example 16.

(b) Making information available for search and use on a database is the supply of intangible personal property. The human element associated with adding information to the database is an input to the supply. See Example 14.

(c) Supplying digitized content (such as information, music, videos and games) to customers while online is a supply of intangible personal property. The human element associated with adding the products to the Web site or in maintaining the Web site occurs "behind the scenes". See Example 15.

(d) The supply to customers of "pushed" customized information (for example, news clippings or stock quotes) which does not involve any human element (as the delivery is automatically performed), is a supply of intangible personal property. See Example 18.

(e) Where technical information is supplied to a customer, the characterization turns on whether the information is sold or licensed to the customer. See Example 17.

　　(i) If the right to use the information is provided by way of license, the supply is intangible personal property. It does not matter whether the information is already in existence or whether it has been specifically developed for the customer.

　　(ii) If the supply is the development of information for a specific customer (for example, a research service), and the customer will own the information at the end of the process, then a service is provided.

(f) Where specific content (for example, information, news stories) is provided, the characterization turns on whether the supplier is providing the right to use copyrighted materials or is developing materials which it will sell to the customer. See Example 19.

　　(i) Where the supplier provides the rights to use copyrighted materials, the supply is intangible personal property. It does not matter whether the copyrighted materials are already in existence or have been specifically developed for the customer.

(ii) Where the supplier develops materials specifically for the customer which are not subject to copyright (and ownership passes to the customer), the supply is a service.

(g) Services rule (c) should not be interpreted too literally. That rule provides that where there is "human involvement in making the supply", this will suggest that a service is being provided. However, it would appear that where the human element is tangential or in the nature of supporting another element, the human element will typically be disregarded in characterizing the supply. The same caution applies to services rule (b) regarding "specific work that is performed by a person for a specific customer". Clearly, specific work may be performed for a specific customer which will not result in a finding that a service has been provided (i.e., where there is a substantial property component to the supply). Technical software support is a leading example of the manner in which this issue commonly manifests.

(d) Secondary Bundling Issues

Each of the bundling examples described above relates to situations where a service was bundled with intangible personal property. However, bundling issues may also arise in other circumstances. For example, bundling issues are required to be resolved where tangible personal property is supplied with intangible personal property. This issue commonly arises in connection with the sale of textbooks supported by online access and is discussed in Chapter 17, Internet Courses, Electronic Books, and Other Educational Offerings.

The requirement to characterize a bundled supply may also arise where all of the elements of the supply are in the nature of services (e.g., telecommunication services bundled with ordinary services). The relevant test for resolving this issue is the "predominant purpose test" and is discussed below.

Bundling issues may also arise where all the elements of the supply are intangible personal property (e.g., intangible personal property which is intellectual property bundled with intangible personal property which is not intellectual property). This issue would relate more to the availability of zero-rating than to the application of the place of supply rules. It would appear that the principal object test would also be used to resolve this type of issue.

5. Evidentiary Issues

In resolving the characterization issues set out above, particularly ones relating to bundled supplies, the CRA has emphasized that it will consider all relevant factors, including:

(a) The nature of the agreement between the supplier and recipient; and

(b) Whether the agreement is in substance for work (or work materials) or for property (including a right or interest of any kind).

This approach will be largely discretionary and will allow the CRA to focus upon the particular considerations which it deems to be most important in the context of any given case. As a result, the weighting which will be applied to any particular factor should be expected to be a subjective exercise.

In resolving bundling issues, taxpayers should be prepared to compare the potential outcomes against existing rulings and administrative examples. These existing materials may assist in advancing a particular position. Tax leakage considerations should always be taken into account in evaluating a particular outcome.

C. DISTINGUISHING TELECOMMUNICATION SERVICES FROM OTHER SERVICES

As indicated at the beginning of this chapter, where it has been determined that a service is being provided, it must be determined whether the service is a telecommunication service.

In the e-commerce setting, distinguishing between a telecommunication service and an ordinary service is complicated because every e-commerce supply will, by its very nature, involve a telecommunications element. In TIB 090, the CRA notes that the distinction to be made is whether a telecommunication service is being supplied or whether telecommunications are used as a means by which other property or services are supplied.

This distinction is particularly important as telecommunication services are subject to a number of special rules. The most important of the special rules relates to the determination of the place of supply both for GST and for HST purposes. The distinction also relates to the availability of zero-rating. Issues relating to determining the place of supply of telecommunication services are discussed in Chapter 5, Place of Supply. Issues relating to zero-rating of telecommunication services are described in Chapter 6, Zero-rating.

1. Predominant Purpose Test

The CRA employs a "predominant purpose" test to determine whether a telecommunication service is being supplied or whether telecommunications are being used as a means to deliver some other supply. Generally, a telecommunication service will be considered to be supplied where the predominant purpose of the supply is:

(a) to provide for the emission, transmission or reception of signs, signals (i.e., voice or data) through a telecommunications network or similar technical system;

(b) to make available a telecommunications facility for the emission, transmission or reception of signs or signals through a telecommunications network or similar technical system; or

(c) to provide a means through which other services or intangible personal property (i.e., content in a digitized format) are delivered, rather than to provide the services or intangible personal property.

Conversely, a supply will generally not be considered to be a supply of a telecommunication service where:

(d) a telecommunication service is used or consumed by the supplier in making a supply of a service or property (other than a telecommunication service);

(e) the supply includes a telecommunication service but only as a means of delivering another service or property; or

(f) the telecommunication service is incidental to the supply of another property or service.

The application of the tests contained in parts (a) and (b) will typically be relatively straightforward. However, the application of the test in part (c) frequently results in interpretative difficulties. This is because in the e-commerce environment, it is not at all unusual for the supplier to provide both the medium (or means), and the content. In those circumstances, the rules in parts (e) and (f) suggest that the supply would typically be characterized as being in the nature of the content. However, those rules must be cautiously applied because it is not uncommon, notwithstanding rules (e) and (f), for this type of supply to be characterized as a telecommunication service. This issue frequently arises where ISPs provide their customers with a connection to the Internet (a telecommunication service) and also provide personalized content or other services (such as security services).

2. Examples of the CRA's Approach

TIB 090 provides a number of examples to demonstrate the manner in which the CRA distinguishes between telecommunication services and other than telecommunication services. These examples are reproduced below.

Example 1: Internet access service

An ISP is a company that provides users with Internet access, for which they pay a fee. The connection is made by a modem, which allows the user to send and receive data over a telephone line. The telephone line is supplied to the user by a third party telephone service provider. To access the Internet, a user "calls" the ISP to log on (if not already connected), and the user's request for a particular Web site is routed to the server hosting the desired data.

This is a supply of a telecommunication service. The predominant purpose of the service is to provide the consumer with a connection, allowing the transmission and reception of data over the Internet. Generally, this is the predominant purpose of the service even where an ISP provides content or access to content as part of its service. The recipient is generally looking to the ISP to supply the means by which access to the Internet is obtained.

Example 2: E-mail

A company contracts with a vendor to provide e-mail services. For a fee, the vendor will ensure that the company's personnel can send and receive intra-office and external e-mails. The vendor dedicates space on a server for the composition, reception and storage of e-mail messages sent to or by the company. The company is provided with e-mail addresses (ID), a mailbox, and the use of a network, thus allowing its employees to send, receive and store information on a secure basis. The company addresses its outgoing e-mail to a mail recipient's e-mail address, and the mail is routed to the server and forwarded to its final destination. Incoming mail addressed to the company is routed to the server and directed to a particular employee.

This is a supply of a telecommunication service. The predominant purpose of the service is to allow the company to send and receive e-mail. The vendor is providing the company with a service of transmitting text, images, etc., by means of its server and the use of a network.

Example 3: Web site hosting

A company enters into an agreement with an ISP to provide Web site hosting services for the company's Web site. Under the agreement, the ISP is responsible for housing the Web site on a server it owns and maintains, which includes ensuring the security of the server and that the Web site is accessible over the Internet. The server is linked to the Internet through dedicated lines acquired from a telephone service provider. The company is responsible for the design and content of the Web site. The agreement only addresses the Web site hosting arrangements and does not deal with Internet access.

This is not a supply of a telecommunication service. The predominant purpose of the supply is the storage and maintenance of the Web site on a server in a manner that allows access to the Web site on the Internet. In making the supply of this service the ISP uses or consumes a number of inputs (e.g., telecommunication services, hardware and software).

Example 4: Internet access services, e-mail and personal web page

A consumer pays a fee to an ISP for Internet access. In addition to the Internet access, the consumer receives e-mail services and space on the ISP's server to create and maintain a personal Web page. The consumer determines the content of the Web page, but it is hosted on the ISP's server.

The service provided by the ISP is a supply of a telecommunication service. This is a typical transaction between an ISP and an individual consumer. The ISP is making a single supply which includes providing the consumer with a connection to the Internet, an e-mail account, and space on the ISP's server. The predominant purpose of the supply to the consumer is the Internet connection. As in the case of Internet access services, the supply of a connection to the Internet is considered to be a telecommunication service.

Example 5: Voice telephony

A consumer pays a fee to a company for long distance "telephone calls" made over the Internet. The consumer is able to place these calls from his or her computer or telephone any place in the world. The calls are routed through the networks that make up the backbone of the Internet.

This is a supply of a telecommunication service. The predominant purpose of the supply is to provide the transmission of voice communication. The supplier of the voice telephony is providing a traditional voice telephone service, except that the service is being provided over the Internet.

Example 6: Electronic data interchange

A company is engaged by an approved EFILE tax preparer to electronically file income tax returns for its clients. The tax preparer completes all of the income tax returns prior to submitting them to the company for electronic transmission. Upon receipt of the returns, the company validates the format of the returns, encrypts the data, validates the values indicated in the tax return boxes (e.g., SIN numbers), and electronically submits the returns to the CCRA.

This is a supply of a telecommunication service. The predominant purpose of the supply is the electronic transmission of data. The validation and encryption are part of the service of transmitting the data.

Example 7: Preparation and EDI transmission of income tax returns

A consumer pays a fee to a tax preparer to prepare and electronically file his or her income tax return with the CCRA. The tax preparer completes the income tax return, validates the format and values, encrypts the data, and electronically transmits the return to the CCRA.

This is not a supply of a telecommunication service. The tax preparer is making a single supply which comprises a number of elements, including preparation of the tax return and its transmission to the CCRA. The predominant purpose of the supply is the preparation of the tax return. Therefore, the supply is not a telecommunication service.

Example 8: Digitized products

A consumer selects and orders a digitized product from a commercial supplier. For a fee, the digitized product is available for downloading by the consumer.

This is not a supply of a telecommunication service. The supply of a digitized product that is readily available for download over the Internet is the supply of intangible personal property. In this instance, a telecommunication service is used or consumed by the supplier in making the supply of the digitized product.

Example 9: Web based broadcasting

A consumer pays a subscription fee for access to a Web site with audio and/or visual content that is streamed (i.e., broadcast in real time) over the Internet. A copy of the content is not provided to the consumer.

The supply of the audio and/or visual content streamed over the Internet is a telecommunication service. The predominant purpose of the supply is to provide the consumer with the broadcast content. This is analogous to a traditional radio or television broadcasting service, which is considered to be a telecommunication service for GST/HST purposes.

3. Guidance Provided by the Examples and Outstanding Issues

The examples set out above provide valuable guidance with respect to the CRA's general approach to resolving the telecommunication service characterization issue. The following features appear evident in the CRA's approach:

(a) Where one of the elements of a supply is Internet access, the supply will typically be considered to be a telecommunication service regardless of the other elements also provided (see Examples 1 and 3). This approach seems to relate to the particular importance of the Internet connection.

(b) Given the approach in (a), it should also be expected that, where a particular supply involves the electronic transmission of data (which would appear to be analogous to the connection issue described above), the supply will similarly be considered a telecommunication service. This position seems to be supported by example 5. In that case, the electronic transmission of income tax returns was considered a telecommunication service notwithstanding that services relating to data verification and formatting were also provided.

However, this should be contrasted with example 8. In example 8, the supplier prepared the income tax returns and then electronically transmitted the returns. This was considered to be other than a telecommunication service. It would appear that the skill, time, and effort required to complete the return was sufficient to relegate the telecommunication portion of the supply to secondary status.

(c) It would appear that the CRA has considerable discretion to make the determination that a particular telecommunication element is merely an input to a supply. In example 3, the CRA concluded that Web site hosting is not a telecommunication service because the connection to the Internet is an input to the supply. This conclusion with respect to the connection seems anomalous given that having a Web site hosted would be of no value if it were not accessible over the Internet.

(d) In each of the nine examples, the conclusion was reached that a single supply had been made. It is not clear why the CRA provided only single supply examples. In offering no multiple supply examples, it may be arguable that the CRA is signaling a general policy direction. Alternatively, it may be possible that the CRA simply determined that this was not an appropriate forum to raise the difficult multiple supply issues. Given that TIB 090 has in connection with other types of supplies similarly avoided broaching the single versus multiple supply issue, it would appear that the latter theory more accurately reflects what has occurred. However, this also suggests that where telecommunication services are in fact supplied with other than telecommunication offerings, the possibility that multiple supplies are being made should be carefully considered.

D. SPECIAL SUBSETS OF SERVICES

As noted above, where it has been determined that a service other than a telecommunication service has been provided, a further distinction may be required to be drawn. For example, services which are considered to be advertising services and consulting, professional and advisory services are subject to special zero-rating rules.

The zero-rating rules which apply to advertising services and to professional, advisory or consulting services are discussed in Chapter 6, Zero-rating. The meaning of "advertising services" is discussed in detail in Chapter 12, Advertising Services. To determine the scope of the term "professional, advisory or consulting services", GST/HST Memorandum 4.5.3, "Exports — Services and Intellectual Property", should be considered.

Chapter 4

Single versus Multiple Supplies

A. OVERVIEW

The issue of whether multiple supplies or a single supply (comprised of multiple elements) is being made is a particularly important and difficult issue. The decision reached on this threshold issue will directly impact on the application of the place of supply rules, the province of supply rules, and the availability of zero-rating.

Once the nature of a single supply has been identified, the place of supply, province of supply, and zero-rating rules will apply based upon the particular considerations which relate to that single supply. However, where multiple supplies are made, each distinct supply is required to be separately analyzed. It is not uncommon for one or more of the separate supplies to each be subject to different tax treatment.

The requirement to distinguish between single and multiple supplies arises very frequently in the e-commerce environment. This is because it is not uncommon for e-commerce suppliers to provide their customers with multiple supplies (or single supplies comprised of multiple elements).

The significance of properly distinguishing between single and multiple supplies is illustrated by the following example:

Example

A non-resident GST registered person supplies its customers with the right to use software applications and provides technical support in respect of the software.

The software, when supplied to Canadian customers, may be used in Canada (and so is considered to be supplied in Canada).

The technical support services are performed wholly outside Canada (and so are considered to be supplied outside Canada).

If the software and the technical support are considered to be separate supplies (and are not subject to the incidental supply rule), the supplier would be required to collect GST in respect of the software (i.e., because it is supplied in Canada). However, it would not be required to collect GST in respect of the services (because they are not supplied in Canada).

However, if the software and technical support are considered to be a single supply, and the principal object of that single supply is the right to use the software, the entire supply will be subject to Division II GST. Conversely, if the software and technical support are considered to be a single supply, and the principal object of that single supply is the technical support, the entire supply would be considered to be made outside Canada and would not be subject to Division II GST. As a practical matter, it should be expected that the technical support would never qualify as the principal object of such a supply. See Chapter 14, Software and Software Related Offerings, for a detailed discussion of these issues.

Other common situations where bundling issues often arise in connection with e-commerce supplies include the following:

- hardware or software provided with set up services;

- online instruction supported by a textbook or CD-ROM;

- services supported by software;

- Web hosting provided with technical assistance; and

- data processing supported by technical assistance.

In addition to the guidance provided in this chapter, specific examples of the manner in which the CRA has resolved these issues are discussed in detail in the rulings chapters (Chapters 12 to 18).

Where the primary issue relating to distinguishing between single and multiple supplies has been resolved, a second level of analysis is always required to be performed in connection with complex offerings:

(a) If *multiple supplies* are being provided, are one or more of those supplies deemed to be a component of another supply because of the application of the incidental supply rule?

(b) If a single supply comprised of *multiple elements* is being provided, what is the nature of that single supply?

The issue raised in (b) above relating to the identification of the nature of the supply is considered in Chapter 3, Characterization of Supply. All other issues relating to single versus multiple supplies and to the incidental supply rule are discussed in this chapter.

B. SINGLE VERSUS MULTIPLE SUPPLIES

1. Approach Adopted in Technical Information Bulletin B-090

As noted above, where e-commerce products and/or services are bundled, the determination of whether single or multiple supplies are being provided is an issue which is typically very difficult to resolve. Given the gravity of this issue, and the complexities associated with its resolution, it would ordinarily be expected that this issue would be subject to considerable discussion in TIB 090. However, unfortunately this has not occurred.

For example, the TIB 090 characterization of supply examples relate for the most part to simple supplies comprised of a single element. In those few examples which relate to bundled supplies, the CRA does conclude on the issue of whether a single or multiple supply has been made. However, it does not in any of those examples discuss how it has reached that particular conclusion.

On this important issue, the CRA has instead cross-referenced Policy Statement P-077R, "Single and Multiple Supplies" as the primary document to be considered.[1]

> As well, each example (i.e. each of the 19 characterization of supply examples) describes a single supply unless otherwise stated. Refer to Policy Statement P-077R, "Single and Multiple Supplies" for more information on single and multiple supplies.

Unfortunately, Policy Statement P-077R2 is not e-commerce specific. Accordingly, it may be difficult to apply the principles established in that policy to e-commerce supplies.

However, notwithstanding that the TIB 090 characterization of supply examples do not explain how the CRA reached any particular single versus multiple supply conclusion, the conclusions may themselves be instructive. The following summarizes the examples which relate to bundled supplies and the conclusions reached by the CRA:

Example	Elements of bundled supply	Conclusion
1	Digitized products and updates to those digitized products	Multiple supplies
4	Software updates and technical support	Single supply
5	Access to troubleshooting database and technical support through live technician	Single supply
7	Right to use software and technical support	Single supply
8	Management of back office function and right to access software	Single supply
15	Right to access digitized content and right to place advertisements on a Web site	Multiple supplies

2. Policy Statement P-077R2

At the outset, P-077R2 notes that the determination of whether single or multiple supplies are being made is a question of fact. The following

---

[1] The most recent version of this document is P-077R2.

general guiding principles are to be considered in resolving this question of fact:

(a) every supply should be regarded as distinct and independent; and

(b) a supply that is a single supply from an economic point of view should not be artificially split.

Policy Statement P-077R2 also provides the following more specific guiding principles:

(a) there is a single supply where one or more elements constitute the supply and any remaining elements serve only to enhance the supply;

(b) two or more elements are part of a single supply when the elements are integral components; the elements are inextricably bound up with each other; the elements are so intertwined and interdependent that they must be supplied together; or one element of the transaction is so dominated by another element that the first element has lost any identity for fiscal purposes;

(c) multiple supplies occur where one or more of the elements can sensibly or realistically be broken out; and

(d) the manner in which the price has been set will not be determinative. A single price does not necessarily mean that a single supply is made. Separately identified fees will not necessarily mean that there are multiple supplies.

Policy Statement P-077R2 also suggests that to resolve the single versus multiple supply issue, the transactions should never be examined in isolation. A more contextual approach will take into account the intent of the parties, the supplier's usual business practices and other circumstances surrounding the transaction. Where the terms of the agreement do not reflect the commercial reality of the transaction, those contractual terms may be discounted.

(a) Threshold Issue: Input or Element of the Supply

The threshold issue which is required to be resolved in every case involving the distinction between single and multiple supplies is whether the element in issue is something which is actually being supplied to the recipient. In many cases, what may appear to be an element of a supply (or a separate supply) will actually be an input to the supply which is being consumed or used by the supplier. The CRA notes that the agreement entered into between the parties will typically provide the guidance required to resolve this issue.

Although in theory this issue may appear to be relatively straightforward, in practice it is typically far more difficult to resolve. This is because agreements are frequently not worded in a sufficiently precise manner to distinguish between supplies and inputs. The matter is further complicated by the fact that in either case (element or input), it is the recipient who ultimately receives the particular benefit (either directly or indirectly).

TIB 090 discusses in considerable detail the distinction between inputs and elements but only in the context of telecommunication related supplies. This guidance is discussed in section D below.

(b) Secondary Issue: Are the Elements Components of a Single Supply?

Where it has been determined that every element in issue is in fact being supplied to the recipient (and is not merely an input), then the issue to be resolved is whether the elements are separate supplies or whether the elements are a constituent part of a single supply.

The CRA notes in Policy Statement P-077R2 that, as a general rule, where there are two or more suppliers or where there are two or more recipients, multiple supplies will be considered to be made. It is not clear to the author why these particular rules are framed as presumptions. Where multiple parties are involved (other than in an agency relationship), the suggestion that a single supply might be made seems to be completely inconsistent with the charging provisions of the ETA.

The CRA also provides three more specific tests in Policy Statement P-077R2 to assist in resolving the single versus multiple supply issue. It would appear from the rulings issued to date in relation to single and multiple supplies that these three issues will typically be determinative.

What Did the Supplier Provide for the Consideration Received?

For an element to be characterized as a supply, the element should be distinct and independent. It should amount to more than merely a component of an overall supply.

It is necessary to determine what the parties agreed to in the context of the recipient's needs. If any one element could be viewed as satisfying the recipient's needs on its own, then the provision of that element could be viewed as a supply distinct from any other supplies or elements.

Is the Recipient Made Aware of the Elements (in Detail) that are Part of the Package?

If the recipient is not made aware of the specific elements, this will suggest that a single supply is being made.

When the recipient is made aware of the elements that make up a package of property and/or services, this information may help to establish the relationship amongst the individual elements and the importance of each element. A detailed indication of specific elements might include the quantity of the particular elements being supplied, their physical characteristics, or the steps to be followed in providing a particular element. If the recipient is made aware of the specific elements, there may be multiple supplies or there might only be a single supply.

In the Context of the Particular Transaction, Does the Recipient have the Option to Acquire the Elements Separately or to Substitute Elements?

The purpose of this question is to establish the strength of the relationship between the elements.

The structure of the transaction should be examined to determine if the provision of a particular element is contingent on the provision of another element. If the recipient does not have the option to acquire the elements separately, then there is likely a single supply.

Conversely, if a supplier were to allow certain elements of a transaction to be substituted for others, then the provision of some elements would not be contingent on the provision of the others, which could indicate that multiple supplies are being made.

Policy Statement P-077R2 provides four examples to illustrate the application of these guiding principles. Unfortunately, none of the examples relates to e-commerce transactions and would be very difficult to apply, even by analogy, to e-commerce transactions.

C. INCIDENTAL SUPPLY RULE

Where it has been determined that a single supply is in fact being made, there is no need to consider the incidental supply rule. However, the nature of the single supply would need to be identified. This will involve applying the "principal object" test. The manner in which this test applies is described in Chapter 3, Characterization of Supply.

Where it has been determined that multiple supplies are in fact being made, the incidental supply rule should be considered. The incidental supply rule is contained in section 138 of the ETA. Where multiple supplies are in fact being made and the incidental supply rule applies, the multiple supplies will be deemed to form part of a single supply. The supplier would then be required to identify the nature of that single supply. This will require the application of the "principal object" test. However, as a practical matter, where a particular supply is considered to be incidental to some other supply (i.e., the dominant supply), then the principal object of the supply should be expected to be in the nature of the dominant supply. These issues are discussed in Chapter 3, Characterization of Supply.

As a threshold matter it should be noted that the incidental supply rule may only apply where a single consideration is charged for the supplies which are in issue. Where separate amounts of consideration are charged in respect of the various supplies, the supplies will always remain as multiple supplies. This particular consideration rule is commonly employed for tax planning purposes. It is particularly useful where one or more of the supplies, if maintained as distinct, will be eligible for preferable tax treatment.

The CRA's administrative policies with respect to the scope of the incidental supply rule are established in Policy Statement P-159R1, "Meaning of the Phrase Reasonably Regarded as Incidental" and in Policy Statement P-160R, "Meaning of the Phrase Where a Particular Property or Service if Supplied Together With Any Other Property or Service".

Generally, a supply is considered to be incidental where the particular supply "plays only a minor or subordinate role in relation to the provision of another supply". This is the technical component of the incidental supply rule. Although the relationship between the particular supplies is important, this consideration is merely one factor to be taken into account. The broader policy issues associated with the use of the incidental supply rule should always be carefully considered. In fact, Policy Statement P-159R1 makes particular note of tax leakage concerns:

> The concept of incidental supply must be viewed in the context of the design and purpose of the section in which it is used. Section 138 is intended to deal with recurring commercial transactions where an allocation of the purchase price between two or more items provided together would be administratively cumbersome for the supplier particularly where the transactions are frequent and the dollar value of the property or service is small. These types of transactions typically involve sales to consumers.

To emphasize its point with respect to low dollar-value transactions, Policy Statement P-159R1 provides a single example of a situation where the rule applies. At issue is a ticket to a performance (valued at $80) provided with a bus ticket (valued at $1.50). In terms of more specific guidance, P-159R1 provides that:

> Generally the provision of one would have to be insignificant, or of little importance relative to the provision of the other... Where the provision of property or services plays an important role by itself in the context of the particular transaction, it is not likely to be regarded as incidental to the provision of the other.

Further, the CRA specifically warns that any use of the incidental supply rule to minimize the application of tax will be carefully scrutinized:

> It generally will not apply to transactions where its application would have significant tax revenue implications.

With these policy issues in mind, the CRA has proposed two tests which are to be applied to determine whether the incidental supply rule might apply to a particular transaction. The CRA notes that ordinarily both questions would be required to be answered in the affirmative before the incidental supply rule would apply:

> (1) Where a transaction involves the provision of two or more properties and/or services, is the supplier's primary objective to provide a particular property or service, or several properties or services together?
>
> This question seeks to determine the objective of the supplier. If the supplier's objective is to provide a particular property or service and not several other properties or services, then the provision of the other properties or services might be regarded as incidental to the provision of the particular property or service. However, if the supplier's objective is to provide several properties or services, then it is unlikely that the provision of one of the properties or services would be regarded as incidental to the provision of any other.
>
> (2) Is the value of the consideration charged for a particular property or service provided together with other properties or services the same as, or only marginally different from, what the value of the consideration for the particular property or service would be if it were provided alone?
>
> Generally, where the value of the consideration for a particular property or service provided together with several other properties or services is the same as, or only marginally different from, what it would be if the particular property or service were provided alone, the provision of the other properties or services may be regarded as incidental to the provision of the particular property or service.

D. TELECOMMUNICATION SERVICES

E-commerce supplies by their very nature will always involve a telecommunication service component. Fortunately, TIB 090 very specifically addresses this important issue. That Bulletin notes at the outset that:

> For GST/HST purposes, it is important to distinguish between a supply that is a supply of a telecommunication service, and the use of telecommunications as a means by which other property and services are supplied.

The CRA has established that a telecommunication service is not typically being provided where:

(a) A telecommunication service is used or consumed by the supplier in making a supply of some other service or property.

(b) The supply involves the provision of a telecommunication service, but only as a means of delivering another service or property.

(c) The supply of the telecommunication service is incidental to the supply of some other property or service.

It would appear that with respect to (a), the telecommunication service is excluded because it is merely an input to the supply. Where (b) applies, the telecommunication service is actually provided to the customer but is a component of a single supply of something which is other than a telecommunication service. Where (c) applies, the telecommunication service is supplied to the customer and is, at least in the first instance, considered to be a separate supply. However, as a result of the application of the incidental supply rule, the supply of the telecommunication service is deemed to be an element of some other supply.

Conversely, the CRA provides that, where the predominant purpose of a particular supply meets any of the following criteria, the supply will typically be considered to be a telecommunication service:

(a) The supplier provides for the emission, transmission or reception of signs or signals through a telecommunications network.

(b) The supplier makes available a telecommunications facility for the emission, transmission or reception of signs or signals.

(c) The supplier provides a means through which other services of intangible personal property are delivered rather than to provide the services.

In each of the examples set out above, the telecommunication service is clearly not consumed by the supplier in order to provide some other supply. In fact, in each example it is apparent that the telecommunication service is the very service which the recipient is seeking. As a result, the telecommunication service cannot be considered an input.

In TIB 090, the CRA has provided a number of examples of supplies which involve a telecommunications service. In each example the CRA has offered its opinion as to whether a telecommunication service is being supplied. The following is a summary of those examples:

Example	Elements of bundled supply	Conclusion
Internet access service	Internet access and content	Single supply of telecommunication service (i.e. the access to the Internet is the object of the supply)
Web site hosting	Hosting for Web site and access to the Internet for the Web site	Single supply of other than a telecommunication service. The telecommunication service is merely an input to the supply of hosting a Web site
Internet access	Internet access, email and personal web page	Single supply of a telecommunication service (i.e., because of the Internet access)
EDI transmission of income tax returns	Supplier verifies and submits customers' income tax returns electronically	Single supply of a telecommunication service (i.e., because the transmission is the object of the supply)
Preparation and EDI transmission of income tax returns	Prepare customers' tax returns and then file electronically	Single supply of other than a telecommunication service (i.e. because the transmission is not the object of the supply)

E. E-COMMERCE PLANNING AND EXPOSURE ISSUES

Making the distinction between single and multiple supplies and determining the circumstances where the incidental supply rule applies will always involve, as a practical matter, some element of uncertainty. The issues are driven by factual determinations and, as a result, the resolution of the issues will be a very subjective exercise. Further, the issues are heavily policy driven. Where a particular outcome will allow for consumption to occur in Canada without attracting any GST, it should be expected that the basis for this position will be carefully scrutinized.

In approaching and resolving these issues, the following should be considered:

1. Notwithstanding that the resolution of single versus multiple supply issues is a very fact-specific exercise, the CRA does aim to be consistent in its approach. Where a particular situation is similar or analogous to a situation considered in an existing ruling (or preferably in a

number of rulings), the advancement of a similar approach should be expected to be more easily justified;

2. Suppliers should, where possible, develop a fall-back position. Given that the particular position which is being advanced may be open to challenge, the supplier should always consider other possible outcomes. Where possible, protection should be enhanced in respect of the primary and fall-back position;

3. Where the supplier is advancing an aggressive approach, consideration should be given as to whether this approach is necessary. For example, if recipients are typically ITC eligible, it may not make sense to adopt an aggressive strategy. Similarly, if customers are accustomed to paying GST (and would pay GST to other competing suppliers), an aggressive tax strategy may not be merited, particularly where it will result in potential exposure for the supplier; and

4. In employing a particular approach, will substantial revenue loss (to the CRA) occur, or will the supplier be enjoying a particular competitive advantage? In either of these circumstances, the particular position should be carefully evaluated to ensure that it will withstand scrutiny on audit.

Chapter 5

Place of Supply

A. OVERVIEW

The identification of the place where a particular supply is considered to be made is a direct function of the nature of the supply. This is because place of supply rules have been implemented in the ETA which are specific to each particular type of supply.

Where a supply has been incorrectly characterized, it follows that the place of supply rules which are applied will not be appropriate. In many cases, particularly in the e-commerce setting, the results will be dramatically different because of significant differences in the place of supply rules.[1]

For example, services (other than telecommunication services) are generally considered to be supplied in the location where the services are performed. Locating the place of performance will, for the most part, turn upon the identification of the locations from which the supplier and its employees operate.

However, with respect to intangible personal property, these employee and performance considerations are for the most part irrelevant. Instead, the focus is on the place where the property may be used. Given that as a practical matter, intangible personal property which is supplied through the Internet may be used anywhere, locating the place of supply will relate to locations where the property is legally allowed to be used.

The broad nature of these place of supply rules very commonly surprises both Canadian residents and non-residents, particularly where supplies are deemed to be made in jurisdictions in which the supplier has very little or no presence.

1. Three-Step Process for Determining Place and Province of Supply

The following three-step process should be undertaken in connection with locating the place and province of supply. The first step relates to determining whether any given supply is deemed to be made in Canada. The rules which govern this process are contained in sections 142 and 142.1 of the ETA and, where applicable, will deem particular supplies to be made in or outside Canada. Step one is discussed in detail under heading B below.

The second step relates to the non-resident override which is contained in section 143 of the ETA. The non-resident override, where applicable, will deem any given supply to be made outside Canada notwithstanding that it has been deemed under either of sections 142 or 142.1 to be made in Canada. Because supplies which are considered to be made outside Canada

---

[1] This will include situations where the single versus multiple supply guidelines, or the incidental supply rule in section 138 have been incorrectly applied.

are not subject to Division II GST (or HST), this rule is particularly important for non-resident suppliers. The operation of the non-resident override is discussed in Chapter 7, GST Registration and the Non-resident Override.

The third step relates to determining the province in which a particular supply is made. This is important because supplies which are considered to be made in Nova Scotia, Newfoundland or New Brunswick are subject to GST (referred to in those provinces as the Harmonized Sales Tax or "HST") at the rate of 14%. All supplies which are considered to be made in Canada but outside of the participating provinces are subject to GST at the rate of 6%.

It should be noted that the third test need only be applied in circumstances where it has first been determined that a supply has been made in Canada. If a supply is considered for any reason to be made outside Canada, there is no need to identify the province of supply because Division II GST will not apply.

It should also be noted that zero-rated supplies are subject to the GST and HST at the rate of 0%. Zero-rating is discussed in further detail in Chapter 6, Zero-rating.

B. TEST 1: PLACE OF SUPPLY — SERVICES OTHER THAN TELECOMMUNICATION SERVICES

1. General Performance Rules

Generally, services other than telecommunication services will be deemed to be supplied in Canada where the service is performed in whole or in part in Canada. This is a result of the rule contained in subsection 142(1) of the ETA.

A service may also be considered to be supplied in Canada if the service is in relation to real property situated in Canada. However, in the e-commerce environment, this real estate rule does not typically apply. This is because most e-commerce service offerings, by their very nature, would not ordinarily relate in a sufficiently direct manner to real property to result in the application of this rule. To illustrate the limited scope of this provision, consider the following example:

Example

A U.S. resident online real estate listing service lists properties which are available for sale in various jurisdictions.

It charges a daily fee to real estate agents to have specific properties listed on its Web site.

A Canadian real estate agent contracts with the online listing service to have a residential property which is located in Ontario listed on the service.

This would not likely be considered to be a service in relation to real property because the nexus between the property and the listing service is not sufficiently direct.

(a) Place of Performance

The place of performance of a particular service will be the critical factor in locating the place where it is supplied. With respect to more traditional service offerings, the identification of the place (or places) of performance has typically been a relatively straightforward exercise. Generally the place of performance would be determined by reference to any location from which the supplier (and its employees) operate. The CRA describes this basic test in the following manner:

> Although the term "performed" is not defined in the Act, the place where a service is performed is traditionally the place where the person physically doing the work is situated.

Accordingly, if employees of the supplier do not visit Canada in connection with a particular supply, then the supply of the service would be considered to be performed (and supplied) wholly outside Canada under the traditional test.

This traditional test does in fact apply to e-commerce transactions. So, for example, where an on-site technical support service is offered by a U.S. resident supplier to a Canadian customer, the service will be considered to be supplied in Canada and will be subject to GST.

Example

A U.S. supplier provides on-site technical support services for U.S. and Canadian customers.

The service includes installing and upgrading software and general troubleshooting.

The service, when provided to a Canadian customer, is considered to be performed in Canada and as a result is deemed to be supplied in Canada under subsection 142(1).

(b) Partial Performance in Canada

The place of supply test for services is often referred to as an "all or nothing test". This is because where a service is performed partially in Canada, and partially outside Canada, the entire supply is deemed to be made in Canada. The rule does not allow for any allocation to be done in connection with the two portions of the service. Many consider this rule to be particularly harsh because it will apply where, for example, only 5% of the service is performed in Canada. Consider the following example:

Example

A U.S. supplier provides technical support services for U.S. and Canadian customers.

The U.S. supplier sends a technical support employee to the customer's location to analyze the customer's hardware and software systems.

Following this visit the vast majority of the services are provided by the technical support service desk which is located in Atlanta, Georgia. Customers call the service desk and strategies for resolving the difficulties are discussed over the phone.

The entire service package when provided to a Canadian resident is deemed to be supplied in Canada. This is because the service was partially performed in Canada.

(c) Unbundling Issues

As noted above, a service performed even partially in Canada will be considered to be supplied in Canada. However, it may be possible to segregate different services so that only those services which are performed in Canada will be subject to GST while other services performed wholly outside Canada would not be subject to GST.

To implement this strategy would require that the supplier establish that two separate supplies have in fact been made. It should be expected that this type of arrangement would be carefully scrutinized by the CRA.

(d) Which Activities are Required to be Taken into Account?

Perhaps the most significant difficulty associated with the application of the place of performance rules relates to the identification of the employee activities which are required to be taken into account. Some employee activities will not, by their very nature, constitute the "performance of the service" and so engaging in those activities in Canada will not result in the supply being made in Canada. For example, where sales employees visit Canada to solicit business, this should not be expected to constitute the performance of the service in Canada. Similarly, other preparatory or auxiliary services which are conducted in Canada might not be required to be taken into account in determining whether performance of the service occurs in Canada. This might include, for example, purely administrative functions such as accepting customer payments in Canada.

Another performance issue relates to whether substantive tasks are required to be taken into account where the task is performed exclusively or primarily for the benefit of the supplier. Consider a U.S. supplier which provides a distant online education service for Canadian corporations. The supplier's employees who provide the online service operate from an office in Washington. However, once a year the supplier sends two employees to the customer's office to obtain feedback as to the adequacy of the service. This feedback is used to improve the supplier's service offerings in the future. It would appear arguable, given that the feedback is obtained for the benefit of the supplier, that this function should not be taken into account in determining the location where the service is performed.

It is clear, however, that where activities such as those referred to above (relating to meeting with the client or preparing reports), are undertaken for the benefit of the customer this will be considered to constitute performance of the service. In TIB 090, the CRA provides an example of a Canadian supplier which provides programming services to U.S. clients. All of the programming services are performed at the recipient's office in the U.S. However, once the programming has been completed, the supplier returns to its offices in Canada where it prepares a client report which summarizes the services provided. The CRA concluded that the place where the report is prepared must be taken into account in identifying the places of performance. The CRA explained that this is because the report is a component of the service supplied.

The determination of whether preparatory activities should be taken into account in locating the place of performance may also be problematic. The CRA has suggested that some preparatory activities may not be required to be taken into account in determining the place of performance of a particular supply. To illustrate the difficulties associated with resolving this issue, consider the following example:

Example

A Canadian service provider provides technical computer training to U.S. corporations.

The training is always delivered on site at the customer's offices in the U.S. However, the instruction manuals and other materials are developed and updated at the supplier's offices in Toronto.

It may be arguable that the development and updating of the instruction manuals at the supplier's office in Canada do not constitute an element of the performance of the service (i.e., they are in the nature of preparatory work). This argument may carry more weight where the manuals have been fully developed prior to the time that the customer has been identified.

(e) Timing Issues

It is not clear how the place of performance rules are to be applied in circumstances where, at the time the supply is made (i.e., when the contract is entered into), it is not clear whether performance might occur in Canada. Consider the following example:

Example

A U.S. supplier provides technical support services to Canadian customers. The customer pays an "up front" annual fee for the services.

The vast majority of issues are handled by the supplier's technical support team which operates from offices in the U.S. and who communicate with customers over the telephone.

The service contract provides that if any particular technical support issue cannot be resolved by the help desk an employee of the supplier will visit the Canadian office to provide technical support in person.

As a practical matter the supplier will only be required to send employees to Canada on rare occasions and most customers will never receive an onsite visit.

In this situation it is not clear whether the services would be considered to be performed in part in Canada. At the time the contract is entered into (which is the relevant time for determining the place of supply), there will be no way of determining whether an onsite visit will be required for that particular customer.

2. Administrative Extensions to Performance of Service Rules

Policy considerations play a very substantial role in the identification of the place of performance of e-commerce services. The examples set out below show that where similar services are provided by a Canadian resident supplier and by a non-resident supplier, the non-resident may, because of its residency status, enjoy a special tax advantage. Where possible, the CRA will take steps to minimize this type of disparity:

Example 1

A Canadian service provider offers technical support to Canadian individuals in respect of issues relating to the use and operation of their home computer.

The advice and technical support is provided over the phone from a location in Canada.

This service would be considered to be performed in Canada and would be subject to Division II GST either at the rate of 6% or 14%.[2]

Example 2

A U.S. service provider offers technical support to Canadian individuals in respect of issues relating to the use and operation of their home computer.

The advice and technical support is provided over the phone from a location outside Canada.

This service would be considered to be performed outside Canada and would not be subject to Division II GST.

As noted above, any relaxation in the application of the place of performance rules would exacerbate tax leakage and "level playing field" concerns. Notwithstanding the significance of these concerns, the establishment of a regime which would fully eliminate these inequities would be impractical. However, the beneficial tax treatment which is afforded to non-residents will more typically result from the operation of the non-resident override than to any relaxation of the place of supply rules.

(a) Deemed Performance in Canada

The CRA has in TIB 090 administratively provided that a service will be deemed to be performed at least in part in Canada in the four following circumstances (referred to further below as rules (a) through (d):

(a) The service requires a person to perform a task (i.e., the supplier acts through one or more of its employees), and the person performing or physically carrying out the task is situated in Canada at the time the activity is done;

(b) The service includes operations performed by a supplier's equipment (e.g., computer equipment), and the equipment is located in Canada;

(c) The supply involves doing something to or with a recipient's equipment by accessing it from a remote location, and the recipient's

---

[2] The rules set out in the Place of Supply (GST/HST) Regulations should be taken into account in locating the province of supply.

equipment is located in Canada. However, this does not apply to a service wholly performed outside Canada, where the results are subsequently delivered electronically to a recipient's computers in Canada, e.g., a programming service carried out at the supplier's location outside Canada and e-mailed to a recipient in Canada; or

(d) Any activity related to the performance of the service is undertaken in Canada.

Unfortunately, TIB 090 does not provide any examples to illustrate the practical application of these four performance rules. As a result the scope of the rules remains in doubt.

(b) Employee-Related Considerations

The employee-related performance rules are those contained in (a) and (d). It appears arguable that rule (a) is merely a restatement of the traditional place of performance test. Accordingly, the scope of this rule may be ascertained by reference to the CRA's traditional approach. However, performance rule (d) is far more problematic. Assuming that the traditional approach is covered off by rule (a), the suggestion seems to be that performance rule (d) must by necessary implication relate to other extended circumstances. The specific wording of the rule in (d) also seems to support the theory that it establishes a more liberal performance test. For example, while the traditional approach only takes into account tasks which are a component of the service which is provided to the customer, performance rule (d) seems to also take into account any activity which is *related* to the performance of the service.

This may suggest that tangential, preparatory, or even administrative tasks (such as server or Web site maintenance) should be taken into account when resolving the place of performance issue including where those tasks are not components of the supply (i.e., the tasks are undertaken to allow for the service to be provided). Further, tasks such as accepting payment for the service might, if a particularly liberal interpretation were to be adopted, be considered to be an "activity related to the performance of the service".

Hopefully, the CRA will not interpret rule (d) in a manner which departs significantly (or at all) from the traditional approach. A more traditional approach would require that a direct nexus exist between the particular activity and the service to be provided. In the event that this rule is interpreted in a more liberal manner by the CRA, it should be expected that the courts may not lend their concurrence.

(c) Equipment-Related Considerations

Performance may also occur in Canada for e-commerce purposes even where employees do not enter Canada. The equipment-based rules (rules (b) and (c)) should be carefully considered by non-residents who supply services to Canadians through computer equipment or other hardware. Similarly, these extended rules should be considered by suppliers who might, under these rules, be considered to be making a supply in a participating province. The following two examples illustrate the operation of these rules in respect of suppliers whose employees do not enter Canada:

Example 1 — Rule (b)

A U.S. resident corporation offers a health-related consulting service to customers located in Canada.

The customers are charged an hourly fee to interact online through a chat room with consultants who are located in the U.S.

The chat room operates through the supplier's Web site which is hosted on a server in Ontario which is leased to the supplier.

This service would likely be considered to be a service which is supplied in Canada because the service involves operations performed by the supplier's equipment located in Canada (rule (b)).[3]

Example 2 — Rule (c)

A U.S. resident corporation provides IT technical support to its subsidiary located in Canada.

Where any user in Canada experiences technical difficulties the user calls the help desk in the U.S. The help desk employee remotely logs onto the user's computer in Canada to resolve the issue.

This service would likely be considered to be a service supplied in Canada because the service involves remote access to a computer located in Canada (performance rule (c)).

Although the scope of rule (c) appears to be relatively straightforward, the same cannot be said of rule (b). Some of the issues which remain outstanding in respect of rule (b) include the following:

(a) Could a Web site or software be considered to be the supplier's equipment?

Given the manner in which the CRA has approached the analogous issue in connection with the identification of permanent establishments, it

---

[3] For a related issue, see for example, ruling 37297 summarized in Chapter 16, Online Content, Services, and Other General Offerings.

would appear that neither software nor a Web site would be considered to be equipment. However, a server will be considered to be equipment.

(b) When is equipment considered to be the supplier's equipment?

Given the approach adopted by the CRA with respect to the circumstances when servers will be considered to be permanent establishments, it would appear that equipment will be the "supplier's equipment" when it is "at the disposal" of the supplier. This may include, for example, an informal arrangement (for example a server belonging to a subsidiary) which results in the supplier being allowed to use the equipment. However, equipment which is accessed in an ISP arrangement will not likely be considered the "supplier's equipment". This is because it would not be at the disposal of the supplier. This conclusion is supported by the manner in which the CRA has approached the permanent establishment issue.

(c) What types of operations will be included in this determination?

The scope of operations to be included is far from clear. It may be arguable that tangential or auxiliary services provided through equipment in Canada should not be included. This would be because tangential or auxiliary services would not typically be taken into account under the traditional place of performance test (rule (a)).

However, the issue may be moot in any event. Even where it is successfully argued that the service "does not include operations performed by the supplier's equipment", the non-resident person may be found to be performing the service under rule (d). In fact, a number of rulings have already held that where the supplier performs any task in relation to equipment in Canada, the service will be considered to be performed in Canada. This will include, for example, maintaining or setting up the Web site or server.[4]

C. TEST 2: PLACE OF SUPPLY — TELECOMMUNICATION SERVICES

1. General Performance Rules

The definition of "telecommunication service" in subsection 123(1) establishes two distinct types of services as follows:

(a) Emitting, transmitting or receiving signs, signals, writing, images or sounds, or intelligence of any nature by wire, cable, radio, optical or other electromagnetic system, or by any similar technical system; or

---

[4] See the rulings in Chapter 16 in particular.

(b) Making available for such emission, transmission or reception tele-communications facilities of a person who carries on the business of supplying services referred to in paragraph (a).

The starting point for determining the place of supply of a telecommunication service is the determination of which of the two types of services is being provided. The place of supply rules for each of the two types of telecommunication services are set out in subsection 142.1(2) of the ETA.

These telecommunication specific rules override the ordinary place of supply rules set out in section 142. However, where a telecommunication service is deemed to be supplied in Canada under the place of supply rules contained in section 142.1, the non-resident override may apply to deem the supply to be made outside Canada.

(a) Type (A) Services

Where it has been determined that the telecommunication service is of the type described in paragraph (a) (i.e., the service of emitting, transmitting or receiving signs, signals . . .), the place of supply rules are contained in paragraph 142.1(*b*). These rules provide that the supply is made in Canada if:

(i) the telecommunication is emitted and received in Canada; or

(ii) the telecommunication is emitted or received in Canada and the billing location for the service is in Canada.

Pursuant to subsection 142.1(1), the "billing location" for the service will be considered to be in Canada in either of the following circumstances:

(a) where the consideration payable for the service is charged or applied to an account that the recipient has with a person who carries on the business of supplying telecommunication services, and the account relates to a telecommunications facility that is used or is available for use by the recipient to obtain telecommunication services, that telecommunications facility is ordinarily located in Canada; or

(b) in any other case, the telecommunications facility used to initiate the service is located in Canada.

The concept of "billing location" is much broader than ordinary usage might suggest. The CRA has described the concept of the "billing location" in TIB 090, as follows:

> The billing location for a telecommunication service is a factor only where the telecommunication is either emitted or received in Canada, but not both emitted and received in Canada. Pursuant to subsection 142.1(1) of

the Act, the billing location is considered to be in Canada if the fee for the service is charged or applied to an account the recipient has with the telecommunication service supplier that relates to a telecommunications facility used or made available for use by the recipient to obtain telecommunication services, and that telecommunications facility is ordinarily located in Canada. The billing location is not necessarily the same as the billing address, or the place to which an invoice is sent.

The definition of "billing location" references the location of the "telecommunications facility used to initiate the service". The term "telecommunications facility" is defined in subsection 123(1) as:

> ... any facility, apparatus or other thing (including any wire, cable, radio, optical or other electromagnetic system, or any similar technical system, or any part thereof) that is used or is capable of being used for telecommunications.

(b) Type (B) Services

Where it has been determined that the telecommunication service is of the type described in paragraph (B) (i.e., making available telecommunications facilities), the place of supply rules are contained in paragraph 142.1(*a*):

> (*a*) in the case of a telecommunication service of making telecommunications facilities available, the facilities or any part thereof are located in Canada;

The CRA in TIB 090 provided a single example of the operation of this place of supply rule in connection with Internet service providers:

> *An ISP located in Canada provides Internet access to customers.*
>
> Internet access is a telecommunication service which involves making available telecommunications facilities. The supply of the Internet access is deemed to be made in Canada as the facilities or part thereof which enables connection to the Internet are located in Canada.

Given the broad definition of "telecommunications facility" (set out above) any hardware located in Canada (including, for example, simple LAN jacks) which is used or is capable of being used in connection with the service, will result in the supply being made in Canada. The broad manner in which this place of supply rule operates is evidenced in a number of the rulings discussed in Chapter 15, Telecommunication Services and Related Supplies.

2. Special Allocation Rule

Section 136.4 of the ETA contains a special rule which relates to the granting of sole access to a telecommunications channel. A "telecommunications channel" is defined as "a telecommunications circuit, line, frequency, channel, partial channel or other means of sending or receiving a telecommunication but does not include a satellite channel".

The rule provides that, where a person supplies a telecommunication service of providing sole access to a telecommunications channel for the purpose of transmitting telecommunications between a place in a participating province and a place in another province, then two separate supplies will be deemed to be made. The consideration attributable to the supply made in the participating province will correspond with the length of the channel located within that province. Similarly, the consideration attributable to the supply made other than in the participating province, will correspond with the length of the channel located outside the participating province. Similar rules will apply where the channel spans additional provinces. This rule represents a significant departure from the typical "all or nothing" approach which applies when locating most supplies.

It would appear that the CRA has administratively allowed for the application of this rule in connection with telecommunication channels which span Canada and another country (i.e., the U.S.). On this issue, see in particular ruling 34339, which is discussed in Chapter 15, Telecommunication Services and Related Supplies.

D. PLACE OF SUPPLY — INTANGIBLE PERSONAL PROPERTY

The place of supply rules which apply to intangible personal property are notoriously broad. Intangible personal property will be deemed to be supplied in Canada under the rule in subsection 142(1) where:

(i) the property may be used in whole or in part in Canada; or

(ii) the property relates to real property situated in Canada, to tangible personal property ordinarily situated in Canada, or to a service to be performed in Canada.

In the e-commerce environment most supplies will be at risk of being deemed to be supplied in Canada in connection with the "may be used in whole or in part in Canada" requirement.

1. "May Be Used" in Canada Requirement

The CRA has emphasized that the term "may be used" is interpreted to mean "allowed to be used". Where intangible personal property is permitted to be used in Canada (i.e., where there are no contractual restrictions which would prohibit use in Canada) the property will be deemed to be supplied in Canada. The fact that, as a practical matter, the particular property will not ever be used in Canada is irrelevant. The CRA has noted in TIB 090 that, for example:

> ... the fact that the supply may be made to a recipient who is outside Canada has no bearing on whether the supply is made in Canada.

This broad place of supply rule is commonly misunderstood by non-resident suppliers. The following example illustrates the broad application of this rule:

Example

A supplier in China provides its customers with the right to download and read electronic books.

All of the customers are individuals who are resident in China. The customers would typically be expected to access the e-books on their home computers.

The customer is not restricted by contract or otherwise from accessing or using the books from a location in Canada.

This supply is considered to be made in Canada because there are no contractual restrictions in place to prevent the customers from accessing the content from a location in Canada.

This example may appear to be anomalous because it seems to suggest that the supplier in China would be required to collect GST from a customer in China. However, this broad place of supply rule is tempered by the non-resident override, and by the non-resident registration rules. This type of supplier would not typically be GST registered, and would not be required to be registered because of the absence of a substantial connection to Canada. All other requirements of the non-resident override (relating to carrying on business in Canada and relating to supplies made through a permanent establishment in Canada), would be easily satisfied by this type of supplier.

2. Mechanisms for Restricting Use of Intangible Personal Property

To avoid the application of this incredibly broad place of supply rule, the supplier is required to restrict the property from being used in any location in Canada. Generally, this restriction will be contained in the agreement entered into between the supplier and the recipient.

However, the CRA has also indicated that other, less formal measures may be undertaken to impose this restriction, particularly with respect to consumer transactions. These less formal measures will generally be sufficient as long as they are clearly communicated to the customer. For example, the CRA has suggested that the restriction may be established on the Web site through which the supply is made. However, the CRA has also signaled that for business-to-business transactions, the CRA would expect to see more formal contractual restrictions in place.

The supplier who has appropriately restricted the use of the property to locations outside Canada will not be charged with the responsibility of monitoring location of use, or otherwise enforcing the restrictions. Accordingly, if a particular customer were to contravene a contractual term which prohibited him from accessing intangible personal property from any location in Canada, the supplier who has acted in good faith should not be expected to face exposure.

E. TEST 3: PLACE OF SUPPLY — HARMONIZED PROVINCES

It is only where a particular supply is deemed to be made in Canada (and has not been deemed to be made outside Canada because of the override) that the province of supply must be identified.

Where a supply is made in Canada but outside of the participating provinces, the supply, unless zero-rated or exempt, will be taxed at the rate of 6%. Where a supply is made in Canada and in a participating province, the supply unless zero-rated or exempt, will be taxed at the rate of 14%.

1. Intangible Personal Property

The general province of supply rules for intangible personal property are contained in Part III of Schedule IX to the ETA.

Rule 1

Where intangible personal property is supplied which does not relate to either real property, tangible personal property, or services to be performed, the primary rule is as follows: if all or substantially all of the Canadian rights in respect of the property can be used only in a single province, then the supply will be made in that province.[5]

"Canadian rights" is defined to mean that part of the intangible personal property that can be used in Canada. The following example illustrates the operation of this rule:

---

[5] Subparagraph 2(*d*)(i) of Part III of Schedule IX.

Example

A supplier licences software to a customer who has offices in Ontario.

The software licence prohibits the customer from using the software outside Ontario.

The software is considered to be supplied in Ontario.

Where this rule applies there is no need to consider the remaining province of supply rules contained in Part III. However, this rule will never apply where there are no restrictions as to the location where the intangible personal property may be used.

Rule 2

The second rule for intangible personal property which does not relate to real property, tangible personal property, or services to be performed is that the supply will be made in a particular province if the place of negotiation of the supply is in that province and the property can be used otherwise than exclusively outside that province.[6] This rule does not apply where rule 1 applies.

The place of negotiation of the supply is the location of the supplier's permanent establishment at which the individual principally involved in negotiating an agreement for the supplier ordinarily works or ordinarily reports in the performance of his or her duties relating to the supplier's activities in the course of which the supply is made. The term "negotiating" includes the making or accepting of an offer.[7]

Where rule 1 does not apply, but the place of negotiation is in Canada, and the property may not be used exclusively outside the province of negotiation, then this rule will locate the supply in the province of negotiation.

Rule 3

Where neither of rules 1 or 2 locate the supply in a particular province, the supply (which does not relate to real property, tangible personal property or services to be performed) will be considered to be made in a participating province if:

(a) the Canadian rights in respect of the property cannot be used otherwise than primarily in the participating provinces; and

(b) where the place of negotiation of the supply is outside Canada, the property cannot be used otherwise than exclusively in Canada

---

[6] Subparagraph 2(*d*)(ii) of Part III of Schedule IX.

[7] Section 1 of Part I of Schedule IX.

Failing the application of all of these rules the supply will be deemed, by default, to be made in other than a participating province.

Special Override Rules for Memberships

Section 3 of Part IX of Schedule IX provides that, notwithstanding any of the rules set out in Parts I through VIII of Schedule IX, a supply will be deemed to be made in a province if that supply is prescribed as made in that province. This is known as the province of supply override.

The specific override rules are contained in the Place of Supply (GST/HST) Regulations. Section 6 of the Regulations provides that a supply of a membership will be deemed to be made in a particular province if the membership is supplied to an individual, the Canadian rights in respect of the membership can be exercised other than exclusively in a single province, and the mailing address of the recipient of the supply is in that province.

In all other cases, the membership will be considered to be a supply of intangible personal property and will be located in accordance with the Part III intangible personal property rules described above.

2. Services (Other than Telecommunication Services)

To determine the province of supply of services which are not telecommunication services, a threshold determination must be made as to whether the service constitutes a "computer related service".

A "computer related service" is defined in the Place of Supply (GST/HST) Regulations to mean:

(a) A technical support service which is provided by means of telecommunications and relates to the operation or use of computer hardware or software; or

(b) A service involving the electronic storage of information and computer-to-computer transfer of information.

The special rules which apply to a "computer related service" are described in heading 4 below. All other services (which are not telecommunication services) are subject to the more general province of supply rules set out in Part V of Schedule IX.

Rule 1

The first rule provides that a service will be considered to be supplied in a particular province if all or substantially all of the Canadian element of the service is performed in that province.[8] The Canadian element of a service is that portion of the service which is performed in Canada. If the service is provincially located with this rule, there is no need to consider the remaining rules.

The identification of the place of performance of a service will require that the extended place of performance rules described in TIB 090 be taken into account. This will require, for example, that the location of any of the supplier's equipment through which the service is provided be considered. It will also require that the location of the recipient's computer be taken into account where the service relates to "doing something to or with a recipient's equipment by accessing it from a remote location".

Rule 2

The second rule provides that a service will be considered to be supplied in a particular province if the place of negotiation for the supply is in the province and all or substantially all of the service is not performed outside that province.

Rule 3

Where neither of rules 1 or 2 apply, a service will be considered to be supplied in a participating province where:

(a) The place of negotiation of the supply is in Canada and the Canadian element of the service is performed primarily in the participating provinces; or

(b) The place of negotiation of the supply is outside Canada, all or substantially all of the service is performed in Canada, and the Canadian element of the service is performed primarily in the participating provinces.

In all other cases (unless the override applies), the supply will be considered to be made in other than a participating province. It should be noted that the rules which relate to the province of supply of services are very closely analogous to those described above with respect to intangible personal property.

3. Telecommunication Services

To determine the province of supply of telecommunication services, two threshold determinations must be made.

---

[8] Paragraph 2(*a*) of Part V of Schedule IX.

The first threshold determination relates to whether the service constitutes the provision of sole access to a telecommunications channel which allows for the transmission of telecommunications between a place in a participating province and a place located in another province. Section 136.4 of the ETA and section 3 of Part VIII of Schedule IX provide that, in those circumstances, two separate supplies will be deemed to be made. The rate at which the GST applies will be a function of the portion of the channel which is within the participating provinces.

The second threshold determination relates to whether the services are considered to be a "computer related service" or the service of providing Internet access. If the service is a computer related service or the provision of Internet access, then special place of supply rules apply. These special rules are described in heading 4 below.

All other telecommunication services are subject to the more general rules described below. The rules are set out in Part VIII of Schedule IX.

The rules draw a distinction between telecommunication services of making telecommunication facilities available and all other telecommunication services. This distinction is similar to that which has been drawn in the general place of supply rules.

Where the service is the making of telecommunication facilities available (other than the granting of sole access to a telecommunications channel), the service is made in a particular province if:

(a) All of the facilities are ordinarily located in that province; or

(b) Where not all of the facilities are ordinarily located in that province, the invoice for the supply is sent to an address in that province.

Where the service is other than the making of telecommunication facilities available, and is not the granting of sole access to a telecommunications channel, then the service is made in a particular province if the telecommunication:

(a) Is both emitted and received in that province;

(b) Is either emitted or received in that province and the billing location for the service is in that province; or

(c) Is emitted in that province and received outside that province, and the billing location for that service is not in a province in which the telecommunication is emitted and received.

Section 1 of Part VIII describes the circumstances when the billing location will be considered to be in a particular province. This description corresponds with the description of the billing location which is contained in subsection 142.1(1). The billing location will be considered to be in a particular province where the telecommunication supplier charges or applies the fee for the service to the recipient's account relating to telecommunication facilities that are used or are available for use to obtain telecommunication services, and all those facilities are ordinarily located in that province.

If the telecommunications supplier does not charge or apply the fee for the service to the recipient's account, the billing location is considered to be in a particular province if the telecommunications facility used to initiate the service is located in that province.

4. Supplies of Internet Access and Computer Related Services

The supply of Internet access, and any service which is a computer related service, are subject to special province of supply rules. These rules are contained in the Place of Supply (GST/HST) Regulations and, where applicable, override the general province of supply provisions.

A "computer related service" is defined as:

(a) a computer support service that is provided by means of telecommunications and relates to the operation or use of computer hardware or software; or

(b) a service involving the electronic storage of information and the computer to computer transfer of information.

Section 10 of the Place of Supply (GST/HST) Regulations provides two separate rules for services relating to Internet access or a computer related service depending on whether there is to be a single final recipient of the service or multiple final recipients of the service. The term "final recipient" is defined as follows:

> "final recipient" in respect of a computer related service or access to the Internet, means a person who is the recipient of a supply of the service or access and who acquires if otherwise than for the purpose of supplying it to another person.

It should be noted that this definition refers to the person who is the recipient of "*a* supply" as opposed to the person who is the recipient of "*the* supply". This means that the person in issue (i.e., the final recipient) may or may not be the person to whom the particular supply is made. As described below, these complex rules will often require that the supplier look beyond the person to whom the particular supply is made (i.e., in a re-supply situation), in order to locate the province of supply.

(a) Single Final Recipient

Where there is a single final recipient of the computer related supply or the supply of Internet access made by a particular supplier and the recipient acquires the supply through an agreement either with the supplier or another supplier, then the rules may be summarized as follows:

Default Rule: if the recipient avails itself of the service or access at a single ordinary location in a particular province, the supply is made in that province if:

(a) the particular supplier maintains information sufficient to determine that location; or

(b) it is the normal business practice of the supplier to obtain information sufficient to determine that location.

Alternative Rule: if the above does not apply (i.e., the recipient does not avail itself of the service at a single ordinary location or if the supplier does not have the relevant information), the supply will be made in a particular province if the mailing address of the recipient of the supply is in that province.

(b) Multiple Final Recipients

Where there are multiple final recipients of a computer related service or Internet access made by a particular supplier, and each recipient acquires the supply either under an agreement with the particular supplier or another supplier, the operation of the rules may be summarized as follows:

Default Rule: Where in the case of each recipient, there is a single location at which the recipient avails itself of the service or access and:

(a) either the particular supplier maintains information sufficient to determine that location; or

(b) it is the normal business practice of the particular supplier to obtain information sufficient to determine that location,

then the determination of the province of supply is as follows:

(a) with respect to a computer related service, the province of supply rules contained in Part V are to be applied on the basis that the service is considered to be performed (for the purpose of applying those rules) in a particular province to the extent to which the final recipients avail themselves of the service in that province.

(b) with respect to Internet access, the province of supply rules contained in Part III are to be applied on the basis that the access is attainable in a particular province to the extent to which the final recipients avail themselves of the access in that province.

Alternative Rule: Where the default rule does not apply, the supply of the computer related service or Internet access will be made in a particular province if the mailing address of the recipient of the particular supply (and not the final recipients) is in that province.

Chapter 6

Zero-rating

A. OVERVIEW

Zero-rating is a concept which relates to the application of Division II GST. Where a supply of property or services is considered to be made in Canada, but qualifies for zero-rating relief, the supply will be subject to GST at the rate of 0%. Where a supply qualifies for zero-rating relief, there is no requirement to consider the province of supply issue. This is because the 0% tax rate would apply to provide relief in respect of both the GST and HST.

All of the zero-rating provisions are contained in Schedule VI to the ETA. That schedule contains 10 separate parts, each of which relates to a particular subject matter. For the purposes of this book, the only relevant zero-rating provisions are those which are contained in Part V of that schedule, and which relate to exported supplies.

B. DISTINCTION BETWEEN ZERO-RATED AND EXEMPT SUPPLIES

At the outset, the distinction should be drawn between supplies which are zero-rated and supplies which are GST exempt. Supplies which may be made on a GST exempt basis are described in Schedule V to the ETA.

From the perspective of the recipient of a supply, it does not matter whether a supply is zero-rated or exempt. The recipient will not be required to pay any Division II GST in respect of the supply. However, the distinction between zero-rated and exempt supplies is very important from the perspective of the supplier because the distinction relates to the eligibility of the supplier to claim ITCs.

The basic test for claiming ITCs is contained in section 169 of the ETA. Where a GST registered person acquires or imports property or a service and incurs GST expense in connection with that acquisition or importation, the person will generally be entitled to claim an ITC to recover the amount of GST paid. However, the ITC will only be available to the extent to which the person acquired or imported the property or service for consumption, use or supply in the course of commercial activities of the person.

As a general rule, a business which is carried on by a person will be considered to constitute a "commercial activity" except to the extent to which the business involves the making of exempt supplies. Similarly, engaging in an adventure or concern in the nature of trade will be considered to constitute a "commercial activity", except to the extent to which it involves the making of exempt supplies.[1]

---

[1] See the definition of "commercial activity" in subsection 123(1) of the ETA. The definition of "commercial activity" also provides for other exclusions relating to the application of the "reasonable expectation of profit test". However, these exclusions are not directly relevant in the e-commerce context.

Given that the making of exempt supplies (either in the course of carrying on a business or in the course of engaging in an adventure or concern in the nature of trade) does not constitute a commercial activity, it follows that a supplier may not claim ITCs to the extent that it incurs expenses to make exempt supplies. For this reason, suppliers would prefer to make supplies which are zero-rated as opposed to supplies which are exempt.

The following two examples are intended to illustrate this distinction:

Example: Exempt Supplies

A financial institution provides a number of services to its clients which are considered to be exempt financial services.

The financial institution incurs a number of GST taxable expenses in connection with the operation of the business which include leasing office space, renting computers, and buying office furniture.

The financial institution would not charge any GST to its customers in respect of the fees charged for the provision of exempt financial services.

The financial institution would not be entitled to claim any ITCs in respect of the GST expenses incurred to lease office space, rent computers, or buy office furniture. This is because the institution provides only exempt supplies.

Example: Zero-rated Supplies

A Canadian firm provides consulting services to customers located in the U.S.

The firm incurs a number of GST taxable expenses in connection with the operation of the business which include leasing office space, renting computers, and buying office furniture.

The firm would not charge the GST to its U.S. customers in respect of the services provided. This is because the services are considered to be zero-rated.

The firm would be entitled to claim ITCs in respect of the GST expenses incurred to lease office space, rent computers, and buy office furniture. This is because the supplies made are taxable, but at the rate of 0%.

C. SCOPE OF ZERO-RATING

Part V of Schedule VI of the ETA establishes the circumstances in which supplies may be made to a non-resident on a zero-rated basis. Although Part V of Schedule VI is commonly referred to as the "export schedule", it is arguable that this term does not fully reflect its broad scope.

For example, zero-rating relief may be available in respect of supplies made from a non-resident supplier to a non-resident recipient.

The policy considerations which resulted in the development of this export schedule are important. The schedule allows for suppliers (who are, in most cases, Canadian suppliers) to supply property or services into the world market without their offerings being encumbered with any GST. This is particularly important because recipients located outside Canada will not typically be GST registered, and accordingly will not be eligible to claim ITCs. In addition to the provisions which ensure that GST is not embedded in supplies made to non-residents who are not registered, some of the provisions allow for zero-rating in respect of supplies made to non-residents who are registered. Although this particular class of recipients would typically be ITC eligible, these provisions provide relief against the administrative burden and interest carrying charges associated with paying the GST and then claiming back ITCs.

However, the zero-rating schedule is not without its problems. The policy imperative of allowing suppliers to sell their offerings into the world market on a GST-free basis is required to be weighed off against tax leakage risks. In particular, there is a substantial risk that overly broad zero-rating relief provisions may allow for some consumption to occur in Canada without attracting GST. Where these two policy imperatives clash, the tax leakage imperative will typically prevail. This delicate balancing act will often result in rules which at times may appear arbitrary and unfair.

D. E-COMMERCE ZERO-RATING PROVISIONS

The most commonly relied upon zero-rating provisions in the e-commerce context are described below. At the outset it should be noted that the following zero-rating provisions are not mutually exclusive. A failure to qualify for zero-rating under a particular provision does not preclude the possibility that zero-rating may be available under a separate provision. Similarly, it is not uncommon for a particular supply to concurrently qualify for zero-rating relief under two or more distinct zero-rating provisions.

1. Services

(a) Section 5: Agency or Representative Services

A supply made to a non-resident person of a service of acting as an agent of the person or of arranging for, procuring or soliciting orders for supplies by or to the person, where the service is in respect of (*a*) a supply to the person that is included in any other section of this Part; or

(*b*) a supply made outside Canada by or to the person.

Section 5 allows for agency services to be provided to a non-resident person on a zero-rated basis where the service is in respect of another supply made to the non-resident person which also qualifies for zero-rating. Alternatively, the agency service may be provided on a zero-rated basis where the services are in respect of a supply made outside Canada by the non-resident person. For example, if the agency services are provided in respect of a supply of tangible personal property, and the property is deemed to be supplied outside Canada under either the section 142 place of supply rules or under the non-resident override, the agency services will be zero-rated.

The section 5 relief is not limited to agency services. Services which are in the nature of arranging for, procuring, or soliciting orders for supplies by or to the non-resident person, may also qualify where either of the conditions described above with respect to the underlying supply are met.

The section 5 zero-rating relief is frequently in issue in connection with third party sales. This issue is discussed in detail in Chapter 13, Third Party Sales of Goods.

(b) Section 7: General Services

A supply of a service made to a non-resident person, but not including a supply of

(*a*) a service made to an individual who is in Canada at any time when the individual has contact with the supplier in relation to the supply;

(*a*.1) a service that is rendered to an individual while that individual is in Canada;

(*b*) an advisory, consulting or professional service;

(*c*) a postal service;

(*d*) a service in respect of real property situated in Canada;

(*e*) a service in respect of tangible personal property that is situated in Canada at the time the service is performed;

(*f*) a service of acting as an agent of the non-resident person or of arranging for, procuring or soliciting orders for supplies by or to the person;

(*g*) a transportation service; or

(*h*) a telecommunication service.

Section 7 is the most commonly applied zero-rating provision for services. The relief provided is particularly broad in that the section allows for zero-rating in respect of services provided to non-residents who are GST registered. However, the many carve-outs associated with this provision should be carefully considered. Some of the leading e-commerce related carve-outs are discussed below.

The distinction between the related carve-outs in paragraphs (*a*) and (*a*.1) should be noted. In paragraph (*a*), the reference to "made to an individual" indicates that it is only where the recipient of the supply is an individual that the carve-out will apply. This should be contrasted with paragraph (*a*.1) where the concept of "rendered" is used. A service may be rendered to an individual (i.e., an employee) in circumstances where the supply is made to a separate person (for example, a corporation). The suggestion is that for the purposes of (*a*.1), contact with individuals in Canada who are associated with the recipient is particularly risky.

CRA Memorandum 4.5.3, "Exports — Services and Intellectual Property", discusses the scope of the carve-outs in paragraphs (*b*) and (*c*). Where the carve-out in paragraph (*b*) (which relates to professional, advisory, or consulting services) applies, section 23 should be considered. Where the carve-out in paragraph (*c*) (which relates to postal services) applies, section 22 should be considered.

The "in respect of" carve out in paragraphs (*d*) and (*e*) also warrants a high level of respect as this issue can be particularly contentious. For example, in ruling 48298 (discussed in Chapter 16), the central issue was whether services were in respect of tangible personal property. The service was accepting and processing customer rebate applications on an outsourced basis. If the service was in respect of tangible personal property, zero-rating would not be available. The CRA concluded that the service was in fact provided in respect of tangible personal property. The tangible personal property in issue were rebate forms which had been filed by the consumers, and which had been shipped in bulk to the service provider. This ruling is but one example of the broad scope of the "in respect of" test.

Policy Statement P-169R, "Meaning of in Respect of Real Property Situated in Canada", provides a detailed description of the issues to be taken into account in determining whether the "in respect of" test is met.

(c) Section 8: Advertising Services

A supply of a service of advertising made to a non-resident person who is not registered under Subdivision d of Division V of Part IX of the Act at the time the service is performed.

This provision is often relied upon to provide relief in circumstances where zero-rating is not available under section 7. Section 8 does not contain the carve-outs which are a component of section 7 (in particular the "in respect of" requirements). However, unlike section 7, relief is only available where the non-resident is not registered.

The term "advertising service" is not specifically defined in the ETA. However, administratively, the CRA interprets the term "advertising service" in an extremely broad manner to include:

> ... the service of creating a message and a service directly related to the communication of such a message. The message must be oriented towards soliciting business, attracting donations, or calling public attention in the form of an information notice, a political announcement or other similar communication.[2]

The scope and operation of this zero-rating provision is discussed in detail in Chapter 12, Advertising Services.

(d) Section 18: Training Services

> A supply made to a non-resident person, other than an individual, who is not registered under Subdivision d of Division V of Part IX of the Act of a service of instructing non-resident individuals in, or administering examinations in respect of, courses leading to certificates, diplomas, licences or similar documents, or classes or ratings in respect of licences, that attest to the competence of the individuals to whom the service is rendered or the examination is administered to practice or perform a trade or vocation.

This zero-rating relief is only available where the recipient of the supply (i.e., the person who is responsible for paying for the supply) is other than an individual (e.g., a corporation). The critical issue in determining whether this relief is available relates to whether the courses in issue lead to "certificates, diplomas, licences or similar documents, or classes or ratings in respect of licences, that attest to the competence of individuals to practice or perform a trade or vocation". The leading Policy Statement on this issue, P-231, "Courses that Qualify for Exemption Pursuant to Section 8 of Part III of Schedule V", was drafted in connection with an exempting provision. However, the principles set out in that document apply equally for the purposes of section 8.

(e) Section 22.1: Telecommunication Services

> A supply of a telecommunication service where the supply is made, by a registrant who carries on the business of supplying telecommunication services, to a non-resident person who is not a registrant and who carries

---

[2] See RITS 6277, "Supply of Products and Services Through the Internet", dated November 6, 2001.

on such a business, but not including a supply of a telecommunication service where the telecommunication is emitted and received in Canada.

This zero-rating provision is unusual in a number of respects:

(a) it requires that the supplier be a registrant (i.e., registered or required to be registered);

(b) it requires that the non-resident be engaged in the business of supplying telecommunication services; and

(c) it requires that the non-resident not be a registrant.

The second and third criteria place a high level of responsibility upon the supplier to obtain assurances from the recipient with respect to the nature of its business, and with respect to its registration status.

(f) Section 23: Professional, Advisory or Consulting Services

A supply of an advisory, professional or consulting service made to a non-resident person, but not including a supply of

(*a*) a service rendered to an individual in connection with criminal, civil or administrative litigation in Canada, other than a service rendered before the commencement of such litigation;

(*b*) a service in respect of real property situated in Canada;

(*c*) a service in respect of tangible personal property that is situated in Canada at the time the service is performed; or

(*d*) a service of acting as an agent of the non-resident person or of arranging for, procuring or soliciting orders for supplies by or to the person.

Where the service relates to acting as agent of the non-resident, or arranging for, procuring, or soliciting orders for the non-resident, then section 5 should be considered. The "in respect of" carve-outs should also be carefully considered when applying this relief provision. Where there is any risk that a service may relate to tangible personal property or real property, Policy Statement P-169R should be consulted to determine whether the nexus is sufficiently strong that zero-rating will be precluded.

The decision of the Tax Court of Canada in *Invera Inc. v. The Queen*, 2006 GTC 17, should also be considered in connection with the interpretation of this section. That decision related to a supplier who provided software training services to non-residents. The Minister argued that these services did not qualify for zero-rating under either of section 7 (as a result of the carve-outs associated with that provision) or under section 23.

The Court's reasons for the decision evidence a particular focus upon the relationship between sections 7 and 23. The Court concluded that section 23 in particular should be afforded a broad and liberal interpretation which would allow for the training services in issue to qualify for zero-rating as "advisory, consulting or professional services".

2. Intangible Personal Property

(a) Section 10: Intellectual Property

A supply of an invention, patent, trade secret, trade-mark, trade name, copyright, industrial design or other intellectual property or any right, license or privilege to use any such property, where the recipient is a non-resident person who is not registered ... at the time the supply is made.

This is the only zero-rating provision which may apply to provide relief in respect of supplies to non-residents of intangible personal property. The scope of this provision might ordinarily appear to be quite broad. For example, not only will "a supply of intellectual property" qualify, but so too will "any right, license or privilege to use any such property". The terms "right" and "privilege" would appear to be terms which are of the broadest possible scope.

Unfortunately, the CRA has consistently interpreted this provision in an extremely narrow manner. For example, it would appear that software will only qualify for zero-rating under this provision where a licence has been granted and the software may be downloaded to the recipient's computer. The suggestion is that the right to access software applications online will not qualify for relief.

The following two examples from TIB 090 further illustrate the difficulties associated with ascertaining the scope of this provision:

Example

A GST/HST registrant operates an interactive Web site. Subscribers pay a fee to access the site, which features digitized content, including music, videos, games, and other activities. The subscribers are not able to download permanent copies of the content to their computers, but can interact with it while online. They are provided with a password to enter the site, and can access it at any time from any location.

This is a supply of intangible personal property, which is made in Canada as there are no restrictions as to where the intangible personal property may be used. The registrant will be required to charge its non-resident subscribers tax at the rate of 7% or 15%, [Note: Now 6% or 14%] as the supply is not a supply of intellectual property, and therefore is not zero-rated under the provisions of section 10 of Part V of Schedule VI.

Example

A non-resident non-registered customer purchases software from a Canadian registrant and downloads the software from the supplier's Web site.

The supply of the software by electronic means is considered to be a supply of intangible personal property, and as there are no restrictions with respect to its use, it is deemed to be made in Canada. However, the supply in this instance is zero-rated under section 10 of Part V of Schedule VI, as the supply of software is a supply of intellectual property.

The narrow scope of this relief provision has long been a contentious issue in the commodity tax community. It would appear that this narrow approach has been adopted because of particular tax leakage concerns. As a result, a number of intangible personal property offerings will not qualify for relief, including the right to access information, or other online electronic resources such as an e-book. Similarly, the CRA takes the position that memberships do not qualify for zero-rating under this (or any other) provisions. The CRA's restrictive interpretation has recently been successfully challenged in the Tax Court case of *Dawn's Place Ltd. v. The Queen*, 2006 GTC 70. However, this decision is currently under appeal. This decision is discussed in detail in Chapter 16, Online Content, Services, and Other General Offerings.

Chapter 14, Software and Software Related Offerings; Chapter 16, Online Content, Services, and Other General Offerings; and Chapter 17, Internet Courses, Electronic Books, and other Educational Offerings, focus particularly upon identifying the types of supplies which will qualify for relief under this provision.

E. PLANNING AND EXPOSURE ISSUES

The application of zero-rating to a particular supply will always involve some element of exposure for the supplier. Where it is subsequently determined that a particular supply does not qualify for zero-rating relief, the supplier would ordinarily be the person who is assessed for the amount of tax owing.

As a result, the supplier should carefully consider both whether zero-rating relief might be available, and whether it is prepared to assume the risk associated with claiming relief. The supplier will typically be in a good position to manage the risks associated with ensuring that the supply falls within the particular relief provision. However, the supplier will not be as well positioned to manage the risks associated with the recipient's residency or registration status.

The CRA addresses some of these potential exposure issues in Policy Statement P-009, "Determining Proof of Residency and Registration Status". For example, the CRA specifically makes note of the exposure risk which is assumed by the supplier:

> The onus to substantiate that all of the requirements (including the status of the customer) of a particular provision are met, will continue to rest with the supplier.

Fortunately, the policy also establishes a certificate mechanism which may be employed to manage the risks. Where a customer has provided written certification that it is not registered, or that it is not resident in Canada, this may be sufficient to relieve the supplier of the exposure normally associated with that status. However, as evidenced in the following excerpt from Policy Statement P-009, the obtaining of a certificate will not necessarily be sufficient to provide supplier relief:

> The supplier is responsible for ensuring that the customer is a non-resident and, where applicable, unregistered for purposes of the Act. If, despite retaining certification from the customer it is determined by audit that the supply should not have been zero-rated because the customer was not a non-resident or, where applicable, unregistered, the supplier may be assessed the tax.

There are a number of other circumstances where zero-rating relief may not be available because of actions taken by the recipient of the supply. For example, section 5, which relates to agency services, is typically contingent upon the underlying supply (which is the supply made by the non-resident) being a supply made outside Canada. Similarly, with respect to section 22.1 (telecommunication services), the recipient must be engaged in the business of providing telecommunication services.

Although Policy Statement P-009 does not reference the use of certificates in connection with issues other than registration or residency status, the use of certificates in those circumstances should be considered. Alternatively, the supplier may want to obtain representations and warranties from the recipient, in the underlying agreement, which relate to the particular zero-rating provision to be relied upon. The supplier may also want to consider obtaining an indemnity from the recipient in the event that zero-rating should fail, particularly where the amounts of consideration in issue are large.

Alternatively, given all the risks set out above, the supplier may wish to consider whether any other options might be available to provide GST relief. For example, if the particular property or service is considered to be supplied outside Canada then there would be no need to consider the zero-rating provisions. Further, where supplies are made outside Canada, the supplier would be in a better position to identify and manage any potential risk associated with this approach.

Chapter 7

GST Registration and the Non-resident Override

A. OVERVIEW

Under some taxation regimes, registration issues are largely an administrative matter which carry very little weight. However, this is not the case with the GST.

Registration issues are among the most important GST issues which a business will face. This is because a person's GST registration status will impact very directly on a number of substantive GST provisions. Where a person misunderstands its GST registration requirements, or engages in poor registration related planning, these discrepancies will often result in derivative problems which impact both on the person and on its supply chain partners.

The following are some of the leading substantive GST issues which are directly linked to a person's registration status:

(a) **Requirement to collect the GST where supplies are made in Canada:** A non-resident who is GST registered, and who is deemed to be making supplies in Canada, will be required to collect the tax from the recipient of the supply. However, a non-resident who is not GST registered (and who satisfies the other requirements of the non-resident override), will not be obligated to collect GST when it makes supplies in Canada. The non-resident override is discussed below.

(b) **Eligibility to claim ITCs:** Only those persons who are registered (or required to be registered) may claim ITCs in respect of GST expenses incurred. Although in a technical sense a person may claim ITCs as soon as they are required to be registered, the ITCs cannot actually be recovered until registration is in place.

(c) **Eligibility for zero-rating on supplies to non-residents:** There are a number of circumstances in which a supply made to a non-resident person will not qualify for zero-rating if the non-resident is registered or is a registrant.

Registration issues are complicated by the fact that there are a number of limitations associated with changing a person's GST registration status. For example, backdating of registrations beyond 30 days is very rarely permitted. Conversely, the deregistration of registered persons is also strictly regulated.

This chapter discusses the leading registration related issues, including the circumstances where registration is permitted or required. The chapter will also discuss the operation of the non-resident override and a number of other leading practical issues which are closely tied to registration.

B. DISTINCTION BETWEEN REGISTERED AND REGISTRANT

The ETA contains numerous references to the terms "registered" and "registrant". These terms are not synonymous.

A person who is registered

A person will be considered to be registered only once it has been issued a nine-digit GST Business Number by the CRA. However, even where the person has been issued a Business Number, the person should ensure that a GST account has in fact been opened. This is because the CRA issues a single Business Number which may relate to any one (or more) of the following accounts:

(a) Corporate income tax account (an RC account)

(b) Payroll source deductions account (an RP account)

(c) GST account (an RT account)

(d) Import/Export account (an RM account)

A person who is a registrant

A registrant is a person who is either registered or who is required to be registered. Accordingly, it is not uncommon for a person to be a registrant without even being aware of the GST registration requirements. This issue frequently arises in connection with non-residents who may not be aware of the manner in which the registration rules apply.

The circumstances in which a person will be required to be registered are discussed in the following section.

C. SPECIFIC REGISTRATION RULES

The basic registration requirement rule is provided in subsection 240(1) of the ETA, which states that:

Every person who makes a taxable supply in Canada in the course of a commercial activity engaged in by the person in Canada, is required to be registered for the purposes of this part except where

(a) the person is a small supplier;

(b) the only commercial activity of the person is the making of supplies of real property by way of sale otherwise than in the course of a business; or

(c) the person is a non-resident person who does not carry on any business in Canada.

1. Taxable Supply in Canada

Whether a person is making a taxable supply in Canada turns on two different issues. First, is any supply considered to be made in Canada under the place of supply rules contained in sections 142 or 142.1 of the ETA? Second, if the supply is considered to be made in Canada under either of those provisions, is the supply deemed to be made outside Canada under the non-resident override? The non-resident override is discussed further below.

2. Commercial Activity

Generally, registration is only required where a supply is made in Canada and that supply is made in the course of a commercial activity engaged in by the person in Canada. A person will be considered to be engaged in a commercial activity in Canada (other than with respect to real property transactions which involve a lower threshold) where either of the following tests are met:

(a) the person carries on a business in Canada (other than a business carried on without a reasonable expectation of profit by an individual, personal trust, or a partnership, all of the members of which are individuals), except to the extent that the business involves the making of exempt supplies; or

(b) the person engages in an adventure or concern in the nature of trade in Canada (other than an adventure or concern engaged in without a reasonable expectation of profit by an individual, personal trust, or a partnership, all of the members of which are individuals), except to the extent to which the adventure or concern involves the making of exempt supplies.

Accordingly, where a person (including a non-resident person) carries on business in Canada or engages in an adventure or concern in the nature of trade in Canada, the person will be considered to be engaged in a commercial activity in Canada. A narrow exception is provided for certain types of suppliers and only to the extent that they are not motivated by profit.

(a) Carrying on Business in Canada

The determination of whether a person is carrying on business in Canada is considered in detail in Chapter 9, Carrying on Business in Canada.

For the purposes of this chapter, it should be noted that the term "carrying on business" is not defined in the ETA. The issue of whether a person is carrying on business in a particular jurisdiction is a question of fact. Further, a substantial body of jurisprudence has been developed in connection with this critical factual issue.

However, as a practical matter, it would only be in exceptional circumstances that a Canadian resident supplier would be able to demonstrate that it is not carrying on business in Canada. In those rare circumstances where the person is not carrying on business in Canada, it should be expected that the person would be considered to be engaged in an adventure or concern in the nature of trade in Canada.

The issue is far more complex for non-resident persons or for Canadian resident persons who operate largely from outside Canada.

(b) Engaging in an Adventure or Concern in the Nature of Trade in Canada

The term "adventure or concern in the nature of trade" is not defined in the ETA. As with carrying on business, it is a question of fact whether a person is engaged in an adventure or concern in the nature of trade in a particular jurisdiction. A substantial body of jurisprudence (much of which does not specifically relate to the GST) has developed in connection with this issue. The jurisprudence for the most part suggests that the adventure or concern threshold is lower than the carrying on business threshold.

Since, as a general rule, a non-resident will not be required to GST register where it merely engages in an adventure or concern in the nature of trade in Canada (and does not carry on business in Canada), the focus in this chapter and throughout the book is on the "carrying on business" standard.

3. Application to Canadian Residents

Any Canadian person who makes supplies in Canada in the course of a business carried on in Canada, or in the course of engaging in an adventure or concern in the nature of trade in Canada, will be required to be registered — unless it qualifies as a small supplier or it qualifies for the exception related to profit expectation. Generally, to qualify as a small supplier, the annual total taxable sales of the person (including sales made outside

Canada) may not exceed $30,000. Sales made by associated persons are also required to be taken into account in calculating total sales.

As a result of this broad registration requirement, virtually every Canadian business is GST registered. Further, where a Canadian resident person is not required to be registered, it may choose to voluntarily register. There are a wide range of circumstances in which a person will be permitted to voluntarily register.

4. Application to Non-Residents

(a) Requirement to Register

Non-residents are subject to a different registration requirement standard than Canadian residents. This special standard is established by the non-resident carve-out contained in paragraph 240(1)(c) of the ETA. A non-resident is only required to be registered where the commercial activity of the non-resident is in the nature of carrying on business in Canada. This means that generally, a non-resident who merely engages in an adventure or concern in the nature of trade in Canada, will not be required to register.

Given that non-residents are subject to a less stringent registration standard maintaining non-resident status is critical. A non-resident, if deemed to be a Canadian resident for GST purposes, will be subject to the same registration standard which is applied to ordinary Canadian business.

The issue of deemed residency often arises in connection with permanent establishments. Pursuant to subsection 132(2) of the ETA, where a non-resident person has a permanent establishment in Canada, the non-resident person will be deemed to be resident in Canada in respect of any activities carried on through that establishment.

This deeming provision is particularly important in the e-commerce environment because a server (or other equipment of the supplier) may be considered to be a permanent establishment of the non-resident person. This means that when the non-resident makes supplies through their Canadian server (or through any Canadian server which is at their disposal), the non-resident person will be deemed to be a resident of Canada. If taxable supplies are made through this server, either in the course of a business carried on in Canada or in the course of an adventure or concern in the nature in Canada, then the non-resident would be required to register.

A non-resident may also be deemed to be resident in Canada in connection with a permanent establishment of a dependent agent in Canada. Where supplies are made through a dependent agent and that agent has a permanent establishment in Canada, the non-resident may be deemed to be resident in Canada.

These important issues are also discussed in detail under the heading "Non-resident Override" and in Chapter 8, Permanent Establishment Issues.

(b) Voluntary Registration

Many non-resident persons who are not required to GST register will choose to voluntarily register. There are a wide range of circumstances in which a person might find that it is advantageous to register. However, it is very common for non-resident persons to voluntarily register either to secure access to ITCs or to simplify arrangements with supply chain partners. Among the persons who may voluntarily register are:

(a) Any person engaged in a commercial activity in Canada;

(b) Any non-resident person, who in the ordinary course of carrying on business outside Canada

(i) regularly solicits orders for the supply by the person of tangible personal property for export or delivery to Canada; or

(ii) has entered into an agreement for the supply by the person of

(a) services to be performed in Canada;

(b) intangible personal property to be used in Canada or that relates to

— real property situated in Canada;

— tangible personal property ordinarily situated in Canada;

— services to be performed in Canada.

(c) Other Registration Requirements

In addition to the registration tests set out above, there are a wide range of special circumstances in which a non-resident may be required to be registered. These rules apply to taxi businesses, non-resident performers, and persons who send prescribed property by mail or courier to Canada. It is beyond the scope of this book to discuss the special registration rules which apply to these persons.

D. BACKDATING ISSUES

It is not uncommon for a person to seek to have a GST registration number issued on a backdated basis. For example, a person who has already incurred numerous GST expenses may wish to have their registration backdated to a period immediately prior to the time when those expenses were incurred. This backdating would typically allow for ITCs to be claimed in respect of the expenses.

The CRA will, as a matter of course, allow for backdating to occur up to 30 days prior to the date when a registration request has been filed. However, backdating beyond that 30-day window is typically far more difficult to achieve. A person seeking to backdate a registration beyond the 30-day period would be required to demonstrate that they were in fact required to be registered as of the date in issue. The person would be obligated to show that they were:

(a) making taxable supplies in the course of a commercial activity on the particular date; and

(b) not a small supplier on the particular date.

Given the difficulties associated with backdating, it is important that any person who incurs GST expense (including Division III GST expense), consider their registration obligations prior to the time when the expenses are incurred.

E. THE NON-RESIDENT OVERRIDE

Perhaps the most important legislative provision for non-residents who supply property or services in Canada is the non-resident override.

The override represents an exception to the general rule that any person making taxable supplies in Canada should collect the GST from its customers. The rule allows non-residents who have minimal presence in Canada to make sales in Canada without any requirement to collect the tax. The non-resident override has been carefully designed to dovetail with the registration rules. Accordingly, in interpreting the override, special consideration should also be given to subsection 240(1) of the ETA.

The non-resident override does not stand for the proposition that the supplies may be made on a tax-free basis. In many cases, other legislative provisions will result in the application of tax to the particular supply. The most common provisions are found in Division IV which, when applicable, will result in the recipient being required to self-assess the tax owing.

Generally, the non-resident override, where applicable, will deem a supply made by a non-resident of tangible personal property or a service to be made outside Canada. Those supplies would otherwise have been deemed to be made in Canada under the place of supply rules contained in sections 142 and 142.1 of the ETA. Where a particular supply is considered to be made outside Canada under the place of supply rules, there is no reason to consider the non-resident override.

If any of the following apply, the non-resident override will not be available:

(a) the supply is made by the non-resident in the course of a business carried on in Canada;

(b) at the time the supply is made the non-resident is GST registered; or

(c) the supply is a supply of an admission.

Other than where admissions are supplied, the non-resident override contains three distinct tests which must be met:

(a) the supplier must be a non-resident;

(b) the supply must not be made in the course of a business carried on in Canada; and

(c) the non-resident must not be GST registered.

Each of these three tests is described below.

1. Test #1: The Supplier Must be a Non-resident

A non-resident is defined in subsection 123(1) of the ETA as a person "not resident in Canada". Subsection 132(1) provides a series of rules pursuant to which a person may be deemed to be resident in Canada. For example, corporations are deemed to be resident in Canada if they are "incorporated or continued in Canada and not continued elsewhere". Other deeming rules are provided with respect to partnerships, societies, clubs, individuals, and other persons. In addition to these statutory provisions, common law residency considerations should also be taken into account. For example, at common law a corporation is considered to be resident in Canada if its "central management and control" are in Canada. With respect to individuals, the common law tests will examine the degree of connection between the individual and the competing jurisdictions.

Section 132 also contains a number of secondary deeming rules which may apply to deem a person to be resident in Canada. The special deeming rule contained in subsection 132(2) is particularly important in the e-commerce setting.

Pursuant to subsection 132(2), a non-resident person who has a permanent establishment in Canada will be deemed to be resident in Canada in respect of any activities of the person carried on through that establishment. Accordingly, if a non-resident corporation were to make supplies through its permanent establishment in Canada, the corporation would be deemed to be resident in Canada in respect of the supplies made through that establishment. The person who is deemed resident in respect of the activities carried on through the particular permanent establishment would remain a non-resident for all other purposes.

Given that making supplies through a Canadian permanent establishment may result in deemed Canadian residency, it is critical to determine what might constitute a permanent establishment. The definition of "permanent establishment" in subsection 123(1) of the ETA provides that either of the following will be considered a permanent establishment of a person:

(a) a fixed place of business of the particular person, including:

(i) a place of management, a branch, an office, a factory, or a workshop, and

(ii) a mine, an oil or gas well, a quarry, timberland or any other place of extraction of natural resources,

through which the person makes supplies; or

(b) a fixed place of business of another person (other than a broker, general commission agent, or other independent agent acting in the ordinary course of business) who is acting in Canada on behalf of the particular person and through whom the particular person makes supplies in the ordinary course of business.

In addition to more traditional forms of establishments, it is now widely accepted that a server (or other equipment) may constitute a permanent establishment of the non-resident person pursuant to the test contained in (a). It is also not uncommon in the e-commerce setting for a non-resident person to be deemed resident in Canada because supplies are made through a dependent agent in Canada.

In either case, the non-resident would be precluded from relying upon the non-resident override (including where the non-resident continues to qualify as a small supplier). Further, given that the non-resident would be deemed to be a Canadian resident in connection with activities carried on through the particular permanent establishment, it would also be subject to the Canadian resident registration standard. Registration would be required where supplies are made either in the course of a business carried on in Canada, or where supplies are made in the course of engaging in an "adventure or concern in the nature of trade" in Canada, except where the non-resident is a small supplier. These permanent establishment issues are discussed in further detail in Chapter 8, Permanent Establishment Issues.

2. Test #2: The Supplier Must not be Carrying on Business in Canada

A non-resident who seeks to avail itself of the non-resident override must ensure that it is not making the supply in the course of a business which is being carried on in Canada. It is a question of fact whether a non-resident is making supplies in the course of a business carried on in Canada. The carrying on business in Canada tests are considered in detail in Chapter 9.

3. Test #3: The Supplier Must not be GST Registered

Any non-resident who is GST registered will not be entitled to take advantage of the non-resident override.

It is interesting to note that the term "registrant", a significantly broader term than "registered" was not used in the override. However, a person who is required to be registered (but who is not in fact registered) will not qualify for the override. The person who is required to be registered will have failed on the "carrying on business in Canada" test and/or may have failed on the deemed residency test.

A second interesting issue relates to the operation of the override where a registration proceeds on a backdated basis. Where a registration is backdated, the benefit of the override will also be lost on a corresponding basis, because the person will on the relevant date be "registered". However, given that a person must demonstrate that they were previously required to be registered in order to have their registration backdated, the person would have in any event failed on test #1 or #2.

A very common registration exposure issue is also worth noting. It is not uncommon for a non-resident person to become GST registered in connection with a particular product line. However, this decision will impact upon other product lines of the person, including those which are distributed through separate divisions. It is for this reason that many non-residents will incorporate a new entity which alone will be registered for GST purposes.

Chapter 8

Permanent Establishment Issues

A. OVERVIEW

The "permanent establishment" concept is one of the cornerstones of the GST. This term is used throughout the ETA as a means by which persons who reside or operate businesses from outside Canada may be linked to Canada.

Once this link has been established, the manner in which the GST will apply to the person will change dramatically. For example, non-residents with a permanent establishment in Canada will typically be required to become GST registered. However, when that person becomes GST registered, it will not be required to post non-resident security because it will have a permanent establishment in Canada.

Some of the other major issues which are impacted by a finding that a non-resident has a permanent establishment in Canada include the following:

(a) non-residents who make supplies through permanent establishments in Canada will not be entitled to rely upon the non-resident override (and will be obligated to collect Division II GST on those supplies);

(b) non-residents with a permanent establishment in Canada may find that their entitlement to acquire supplies on a zero-rated basis is limited to the extent that those supplies relate to that permanent establishment; and

(c) a non-resident with a permanent establishment in Canada may find that it is required to pay Division IV GST on a self-assessing basis on imported taxable supplies.

The permanent establishment concept is equally important for Canadian businesses. For example, the province of supply rules (contained in Schedule IX) for services, intangible personal property, and real property, all rely heavily upon the concept of the "place of negotiation" for the supply. The supplier's permanent establishment (or one of its permanent establishments) may constitute the place of negotiation.

There are many other situations in which a determination that a permanent establishment exists in Canada will alter the manner in which the GST applies.

B. WHEN WILL A NON-RESIDENT HAVE A PERMANENT ESTABLISHMENT IN CANADA?

1. General Considerations

By definition there are two distinct circumstances in which a person may be deemed to have a permanent establishment for GST purposes. The term "permanent establishment" is defined in the ETA as follows:

(a) a fixed place of business of the particular person, including

  (i) a place of management, a branch, an office, a factory or a workshop, and

  (ii) a mine, an oil and gas well, a quarry, timberland or any other place of extraction of natural resources

through which the particular person makes supplies, or

(b) a fixed place of business of another person (other than a broker, general commission agent or other independent agent acting in the ordinary course of business) who is acting in Canada on behalf of the particular person and through whom the particular person makes supplies in the ordinary course of business.

Notwithstanding that the term "permanent establishment" is legislatively defined, the scope of this provision is heavily influenced by a lengthy body of jurisprudence. The common law which is taken into account in interpreting the definition may be GST related, income tax related, or otherwise.

It is interesting to note that the corresponding *Income Tax Act* (Canada) definition of "permanent establishment" is not identical to the GST definition. One of the most important distinctions between the income tax and GST definitions of permanent establishment relates to the GST requirement that a person make supplies through the permanent establishment. The income tax definition contains no similar requirement.

As a result of the difference between the income tax and GST definitions, it is not uncommon for a person to be deemed to have a permanent establishment for the purposes of one tax but not for the other.

2. Paragraph (a): Fixed Place of Business of the Particular Person

There are three distinct tests, each of which must be passed before a person will be deemed to have a permanent establishment in Canada under the rule in paragraph (a):

(i) there must be a "place of business";

(ii) that place of business must be "fixed"; and

(iii) the person must "make supplies" through this particular place.

(a) What Constitutes a "Place of Business"?

In determining whether a particular location constitutes a place of business, the starting point should be the list of specifically included places of business. There are two reasons for this approach:

(a) any "place" listed is specifically deemed to be a place of business even if it would not ordinarily be considered a place of business. For example, most people would not consider an oil well to be a place of business; and

(b) the scope of the items listed suggests that the term "place of business" is intended to be extremely broad. Any other location which is not specifically listed should be expected to be considered a place of business if it is analogous to any of the places listed.

Where the particular place which is in issue is not specifically deemed to be a place of business, consideration should be given as to whether that place may in any event constitute a place of business. Administratively, the CRA has adopted an extremely broad approach with respect to the issue of what constitutes a "place of business". This approach is reflected both in TIB 090 and in Policy Statement P-208R, "Meaning of Permanent Establishment in subsection 123(1) of the *Excise Tax Act*".

In fact, it may even be arguable that the CRA has developed two distinct but parallel sets of tests for resolving the issue of whether a place of business exists. If this theory is correct, the first set of tests seem to relate to traditional places of business (i.e., office space). A second set of more liberal tests appears to have been developed in connection with other than traditional arrangements.

The primary rules which seem to relate to traditional types of business locations are as follows:

(a) A place of business will only exist where there is a "space". However, any "premises used for conducting business activities" will be considered a space.

(b) There is no requirement that this space be owned by the particular person in order to qualify as a place of business. Any space which is available to the person (including where there is no formal legal arrangement as to its use), will qualify as a space. The CRA explains this important concept in the following manner:

> A person need not have a formal legal right to use the space by owning or leasing it for it to constitute a place of business of the person. Rather the fact that the space is at the person's disposal is sufficient. ... For instance this could include space at the disposal of a non-resident at its client's premises. ...[1]

The application of this rule often leads to a finding that a non-resident person has a place of business in Canada as a result of an informal arrangement with a related entity. For example, office space of a Canadian subsidiary may be "at the disposal" of the non-resident parent corporation notwithstanding that there is no specific agreement in place allowing for access to this space. This liberal approach to the identification of potential places of business often surprises non-residents.

(c) The particular person must control the space. This requirement is satisfied where there is someone at the space who has the authority to make operational decisions. If this person is an employee, this person will only have the requisite authority where he or she is authorized to "make important business decisions".

The secondary (or alternative) "place of business" rules seem to be aimed squarely at machinery and equipment. This will include for example servers and other computer hardware. The secondary guidelines provide that:

(a) Machinery and equipment can constitute a space.

(b) The machinery and equipment need not be owned by the particular person to qualify as a place of business as long as the equipment is made available to the person. In determining whether machinery or equipment is being made available to the person, the "at the disposal" guidance set out above should be considered. The suggestion is that informal arrangements as to use may be sufficient to result in the standard being met.

(c) The particular person must control the space. However, control can exist even where no employees are required to be present to operate

---

[1] Policy Statement P-208R.

the machinery or equipment. The control test will be satisfied if the equipment which is at the disposal of the person is capable of performing its intended function on an automatic basis.

Given the guidance set out above, it follows that a server which is neither owned nor leased by the non-resident (i.e., a server which the non-resident is merely allowed to use), and which does not require employees for its operation, could constitute a permanent establishment.

(b) When is a Place of Business Considered to be Fixed?

Administratively, the CRA has explained that there must be a certain degree of continuity and permanency associated with a particular place of business in order for it to qualify as a permanent establishment. However, the application of this requirement is fraught with difficulties. In particular, it would appear that the CRA may at times be prepared to relax this permanency requirement in order to achieve certain policy objectives. Accordingly, it is hardly surprising that the CRA has described the permanency requirement in the following broad manner:

> The determination of whether the place of business is fixed will take into account the period of time the place is used and the frequency of such use.[2]

The CRA has explained that in order to constitute a fixed place of business, the place should be lasting or intended to last "indefinitely". As an evidentiary matter, the CRA has suggested that this intention requirement is met where the physical address of the business is listed in a directory or on a Web site.

The CRA's flexible approach to the permanency requirement is evidenced throughout the relevant administrative materials. For example, in Policy Statement P-208R, the CRA explains that where work occurs at a particular location for a finite period of time (e.g., because of the limited nature of the work to be performed), this location may constitute a fixed place of business. Further, the continuity and permanence requirements may even be met where a person returns to the same location on a recurring basis. The CRA illustrates this concept in Policy Statement P-208R with an example which relates to a non-resident returning to a booth at an annual convention. The CRA explained that the booth would meet the continuity and permanence requirements.

This latter example, if taken literally, seems to suggest that returning to Canada annually for a period of only two or three days for any purpose might be sufficient to constitute a fixed place of business. Although the particular trade booth example does not relate directly to e-commerce

---

[2] Policy Statement P-208R.

activities, the liberal manner in which the CRA has interpreted the "fixed place of business" requirement should not be ignored.

It has been argued by some tax professionals that a server cannot constitute a permanent establishment because, as a matter of real estate law, the server is not typically affixed to the ground. Most servers would rest upon the ground, or upon another chattel such as a desk, shelf, or other supporting structure. The CRA has administratively dismissed this argument. In support of its position the CRA has explained that where machinery or equipment is in issue, there is no requirement that it be fixed to the ground to qualify as a permanent establishment:

> ... the equipment must merely remain at the place of business for a sufficient period of time to be considered fixed.

(c) When is a Person Making Supplies Through a Place of Business?

At the outset, the CRA has emphasized that the supply test is not intended to be interpreted in a literal manner. In order for this test to be met, the activity carried on at (or through) the place of business must be an "essential and significant" part of the overall business activities.

In determining whether a particular activity is an essential and significant part of the overall business activity, the CRA offers that any activity which is not of a strictly preparatory (i.e., making the business ready) or auxiliary (i.e., to help or support the business) nature should be taken into account. The CRA has suggested that the following are considered to be either preparatory or auxiliary (although it would appear that this list is by no means exhaustive):

(a) using a fixed place of business strictly for storage, display or delivery of goods;

(b) maintaining a fixed place strictly for the purpose of purchasing goods or for collecting information; or

(c) maintaining the fixed place solely for the purpose of carrying on any combination of the above as long as the activities are preparatory or auxiliary.

However, any one of the activities noted above could in some circumstances be considered essential and significant in the context of certain business activities. For example, if a person is in the business of storing goods, then operating a storage facility would not in that context be considered to be merely preparatory or auxiliary.

The CRA has established a list of criteria to be considered in resolving the issue of whether the activities carried on are essential and significant. The criteria are broken down between a primary list of factors and a secondary list of factors.

(i) Primary Factors

The primary factors list establishes the following four factors. If any of these tests is met, supplies will be considered to be made through the particular place of business:

(a) there is authority (and that authority is regularly exercised) at the fixed place of business to enter into contracts or accept purchase orders relating to supplies to other persons;

(b) the tangible personal property which is being supplied is manufactured or produced at the fixed place of business;

(c) if a service is being supplied, then the service is performed at the fixed place of business;

(d) if the service is maintaining equipment supplied by the non-resident, then that service is performed at the fixed place of business (i.e., authorized factory repair outlet).

Criteria (a), (b) and (d) do not appear to be particularly relevant in connection with the use of servers. With respect to criterion (a), a supplier with a server in Canada would not ordinarily have an employee present at the location of the server unless an office was also maintained in Canada. It should be expected in those circumstances that the office, and not the server, would be the central focus. Criterion (b) is not relevant because it relates to tangible personal property.

However, criterion (c) is more problematic because its scope may be quite broad. As noted in Chapter 5, Place of Supply, where a service is provided through equipment (such as a server), the service will be considered to be performed, in part, at the location of the equipment. It seems to follow that if a server (or for that matter any other automatic equipment) is used to automatically provide a service, then criterion (c) might be satisfied and a supply will be considered to be made through the equipment. This issue should be carefully considered by providers of telecommunication services because the equipment requirement might be satisfied by a simple, inexpensive item such as a LAN, jack or wire.

None of the four primary criteria relates specifically to circumstances where a server (or other equipment) is used to dispense intangible personal property. This silence might ordinarily suggest that where only intangible personal property is dispensed through an automatic server, the server will not constitute a permanent establishment of the supplier. However, the example described below demonstrates that the CRA does take the position that where a server is used to automatically dispense intangible personal property, the "supplies made through the place of business" test may be met. As a result the server may constitute a permanent establishment of the person.

In example 8 of Policy Statement P-208R, the CRA considered whether a server located in Canada which was leased by a non-resident could be considered a permanent establishment of the non-resident. The server was used to host the non-resident's Web site. Through the Web site the non-resident sold the rights to download music files which were stored on the server. All elements of the transaction were automatic, including accepting payments and payment processing. The server operated in a completely automatic manner.

The CRA ruled that the server was a permanent establishment of the non-resident. This is because the server is a fixed place of business which is at the disposal of the non-resident and because supplies were made through the server which are an essential and significant part of the non-resident's overall business.

The example described above should be contrasted with example 7 (also from Policy Statement P-208R). In example 7, the CRA concluded that supplies were not being made through the server and, accordingly, the server did not constitute a permanent establishment. The server in issue was located in Canada and operated in an automatic manner. The server had been leased by the non-resident person to be used solely as a place where business records would be stored. The non-resident person was in the business of selling tangible personal property, the sales of which did not involve the server.

The CRA concluded that the server was in fact a fixed place of business which was at the disposal of the non-resident person. However, it was concluded that the server performed only an auxiliary function in relation to the business of selling goods. Accordingly, the server did not constitute a permanent establishment of the non-resident.

(ii) Secondary Factors

Where none of the primary criteria tests have been met, the following secondary criteria should be considered in order to determine whether supplies are being made through the fixed place of business. The CRA has indicated that an affirmative response would be required in combination with two or more of the secondary factors to support the conclusion that supplies are made through the particular place of business. The central issue is whether any of the following occur at the particular fixed place of business:

(a) solicitation of orders;

(b) taking or receiving orders;

(c) arranging for customer contracts;

(d) providing for storage, packing, shipping or transport of goods;

(e) providing general administration of accounts (including collection and depositing payments);

(f) providing advertising for the supply; and

(g) providing after sales support.

It is not at all clear how these secondary factors might be applied in connection with a server which may potentially be a permanent establishment. In particular, it is arguable that virtually every server arrangement will invariably satisfy several of these tests:

(a) the server would solicit orders by advertising a product or service for sale (e.g., a digitized product offered for sale through a Web site);

(b) the server might take or receive orders when it automatically accepts order submitted online;

(c) the server could be used to provide general administration of accounts by accepting payments made by customers;

(d) advertising could be provided through the Web site; and

(e) after sales support could be provided by means of an automatic information service or database set up on the Web site.

The secondary tests even further emphasize that where automatic sales are made through a Web site hosted on a server in Canada, that server may be at an enhanced risk of being considered a permanent establishment of the non-resident in Canada.

(iii) Important Carve-outs for E-Commerce

Notwithstanding the broad circumstances in which a permanent establishment will be considered to exist in connection with a server or other equipment, a number of important exceptions have been firmly established. For example, the CRA has confirmed that a Web site itself cannot ever be considered to be a permanent establishment. This is because the Web site by its very nature does not have a physical location:

At a minimum a "place of business" of a person requires that a certain amount of physical space be at the disposal of the person. A Web site which merely consists of software and electronic data is not tangible personal property and therefore does not have a location that can constitute a place of business.[3]

This conclusion is also confirmed in Policy Statement P-208R (example 5). In that example, a non-resident had its Web site hosted in Canada by an ISP. The CRA ruled that there was no permanent establishment because the Web site was not tangible personal property and did not have a location. Further, in these particular circumstances the server in issue was not at the disposal of the non-resident.

The CRA has also clarified that a server will not be considered to be "at the disposal" of a person where the person has contracted with an ISP to have their Web site hosted.

A server on which a website is stored is tangible personal property having a physical location. The server may constitute a place of business of a non-resident person, if it is at the disposal of the person (i.e., operated and owned or leased by the person). A non-resident person who has its website hosted on a server of an independent ISP in Canada would not generally be regarded as having the ISP's server at its disposal ...[4]

The CRA has explained that the person who contracts with the ISP is not being provided with the right to use a particular server. Rather, the person is purchasing the right to have their Web site hosted by the ISP. For example, the ISP would be free to host the Web site on any server of its choosing, and may transfer the Web site between servers in connection with upgrade or maintenance activities without in any way diminishing the quality of service offered.

The approach which has been adopted by the CRA to reach the conclusion that an ISP server is not "at the disposal" of the Web site owner should be carefully considered in connection with other ambiguous issues. The CRA's approach may be capable of being applied by way of analogy to other related situations.

2. Paragraph (b): Fixed Place of Business of Another Person

(a) Overview

Paragraph two of the definition of "permanent establishment" relates to supplies made through the permanent establishment of dependent agents.

---

[3] TIB 090.

[4] *Ibid.*

The rule provides that the following will constitute a permanent establishment of a particular person:

> (*b*) a fixed place of business of another person (other than a broker, general commission agent or other independent agent acting in the ordinary course of business) who is acting in Canada on behalf of the particular person and through whom the particular person makes supplies in the ordinary course of business

As a preliminary matter, it should be noted that many of the elements of this test are analogous to those which are established under paragraph (a) above. For example, for a permanent establishment to exist the following tests must be met:

- the other person must have a place of business;
- the other person's place of business must be fixed; and
- supplies must be made through the other person's place of business.

It should be expected that these tests will be interpreted in the same manner as described under paragraph (a) above. For example, for supplies to be made through the other person's place of business, the supplies should be required to also meet the "significant and essential" test in relation to the overall business activities of the person.

(b) "Ordinary Course of Business" Issue

Although there are a number of parallels between the two distinct "permanent establishment" tests, the scope of the paragraph (b) test is qualified in one very important manner. It is only where supplies are made through the dependent agent's place of business *in the ordinary course of the supplier's business* that the place of business of the dependent agent may constitute a permanent establishment of the supplier. The suggestion is that the supplies made through the dependent agent must be other than merely "one off" or isolated transactions.

(c) Dependent Agent Issue

A permanent establishment will only exist under paragraph (b) where the third party is a dependent agent of the particular person. This raises two distinct issues:

(a) Is the third party an agent?

(b) If the third party is an agent, is the third party a dependent agent?

The circumstances in which a person is considered an agent (and is considered a dependent agent) are discussed in Chapter 10, Agency.

(d) Special Issue Relating to ISPs

As noted above, where a supply is made through a Web site which is hosted on a server in a typical ISP arrangement, the supplier will not be considered to have a permanent establishment in Canada under heading (a) (i.e., a fixed place of the person). This is because the ISP's server will not be considered to be "at the disposal" of the person.

However, it might appear that in these circumstances the test in heading (b) of the definition of "permanent establishment" would be met. Fortunately, the CRA has laid this concern to rest. The CRA notes in TIB 090 that although the server is in fact at the disposal of the ISP, the ISP will not typically be considered an agent of the supplier. In fact, the relationship would typically be in the nature of an independent contractor relationship. Further, even if the ISP were considered to be the agent of the supplier, the ISP would not be considered to be the dependent agent of the supplier. The primary test of dependency will not be met because the ISP will provide its services to other parties too.

> ... an ISP that hosts a Web site of a non-resident person on its servers in Canada will not generally be an agent of the non-resident person, either because the ISP does not usually have the authority to conclude contracts in the name of the non-resident person, or because the ISP is an independent agent acting in the ordinary course of its business, as evidenced by the fact that it typically hosts websites of many different businesses.[5]

Notwithstanding that typical ISP arrangements will not result in the non-resident having a permanent establishment in Canada, other hosting arrangements may result in a finding that the non-resident has a permanent establishment in Canada. One example might be where a non-resident entity hosts its Web site on a server belonging to (or otherwise at the disposal of) its Canadian subsidiary.

C. SPECIFIC PERMANENT ESTABLISHMENT IMPACT ISSUES

The primary impact of a finding that a non-resident has a permanent establishment in Canada is that the non-resident will be deemed to be resident in Canada in respect of any supplies made through that permanent establishment. This rule is found in subsection 132(2) of the ETA. The permanent establishment in issue may be "at the disposal" of the non-resident (the rule in heading (a) above), or it may be a permanent establishment which is "at the disposal" of a dependent agent of the non-resident (the rule in heading (b) above). This means that a non-resident

---

[5] TIB 090.

may have a permanent establishment in Canada in connection with a place of business to which it does not even have access.

The finding that a person has a permanent establishment in Canada (and is deemed to be resident in Canada in respect of activities carried on through that permanent establishment) will impact very directly on the following:

1. Requirement to Register

A non-resident is only required to register where it makes supplies in Canada in the course of a business carried on in Canada. This is the rule in subsection 240(1). However, as a deemed Canadian resident, registration would be required if supplies are made either in the course of a business carried on in Canada or in the course of engaging in an adventure or concern in the nature of trade. It is generally accepted that the "adventure or concern" test represents a lower threshold. Accordingly, a finding that a non-resident person has a permanent establishment in Canada will dramatically increase the likelihood that the person will be required to become GST registered.

Further, the fact that supplies are made through a permanent establishment in Canada will be an important factor to be taken into account in resolving the issue of whether the person engages in an adventure or concern, or carries on business, in Canada.

2. Availability of Non-resident Override

The non-resident override is not available in respect of supplies made by Canadian resident persons. Given that a non-resident will be deemed to be resident in Canada in respect of any supplies made through a permanent establishment in Canada, any finding that a permanent establishment exists in Canada will severely limit the availability of the override.

However, this particular limitation operates in a flexible manner which may allow for some supplies to continue to be made by way of the override. This is because subsection 132(2) establishes that the non-resident person who has a permanent establishment in Canada will be deemed resident "in respect of, but only in respect of activities carried on through that establishment".

The non-resident will remain a non-resident in connection with all activities which are not carried on through the permanent establishment. Accordingly, if the non-resident can show that a particular supply was made in its capacity as non-resident (i.e., other than through the permanent establishment), it will remain eligible for the override in respect of that supply.

Many tax practitioners have struggled with determining the scope of the special rule which is contained in subsection 132(2). In particular, the rule appears in many respects to be inimical to the very foundation of the GST because it does not operate in the typical "all or nothing" manner. For example, first principles would ordinarily suggest that where a person becomes GST registered, that person would be registered for all purposes. However, subsection 132(2) raises the possibility that a person may be considered GST registered for some purposes but will not be considered registered for other purposes.

All of the issues described above are further complicated by the rule in subsection 132(4). That subsection provides that where a person carries on business through a permanent establishment in Canada, and another permanent establishment outside Canada, any transfer of property or provision of a service from the Canadian establishment to the non-resident establishment shall be deemed to be a supply. The rule also provides that tax will apply as if the permanent establishments are separate persons who operate at arm's length. The suggestion is that a person who is GST registered because of a permanent establishment in Canada may be required to charge GST to itself. Further, given that the person may not be considered to be registered in connection with activities carried out other than through the permanent establishment in Canada, the amounts of GST charged might not be recoverable as ITCs.

A related issue arose in the case of *State Farm Mutual Insurance Co. v. The Queen*, 2003 GTC 632 (T.C.C.), in the context of section 220 of the ETA. That provision establishes that where a person carries on business through a permanent establishment in Canada and another permanent establishment outside Canada, any transfer of property or services between the establishments shall be deemed to be a supply. Pursuant to that rule, the permanent establishments are to be treated as separate persons, and any supply shall be considered to be made at fair market value.

The Tax Court of Canada in that case ruled that section 220 did not apply because the administrative services in issue were not taxable. In so concluding, the Court dealt a severe blow to the CRA's attempts to apply tax to "transactions" of this nature. It should also be noted that the Court's reasons for the decision appeared to evidence a particular disdain for this type of taxing provision.

3. Zero-rating Issue

Each of the zero-rating provisions described in Chapter 6 are premised on a supply being made to a non-resident person. Accordingly, where supplies are made to a person in circumstances in which the person is deemed to be a resident in Canada, zero-rating will not be available.

However, given that a non-resident with a permanent establishment in Canada will only be deemed to be resident in Canada in respect of activities carried on through that permanent establishment, there should be ample opportunities for the non-resident to acquire supplies in its capacity as a non-resident.

D. SUMMARY CHART OF EXAMPLES FROM POLICY STATEMENT P-208R

The CRA, in Policy Statement P-208R, provided a number of examples of situations where it applied the principles set out above to determine if a non-resident has a permanent establishment in Canada. The following chart summarizes the results in those leading examples:

Category	Overview	How does it work?	What do they do?	What is the supply?	PE in Canada?	Why?
Banking	Bank sets up branch in Canada	Employees on site (but with limited authority) Major decisions are made in the U.S.	Solicit sales from Canadians	Banking services are provided from the U.S. if customer signs on	No	Supplies are not made through the fixed place of business Only auxiliary and incidental tasks are performed in Canada The underlying services are provided in the U.S.
Insurance	Sale of insurance in Canada through office	Regulatory work done in Canada, administrative work in Canada	Sells insurance	Insurance products	Yes	The insurance products sold through the Canadian office are an essential and integral part of the insurance business

Category	Overview	How does it work?	What do they do?	What is the supply?	PE in Canada?	Why?
Sales Representative	Works from home to solicit sales	Sales representative has office in his apartment. Employee is reimbursed for expenses	Orders are approved by head office. Equipment sold goes direct to customer. Canadian employee hires subcontractors to install equipment	Equipment	Yes	There is a location/space and it is listed in a directory. There is constant presence in that location (by the employee) and by an answering machine
Sales Representative (traveling)	Sales representative travels to local fairs to sell products	Sales representative travels around in a motorhome	Sales are concluded at booth	Herbal remedies	Yes	He returns to the same locations each year. He makes sales at this location (either immediate delivery or to be shipped later)
ISP	Non-resident ISP hosts Web sites on a Canadian server	Server operates automatically		Web site hosting	Yes	The server is at the disposal of the ISP
Data Storage	Non-resident leases server in Canada	Server is used to store records		No supply	No	Only auxiliary functions performed through server
Digitized Products	Non-resident leases server in Canada	Server hosts Web site	Digitized products sold through Web site	Digitized products	Yes	Significant and essential supplies made through server

Chapter 9

Carrying on Business in Canada

A. OVERVIEW

The issue of whether a non-resident person is carrying on business in Canada is critical from a GST perspective. This is because the carrying on business in Canada test is one of the primary means by which the activities of a non-resident may be linked to Canada. In this sense, the concept of carrying on business in Canada is analogous to the very important "permanent establishment in Canada" issue.

Some of the leading e-commerce issues which are very directly impacted by the concept of carrying on business in Canada include the following:

(a) requirement to register for GST (and eligibility to backdate registration);

(b) requirement to collect the GST (and in particular eligibility for the non-resident override);

(c) eligibility to claim non-resident zero-rating relief; and

(d) application of Division IV GST.

The connections between these leading issues and the concept of carrying on business in Canada are described below.

1. Requirement to Register for GST (and Eligibility to Backdate Registration)

Generally, a non-resident will be required to register for GST purposes if the person makes taxable supplies in the course of a business carried on in Canada. This requirement is established in subsection 240(1) of the ETA.[1] There is no requirement that the person have a permanent establishment in Canada to be considered to be carrying on business in Canada.

Once registered, the non-resident will be obligated to regularly file GST returns (typically monthly or quarterly). If the non-resident does not have a permanent establishment in Canada it will be required to post security with the CRA.

Registration will in some cases be advantageous to the non-resident. For example, if the non-resident in the course of making taxable supplies incurs expenses which are subject to GST, registration will typically allow for those expenses to be recovered. The ITC mechanism allows for the recovery of the GST expenses incurred.

---

[1] This requirement is discussed in detail in Chapter 7, GST Registration and the Non-resident Override.

For recovery reasons it is not uncommon for non-residents to request that their GST registration be backdated. However, as discussed in Chapter 7, GST Registration and the Non-resident Override, backdating will only be allowed where the non-resident is able to show that it was previously required to be registered. To demonstrate that it was previously required to be registered, the non-resident would need to be able to support that it was carrying on business in Canada at the relevant time. The following is an example of a situation in which a person might advance the position that it was carrying on business in Canada:

Example

Non-resident Corporation A for years regularly makes supplies of zero-rated groceries to customers located in Canada. The supplies are made in the course of a business which is considered to be carried on in Canada.

Some of Corporation A's suppliers have for years been charging GST to Corporation A in respect of goods or services provided to Corporation A.

Corporation A is not registered for GST purposes and so does not claim input tax credits in respect of the taxable expenses which it incurs.

The facts set out above present an opportunity for Corporation A. If Corporation A can show that it was carrying on business in Canada during the relevant period (and that it was not a small supplier), then Corporation A will be entitled to become GST registered and to have its GST registration backdated to the period when it first began making taxable supplies in the course of a business carried on in Canada. This will allow for the claiming of previously unrecoverable ITCs.

2. Requirement to Collect GST

The obligation to collect GST is linked to the requirement to register. A person who is registered, or who is required to be registered, will be required to collect Division II GST on any taxable supply which is made in Canada.

This requirement to collect the GST applies equally to non-resident persons because, as discussed in Chapter 7, the non-resident override is not available to a non-resident who is GST registered. Similarly, the override is not available if the non-resident makes supplies in the course of a business carried on in Canada (i.e., circumstances where the non-resident is not registered because it has not recognized its registration obligations, or it is a small supplier).

The above represents a substantial source of audit exposure for non-residents. A non-resident who does not recognize that it is carrying on business in Canada will remain unregistered. The non-resident would then rely upon the override to make taxable supplies to Canadian customers without charging any amount of GST. Where it is subsequently determined that the override was not available (i.e., because the non-resident was in fact carrying on business in Canada), the non-resident will be liable to remit to the CRA the amounts of GST which should have been collected on supplies previously made in Canada. Penalties and interest will also attach to these amounts.

In the circumstances described above, the non-resident's exposure may be exacerbated by supply chain difficulties. The non-resident may encounter difficulties in attempting to subsequently collect amounts of GST from its customers (i.e., when it re-issues the invoices). Collection efforts will be particularly difficult where sales were made to a large number of customers, where customers have relocated or have experienced financial difficulties, or where customers are not GST registered. The CRA will not assist the non-resident supplier in these GST collection efforts.

Accordingly, non-residents should be very cautious when applying the carrying on business in Canada test. These risks should be even more carefully managed by non-resident e-commerce suppliers where the supplies in issue are made to a large number of customers or where the customers are not GST registered.

3. Availability of Zero-rating

Many of the export-related zero-rating relief provisions (described in Chapter 6) will only be available where the recipient of the particular supply is not registered. To ensure that this zero-rating relief remains available, non-residents will need to ensure that they do not engage in activities which will obligate them to become GST registered. Given that non-residents generally are only required to register when they carry on business in Canada, managing the jurisdictions in which business is carried on is a leading way of avoiding the registration requirement.

4. Application of Division IV GST

Division IV GST applies to a supply which is deemed to be an "imported taxable supply". Where a supply is subject to Division IV GST, the recipient of the supply is the person who is required to pay the amount of GST owing on a self-assessing basis.

There are a wide variety of circumstances in which a supply of property or a service will be deemed to be an imported taxable supply and subject to Division IV GST. However, typically the Division IV GST will apply where a consumer or other person who is not GST registered acquires a supply from a non-resident supplier who did not charge any Division II GST. Division IV

GST very commonly applies to e-commerce supplies particularly where the recipients of a particular supply are individual consumers or are otherwise not GST registered. Given that Division IV GST very commonly applies in circumstances where Division II GST does not apply, the application of Division IV GST is very closely linked to the issue of whether a non-resident is carrying on business in Canada.

If a non-resident supplier makes a supply in the course of a business carried on in Canada, the non-resident override will not apply and the supply will be deemed to be made in Canada. Division IV GST will not apply in these circumstances. Conversely, where the non-resident makes a supply to a Canadian purchaser which qualifies for the override, then the Division IV GST might apply. In effect the carrying on business in Canada test will determine whether the supplier is responsible for the collection of the GST (i.e., the Division II GST) or whether the recipient is responsible for the payment of the GST (i.e., the Division IV GST).

B. WHEN IS A PERSON CARRYING ON BUSINESS IN CANADA?

1. General Issues

The term "carrying on business" (and similar related terms such as "business carried on") is not defined in the ETA. The issue of whether a person is carrying on business in a particular jurisdiction is a question of fact in respect of which an extensive body of jurisprudence has been developed. Much of this jurisprudence does not specifically relate to the GST.

Notwithstanding that the term "carrying on business" is not specifically defined, there are circumstances where a person will be deemed to be carrying on business in Canada for GST purposes. For example, subsection 240(4) of the ETA deems a person to be carrying on business in Canada where the person solicits orders for the supply of prescribed property which is sent by mail or courier to the recipient of the supply in Canada. Regardless of whether a person is considered at common law to be carrying on business in Canada, the matter is settled for GST purposes if a person is legislatively deemed to be carrying on business in Canada.

In the absence of a specific deeming provision, the meaning of the term "carrying on business" is required to be ascertained with regard to the common law.

2. Policy Considerations

There are two main issues to consider in determining whether a non-resident may be considered to be carrying on business in Canada. The first is the interpretation of the common law of "carrying on business". The second relates to the important policy considerations which drive the interpretation of carrying on business. In particular, where a finding that a person is not carrying on business in Canada would result in considerable tax leakage, or would provide non-resident suppliers with a particular tax-related advantage (as compared to Canadian resident suppliers or non-resident registered suppliers), it should be expected that these considerations will impact upon the manner in which the carrying on business test is interpreted by the CRA.

E-commerce activities present a number of special tax leakage concerns which are not typically associated with other, more traditional types of business activities. The following example illustrates how tax leakage concerns are minimized where a non-resident makes a traditional sale to a Canadian resident.

Example

A non-resident vendor sells tangible personal property to Canadian customers. If the non-resident person is not considered to be carrying on business in Canada, does not make supplies through a permanent establishment in Canada and is not registered, the person will be entitled to make the sales without any obligation to charge Division II GST.

However, in this scenario, tax leakage concerns are minimal because the goods will be subject to Division III GST when they enter Canada. Further, the ETA contains a number of complex mechanisms to ensure that the Division III GST will not be recoverable in any circumstance where such recovery could potentially result in tax leakage.

The CRA is also well positioned to ensure that tax leakage does not occur in connection with traditional service offerings (i.e., hands on services which require employees of the supplier to enter Canada). For example, where employees of a supplier enter Canada for business purposes, they are required to report the nature of their intended activities to the Canada Border Services Agency. This reporting requirement is one of the many mechanisms which allows the CRA to monitor the nature and duration of activities undertaken in Canada in order to determine whether the person might be carrying on business in Canada.

In contrast however, the offering of e-commerce supplies from outside Canada presents a number of special challenges. The most significant challenge relates to the non-resident's physical presence in Canada. Intangible personal property and most e-commerce services can, as a practical matter, be provided to Canadian customers without the supplier being required to establish any physical presence in Canada.

Although the Division IV GST provides a fallback position for the CRA in circumstances in which the Division II GST is not levied, enforcing the Division IV GST can be very difficult. The first limitation relates to detection of the supplies which are being made. It is generally very difficult for the CRA to determine to whom a supply of intangible personal property (or an e-commerce service) is made especially where the non-resident supplier is not registered. The second limitation relates to the difficulties associated with taking enforcement action against certain Canadian recipients. For example, enforcement against individuals is not particularly cost-effective where the amounts in issue are relatively small. To illustrate this limitation, consider the following example:

Example

A consumer in Ontario purchases the right to access and use online software. The rights are purchased over the Internet from a non-resident supplier who is not GST registered.

The consumer pays $100 for the rights to use the software.

Because the supplier is not GST registered and does not collect the GST the consumer is required to self-assess the GST owing under Division IV. However, the amount owing would be only $6.

Given the considerable challenges associated with enforcing the payment of GST under Division IV, it should be expected that the CRA would prefer that the GST be collected under Division II. It follows that where the non-resident establishes any form of physical presence in Canada, this presence will be very carefully scrutinized to determine whether the person might be required to be registered.

Further, given that e-commerce has provided a means by which products or services may be distributed to Canadian purchasers with only minimal supplier presence in Canada, it should be expected that the CRA will, in the e-commerce environment, consider a wider range of "presence" factors in resolving the carrying on business issue than might be taken into account for more traditional lines of business.

3. When is a Person Carrying on Business at Common Law?

The following two issues must always be considered:

(a) is the person carrying on a business; and

(b) is the person carrying on the business in Canada.

Each of these issues is discussed below.

4. When is a Business Carried On?

The term "business" is defined in the ETA in an extremely broad manner as follows:

> "business" includes a profession, calling, trade, manufacture or undertaking of any kind whatever, whether the activity or undertaking is engaged in for profit, and any activity engaged in on a regular and continuous basis that involves the supply of property by way of lease, license or similar arrangement, but does not include an office or employment.[2]

It should be noted that this definition of "business" is not intended to be comprehensive. The use of the word "includes" suggests that other activities may also be considered to constitute a business. At common law there are a wide range of circumstances in which a person will be held to be carrying on business. The CRA has summarized the relevant common law test of "carrying on business" as:

> ... anything which occupies the time and attention and labour of a man for the purpose of profit ...[3]

Ordinarily it would be expected that the common law meaning of "business" would be broader than the statutory definition of "business". However, the generally held view is that the ETA definition of "business" is broader than the CRA's description of the common law test. Among the more important distinctions between the common law and statutory meaning are the following:

Difference #1: While the common law test for a business references "anything that occupies the time and attention and labour of a man for the purpose of profit", the statutory definition specifically references an "undertaking of any kind whatever". It would be difficult to conceive of any type of commerce related situation which would not be considered to be "an undertaking of any kind whatever".

Difference #2: The common law test requires that the particular activity be motivated by profit. The statutory definition specifically deems activities which are not motivated by profit to be included.

Difference #3: At common law, by the CRA's own admission,[4] a business is only carried on where the activities in question are considered to occur on a regular and continuous basis. In contrast, only the second branch of the

---

[2] Subsection 123(1).

[3] Policy Statement P-051R2, "Carrying on Business in Canada".

[4] See Policy Statement P-051R2.

statutory definition contains a similar frequency or duration requirement. The broad wording of the first branch of the ETA test, if taken literally, suggests that even "one-off" or isolated transactions could be considered to constitute a business. The better view however, is that notwithstanding the apparent broad wording of the statutory definition, the courts may choose to "read in" some elements of the common law standard when interpreting its scope. This would likely include a requirement that the activity in issue be carried out on more than an isolated basis. An alternative view is that even though a business might exist in circumstances involving only isolated transactions such a business would not be considered to be "carried on".

(a) Comparison to Income Tax Standard

In resolving issues relating to the interpretation of the term "business" as defined in the ETA, the corresponding income tax definition is often referenced. The differences between the two definitions provide insight into the scope of the respective provisions.

The first branch of the GST statutory definition of "business" is similar to the general income tax definition of "business".[5] However, unlike the income tax definition the GST definition includes a second branch which relates to "any activity engaged in on a regular and continuous basis that involves a supply by way of lease, license or similar arrangement".

Another important distinction relates to the fact that the ETA, for the most part does not specifically deem any particular activity to constitute carrying on business.[6] In contrast, the *Income Tax Act*, specifically deems certain activities to constitute carrying on business. For example, a non-resident who produces, grows, mines, creates, manufactures, fabricates, improves, packs, preserves or constructs anything in Canada will be deemed, for income tax purposes, to be carrying on business in Canada.[7]

There are a number of other important distinctions between the definitions which may be useful as interpretation tools.

(b) Other Interpretation Issues Relating to "Carrying on Business"

In addition to the "carrying on business" test the ETA relies extensively upon the related "adventure or concern in the nature of trade" test for establishing threshold obligations. For example, to determine whether a

---

[5] See subsection 248(1) of the *Income Tax Act*.

[6] Except for subsection 240(4), which actually deems a person to be carrying on business in Canada.

[7] Section 253 of the *Income Tax Act*.

particular supply is made in the course of a commercial activity, consideration would be given to each of the two distinct tests.

The very presence in the ETA of this second "adventure or concern" standard suggests that the "carrying on business" test was intended to be of limited scope. For example, with respect to non-resident registration, registration is only required where the non-resident is carrying on business in Canada (and not where the non-resident merely engages in an adventure or concern in the nature of trade). The fact that the ETA does not reference the "adventure or concern" standard suggests that a non-resident person may engage in certain limited commerce related activities in Canada without triggering the registration requirement.

5. When is that Business Carried on in Canada?

(a) Threshold Interpretation Issues

A lengthy body of jurisprudence has been developed with respect to the issue of whether a person who is carrying on business is in fact carrying on business in a particular jurisdiction. Most of this jurisprudence does not specifically relate to the GST.

This raises a particular interpretive difficulty. Could there be circumstances where a person would be considered to be carrying on business in Canada at common law but would not be considered to be engaged in a business as a result of the definition of "business"contained in the ETA? One view is that the statutory definition of business is merely an extension of the common law. If this is the correct interpretation, it would follow that where a person is found to be carrying on business at common law they would also be carrying on business for ETA purposes. However, a competing view is that the statutory definition of "business" might actually preclude the full operation of the common rules. If this latter interpretation is correct, there may be circumstances where a person is considered to be carrying on business in Canada at common law but is not carrying on business in Canada for GST purposes. Given the broad nature of the ETA definition of "business", this concern is likely more academic than real.

A second very significant interpretation limitation is typically associated with relying upon the common law meaning of "carrying on business". Most of the existing "carrying on business" jurisprudence relates to the resolution of that issue in the context of the sale of goods. This is not surprising, given that many of the leading decisions were released during an era when services were very rarely provided beyond the primary jurisdiction of the service provider. Similarly, issues relating to carrying on business in connection with the distribution of intangible personal property rarely arose.

As a result, the CRA has been faced with the challenge of applying rules which were developed in connection with the sale of goods to transactions relating to the provision of services and intangible personal property. The development and enforcement of these new rules has thus far been extremely contentious.

These difficulties have been exacerbated by technological advances which allow suppliers to distribute products or services in a manner which does not rely upon traditional distribution channels. E-commerce products and services in particular can now easily be provided to customers in a particular jurisdiction with minimal or no supplier presence in that jurisdiction.

In response to these apparent tax leakage concerns, it appears arguable that the CRA's response has been to adopt a more liberal interpretation of the carrying on business in Canada standard. To many this new direction may best be described as a "commercial reality" approach.

The following two sections discuss the CRA's traditional approach and current approach to resolving "carrying on business in Canada" issues.

(b) Traditional Common Law Approach

The traditional common law approach to evaluating whether a person carries on business in a particular jurisdiction has been to examine a wide range of criteria which relate to the person's "presence" or "nexus" in the particular jurisdiction. Generally, as the number and strength of the factors which link the person to a particular jurisdiction increases, so too will the likelihood that they will be found to be carrying on business in that jurisdiction.

However, notwithstanding that all of the listed connecting factors were to be considered in applying this test, the following two factors always carried a much higher degree of weight with the CRA:

(a) the place where the contract was concluded; and

(b) the place of the operations from which the profits arose.

Under this traditional weighted approach, if the non-resident concluded contracts in Canada or had operations in Canada, it would invariably follow that the non-resident would be considered to be carrying on business in Canada. This conclusion would be strengthened if one or more of the secondary factors were also met. The secondary factors which were typically considered included (but were not limited to) the following:

(i) the place where delivery of the goods is made;

(ii) the place where payment is made;

(iii) the place where the goods in question are manufactured;

(iv) the place where the orders are solicited;

(v) the place where an inventory of the goods is maintained;

(vi) the existence of any branch or office in the particular place;

(vii) the existence of any agents or employees authorized to transaction business on behalf of the non-resident in the particular place;

(viii) the place where bank accounts are maintained;

(ix) the place where back-up services under the contract are maintained; and

(x) a list of the names and business of the non-resident person in a directory in the particular place.

Given that the secondary factors did not carry as much weight as the primary factors, the suggestion has always been that several of the secondary factors would be required to be met where neither of the primary factors was met.

In recent years, a number of deficiencies have been identified in connection with this traditional approach. The primary deficiency related to the fact that the factor list was heavily weighted towards business activities relating only to the trade in goods. For example, the revised version of Policy Statement P-051R, "Carrying on Business in Canada" (which has since been replaced by Policy Statement P-051R2, discussed further below), contained very little discussion of issues relating to the trade in services or intangible personal property.

Given that the factor list did not, for the most part, specifically address issues relating to supplies of services or intangible personal property, many viewed this silence as an assertion that non-residents engaging in these types of activities would only rarely be found to be carrying on business in Canada. However, more recently the CRA has made clear (through new administrative policies and enforcement activities) that there are a wide range of circumstances in which, non-resident persons who provide only services or intangible personal property in Canada will be considered to be carrying on business in Canada.

A second deficiency associated with the traditional approach relates to the seemingly arbitrary nature of some factors. For example, many have argued that the place where the contract is concluded is a weak and outdated connecting factor. This is because it would be relatively simple for a non-resident supplier to arrange that contracts always be concluded outside Canada.

(c) The CRA's New Approach: Policy Statement P-051R2, "Carrying on Business in Canada"

The CRA seems to have recognized that its traditional administrative approach was no longer adequate given the many commercial changes which had occurred. In 2005, Policy Statement P-051R2, the CRA's leading position paper on carrying on business in Canada was released. This policy bears little resemblance to the previous version of that policy which had been released only six years earlier.

The new policy statement reconfigured the factor list to more appropriately reflect the trade in other than goods. The new policy also specifically introduced a series of guiding principles in connection with e-commerce offerings. Most importantly, the new policy signalled, in the clearest manner possible, that the CRA would be prepared to more carefully scrutinize the activities of non-residents who offer services or intangible property in Canada.

From a mechanical perspective, the new policy collapsed the former two-part factor list into a single stage factor list. As a result, the two primary factors referenced above (including the very problematic "place of contract" factor) were relegated to standard weighting status. Further, many of the former factors were redrafted or replaced in order to more accurately reflect the CRA's new position. As a result, the new factor list is as follows:

(i) the place where agents or employees of the non-resident are located;

(ii) the place of delivery;

(iii) the place of payment;

(iv) the place where purchases are made or assets are acquired;

(v) the place from which transactions are solicited;

(vi) the location of assets ("profit making apparatus") or an inventory of goods;

(vii) the place where the business contracts are made;

(viii) the location of a bank account;

(ix) the place where the non-resident's name and business are located in a directory;

(x) the location of a branch or office;

(xi) the place where the service is performed; and

(xii) the place of manufacture or production.

The CRA also released new guidance in connection with the interpretation of the factor list which emphasized that the list is not to be interpreted in a mechanical manner. More specifically, the CRA has advised that the process may not be reduced to simply counting the number of factors which point to or away from Canada.

The CRA also indicated that the weight provided to different factors will turn on the nature of the particular supply which is being offered. For example, a determination that a service provider does not manufacture or produce goods in Canada (factor 12) is not to be interpreted as support for the proposition that the nexus to Canada is not strong. This is because in the context of providing services this factor would be irrelevant.

In addition to the requirement to disregard certain factors where inapplicable, the CRA has also specifically noted that some of the factors are to be interpreted differently (i.e., more liberally) in the e-commerce environment:

> ... some factors must be interpreted to take into account the particular nature of e-commerce. For example, in determining the place where payment is made, it may be more appropriate, depending on the circumstances, to consider the place where approval for the electronic transfer of funds takes place, rather than the place of posting or receipt of cheques.[8]

Given that payment for many electronic products is typically made on an automatic basis to the server and Web site which dispenses the product, this factor should be of particular concern to non-residents who are contemplating their registration obligations.

C. EXAMPLES OF THE CRA'S NEW POSITION

There is perhaps no better way to ascertain the scope of the CRA's new administrative position than to consider specific examples. Policy Statement P-051R2 sets out 21 distinct factual scenarios where the CRA has ruled on the issue of whether, in its opinion, the non-resident is, in fact, carrying on business in Canada. Examples 1 through 13 consider issues relating to the supply of goods, examples 14 through 17 address e-commerce supplies, and examples 18 through 21 consider issues relating to supplies of services. The focus in the following section will be on providing a summary of examples 14 through 21.

It should be emphasized that the conclusions set out below represent the CRA's interpretation of the "carrying on business in Canada" test. These conclusions may not necessarily be supported by the courts.

---

[8] Technical Information Bulletin B-090 "GST/HST and Electronic Commerce".

Example 14: Digitized Audio Files — Non-resident is not carrying on business in Canada

A non-resident supplies downloadable audio files through its Web site. The audio files may be used in Canada.

The Web site is hosted on a server located outside of Canada which is owned by the non-resident.

Advertising aimed at the Canadian market is contained on the Web site.

When payment is made in Canada by the purchaser (by way of credit card) the payments are processed in Canada by a Canadian independent service provider. The contracts are concluded in Canada.

Technical support is provided to the customer by phone or email by employees of the non-resident who work from offices outside of Canada.

The non-resident does not have any agents or employees in Canada, is not listed in a directory in Canada, has no bank account in Canada, and has no equipment or office in Canada.

Decision and Rationale

The non-resident is not carrying on business in Canada notwithstanding the presence of the following factors:

(a) the contract was concluded in Canada;

(b) sales were solicited in Canada (by way of Web site); and

(c) payment was made in Canada.

Example 15: Software Applications — Non-resident is carrying on business in Canada

A non-resident supplies the right to use various software applications through its Web site. The software may be used in Canada.

The Web site is hosted on a server located in Canada which is owned and operated by a Canadian ISP (the server is not at the disposal of the non-resident).

The software applications are stored on the server in Canada.

Advertising aimed at the Canadian market is contained on the Web site. Further advertising aimed at the Canadian market is contained in Canadian newspapers.

Customers order the software online. The application is processed automatically with the user being provided a computer generated user ID and password. The contract is concluded in Canada.

Customers are invoiced electronically according to the number of hours which they use the applications. Payment may be made by cheque or credit card.

A Canadian independent service provider processes the payments.

After sales customer support (technical support) is provided by an independent Canadian service provider.

Decision and Rationale

The non-resident is carrying on business in Canada. The factors which support this conclusion are:

(a) Canadian independent service providers are used for after sales support (this is the primary determinant);

(b) The non-resident solicits sales in Canada (through its Web site and newspapers);

(c) Payments are processed in Canada;

(d) The place of contract is in Canada; and

(e) Activities are carried out by the automated Web site in Canada.

Notes

Ruling 15 should be contrasted with ruling 14. The most significant factual differences appear to be as follows:

(a) The involvement in example 15 of Canadian service providers for after sales technical support;

(b) The supplies in example 15 are provided automatically through a Web site which is hosted in Canada. In example 14 the supplies are made through a Web site which is hosted outside Canada; and

(c) In example 15, the non-resident solicited sales through both its Web site and through an independent medium. In example 14 sales were only solicited through the Web site.

The ruling is also important because it demonstrates how a non-resident may be required to register due to the application of the carrying on business test in circumstances where the non-resident does not have a permanent establishment in Canada. As noted in Chapter 8, a non-resident is not considered to have a permanent establishment in Canada where their Web site is hosted on a server in Canada which is operated in a typical ISP relationship.

Example 16: Application Hosting — Non-resident is not carrying on business in Canada

A non-resident application service provider supplies access to a web based software application. The application is hosted on the non-resident's server which is located outside Canada.

The customer is assigned a user ID and password to access the application on the Web site.

The software tracks and processes the customer's data to assist with inventory management.

The Web site contains advertising aimed at the Canadian market.

The contract is concluded in Canada.

Payment for the supply is made outside Canada and the non-resident has no equipment, offices or agents or employees in Canada.

The non-resident is not listed in any directory in Canada and has no bank account in Canada.

Technical support is provided by phone or email by the non-resident's own technicians who operate from outside Canada.

Decision and Rationale

The non-resident is not carrying on business in Canada because the factors which suggest a connection to Canada are insufficient to constitute carrying on business. Those factors include:

(a) Sales are solicited in Canada (but only through the supplier's Web site); and

(b) The contract is concluded in Canada.

Example 17: Web Site Hosting — Non-resident is carrying on business in Canada

A non-resident Internet service provider hosts websites for customers located around the world.

The server on which the websites are hosted is located in Canada and is owned by the ISP.

Employees of the ISP enter Canada to set up the server but are not required to return for maintenance. There are no other employees or agents in Canada.

Payment is made outside Canada. The place of contract is outside Canada.

The non-resident does not have a bank account in Canada and is not listed in a directory in Canada.

Decision and Rationale

The non-resident is carrying on business in Canada. The factors which support this conclusion are:

> (a) The service which is supplied is performed in Canada. Services which are performed through an automatic machine are performed in Canada if that equipment is located in Canada; and

> (b) The server is also a permanent establishment of the non-resident. The service which is performed through the permanent establishment is a significant service in relation to the non-resident's overall business (of hosting websites). In fact this service is the supplier's core offering.

Example 18: Supply of Engineering Services — Non-resident is not carrying on business in Canada

A non-resident engineering firm has contracted with a Canadian to perform services on an oil rig stationed in a Canadian port.

The non-resident has no other contracts with Canadian customers.

Under the contract a single employee will enter Canada for one week to perform services on the rig.

The contract is concluded outside Canada and payment is made outside Canada. The non-resident does not solicit business in Canada, is not listed in directories in Canada, does not have a bank account in Canada and has no agents or employees in Canada (other than the sole employee who enters Canada for one week).

Decision and Rationale

The non-resident is not carrying on business in Canada.

The sole nexus to Canada relates to the employee. This factor alone is insufficient to constitute carrying on business in Canada where a single employee is involved.

Example 19: Supply of Services (cleaning services) — Non-resident is carrying on business in Canada

A non-resident has contracted with a Canadian to provide cleaning services in respect of a power generation facility.

Under the contract 10 employees will enter Canada for one month to perform the services. The employees will bring with them specialized cleaning equipment.

The non-resident solicits business in Canada through advertising.

The contract is concluded outside Canada and payment is made outside Canada. The non-resident is not listed in directories in Canada and does not have a bank account in Canada. It has no office or equipment in

Canada (other than the equipment noted above) and has no agents or employees in Canada (other than the employees noted above).

Decision and Rationale

The non-resident is carrying on business in Canada. The factors which support this conclusion are:

(a) The service is to be performed in Canada (which service is significant to the overall business activity of the non-resident);

(b) Several employees will be in Canada to perform the service; and

(c) Business is solicited in Canada.

Notes

Examples 18 and 19 should be compared because a different conclusion was drawn in connection with very similar facts. The suggestion seems to be that with respect to services performed in Canada the determination of whether the non-resident is carrying on business in Canada will relate in large part to the number of employees in Canada and the duration of time which they will spend in Canada. This conclusion is consistent with the result in example 20.

Example 20: Supply of Services (consulting and training) — Non-resident is carrying on business in Canada

A non-resident provides consulting and training services with respect to improving productivity.

The services are delivered to customers in the following manner:

(a) Employees of the non-resident visit the customer's facilities to analyze the customer's operations;

(b) Recommendations are provided to management;

(c) Customer on site training is provided to employees of the customer; and

(d) Employees of the non-resident remain on site following training to respond to questions and to monitor progress of implementation.

The non-resident has a single contract in Canada. The non-resident's employees will be in Canada for at least 2 months.

The contract is concluded outside Canada and payment is made outside Canada. The non-resident is not listed in a business directory in Canada, does not solicit business in Canada and does not have a bank account in Canada. The non-resident has no premises in Canada.

Decision and Rationale

The non-resident is carrying on business in Canada. The service which is provided is performed in Canada and is central to the overall business of the non-resident. Several employees enter Canada to provide this service.

Example 21: Supply of Services (painting) — Non-resident is not carrying on business in Canada

A non-resident is awarded the contract to paint a customer's building in Canada. The work will take seven months to complete.

The non-resident subcontracts the job to a Canadian company. The Canadian agrees to paint the building in the color specified by the non-resident and in the time frame allowed. The non-resident does not provide further instructions as to how the work is to be completed.

The non-resident will not visit Canada to monitor the work. Progress will only be monitored by telephone from outside Canada.

Apart from the payment to the subcontractor (which is made in Canada), and the conclusion of the contract with the subcontractor (which contract is concluded in Canada), no other factors point to a connection with Canada (i.e., no soliciting business, no listing in directories etc.).

Decision and Rationale

The non-resident is not carrying on business in Canada. The non-resident has no presence in Canada in the form of employees or agents.

D. GUIDING PRINCIPLES TO BE TAKEN FROM THE EXAMPLES

The examples described above suggest that the presence of any of the following should result in a heightened awareness when considering whether a person might be carrying on business in Canada:

(a) Where supplies are made through a permanent establishment of the non-resident in Canada, the non-resident will likely be considered to be carrying on business in Canada. This presumption is strengthened where the supplies are ongoing and are significant in relation to the overall business. A server which is owned by the non-resident may constitute the permanent establishment (see example 17).

(b) The use of automated equipment located in Canada poses two distinct risks. The equipment might be considered a permanent establishment of the non-resident. However, even where the equipment does not constitute a permanent establishment, the equipment may constitute a place where services are performed which will be taken into account in determining "presence" in Canada (see example 17).

(c) Where employees enter Canada to provide services, there is a substantial risk that this may lead to the conclusion that the non-resident is carrying on business in Canada. The risk is increased where the services performed are central to the overall business of the non-resident. The risk is also increased as the duration of visits and number of employees who enter Canada increases (see examples 18, 19, and 20).

(d) Soliciting sales in Canada through the person's Web site is typically a relatively innocuous factor with respect to the application of the carrying on business test. However, where the solicitation occurs other than through the supplier's Web site (i.e., through an independent medium such as a newspaper) this risk will be significantly heightened (see example 15).

(e) Concluding a contract in Canada does not appear on its own to be a particularly important factor. However, this factor will cumulate with other factors (see examples 14, 15, and 16).

(f) The involvement of third parties in Canada is typically risky, particularly if the third parties provide a supply related function (see example 15). However subcontracting work to a third party in Canada does not appear to involve the same element of risk (see example 21).

1. Role of Policy

In reconciling these examples, it may be possible that the conclusions which have been drawn are in part a function of the potential for tax leakage. To illustrate this possibility, the conclusion reached in example 15 should be contrasted with the conclusion reached in example 21.

In example 21, it was determined that the non-resident who subcontracted an entire painting contract out to a Canadian third party was not carrying on business in Canada. However, a number of factors in that example suggested that business was in fact being carried on in Canada, including:

(a) the contract was concluded in Canada;

(b) the payment was made in Canada; and

(c) the work was entirely performed within Canada.

The conclusion that the person was not carrying on business in Canada may have related in part to the fact that the risk for tax leakage in this situation would be quite low. The Canadian service provider would likely be GST registered and would be required to charge GST to the non-resident in respect of its services because the services are performed in Canada. Zero-rating would not be available for these services because the services are "in respect of" real property which is situated in Canada. Accordingly, the non-resident who is not carrying on business in Canada and who does not GST register would typically be required to pay non-refundable GST. This would provide a strong incentive for the non-resident to consider voluntarily registering.

This should be contrasted with example 15 where the conclusion was reached that the non-resident was in fact carrying on business in Canada. One of the factors which was relied upon to support this conclusion was the involvement of a Canadian service provider who provided technical support. However, in this example, unlike example 21, the services provided by the Canadian third party would ordinarily qualify for zero-rating.

As a result, the non-resident in example 15 who remains unregistered (unlike the non-resident in example 21) would not incur any tax expense in connection with the activities of the Canadian service provider. The non-resident in this example would not be likely to seek out voluntary registration.

E. EXPOSURE AND PLANNING ISSUES

Non-residents who make taxable supplies in Canada and who may or may not be carrying on business in Canada are faced with a difficult dilemma. This is because the costs associated with erring on this issue can be very substantial. If the person does not register and it is subsequently determined that they were required to have been registered, the person will be subject to considerable Division II tax exposure. This exposure may be exacerbated by the fact that many suppliers will find only limited success in attempting to collect Division II GST from Canadian customers after the sale has occurred.

Where the non-resident person is contemplating registering, the following should be taken into account and weighed off against the risks described above:

> (a) the administrative burden associated with collecting, reporting and remitting GST;

> (b) the risk of exposure associated with failing to collect or report the appropriate amount of GST;

(c) the possible impact of registration upon others in the supply chain. For example many suppliers to the non-resident person will no longer be entitled to zero-rate their supplies; and

(d) supplies made to other non-resident recipients may become subject to Division II GST unless specific planning measures are adopted.

.

Chapter 10

Agency

A. OVERVIEW

Recognizing the existence of an agency relationship and understanding the impact of this type of relationship is very important when applying the GST. The ETA contains a number of deeming provisions which are intended to ensure that tax leakage does not result where sales are made through agents. In addition to these specific legislative rules, general common law principles of agency may also apply. As a result agency impacts upon the circumstances in which ITCs may be claimed and upon the requirements to collect, report and remit GST. However, it is not uncommon for parties to an agency relationship to be unaware that these specific rules exist.

Agency relationships may also impact very substantially upon the manner in which certain threshold GST issues are resolved. For example, the making of supplies through a Canadian agent may result in a finding that a non-resident has a permanent establishment in Canada. This issue is discussed in Chapter 8, Permanent Establishment Issues. Certain agency arrangements may also suggest that a non-resident is carrying on business in Canada. This issue is considered in Chapter 9, Carrying on Business in Canada.

Agency is particularly important in the e-commerce environment because so many e-commerce supplies involve agency relationships. For example, one very common means by which parties transact business through the Internet involves an agent making third-party sales on behalf of a principal.

The focus in this chapter is on identifying the circumstances in which an agency relationship will be considered to exist. This chapter will also discuss the obligations of the respective parties where an agency relationship exists.

B. RECOGNITION OF AN AGENCY RELATIONSHIP

1. General Overview

Where parties are operating together the threshold distinction which must be made is whether the particular relationship is in the nature of agency or whether the relationship is an independent contractor relationship. The most common means by which this issue is resolved is to consider whether the facts support the existence of an agency relationship. Where the facts do not support an agency relationship, then by default an independent contractor relationship will be considered to exist.

Determining whether an agency relationship exists (or alternatively making the distinction between an agency and independent contractor relationship) is a question of fact. A substantial body of jurisprudence has been developed in connection with this difficult issue. Much of this jurisprudence relates to areas of law which are not tax related, including contract law and employment law.

The CRA has summarized its interpretation of the relevant common law in Policy Statement P-182R, "Agency". In that policy the CRA has explicitly acknowledged the difficulties associated with making an agency determination in the following manner:

> Despite an extensive body of jurisprudence, whether a person is acting as an agent in a transaction is not always clear. Where there is uncertainty ... only a court can provide a definitive ruling. In the absence of a court ruling, one can only assess the likelihood of whether a court would find a transaction to have been made by an agent on behalf of a principal based on established legal principles.

2. The Three Essential Qualities of Agency

Policy Statement P-182R summarizes the common law of agency by establishing that there are three essential qualities of an agency relationship. These three essential qualities are as follows:

(a) consent of both the principal and agent;

(b) authority of the agent to affect the principal's legal position; and

(c) the principal's control of the agent's actions.

Each of these three essential qualities is briefly summarized below.

(a) Consent

For agency to exist, the parties must have intended to have established such a relationship. However, that is not to say that there is any requirement that an express written agreement have been established. The intention of the parties may, for example be inferred from their respective conduct.

It is also conceivable that an agency relationship may exist notwithstanding that the parties have not specifically contemplated agency. In these circumstances the parties would not even be aware that they have entered into an agency relationship. The CRA notes that agency may exist in these circumstances if it is "... evident that the purported agent is arranging transactions for the principal and is not trading on its own account".

(b) Authority

To constitute an agent, the person must have the authority to affect the principal's legal position. This commonly occurs where the agent is provided with the authority to enter into third party contracts on behalf of the principle.

The CRA notes that it should be evident that the principal has empowered the agent to act on its behalf. This means that any transactions undertaken by the agent should be clearly authorized by the principal. This authority may be expressly provided, or it may even be inferred from a positive finding with respect to the other two tests of agency.

The CRA also notes that the authority test will be met where the agent has the authority to discharge obligations of the principal. P-182R illustrates this concept with an example relating to a lawyer who is provided with the authority to pay property taxes on behalf of a client. The example notes that the lawyer is considered to have been provided with the authority to act to affect the client's legal position.

(c) Control

The element of control is one of the leading mechanisms which is used to distinguish between an agency and an independent contractor relationship. The degree of control exerted by the principal in an agency relationship will typically exceed the control exerted in an independent contractor relationship.

The control test, however, will typically be met in circumstances where the control exerted is minimal. For example, the control test may be met where the agent is merely required to regularly provide reports to the principal. The control test may also be met where the principal merely ensures that the agent acts in a competent manner or within the scope of its particular mandate.

3. Other Qualities of Agency

The CRA has also established a secondary list of indicators which may be of assistance in distinguishing between an agency and independent contractor relationship. The factors contained within the secondary list are each consistent with the existence of an agency relationship.

The most important of these secondary indicators is the presence of a fiduciary relationship. This is because agency relationships are always considered to be fiduciary in nature. In practical terms, this means that the agent is required to disclose and account for any secret profits which it earns in the course of acting as agent. The agent is also required to ensure that it does not undertake or engage in any activity which might conflict with the interests of the principal. Other secondary factors include the following:

(a) **Assumption of risk:** an agent would not typically be responsible for the assumption of any loss in connection with a third party transaction. This corresponds with the fiduciary nature of the relationship;

(b) **Accounting practices:** the agent would not typically record in its book of account as revenues amounts received for supplies made by the agent on behalf of the principal;

(c) **Remuneration:** the remuneration of an agent would typically take the form of a set fee for the provision of agency services;

(d) **Best efforts:** an agent will typically undertake to provide its best efforts in connection with a task, but will not guarantee a certain result;

(e) **Alteration of property acquired:** an agent would not typically alter property acquired from a third party which is for a principal;

(f) **Use of property or service:** an agent would not typically consume or use property or services acquired from a third party for a principal;

(g) **Liability for payment:** generally the purchaser of a supply provided through an agent will have recourse against the principal in the event of default; and

(h) **Ownership of property:** typically an agent does not acquire ownership of property which it acquires on behalf of a principal.

Given the many complex and subjective factors which are to be considered in connection with identifying an agency relationship, it is not surprising that the CRA and taxpayers will often reach disparate conclusions as to the nature of the relationship on the same facts.

4. Independent vs. Dependent Agents

Generally, a finding that a third party is (or is not) an agent of another person will be sufficient to resolve most agency related GST issues. However, there will be circumstances where it must be determined whether the agent is a dependent or an independent agent. For example, under the second branch of the definition of "permanent establishment", the fixed place of business of a dependent agent may be considered to be a permanent establishment of the principal.

Policy Statement P-182R, "Agency", does not address the distinction between dependent and independent agents. However, Policy Statement P-208R, "Meaning of Permanent Establishment in Subsection 123(1) of the *Excise Tax Act* (the Act)" does provide the following limited guidance:

Generally, an agent will be considered to be independent if the agent is both legally and economically independent of the principal.

To determine if an agent is legally and economically independent, the following factors should be considered:

(a) whether the agent is subject to detailed instructions or comprehensive control by the principal. An independent agent will not typically be subject to significant control in terms of how they carry out the work or subject to detailed instructions with respect to the conduct of the work. The principal will typically be more interested in the results of the agent's work and will rely on the special skills, knowledge and strength of the agent;

(b) whether the entrepreneurial risk must be borne by the agent or the principal;

(c) whether the agent sells goods in its own name rather than in the name of the principal; and

(d) whether the agent acts as agent for other persons.

The application of the first three tests set out above should be expected to be far from straightforward. For example, test (a) notes that an enhanced level of control will be suggestive of dependent agency. However, it may be difficult to measure control given that all agency relationships, including independent agency relationships, will by their very nature involve a higher degree of control. The test in (b) relates to the assumption of entrepreneurial risk. The inclusion of this reference to risk is confusing given that P-182R provides that agents generally will not assume any risks. Further, with respect to the tests contained in (b) and (c), the CRA does not explain which of the two potential outcomes would be considered to be consistent with an independent agency relationship. For example, if an agent bears entrepreneurial risk or sells goods in its own name, then it is not clear whether the agent would be more likely or less likely to be considered a dependent agent.

The suggestion from all of the above is that the leading indicator of whether a person is a dependent agent will be a function of whether the person acts for other principals (the test in part (d)). Where an agent acts for several principals, the *prima facie* presumption would seem to be that they are an independent agent. Conversely, where an agent acts for only one principal (or possibly a small number of principals), then the agent may be a dependent agent. This presumption, in favour of dependent agency would also be strengthened if, for example, the agent acted only for principals who were related parties.

Policy Statement P-208R provides an example of a situation where it considers that a particular person is a dependent agent. In example 13, the non-resident supplier sells software. To encourage sales in Canada, it has entered into a distribution agreement with a Canadian arm's length corporation. The Canadian, who acts for no other person, will sell and distribute the product on behalf of the non-resident. The Canadian is provided with the authority to conclude contracts but is subject to considerable control from the non-resident. The elements of control include:

— prices set by the non-resident;

— sales techniques specified by the non-resident; and

— terms of sale set by the non-resident.

The CRA ruled that the Canadian is considered a dependent agent of the non-resident. The CRA seemed to focus in particular upon the elements of control and the fact that the Canadian acts for no other person.

C. SUPPLIES MADE BY AGENTS

At common law, acts performed by an agent on behalf of a principal are considered to have been performed by the principal. Accordingly, at common law, if supplies are made by an agent on behalf of a principal, the supplies would be considered to be supplied by the principal.

Absent any legislative alterations to this common law rule, the principal would be the person who is required to register for GST purposes and the person who is responsible for collecting and remitting the GST. The agent would merely be responsible for collecting GST from the principal in connection with its agency services.

General principles of common law will still apply for the purpose of determining whether an agency relationship exists. However, once it has been determined that an agency relationship exists, the common law rules are for the most part overridden by specific rules which have been established in section 177 of the ETA.

These statutory rules have been implemented in large part to ensure that tax leakage does not occur when supplies are made through agents. Although the codified rules are extensive there will still be situations (described below) where no specific statutory rule exists. In those circumstances, the common law rules will continue to apply.

Although for the most part it is beyond the scope of this book to discuss issues relating to the supply of goods, an exception has been made in this chapter. This is because many e-commerce transactions involve agents making supplies of goods over the Internet on behalf of principals. The rules are summarized below.

1. Supply of Tangible Personal Property Supplied on Behalf of a Principal Who is not Required to Collect Tax

The default rule for supplies of tangible personal property made through agents is contained in subsection 177(1) of the ETA. This is an avoidance provision which has been developed to ensure that supplies of goods made through agents are subject to GST in situations where the principal is not a person who is required to collect GST.

The default rule applies in the following circumstances:

(a) a principal makes a supply of tangible personal property, but the principal is not required to collect tax;

(b) the supply is not a zero-rated or exempt supply; and

(c) an agent who is a registrant, in the course of a commercial activity acts as agent in making the supply on behalf of the principal.

The most common situations in which a principal will not be required to collect tax are as follows:

(a) the principal is not registered (and is not required to be registered); or

(b) the principal, regardless of registration status, last acquired the property for use other than in the course of a commercial activity.[1]

Where the above three tests are met, the parties have the option of entering into an election. Assuming that the parties do not enter into this election, the GST will apply in the following manner:

(i) the supply of the property is deemed to have been made by the agent (and not by the principal); and

(ii) the agent is deemed for all purposes (other than for the purposes of section 180) not to have made a supply of agency services to the principal.

This rule is particularly important for non-resident principals. The rule ensures that where goods are supplied in Canada by non-resident principals who are not required to collect tax (because of the application of the registration rules and the non-resident override), the goods will, when supplied through registrant agents, attract Division II GST. The rule will also apply to Canadian resident principals who are not required to collect tax (for

---

[1] See paragraph 141.1(1)(*b*).

example, principals who are small suppliers). The rule does not however deem the supply to have been made in Canada. The ordinary place of supply rules must still be considered to resolve this critical issue.

Another important feature of the default rule is that it removes the obligation of the agent to collect GST from the principal in respect of the agency services. This is because the principal will, where this rule applies, be a person who is not entitled to claim ITCs.

It is interesting to note that the rule in subsection 177(1) applies where the principal is a person who is not required to collect tax. However, it should be noted that a principal may be a person who is required to collect tax, even though it is not GST registered. For example, a non-resident person who supplies goods in Canada in the course of a business carried on in Canada (and who is not a small supplier), would ordinarily be a person who is both required to be registered and a person who is required to collect tax.

As noted above, subsection 177(1) provides for an election. The election may only be entered into where the principal is a registrant (registered or required to be registered), and where the property was last used or acquired by the principal for consumption or use in an endeavour of the principal as defined in subsection 141.01(1). Where the election has been entered into, the GST applies in the following manner:

(a) the supply of the tangible personal property is deemed to be a taxable supply, and is considered to have been made from the principal to the recipient;

(b) the principal will be required to collect and remit the tax;

(c) the agent's services (unless zero-rated or provided outside Canada) will be taxable;

(d) the agent will be responsible for collecting and remitting the tax in respect of the agent's services; and

(e) the principal will be entitled to claim ITCs in respect of any tax paid on the agent's services.

The circumstances in which the election will be available are narrow and do not typically arise in connection with e-commerce transactions.

(a) Exposure Issues for Principals

Where the default rule in subsection 177(1) applies, and no election is entered into, it might ordinarily be expected that there would be very little risk of exposure for the principal. The principal is not the person who is required to collect or remit the tax, and is also not required to pay GST in respect of the agent's services.

Unfortunately, the principal may encounter other more derivative difficulties. For example, a principal who ships the goods into Canada (and clears the goods through Customs) will be required to pay the Division III GST in respect of the goods. However, a person who is not registered cannot claim the Division III ITC itself. Ordinarily a non-resident person who is not registered and who sells goods directly to Canadian customers with delivery in Canada will be entitled to "shift" the Division III ITC claim to its customer by using the mechanism in section 180. However, where the principal makes the supply to the Canadian customer through an agent, it does not appear that the section 180 mechanism will be available. This is because the first branch of section 180 relief is only available where the non-resident person "makes a supply of tangible personal property" to the recipient. The deeming rules in subsection 177(1) establish that it is the agent (and not the principal) who makes the supply to the recipient. As a result, it would appear that this critical requirement will not be met.

It is not clear whether the principal might in the circumstances described above be able to obtain relief under the second branch of the section 180 test. The second branch allows for relief where the non-resident person causes physical possession of the goods to be transferred to a particular person (i.e., the agent), and the particular person is acquiring the property for the purpose of supplying a commercial service in respect of the property to the non-resident. Subsection 177(1) seems to dovetail neatly with this provision in that it deems the agent to be a person who provides services to the non-resident specifically in relation to section 180. However, that being said, two major interpretation concerns remain:

(a) is the principal providing the agent with possession of the goods? Normally, the principal would ship the goods directly to the customer; and

(b) although the agent is providing a service to the non-resident, is it providing a "commercial service"? A "commercial service" is defined as any service in respect of tangible personal property other than "a service of shipping the property supplied by a carrier" and "a financial service". Although this definition appears to be quite broad (and would seem to include ordinary agency services), there is some question as to whether the CRA would adopt this same liberal interpretation.

Given these considerable interpretive difficulties, the better view is that the non-resident supplier should make every effort to avoid being the person who pays the Division III GST. If the customer or the agent were to clear the goods through customs, that person would ordinarily be entitled, assuming that they are GST registered, to claim the corresponding ITC.

(b) Exposure Issues for Agents

The agent bears considerable risk when making sales on behalf of a principal who is not required to collect tax. This is because the agent is the person who is required to collect and remit the GST in respect of the sale of the goods to the customer (assuming that the goods are delivered or made available to the customer in Canada). Many agents do not recognize that they have been charged with this responsibility.

The risks of exposure are exacerbated by the fact that the agent may not have sufficient information to determine whether a particular supply is taxable or exempt or whether the particular taxable supply is being delivered to the customer in Canada.

2. Supply on Behalf of Principal Who is Required to Collect Tax

Where an agent makes a supply on behalf of a principal who is required to collect tax, the manner in which the tax will apply will turn on whether the parties enter into the election set out in subsection 177(1.1).

If the election is not entered into, the ordinary common law rules will apply. The principal will be the person who is required to collect and remit the tax on the supply to the customer (assuming the supply is made in Canada). The agent will be required to collect GST from the principal in respect of the agency services (unless those agency services are provided outside Canada or are zero-rated).

The parties will have the option of electing out of the common law rules where the following conditions are met:

(a) the principal is a person who would be required to collect the tax on the supply other than as a result of the rule in subsection 177(1);

(b) the agent is a registrant and provides its agency services in the course of a commercial activity; and

(c) the supply is not made by way of auction.

Where the election has been entered into, the supply to the customer is deemed to have been made by the agent for the following purposes:

(a) for the purpose of determining the net tax of the agent and of the principal; and

(b) for the purpose of the rules set out in sections 222 and 232.

As a result, the agent will collect and remit the tax as if the supply had been made directly by the agent (and not by the principal). The reference to section 222 ensures that the agent is deemed to hold amounts of GST collected from customers in trust (which involves the special GST priority rules). The reference to section 232 clarifies that the agent has the authority to issue credit or debit notes where the consideration charged is subsequently reduced or where an excess amount of tax was charged or collected. This mechanism is particularly important where the recipient of the supply is not entitled to claim full ITCs (e.g., the person is a consumer).

However, subsection 177(1.1) establishes that the principal who elects to shift GST responsibilities to the agent is not absolved from all potential exposure. Paragraph 177(1.1)(*b*) provides that the principal and agent are jointly and severally liable for all GST obligations, including discrepancies which are attributable solely to the actions of the agent.

Accordingly, prior to entering into any such election with an agent, the principal should be certain that the agent is trustworthy, solvent and fully understands its GST obligations. A principal might also consider monitoring the activities of the agent to ensure that the GST is in fact being collected and remitted.

The following examples demonstrate the operation of the rules where the principal is a person who is required to collect tax:

Example 1: Parties Enter Into Election

The principal is a non-resident GST registered entity which sells taxable tangible personal property to customers located in Canada and the U.S.

For sales in Canada the non-resident relies upon a Canadian sales agent who is a GST registered person.

Where sales are made to a Canadian customer the non-resident ships the goods to the agent in Canada and the agent delivers the goods to the customer's premises.

The agent clears the goods through customs.

The principal and agent enter into a subsection 177(1.1) election.

Application of GST

The agent would pay the Division III GST owing in connection with the clearing of the goods through customs and would claim an ITC for the amount paid.

The agent would collect the GST owing on the sale of the goods to the customer and would remit those amounts to the CRA.

The agent would charge GST to the principal on its agency services but the principal would be entitled to claim an ITC in respect of these amounts.

Example 2: Parties Do Not Enter into Election

The principal is a non-resident GST registered entity which sells taxable tangible personal property to customers located in Canada and the U.S.

For sales in Canada, the non-resident relies upon a Canadian sales agent who is a GST registered person.

Where sales are made to a Canadian customer, the non-resident ships the goods to the customer in Canada.

The customer clears the goods through Customs.

The principal and agent do not enter into a section 177(1.1) election.

Application of GST

The customer would pay the Division III GST owing in connection with the clearing of the goods through Customs. The customer, if registered and if acquiring the goods for consumption, use, or supply in the course of a commercial activity, would be entitled to claim ITCs in respect of the Division III expense incurred.

The principal would collect the GST owing on the sale of the goods to the customer (if the goods are delivered in Canada) and remit those amounts to the CRA.

The customer, if registered and if acquiring the goods for consumption, use or supply in the course of a commercial activity would be entitled to claim ITCs in respect of the Division II expense incurred.

The agent would charge GST to the principal on its services but the principal would be entitled to claim an ITC in respect of these amounts.

(a) Special Rules

Notwithstanding all the rules described above, it should be noted that special agency rules exist in respect of the following:

(a) agents who act only in the capacity of a billing agent (but who are not agents in respect of the making of the supply). This rule may permit the limited purpose agent to elect under subsection 177(1.1);

(b) agents who act as auctioneers; and

(c) certain agents who make supplies of intangible personal property on behalf of principals who are authors, performing artists, painters, sculptors, or other artists. However, these rules only apply where the agent is listed in the Artists' Representatives (GST/HST) Regulations. That list includes such agents as the Directors Guild of Canada.

D. DOCUMENTARY REQUIREMENTS

The ETA has established a number of procedural documentary rules which must be adhered to by all suppliers. These rules allow for the CRA on audit to follow the chain of supplies through different suppliers.

Where these rules are not followed by the supplier, the recipient of a particular supply may not be entitled to claim ITCs. This will include circumstances where all of the substantive requirements for claiming an ITC have been met (i.e., the supply has been consumed, used, or re-supplied in the course of a commercial activity).

Supplies involving agency relationships require special rules, in part because the agent will often be the person who issues the invoice to the customer. The Input Tax Credit (GST/HST) Regulations specifically allow for the agent who makes a supply on behalf of a principal to provide an invoice to the customer bearing information relating to the agent which will meet the documentary requirements. This will include situations where, as a result of the application of the rules in section 177, the supply is deemed to be made by the principal.

E. SUPPLIES ACQUIRED THROUGH AGENTS

The ETA, when first introduced, contained specific statutory rules relating to the application of GST where supplies are acquired by an agent on behalf of a principal. It was subsequently determined that this section was not required because general legal principals of agency provided for the same result. The statutory rules were accordingly abolished.

As a result, the current approach requires that where any given expense is incurred by a third party, the nature of the relationship between the parties be examined to determine whether:

(a) the expense is incurred as an agent for the principal; or

(b) the expense is incurred as the third party's own expense.

The tests set out in Policy Statement P-182R may be used to determine whether an expense is incurred as an agent on behalf of a principal. However, admittedly the focus in that policy statement is upon situations involving supplies made through agents. More specific guidance may also be found in Policy Statement P-209, "Lawyers' Disbursements".

At common law, where expenses are incurred by a person as an agent for the principal, it is the principal who is considered to have incurred the expense. The agent would typically pass through the particular expense (which will include any GST originally charged) to the principal. The principal would then consider whether it is entitled to claim an input tax credit in respect of the expense.

Where expenses are incurred by a person on its own account, that person would determine whether the GST portion of the expense may be recovered as an ITC. Typically, where the expense relates to the making of taxable supplies in the course of a commercial activity and the person is registered, an ITC would be available.

Chapter 11

Introduction to the Rulings Chapters

A. OVERVIEW

The previous chapters have been organized to correspond with specific issues raised by the ETA. Chapters 12 through 18 are organized along e-commerce subject matter lines. The purpose of the following chapters is to provide a comprehensive description of the manner in which the CRA applies the GST to a wide variety of e-commerce related supplies. Accordingly, the chapters consider a full range of GST issues, including characterization of supplies, identification of single and multiple supplies, the resolution of place of supply (GST and HST), zero-rating, and other jurisdictional issues.

In each of the following chapters, the CRA's leading administrative policies which relate to that particular subject matter are discussed. The chapters focus in particular upon CRA rulings and interpretation letters. To the extent that rulings appear anomalous, or where the rulings do not appear to fully explore a particular issue, specific commentary has been added by the author.

It should also be noted that each of chapters 12 through 18 discusses a broad range of e-commerce offerings. This highly consolidated approach was adopted in order to allow for direct comparisons to be made with respect to the manner in which the GST applies to similar or related offerings. This approach is also a reflection of the fact that in the e-commerce environment activities which, from a commercial perspective, may appear to be divergent, will from a GST perspective be considered to be quite similar.

B. SPECIFIC INTERPRETATION ISSUES

The rulings and interpretation letters which are referenced in the following chapters offer particular insight into the CRA's administrative policies. However, there are a number of limitations associated with relying on such materials which should be fully considered. Among the limitations are the following:

1. Administrative Policies Do Not Have the Force of Law

The manner in which the GST will apply in any situation is a function of the laws which have been passed by the Canadian federal government, Regulations promulgated in accordance with those laws, other subordinate forms of legislation such as Remission Orders, and principles of common law established by Canadian courts.

In the event of conflict between any of the above, and a particular position which has been adopted by the CRA, it should be expected that the position which is supported by the legislation or common law will prevail. However, that is not to say that the CRA's administrative position will not carry considerable weight, particularly given that it is the government entity which is responsible for administering the ETA. A party seeking to advance a position which is contrary to the administrative policies of the CRA, would typically be required to demonstrate that the CRA's position is inconsistent with, or unsupported by, the existing legal framework (including common law).

2. Administrative Policies Are Very Easily Changed

The CRA regularly updates or revises its formal administrative policies. Further, rulings and interpretation letters are from time to time revoked or specifically reversed. These changes are implemented for a number of reasons.

The CRA will also from time to time determine that the system which it previously adopted is no longer sufficient to meet its current policy objectives. As new situations come to the attention of the CRA, policies are revised to reflect the new issues. One example of a very substantial change is reflected in the CRA's Policy Statement P-051R2, "Carrying on Business in Canada". The April 29, 2005 revision of that document bears little resemblance to the former version of that policy.

Generally, where such administrative changes are made, the new regime will be applied with retroactive effect.

3. Administrative Policies May Themselves Be Ambiguous

An extremely high level of care is associated with the drafting of legislative provisions. As a result, the drafting of legislation is an extremely time-consuming practice.

Although administrative policies and rulings are also drafted in a careful manner, the level of care associated with this type of document is not typically commensurate with that of legislative provisions. As a result, it is particularly dangerous to interpret administrative policies in a literal manner or to assume that the particular policy relates in a comprehensive manner to every situation.

4. Administrative Policies May Not Be Correct

Administrative policies reflect the CRA's interpretation of the *Excise Tax Act*, corresponding regulations, other relevant legislation, and principles of common law. The CRA's interpretation may or may not be correct.

5. Administrative Policies May Reflect a Bias

Administrative documents are drafted in a manner which is intended to be consistent both with the underlying legal framework and with the CRA's policy objectives.

In the course of reconciling what may be two different approaches, there is always the potential for a particular bias to emerge. For example, given a choice between two possible interpretations, one of which may lead to an increased risk of tax leakage and the second of which will preclude these concerns, it should be expected that the CRA will adopt the latter.

6. Administrative Policies May Not Address Every Situation

This issue is particularly important in connection with rulings and interpretation letters. Typically, the CRA, in drafting ruling and interpretation letters, will restrict the scope of its analysis to only those specific issues raised by the particular applicant. As a matter of courtesy, the CRA may, where practical, bring to the attention of the applicant other issues which should have been raised or which might be relevant. However, in many cases it simply will not be practical or reasonable to expect the CRA to do so.

The likelihood that tangential issues will be flagged by the CRA is even lower where the particular issue relates to a person other than the ruling applicant. For example, a particular non-resident applicant may enquire as to its obligation to collect Division II GST when supplies are made to a Canadian resident. Where the particular supply is considered to be made outside Canada, the CRA would rule that the supply is not subject to Division II GST. It would be dangerous for the Canadian purchaser, however, to rely upon this ruling as standing for the proposition that it may acquire the particular supply on a tax-free basis. This is because Division III or Division IV GST may still apply to the particular supply. However, given that the Division III and Division IV GST may not directly involve the supplier (i.e., the applicant), it should not be expected that the CRA would reference either of these divisions.

This fundamental limitation should be noted both by third parties who intend to rely upon existing rulings or interpretation letters, as well as by the applicant.

7. Rulings Relate to Specific Factual Situations

A person reviewing an existing ruling may not be aware of all the facts which were taken into account in arriving at the particular conclusion. For example, the third party will not have had the benefit of reviewing the underlying documentation, including sales contracts.

8. Administrative Policies Are Not Issued to Assist in Effective Tax Planning

Opportunities to engage in effective tax planning techniques are not typically described in administrative policies. It would be contrary to the CRA's mandate and policy objectives to describe mechanisms or strategies which could be implemented to reduce tax obligations.

9. Sanitization May Lead to Interpretative Difficulties

Rulings and interpretation letters issued by the CRA are "sanitized" prior to their release to any person other than the applicant or its authorized representative. This process ensures that the privacy rights of the applicant (and of other parties referred to) are protected.

The degree of sanitization which is performed will take into account a number of factors, including the likelihood that any information, if provided, could be used to identify the applicant. Deletions will typically include the identity of any parties, the location of their offices, and the specific details of the subject matter in issue.

Given that critical information may have been deleted from the rulings or interpretation letters, issues will always arise as to the correct interpretation of the documents. These issues may be compounded where there are multiple parties or where the issues are more complex.

Chapters 12 through 18 have been drafted with these limitations in mind. The chapter materials reference situations where policies or rulings do not appear to provide a complete answer, where administrative policies may not be correct (or appear overly aggressive), where further work is required to be done to properly reconcile the issues, or where simple planning opportunities may be available.

C. OTHER ISSUES

At the time of issuance of the rulings discussed in this book, Division II GST was levied at the rate of 7% for supplies which were considered to be made in other than a participating province. Supplies made in a participating province were subject to HST at the rate of 15%. The other divisions of the *Excise Tax Act* also levied corresponding rates of tax.

On July 1, 2006, the GST and HST rates were legislatively reduced throughout the *Excise Tax Act* to 6% and 14%, respectively. The discussion of the rulings which follows takes into account this rate reduction, even though the rates described in those rulings were in fact the former higher rates. However, where direct quotes from rulings are referenced, the former higher rates have been left in place. Similarly, any references to the former Canada

Customs and Revenue Agency ("CCRA") are described in the following chapters as references to the Canada Revenue Agency ("CRA").

On a final note, Chapters 12 through 18 reference the generic term "CRA rulings". In fact, some of the documents referenced in the chapters which follow may be either "advance rulings" (time-limited rulings), "application rulings" (rulings in respect of ongoing transactions which are not time-limited), or "interpretation letters" (more general explanations of the manner in which the law applies).

Unlike advance or application rulings, interpretation letters are not binding on the CRA. In many cases, a request for a ruling will result in the issuance of an interpretation letter by the CRA. This is typically because the applicant has not provided sufficient information to allow for a ruling to be issued. For the purposes of this book, rulings and interpretation letters have been referred to collectively by the generic term "rulings" or "GST rulings".

Chapter 12

Advertising Services

A. OVERVIEW

The delivery of advertising messages is one of the more significant means by which business is conducted over the Internet. The recent proliferation in Internet advertising is primarily attributable to the fact that the Internet allows for the dissemination of messages to a very large number of people located anywhere in the world in a relatively inexpensive manner. Notwithstanding this broad reach, Internet messages may be directed very effectively at a particular target market through a self-selecting process. For example, it may be expedient to advertise sports memorabilia through a sports informational Web site.

Among the unique features associated with Internet advertising are the following:

(a) Any person may, through its Web site, provide Internet advertising. The person may be resident anywhere in the world. Further, the person for whom the Internet advertising is provided may be resident anywhere in the world.

(b) In many cases, the person providing the Internet advertising will be engaged primarily in some line of business which is other than Internet advertising.

(c) The advertising message may typically be accessed by users located anywhere in the world.

1. Traditional E-Commerce Advertising

One of the more traditional means of providing Internet advertising has been to create a Web site specifically to showcase products (or services) which are available for sale from third parties. The Web site would typically provide product specific information and vendor contact information. A fee would be charged (typically a flat rate or a time-based fee) to the third party for inclusion on the Web site.

In some cases, the advertiser will allow the third party to place a customized advertisement on its Web site in order to enhance the offering. Alternatively, a simple list with third party contact information will be provided.

2. More Elaborate E-Commerce Advertising

There has in recent years been a dramatic evolution in Internet advertising, because more elaborate forms of advertising are constantly being developed.

Further, advertising is increasingly being provided by entities which are primarily engaged in lines of business which are other than Internet advertising. For example, it is not unusual for persons with high traffic Web sites (i.e., news, weather, sports, cooking, gardening, fashion or general interest) to allow for advertising to be placed on their Web sites. This form of directed advertising is particularly effective when aligned with the subject matter of the Web site because visitors have already demonstrated a subject matter specific interest. This advertising may take the form of banner advertising (i.e., banners which scroll across Web sites), pop-up windows (which open automatically when a particular Web site is visited), or dialogue windows.

However, a far more subtle approach has also proven to be particularly effective in the Internet environment. In many cases, advertising is provided in such a way that the person to whom the message is directed will not be aware that they have received an advertising message. The leading means by which this approach is implemented is the Web site which contains "reviews" of various competing product offerings. The Web site may contain what appears to be objective third party information (from a person who is technologically sophisticated and who has an interest in the particular subject matter), on the offerings of various suppliers. However, it is not uncommon for the person hosting the Web site to be receiving payments from various suppliers in return for the positive reviews or recommendations. To enhance the credibility of the author and the Web site, the author will often provide general discussion material or unbiased information in connection with the subject matter.

Advanced advertising techniques may involve communicating the message in a very active and unconventional manner. For example, instead of (or in addition to) delivering a traditional message to the viewer, a URL to a target Web site may be established. A customer who is potentially interested in a product (or in a particular vendor) may choose to link through to the target Web site. A more aggressive technique may involve linking a user through to a target Web site in circumstances where the user has not specifically selected or agreed to this option. Whether this type of activity constitutes "advertising" for GST purposes, is discussed below.

Search engines have enjoyed a very high degree of success by providing "link through" advertising. Many (or perhaps all) search engines accept third party compensation in return for more preferable search rankings. In addition, where certain search terms have been entered, many search engines will also specifically list their customers' Web sites in a separate (and very prominent) category, apart from the ordinary search results. The issue of whether this type of activity constitutes "advertising" for GST purposes is also discussed below.

Payment structures for advertising services may take any one, or a combination of forms. The following is an example of a typical payment structure with respect to advertising services:

Example

ABC Co sets up a Web site which provides information relating to the purchase of a home stereo. It writes articles and performs reviews which compare the offerings of various manufacturers. The site will provide for link through URLs to various vendors of stereos.

ABC Co would typically be compensated in one or more of three forms:

(a) A click-through fee where each time a person clicks through, a fee is awarded. Sometimes the click-through fee is tied to performance. For example, the click-through fee is only paid in the event that the customer actually goes beyond the initial home page of the vendor or the customer actually makes a purchase.

(b) A fixed fee for advertising (not related to the click-through fee).

(c) A fee paid as a percentage of sales made. This fee is only paid in the event that the customer makes the purchase and the fee is a function of the sale price.

3. Distinction Between Advertising and Third Party Sales

Advertising and third party sales may be distinguished on the basis that advertising does not relate to an active involvement in the sale of the underlying product or service. The advertiser merely communicates the message or leads the consumer to the underlying supplier.

Third party sellers on the other hand, in addition to promoting a particular offering, will become centrally involved in the underlying sale. Chapter 13, Third Party Sales of Goods, discusses the GST consequences where the third party takes on a more active role with respect to the sale of the underlying product or service.

B. CHARACTERIZATION OF ADVERTISING SUPPLIES

1. Scope of Advertising Service

The ETA does not define the term "advertising". Accordingly, the determination of whether a particular supply constitutes an advertising supply will turn in large part upon the administrative policies of the CRA.

The CRA characterizes "advertising" in an extremely broad manner. Administratively, the CRA describes an "advertising service" as:

> ... the service of creating a message and a service directly related to the communication of such a message. The message must be oriented towards soliciting business, attracting donations, or calling public attention in the form of an information notice, a political announcement or other similar communication.[1]

This suggests that there are two distinct types of services which may qualify as an advertising service:

(a) the service of creating a message; and

(b) a service directly related to the communication of such a message.

(a) What is a "Service of Creating a Message"

In paragraph 26(a) of GST/HST Memorandum 4.5.3, "Exports — Services and Intellectual Property", the CRA notes that the term "creating a message" refers to the following:

> A service of creating a message oriented towards soliciting business, attracting donations, or calling public attention in the form of an information notice, a political announcement or other similar communication by any means including oral, written, or graphic statements and representations disseminated by any means including:
>
> (i) in a newspaper or other publication;
>
> (ii) on radio or television;
>
> (iii) in a notice, handbill, sign, catalogue or letter; or
>
> (iv) on a billboard or on real property.

(b) What is a "Service Directly Related to the Communication of a Message"

In paragraph 26(b) of GST/HST Memorandum 4.5.3, the CRA notes that this term refers to the following:

> A service directly related to the communication of such a message (e.g., air time on a broadcasting service, space in a publication) where,
>
> (i) the communication service is supplied as part of the supply of a message as defined in paragraph (a) above [i.e., the creation of the message], or

---

[1] See RITS 6277, "Supply of Products and Services Through the Internet", dated November 6, 2001.

(ii) the person providing the communication service can demonstrate that, at the time the supply is made, the service is in relation to the supply of a message as defined in paragraph (a) above.

The CRA further clarifies that the creation and communicating of the message may or may not be performed by the same person:

There are occasions where the person broadcasting or communicating the message within the meaning of (b) above will not be the same person supplying the message (i.e., the creative aspect). Generally the person supplying the broadcast or communication service will be in possession of the message or will have received sufficient information as to the content of the message prior to the supply of the service to know that the message is in the nature of advertising. In these situations the supply of the broadcast or communication service will be considered to be a supply of an advertising service.

The suggestion seems to be that the creative services supplied to a person in connection with the development of an advertisement will be "advertising services" under the rule in heading (a). These services might include typesetting, design, or developing wording for the advertisement. There would be no requirement that the person providing the services be involved in the dissemination of the message in order for this to constitute an advertising service.

The service of communicating the message would be considered "advertising services" under the rule in heading (b). This would include owners of Web sites who communicate a particular message through their Web site. There would be no requirement that the Web site owner be the person who actually created the message. For example, the message may have been created by the customer or even by a third party (for example a graphic designer).

(c) Application of the Tests

With respect to traditional forms of advertising, it should be expected that the identification of an advertising service will be relatively straightforward. Consider the following example of a traditional advertising scenario:

Example

An auto dealership wishes to promote its business on the radio. The dealership hires an advertising firm to create the advertisement which will include music and an oral description of the business. The auto dealership then contracts with a radio station to run the advertisement.

The supply by the advertising firm would be an advertising service under heading (a). The supply by the radio station would be an advertising service under heading (b).

The identification of an advertising service may be more complex in an Internet setting. The difficulty relates to the fact that the Internet allows for promotional activities to be conducted in a far more elaborate manner than with more traditional media. For example, is a person performing a service which is "directly related to the communication of a message" where the person:

(a) provides only a URL link to a third party Web site;

(b) automatically redirects a person to a third party Web site; or

(c) ranks a person's Web site higher on a search list through a search engine.

The reconciliation of these examples with traditional definitions of advertising raises a number of conceptual difficulties. In examples (a) and (b), the URL link itself may be the message. However, this approach is more difficult to justify where the link is not visible to the user (i.e., the automatic redirect scenario). Alternatively, the relevant message might be the information which is contained on the customer's Web site (i.e., the target link), and the advertiser is providing a means by which people are led to this particular message. Similarly, where a search engine features a particular URL more prominently (i.e., higher in the search rankings), this elevated ranking may constitute the message. Alternatively, the relevant message may be contained within the target Web site and the advertiser is providing the means by which this message is disseminated.

The CRA has acknowledged that advertising provided through the Internet will typically be very different than advertising which is provided through other more traditional channels. More importantly, the CRA has thus far chosen to interpret the advertising services tests in a very liberal manner with respect to the Internet. As a result, many promotional activities conducted through the Internet, including some very elaborate promotional activities, will qualify as "advertising services". For example, rulings 4, 5, and 7 described below, suggest that the three services noted above (i.e., providing URL links, providing automatic redirects, and providing preferential rankings) would likely qualify as advertising services.

The CRA's interpretation of the term "advertising services" is quite broad in another important respect. Much of this chapter focuses on advertising provided for business purposes. However, advertising services will also be provided where the message relates to "attracting donations or calling public attention to a particular issue". For example, a political announcement or even a birth notice may qualify as an advertising service. Most people would not ordinarily consider such messages to be in the nature of advertising.

2. The CRA's Approach to Characterizing Advertising Supplies

The CRA has consistently held that advertising related supplies are a supply of a service (and not a supply of property). This relates to the fact that the advertiser would not typically provide any property rights to its customer.[2] The CRA provides the following example of an advertising service in TIB 090:[3]

> Companies pay a fee to Web site operators to place advertisements on their Web sites. Advertising rates may be determined in a number of ways, including the cost per thousand impressions (i.e., the number of times the advertisement is displayed to a user) or the number of click throughs (i.e., the number of times the advertisement is clicked by a user). For example banner ads, which are small graphic images embedded in a web page, allow a customer's web page to be loaded to a user's computer when clicked by the user.
>
> An advertising service is a service of creating a message and a service directly related to the communication of such a message. The message must be oriented towards soliciting business, attracting donations, or calling public attention in the form of an information notice, political announcement, or other similar communication.
>
> By publicizing companies' messages on the Internet (i.e., placing advertisements on Web sites) the Web site operators are supplying an advertising service to the companies.

This approach is consistent with the general guidelines in TIB 090 which relate to the distinction between property and services. The guidelines provide that supplies made by electronic means will generally be considered to be a service where:

(a) the supply does not include the provision of rights, or if there is a provision of rights, these rights are incidental to the supply;

(b) the supply involves specific work that is performed for a specific person; or

(c) there is human involvement in making the supply.

Advertising will generally involve specific work that is performed for a specific customer and there will be human involvement in making the supply.

---

[2] A "service" as defined in part in subsection 123(1) of the ETA as anything other than property.

[3] Characterization of Supplies, Example 11.

3. Possibility that Advertising Could be a Supply of Intangible Personal Property

Although the rulings issued to date consistently hold that advertising is a supply of a service, the possibility that some forms of advertising might be considered to be a supply of intangible personal property should not be ruled out. TIB 090 provides that a supply made by electronic means may be considered to be a supply of intangible personal property if:

(a) a right in a product or a right to use a product for personal or commercial purposes is provided; or

(b) a product is provided that has already been created or developed or is already in existence.

As a result, advertising related design work would likely be considered to be intangible personal property where the designer retains rights in respect of the creation. It is conceivable that a wide range of other advertising related supplies might also be considered to be property related supplies. This risk that the characterization might shift would seem to be enhanced where the human element involved in the making of the supply is minimal.

For example, consider a Web site owner who has established a system whereby a customer may pay for the right to have a particular message posted (for example, a business listing). The customer posts the message and makes payment automatically by interacting with the particular Web site.

It is arguable that this might be a supply of property because the right to use an existing product is being provided (i.e., the Web site which will host the advertisement). This characterization is also supported by the minimal human involvement in the making of the supply.

Fortunately, the CRA has to date adopted a very liberal approach with respect to the scope of activities which will qualify as advertising services. This approach is extremely favourable both with respect to the application of the place of supply rules, and with respect to the application of the zero-rating rules.

C. PLACE OF SUPPLY ISSUES

1. GST

The ETA does not contain any place of supply rules which are specific to advertising services. Accordingly, determining the location where an advertising service is supplied will be a function of the ordinary place of supply rules for services. However, the distinction between an ordinary service and an advertising service is relevant for the purposes of applying the zero-rating rules in respect of supplies made to non-residents. The zero-rating rules are discussed below.

The general place of supply rules for services establish that a service will be considered to be supplied in Canada if the service meets any of the three tests set out below:

(a) the service is in relation to real property which is located in Canada (paragraph 142(1)(*d*));

(b) the service is a prescribed service (paragraph 142(1)(*f*)); or

(c) the service is, or is to be, performed in whole or in part in Canada (paragraph 142(1)(*g*)).

As a preliminary matter, no regulations have been prescribed in connection with paragraph 142(1)(*f*). Further, the rulings issued to date suggest that the advertising service will not typically be considered to be a service in relation to real property even if the subject matter of the advertising is real property (either in or outside Canada). For example, if a Web site owner provides banner advertising for a real estate developer, the advertising service will not be considered to be a service in relation to real property. The rationale seems to be that the nexus between the services and the real property is insufficient to meet the "in relation to" test.

As a result, an advertising service will generally be considered to be supplied in Canada only if the service is considered to be performed in whole or in part in Canada.

(a) Service Performed in Whole or in Part in Canada

It is a question of fact whether a service is performed in a particular jurisdiction. However, the CRA has adopted a very broad regime for determining the location where services are performed.

There are two different means by which a service may be considered to be performed in Canada. The first relates to the performance of services in Canada as a result of employee activities. The second relates to the performance of services in Canada as a result of equipment (i.e., servers). These two issues are discussed below.

(b) Performance in Canada as a Result of Employees

In TIB 090, the CRA notes that:

> ... the place where the service is performed is traditionally the place where the person physically doing the work is situated. For example, if a

non-resident supplier sends a technician to Canada to provide programming services, the place of performance is in Canada ...

The CRA also notes that a service is typically performed in Canada where:

The service requires a person to perform a task (i.e., the supplier acts through one or more of its employees) and the person performing or physically carrying out the task is situated in Canada at the time the activity is done.[4]

Where a particular supplier operates from a location in Canada, it will follow (absent exceptional circumstances) that the service will be performed in Canada under this rule. Similarly, where a non-resident provides services from a location in Canada, the service will be considered to be performed in Canada. Even the performance of tangential tasks in Canada may result in a finding that services are performed in Canada. In TIB 090, the CRA notes that:

... a supplier may prepare a report in Canada in respect of programming services carried on outside Canada. As the report is a component of the services supplied, the place where the report is prepared must be considered when determining the place of supply.

The example set out above suggests however that there may be some employee activities undertaken in Canada which would not constitute performance in Canada. For example, if the report described above were prepared in Canada, but the report was not a component of the services supplied, it would be arguable that services are not performed in Canada.

Unfortunately, even if this argument were to be successfully advanced, performance may still be considered to occur in Canada because of another, far broader place of performance rule. This alternative rule establishes that where any activity related to the performance of the service is undertaken in Canada, the service will be considered to be supplied in Canada. The suggestion seems to be that the performance of any task in Canada (including tasks which are not a component of the service) will constitute performance of the service in Canada.

It is not clear which types of tangential activities are intended to be captured under these rules. Although the tests are quite broad, it would appear that the activity in issue would need to be a part of the service (test #1), or an activity which is related to the performance of the service (test #2) before the performance rules would apply. The suggestion is that preparatory work, sales work, and perhaps even general support or administrative functions, would not constitute performance of services in Canada.

---

[4] TIB 090.

(c) Application to Advertising Services

Where a supplier provides advertising services and operates from a business location in Canada, the advertising services will clearly be supplied in Canada. However, if the advertising services are provided by a person who operates from offices located outside Canada, and none of the employees involved in providing the advertising services enters Canada, then it should be expected that the services will not be considered to be provided in Canada.

The following examples demonstrate how the employee-based performance rules should be expected to apply:

Example 1

A Canadian resident corporation with offices in Toronto establishes a Web site which posts links to third party service providers who are home renovators. The home renovator pays a fee to the advertiser every time a potential customer links through the advertiser's site to their own Web site.

The advertiser performs all of its functions (posting URLs and other monitoring and maintenance functions) from its offices in Toronto.

The CRA would consider this service to be performed in Canada as the service provider's employees who work on the Web site are located in Canada.

Example 2

A non-resident corporation with offices in Detroit provides an advertising service.

Where the customer is a Canadian entity, the non-resident sends employees to Canada to assist in the development of the advertisement campaign and to provide general advice on how to maximize the effectiveness of the advertisement.

All other functions are performed from Detroit.

The CRA would likely consider this service to be performed in part in Canada because of the critical functions performed in Canada.

(d) Performance in Canada as a Result of Equipment

Services may be performed in Canada even where employees do not visit Canada. The CRA notes in TIB 090 that "A supplier can provide a service to a customer in Canada without physically being in Canada". The CRA has established the following two tests for determining whether performance occurs in Canada as a result of equipment:

(a) the service includes operations performed by a supplier's equipment which is located in Canada; or

(b) the supply involves doing something to or with a recipient's equipment by accessing it from a remote location and the recipient's equipment is located in Canada.

(e) Application to Advertising Services

Ordinarily, a supply of an advertising service will not involve the supplier being provided with remote access to the customer's computers. Accordingly, the second heading referred to above (which typically relates to technical support services), will not normally result in advertising services being performed in Canada.

It would be far more typical that advertising would be deemed to be supplied in Canada because it is provided through the supplier's equipment which is located in Canada. For example, if a non-resident supplier were to provide advertising through a Web site which is hosted on the supplier's server in Canada, the supply would likely be considered to be made in Canada. In ruling 37297 (discussed in Chapter 16, Online Content, Services, and Other General Offerings), an online consulting service was considered to be supplied in Canada because a server in Canada was used to deliver the service.

The equipment which will constitute the supplier's equipment for the purposes of this rule appears to be any equipment which is at the disposal of the supplier. This may include servers which are leased to the supplier or even servers in respect of which the supplier has been granted access under an informal arrangement (for example, with a related corporation). However, it would appear that where access to servers is provided in a typical ISP arrangement, the servers will not be considered to be at the disposal of the supplier. Further, the Web site itself will not be considered to be equipment.

2. HST

A supply may only be considered to be made within an HST province if the supply is first considered to be made in Canada. This is because of the threshold place of supply rule contained in section 144.1. Any supply which is made in Canada, and which is not considered to be made in an HST province, will be deemed to be supplied in a non-participating province.

The general rule with respect to services is that they are supplied in a particular province if "all or substantially all of the Canadian element of the service" is performed in that province.[5] The "Canadian element" of a service is defined as the portion of the service that is performed in Canada.

Given that performance will take into account the location of the supplier's employees, and will also take into account the location of the supplier's equipment, it should be expected that this test may be extremely difficult to apply in a multi-jurisdictional setting. This is because, unlike the country of supply rules which rely upon an "all or nothing" approach, the province of supply rules require that a much more complex allocation be performed. This province of supply test requires that the person determine which portion of the supply is performed in Canada in order to identify the Canadian element of the service, and then determine which portion of the Canadian element of the service is performed in a particular province.

Consider the following example:

Example

A corporation which operates from an office in Ontario provides advertising services to a customer located in Nova Scotia.

The advertisement will be displayed on the supplier's web page which is hosted on the supplier's server in Ontario.

The supplier will send employees to the customer's office in Nova Scotia to assist in developing the advertisements. However, development work will also be done at the supplier's office in Ontario.

It would appear that the service is performed both in Nova Scotia (an HST province) and in Ontario (a non-HST province).

It is not clear how the supplier would determine if all or substantially all of the service is performed in one of those provinces. This task will be complicated by the fact that the service is performed both by employees and by equipment.

Where the first province of supply rule does not apply, the alternative services rule provides that a supply will be considered to be made in a particular province where:[6]

(a) the place of negotiation for the supply is in the province; and

(b) it is not the case that all or substantially all of the service is performed outside that province.

---

[5] Paragraph 2(*a*) of Part V of Schedule IX.

[6] Paragraph 2(*b*) of Part V of Schedule IX.

The reference to the place of negotiation is a reference to the permanent establishment of the supplier at which the individual principally involved in the negotiation for the supplier ordinarily works.

Where neither of the rules set out above locate a service in any particular province, and where the Canadian element of a service is performed primarily in the participating provinces, the supply of the service will be made in the participating province in which the greatest proportion of the Canadian element of the service is performed. This will be the case unless the place of negotiation of the supply is outside Canada, and not all or substantially all of the service is performed in Canada.[7]

D. NON-RESIDENT ISSUES

A non-resident who provides advertising services in Canada may be entitled to take advantage of the non-resident override so that it is not required to collect Division II GST. The following conditions must be satisfied:

(a) the non-resident is not deemed to be resident in Canada because of a permanent establishment in Canada;

(b) the non-resident does not carry on business in Canada; and

(c) the non-resident is not registered.

The application of the first two issues is discussed below in the context of advertising services.

1. Deemed Residence Because of Permanent Establishment

A non-resident person who has a permanent establishment in Canada will be deemed to be resident in respect of any supplies made through that permanent establishment. A permanent establishment is generally defined in subsection 123(1) as:

(a) a fixed place of business through which the person makes supplies; or

(b) a fixed place of business of another person (other than an independent agent) who is acting in Canada on behalf of the particular person and through whom the particular person makes supplies in the ordinary course of business.

A person would not ordinarily be expected to provide advertising services through a dependent agent located in Canada (i.e., the test in part (b)). However, a non-resident person might be considered to be making supplies

---

[7] Section 3 of Part V of Schedule IX.

through its own fixed place of business in Canada when it provides the service through a Canadian server which is at its disposal.

The CRA considers a server to be at the disposal of the non-resident person when it is leased or owned by the non-resident person. However, when a Web site is hosted in a typical ISP arrangement, the server will not be considered to be at the disposal of the non-resident.

The activities carried on through the server would only be sufficient to constitute a permanent establishment if the activities are significant and essential in relation to the overall business activities of the supplier. Where advertising services are provided through a Web site hosted on a server in Canada which is at the disposal of the non-resident, and compensation is being received for those services, it should be anticipated that those services would be viewed as significant and essential. This presumption would be strengthened where the supplier is a person for whom the advertising services constitute a core line of business. For example, if the Web site were established primarily for the purposes of generating advertising revenues, this test would be easily met.

2. Non-Resident is Carrying on Business in Canada

Where a non-resident provides advertising services in Canada in the course of a business carried on in Canada, the services will not be eligible for the non-resident override. The non-resident would be required to collect the Division II GST in respect of the services.[8]

Generally, where a non-resident person operates a Web site which is aimed at Canadians and provides advertising services to Canadian customers, these activities, in and of themselves, would not be considered sufficient to constitute carrying on business in Canada. The CRA notes in TIB 090 that:

> In general, a non-resident person must have a significant presence in Canada to be considered to be carrying on business in Canada. Isolated transactions carried on in Canada as part of a business that is carried on by a non-resident person outside Canada may not result in the person being considered to be carrying on business in Canada ...

However, if the non-resident were to engage in other activities which establish a stronger nexus to Canada, then the non-resident may be considered to be carrying on business in Canada. This may include, for example, accepting payment in Canada, maintaining a bank account in Canada, or working with agents located in Canada. The non-resident in those circum-

---

[8] Carrying on business in Canada would also trigger the obligation to register pursuant to section 240 unless the person is a small supplier.

stances would lose the benefit of the non-resident override in respect of any supplies made in Canada.

E. ZERO-RATING ISSUES

Given that advertising supplies will typically be considered to be services, the general services provision (contained in section 7) will be available to zero-rate supplies made to non-residents. Advertising services will qualify for zero-rating under section 7 when provided to a non-resident person (including where the non-resident is registered), except if any of the exclusions apply. Two of the exclusions which commonly apply in respect of advertising supplies relate to circumstances where:

(a) the service is made to an individual who is in Canada at any time when the individual has contact with the supplier in relation to the supply; or

(b) the service is rendered to an individual while that individual is in Canada.

To avoid the application of the second exclusion described above, it is important that the non-resident customer not have employees enter Canada in connection with the supply of advertising services.

Where the supply in issue does not qualify for zero-rating under section 7, zero-rating might still be available under section 8. Section 8 provides that zero-rating is available for:

A supply of a service of advertising made to a non-resident person who is not registered [for GST purposes] at the time the service is performed.

It should be noted that while section 8 avoids the numerous carve outs which are associated with section 7, section 8 will only apply where the recipient is not registered.

F. RULINGS

1. General Advertising Rulings

Ruling 1: Real Estate Advertising

Ruling 30777[9] relates to a non-resident supplier of advertising services. The GST registered non-resident is engaged in the primary business of selling maps and books over the Internet (i.e., by way of its Web site). The

---

[9] September 11, 2002.

applicant also sells advertising on its Web site to businesses located both in Canada and the U.S. The advertisements are typically for RV parks.

The Ruling

The CRA concluded that the supply of an advertising service is considered to be made outside Canada, including where the supply of advertising is provided to a Canadian resident.

In reaching the conclusion that the supply is made outside Canada, the CRA noted that the employees who work on the Web site (in posting advertisements) operate from outside Canada. The fact that the subject matter of the advertising services related in many cases to real property (RV parks) located in Canada did not result in the services being supplied in Canada. The CRA apparently adopted the position that the services were not "in relation to real property located in Canada". If the services had been in relation to real property located in Canada, then the supply would have been deemed to be made in Canada.

The CRA did specifically note (in the assumptions portion of the ruling), that the servers which hosted the Web site were located outside Canada, and that all updates and maintenance to the Web site is done outside Canada. The reference to the servers seems to suggest that if the supplier's Web site were hosted on a server in Canada, then the supply might have been considered to have been made in Canada (because of the equipment based place of performance rule).

Although the ruling does not mention Division IV GST, the recipient of the service should consider its potential application. Any Canadian resident who is not registered or who is not acquiring the supply for consumption, use, or supply in the course of a commercial activity, would be required to pay this tax on a self-assessing basis.

Conclusions

1. The advertising supply was considered to be supplied outside Canada because the employees of the supplier operated from outside Canada and because the supplier did not make the supply through equipment located in Canada.

2. Although the subject matter of the advertising service was real property situated in Canada, the services are not considered to be in relation to real property in Canada.

3. Where the advertising service is supplied through equipment located in Canada, it would appear that the supply might be considered to be made

in Canada (including in circumstances where the employees of the supplier operate from outside Canada).

Ruling 2: Listing of Vendors

Ruling 32525[10] considers advertising services provided by a GST registered non-resident. The supplier initially charged GST to its Canadian customers (apparently because the advertising provided to Canadians related to Canadian subject matter) and is now questioning whether this position was correct.

The non-resident publishes a Web site where it provides the names and contact information for various service providers (including Canadian resident service providers) in return for a listing fee. The non-resident also supplies a "hot link" system through its Web site. It would appear that a user who clicks on the hot link is redirected to the email address of the service provider.

The non-resident operates from offices located outside of Canada.

The Ruling

The CRA agreed that the services provided constitute advertising services. These services are supplied outside Canada and accordingly, Division II GST should not have been charged. The supply was made outside Canada because the supplier's employees did not enter Canada. However, the CRA did specifically note that the supplier's Web site and server were also located outside Canada.

The CRA cautioned that the Canadian customer may be required to self-assess under Division IV in the event that the services are not acquired for use or consumption in the course of a commercial activity.

Conclusions

1. Where employees of the supplier do not enter Canada, the supply will be considered to be made outside Canada (unless the equipment based place of performance rule applies).

2. Neither of the subject matter of the message nor the location of the recipient of the supply is relevant in determining whether the supply is made in Canada.

3. The ruling suggests that the location of the server which hosts the Web site may be a relevant factor in locating the service.

---

[10] October 12, 2001.

2.   More Elaborate Advertising Services

Ruling 3: Customer Adds Information to Supplier's Web Site

Ruling 40148[11] considers a more elaborate type of advertising service. The Canadian supplier of the service allows its customers to set up an online store on its Web site to sell the customer's own products. The customer is responsible for adding and deleting products and for selling its own products.

The online store operates by using software which the supplier has developed. However, the customer is not provided with a licence for the software and may not download the software. The customer is merely provided with the right to interact with the software from a remote location for the purpose of promoting and selling its products. The customer would use the software to add and delete products, change prices, and print reports.

The Ruling

The CRA ruled that the supply is a supply of an advertising service because it is the service of creating a message for the purpose of making a sale. The CRA was required in this ruling to determine whether the principal object of the supply was the right to use and interact with the software, or whether the principal object was the right to receive advertising services. The CRA concluded that the object of the supply was the latter:

> ... the supply ... is essentially the provision of space on its Web site that allows the customer to place product information to solicit business for the customer.

The fact that much, if not all, of the work relating to creating the message was performed by the customer did not detract from the conclusion that an advertising service had been provided.

The CRA ruled that the supply was in fact made in Canada. This was because the supplier of the service is a Canadian who operates from offices located in Canada, and because the Web site is hosted on servers located in Canada.

The CRA noted that the supply of advertising, if provided to non-residents (including if the advertising is aimed at Canadian residents), could be zero-rated under section 8 where the non-resident is not registered. In the event that the customer is registered, zero-rating may be available under section 7.

---

[11] January 9, 2003.

Conclusions

1. An advertising service may be provided even where the supplier merely provides the forum for the message.

2. The service will be performed in Canada if the employees of the supplier operate from Canada in providing the service.

3. The advertising service when provided to a non-resident could be zero-rated under either section 7 or section 8.

Ruling 4: Link-through Advertising

Ruling 37725[12] considers a Canadian resident supplier who provides link-through advertising. The supplier operates a Web site which contains link-through URLs to the Web site of its sole customer, a supplier of goods. The customer is a non-resident of Canada who is not registered.

Each time a visitor to the supplier's Web site links through to the customer's Web site and registers at the destination site, a fee is paid by the customer to the supplier. The non-resident customer provides the URLs to the supplier for posting on the supplier's Web site. The supplier does not ever interact with the customer's clients.

The Ruling

The CRA ruled that this provision of space on the supplier's Web site is the provision of an advertising service.

> … you are essentially providing space on a web site for text or image links that are intended to solicit business for other suppliers. Based on the information provided, this supply is considered to be a service directly related to the communication of a message.

The service is performed in Canada because there are activities (including maintenance of the Web site) which occur in Canada:

> Given that you are carrying out activities (e.g. maintenance of your Web site) in Canada that are part of the provision of the advertising service to the non-resident your supply of the advertising service is performed in whole or in part in Canada.

The CRA noted that this supply should qualify for zero-rating under section 8.

---

[12] February 10, 2003.

Conclusions

1. The provision of the right to post links on a Web site which are intended to solicit business for another person, is considered to be a supply of an advertising service.

2. Where any activities which are part of the advertising service are carried out in Canada, including maintaining the Web site, the supply will be made in Canada.

3. Zero-rating may be available in respect of supplies of advertising made to non-residents.

Ruling 5: Traffic Diversion

In ruling 31697[13], the supplier is a GST registered Canadian resident. It operates high traffic Web sites which attempt to divert traffic to its customers' Web sites for a fee. The following three diversion techniques are used:

(a) **Graphic banners:** images which, if clicked upon, will redirect the person to the target site;

(b) **Pop-up windows:** windows which pop-up within the site; and

(c) **Dialogue-pop-ups:** these pop-ups ask questions which when answered in a particular manner, will redirect the person to the target site.

Most of the visitors to the sites are U.S. residents. The customers of the supplier are located in Canada and the U.S. It would appear that the server of the supplier upon which its high traffic Web sites are hosted, is located outside Canada.

The Ruling

The CRA ruled that all three methodologies for redirecting traffic constitute advertising services. This is because each of the services relates to publicizing another person's message which is oriented towards soliciting business.

The CRA concluded that the supplies are deemed to be made in Canada. This conclusion appears to have been reached on the basis that the supplier operates from offices located in Canada:

> Whether the server hosting the Web site is situated outside Canada, where
> any activity relating to the performance of the service supplied by your

---

[13] June 25, 2002.

client is undertaken in Canada, the service is considered to be performed at least in part in Canada ...

The CRA also noted that zero-rating could be available under either of section 7 or section 8.

In terms of the HST, the CRA noted that under paragraph 2(*a*) of Part V of Schedule IX, the service will be performed in a particular province where all or substantially all of the Canadian element of the service is performed in that province. Where this rule does not apply, the rule in paragraph 2(*b*) provides that if the place of negotiation for the supply is in a particular province and all or substantially all of the service is not performed outside that province, the supply will be deemed to be made in that province.

Conclusions

1. The provision of graphic banners, pop-up windows, and dialogue pop-ups all constitute advertising services where they are oriented towards soliciting business.

2. Advertising services which are delivered through a server located outside Canada will be supplied in Canada where the supplier performs any activity relating to the supply in Canada.

3. The advertising service will be supplied in a particular province where all or substantially all of the Canadian element of the service is performed in that province. Alternatively, the service will be supplied in the province of negotiation unless all or substantially all of the service is performed outside that province.

Ruling 6: Posting Web Pages

Ruling 41917[14] demonstrates that advertising may take any one of a number of forms. The advertising in this case is in the form of allowing people to post their own materials on the supplier's Web site.

The supplier is a GST registered person who has Web sites hosted on servers located in the U.S. The Web site maintenance is performed from the supplier's offices in Canada. Customers can sign on to the supplier's Web site to obtain tools to build a personal web page. They can then post certain content onto the applicant's Web site for a fee.

---

[14] January 29, 2003.

The Ruling

The CRA ruled that allowing people to post information (including a Web page) is a supply of an advertising service:

> ... the supply of a single XXXX posting made by XXXX to XXXX is considered to be a supply of a service directly related to the communication of a message. Given that XXXX is providing the space to the XXXX to enable the XXXX to call public attention to the message that a XXXX is available, the supply is considered to be an advertising service.

The CRA ruled that this service is performed in Canada and is subject to GST. It appears that this is because the supplier operates from a location in Canada from which it performs maintenance on the Web sites (which are hosted in the U.S.).

It would appear that the supply will never be considered to be made outside Canada where the supplier performs any tasks which relate in any way to the supply in Canada (including maintenance of the Web sites).

This ruling also discusses the supply of memberships. Memberships are discussed in detail in Chapter 16, Online Content, Services, and Other General Offerings.

Conclusions

1. The provision to a customer of the right to post materials on the supplier's Web site will qualify as an advertising service where the materials are posted for one of the specified purposes.

2. The service will be performed in Canada if the employees of the supplier perform any tasks in Canada in connection with the service including the maintenance of the Web site.

Ruling 7: Search Doorways

Ruling 33996[15] considers the provision of search doorways. The supplier is a Canadian GST registered entity. Under the first of two scenarios, the supplier creates a doorway search page for its customers. The supplier submits those pages to various search engines with the objective that the engine will pick up and prioritize those pages. Where a Web user goes through these search pages to access a Web site and then makes a purchase, a commission is charged to the customer.

In the second scenario customers pay a set fee to have web users redirected from the supplier's Web site to the customer's Web page. The fee

---

[15] July 15, 2003.

is only paid to the supplier in the event that the Web user proceeds beyond the initial home page of the customer.

The Ruling

The CRA ruled that both of these services are advertising services. To determine the location of the supply would require that the four-part performance of services test be examined. The CRA suggested that, given that the supplier operates from offices in Canada, it would appear likely that the services would be considered to be supplied in Canada.

The CRA also noted that the rules contained in paragraphs 2(*a*) or 2(*b*) of Part V of Schedule IX would typically be used to locate the province of supply. The rule in paragraph 2(*a*) provides that a service is supplied in a province if all or substantially all of the Canadian element of the service is performed in that province. Alternatively, the rule in paragraph 2(*b*) provides that the supply will be made in a particular province if the place of negotiation is in that province and all or substantially all of the service is not performed outside that province.

This ruling underscores the broad range of services which will qualify as advertising services. These services could easily have been characterized as something other than advertising (for example, "referral services" or "promotional services"). In fact, in the first of the two scenarios, the supplier does not even appear to be posting any type of message on its own Web site. The message appears to be in the form of doorway search pages which are submitted to search engines.

The conclusion that advertising services are being supplied is very positive in that zero-rating is allowed under sections 7 and 8.

Conclusions

1. Redirecting users to a customer's Web site will qualify as the provision of an advertising service where the message relates to a specified purpose.

2. The development of search doorways (which are submitted to search engines) is also the provision of an advertising service where the message relates to a specified purpose.

3. To determine the place of supply of an advertising service, the location of the supplier's equipment should be taken into account as well as the location from which the supplier's employees operate.

4. The supply will be made in a particular province if all or substantially all of the service is performed in that province. Where this rule does not

apply, the province of supply will be the province of negotiation unless all or substantially all of the service is performed outside that province.

Ruling 8: Posting of Literary Materials

Ruling 33013[16] considers an important threshold issue in connection with advertising services. The supplier is a Canadian resident which charges a fee to non-residents in return for allowing them to post literary materials on its Web site. The Web site is hosted on a server located in Canada.

Any person who has access to the Internet and who is interested in the materials may review the materials for no charge. The only charge levied by the supplier is applicable to the non-residents who post materials. The non-resident customer retains all rights in the literary material and accordingly there is no supply of property to any person.

The Ruling

The CRA ruled that it is not clear whether this supply would constitute an advertising service. Although a message is being communicated, the purpose for which the message has been created is not clear.

The CRA noted that if the message is posted strictly for general interest purposes or to share information, the supply will not be an advertising service. However, if the message is intended to encourage sales, or is provided for one of the other listed purposes, it will be an advertising service.

Given that Web site maintenance and other related supplier activities take place in Canada, the service will be considered to be performed in Canada.

Conclusions

1. A service will only be an advertising service if the message is provided for one of the specified purposes.

2. Messages provided for the purpose of sharing information, or for general interest purposes, will not be considered advertising services.

3. A service which is not an advertising service will not be eligible for zero-rating under section 8.

---

[16] August 22, 2002.

Ruling 9: Designing Advertisements

Ruling 6277[17] considers supplies related to designing advertisements. The supplier in this ruling is a Canadian resident who designs advertisements for its customers. The customers either host the completed advertisements on their own Web sites or make arrangements to have the advertisements hosted on a third party Web site. The supplier also designs Web sites for customers.

The Ruling

The CRA ruled that the services of creating a message (i.e., the development of a web page advertisement) which relates to soliciting business would constitute an advertising service including where the supplier will not be the person who communicates the message.

The CRA also ruled that the creation of a Web site for a customer would be considered a service as long as the supplier does not retain any rights in the Web site once completed. If the supplier were to retain rights in the Web site, the supply would be considered to be in the nature of intangible personal property.

The CRA seemed to suggest that where creating the Web site is a service (i.e., where the supplier does not retain any rights in the Web site), this service would not be an advertising service. Given that many Web sites are created to communicate a message for the purpose of soliciting business, it is not clear why the Web site design service would not also potentially qualify as an advertising service.

Conclusions

1. The service of creating a Web page advertisement which will be used for the purpose of soliciting business will qualify as an advertising service.

2. The service of developing a Web site which may be used for the purpose of soliciting business does not appear to qualify as an advertising service.

3. Distinction Between Advertising and Third Party Sales

Third party sales are discussed in detail in Chapter 13. However, the following two rulings relate to making the distinction between advertising services and third party sales.

---

[17] November 6, 2001.

Ruling 10: Third Party Sales and Advertising

In ruling 31695[18], the supplier is a GST registered Canadian entity who through its Web site displays works of art which are available for purchase. The art is owned by the artists who are the customers of the supplier. The artists are located both in Canada and in the U.S. Many of the artists are not GST registered.

Persons interested in purchasing particular items of art notify the supplier. The supplier accepts the money as payment for the art and on account of shipping and handling. The supplier notifies the artist that a sale has been made, so the artist can ship the product directly to the customer. The supplier forwards the money received to the artist (including the shipping and handling fee) less a commission charge which is retained by the supplier.

The supplier also provides banner advertising to artists for an additional fee.

The Ruling

The CRA ruled that the supply of banner advertising is a separate supply from the supply of selling the goods. The banner advertising qualifies as an advertising service and is considered to be supplied in Canada. Presumably this conclusion was reached on the basis that the Canadian operates the Web site from Canada. The CRA also noted that zero-rating would be available under either of section 8 or section 7 in respect of the banner advertising.

The manner in which the tax applies to the sale of the goods is discussed in Chapter 13.

Conclusion

Where a supplier provides advertising services and assists in the sale of its customer's goods the two supplies will be considered separately.

Ruling 11: Online Shopping Portal

In ruling 40372[19], the supplier is a GST registered Canadian entity which operates an online shopping portal where it advertises products available for sale from various vendors.

The supplier would create the electronic messages (advertisements) for each of the products listed for sale on its Web site. Customers would pay a

---

[18] January 17, 2003.

[19] March 28, 2003.

fee for advertising on the Web site and would also pay a commission fee for each sale concluded.

The Ruling

Again, the CRA ruled that two supplies were being made. The advertising related supply would be considered to be an advertising service.

The third party sale would be considered as a distinct supply with its own particular tax consequences. The third party sale is discussed in Chapter 13.

Conclusion

The supply of advertising will be considered separately from supplies which relate to selling the goods of a third party.

Chapter 13

Third Party Sales of Goods

A. OVERVIEW

1. General Scope of Supplies

The third party sales technique allows vendors of goods to rely upon the special marketing skills of a third party to actively promote and sell products. The Internet has proven to be the ideal forum for this sales technique.

Ordinarily, the underlying supplier will provide the third party with the rights to promote and sell the supplier's products to customers through the third party's own Web site. The third party will typically be a person who operates a high traffic Web site and who has a particular expertise in Internet marketing and promotion.

The third party sales technique does not involve the third party assuming ownership of the product.[1] Similarly, the third party does not typically take possession of the product. The underlying product would normally be shipped directly to the customer by the owner of the goods.

The purchaser, if interested in purchasing the product, makes all arrangements relating to the purchase directly with the third party, and not with the owner of the goods. This arrangement is unique in that the customer in most cases will be unaware that the third party is not the owner of the goods. The third party would also typically field queries relating to the product and would accept payment for the product. The third party may or may not be authorized to accept the order for the purchase of the product.

2. Advantages of This Approach

This type of sales arrangement is particularly effective for a number of reasons. The third party sales technique minimizes the responsibilities of the owner of the goods in connection with sales, marketing and certain administrative functions. Third party vendors are typically well equipped to position their Web sites to reach the desired target market. Third parties may also engage in various techniques to attract potential customers, including paying fees to search engines for an increased number of hits.

The third party may enhance its own credibility by offering "educational" content or other informational materials which assist the potential customer in making a purchase decision. For example, a third party seller of kitchen appliances may write reviews of various products which are offered for sale to compare and contrast their respective performance and value. The offering of what may appear to be unbiased and neutral information

---

[1] The nature of the transaction would not be a third party sale if the third party were to assume ownership.

and "side by side" pricing on similar products are the keys to success for this sales technique.

As noted above, the third party is also typically the person who accepts the customer payment. This system assists in preserving the integrity of the commission structure because the owner of the goods is effectively precluded from selling goods directly to a customer who has been identified by the third party.

3. Distinguishing Between Third Party Sales and Advertising Services

Although in some respects third party sales and advertising services are similar because both are promotional in nature, there is one very distinct difference. In the advertising scenario, the third party does not become directly involved in the supply of the underlying product or service, including where the advertising compensation is tied to sales. In contrast, with respect to third party sales, the third party is centrally involved in the sale of the product.

This is not to say, however, that a third party vendor cannot provide an advertising service. For example, it is not uncommon for a third party to provide an advertising service in return for a separate, additional fee. In these circumstances, the advertising service would be considered as a separate supply for GST purposes. However, where a third party seller promotes a product but does not charge any additional promotional fee, this will generally not be considered to be a supply of an advertising service. Advertising services are discussed in Chapter 12, Advertising Services.

B. CHARACTERIZATION OF THIRD PARTY SUPPLIES

Third party sellers, and the vendors for whom they act, may be located anywhere in the world. In many cases either or both the third party and the vendor will not be GST registered. As a result, the potential for GST leakage in connection with third party sales would, absent specific legislative provisions, be extremely high.

1. Exposure Issues

Third party sales have the potential to result in considerable GST exposure for the parties who are involved in the transaction. In fact, the parties are often surprised by the harsh consequences associated with the application of these rules. Fortunately, relatively simple planning steps may be taken to minimize potential exposure.

The principal areas of exposure relate to the tax status of the third party services and to the identification of the person who is required to account for the tax on the supply of the underlying product. Where a third party assists a vendor in making a sale, it is beyond dispute that the third party is supplying a service to the vendor of the goods. However, the determination of whether this service is taxable requires that all of the following be taken into account:

(a) is the service provided by an agent;

(b) is the service provider registered;

(c) are the underlying goods subject to tax; and

(d) is the vendor registered.

With respect to the underlying supply, either the third party or the underlying supplier may be responsible for the collection, reporting and remittance of GST. Among the issues which are required to be considered in order to identify the parties' respective obligations are the following:

(a) whether the supply is subject to tax;

(b) whether the third party is an agent of the underlying supplier;

(c) whether the principal is a person who is required to collect tax; and

(d) if a party is not registered, whether it is obligated to be registered.

The manner in which these complex exposure issues are to be resolved is discussed below.

2. Where the Third Party is an Independent Contractor

The most critical issue which must be resolved in any third party scenario is whether the third party is acting as the agent of the underlying supplier or whether it is an independent contractor. The tests to be used to distinguish between an agency and an independent contractor relationship are described later in this chapter.

Where it has been determined that the third party is not the agent of the supplier (i.e., it is an independent service provider), the responsibilities of the parties may be summarized as follows:

(a) The third party would not be responsible for collecting the GST in respect of the underlying supply of the product. None of the special rules in section 177 would apply because the rules relate only to agency relationships.

(b) The vendor of the goods would be responsible for collecting, reporting and remitting GST in connection with the underlying supply. The manner in which the GST would apply to the supply would be determined in the same manner as with any other sale made directly from a vendor to a customer.

(c) The services provided by the third party would not be subject to any of the special rules contained in section 177 of the ETA. The third party would determine whether its services are taxable in the same manner as with any other service.

For example, if the services are considered to be performed in Canada and the third party is GST registered, it would collect Division II GST in respect of the services. The third party would also be required to consider the possible application of the HST by applying the rules in Schedule IX. The third party may be able to take advantage of the special zero-rating rules contained in section 5 of Part V of Schedule VI because its services would relate to arranging for, procuring, or soliciting orders for supplies to be made by another person. The third party services may also qualify as advertising services which are subject to special zero-rating relief pursuant to section 8.

In TIB 090, the CRA provided the following example of the manner in which the tax applies where the third party is not the agent of the seller.[2]

> *A Web site operator hosts electronic catalogues of various vendors on its servers. Shoppers can select products from these catalogues and place orders online. The Web site owner has no contractual relationship with the shoppers, and merely transmits orders to the merchants, who are responsible for accepting and filling them. The merchants pay the Web site operator a commission based on a percentage of the value of the orders placed through the site.*
>
> By hosting the catalogues, the Web site operator is communicating a message intended to solicit business for the merchants. This is a supply of an advertising service.

It is clear from the example that the CRA drew the conclusion that the third party was not acting as the agent of the vendor. The CRA noted in particular that the third party did not have the authority to conclude the contracts with the shoppers. Accordingly, the service was an advertising service. The manner in which the GST will apply to supplies of advertising services is described in Chapter 12, Advertising Services.

Where the third party is not the agent of the vendor, and as a result is not responsible for collecting GST in respect of the supply of the goods, the third party may still be subject to exposure in connection with the goods.

---

[2] TIB 090, Characterization of Supply, example 11.

For example, where the third party collects amounts as, or on account of GST from the customer in respect of the sale of the goods (which were sold to the customer by the vendor), the third party may be held liable for the GST amounts collected if the vendor does not make the corresponding remittance. The vendor may fail to make the appropriate remittance as a result of not being registered, as a result of error, or as a result of a deliberate act of avoidance. It would appear that in any of these circumstances, the third party would be held liable for the amounts of GST collected.

The CRA suggests that the third party may avoid this exposure by remitting the tax directly to the CRA. Further, the suggestion seems to be that the vendor will not be held liable where the third party has made the remittance (even though technically the tax should have been remitted by the vendor).

These exposure issues should be carefully considered by the parties to any such transaction.

3. Where the Third Party is an Agent of the Underlying Supplier

A very different GST regime applies where the third party is the agent of the vendor. As a practical matter, in most cases where a third party is provided with the authority to conclude the sale with the customer, the third party will be considered an agent of the vendor. However, all of the relevant facts must be taken into account in order to make this determination.

Assuming that the third party is acting as the agent of the underlying supplier in respect of the supply, the rules which will apply are summarized below. A more detailed discussion of the intricate agency rules is provided in Chapter 10, Agency.

(a) Where Principal is a Person Who is not Required to Collect GST

The default rule applies where:

(a) a principal makes a supply of tangible personal property but the principal is not required to collect tax in respect of the supply;

(b) the supply is not a zero-rated or exempt supply;

(c) an agent who is a registrant, in the course of a commercial activity of the agent, acts as agent in making the supply on behalf of the principal;

(d) the election contained in subsection 177(1) has not been entered into; and

(e) the supply is not made by way of auction.

Application of default rule:

(a) the supply of the property is deemed to have been made by the agent (and not by the principal); and

(b) the agent is deemed for all purposes (other than for the purposes of section 180) not to have made a supply of agency services to the principal.

The result is that the agent would be responsible for the collection, reporting, and remitting of tax in connection with the supply of the goods. The agent would not, however, charge GST to the vendor on its agency services. This is because the vendor, as a person who is not required to collect tax, would not be eligible for an ITC.

Where the agent is not a registrant or is not acting in the course of a commercial activity, and the principal is not a person who is required to collect tax, the manner in which the tax would apply is as follows:

(a) the agent is not responsible for the collection of tax on either the underlying supply or on the agency services; and

(b) the principal is not responsible for the collection of tax on the underlying supply.

Given that neither party would be responsible for the collection of tax in this scenario, it should be expected that attempts to advance this position would result in considerable CRA scrutiny.

(b) Where the Principal is a Person Who is Required to Collect GST

The default rule applies where:

(a) the principal is a person who is required to collect GST; and

(b) a subsection 177(1.1) election has not been entered into.

Application of the default rule:

(a) the principal would be responsible for collecting, reporting and remitting the GST in respect of the underlying supply; and

(b) the agent would collect GST in respect of its agency services if the agent is registered and provides those agency services in Canada in the course of a commercial activity.

The subsection 177(1.1) election is available where:

(a) the principal is a person who would be required to collect the tax on the supply, other than as a result of the rule in subsection 177(1);

(b) the agent is a registrant and provides its agency services in the course of a commercial activity; and

(c) the supply is not made by way of auction.

Where the election has been entered into the tax applies in the following manner:

(a) the underlying supply is deemed to be made by the agent for the purposes of:

(i) determining the net tax of the agent and of the principal; and

(ii) applying the rules set out in sections 222 and 232.

(b) the agent would collect GST on its agency services (if supplied in Canada); and

(c) the principal and agent would be jointly and severally liable for the amounts of GST to be remitted by the agent (and for any other related discrepancies on the part of the agent).

The election shifts the responsibility for reporting the tax from the principal to the agent. However, even where the election has been entered into, the principal remains liable for any amounts of GST not properly reported or remitted by the agent. For this reason, the principal should not consider entering into this election unless it is satisfied that the agent will properly account for tax.

(c) Special Situations

Auctions

Where a registrant agent who is an auctioneer (and who acts as agent for another person in the course of a commercial activity of the auctioneer) makes a supply of tangible personal property to a recipient:

(i) the agent is deemed to have made the supply to the recipient of the tangible personal property; and

(ii) the agent is deemed not to have made a supply of agency services to the principal.

An election may be available to opt out of these rules where "prescribed property" is supplied by way of auction.

Billing Agents

A special rule applies where the agent acts as the vendor's agent only for billing purposes and does not act as the agent in making the supply. The agent is deemed to have acted as the agent of the principal for the purposes of applying the rule in subsection 177(1.1). This allows the election in subsection 177(1.1) to be entered into, notwithstanding that the third party's agency authority is limited in scope.

Special Rule for Supplies of Artists

A special rule applies where intangible personal property in respect of a product of an artist is sold by a third party who is a "prescribed registrant". A person is considered to be a prescribed registrant only if they are listed in the Artists' Representatives (GST/HST) Regulations. Those regulations list approximately 40 organizations (including, for example, the Director's Guild of Canada) which are deemed to be prescribed registrants.

These rules may also apply where the third party is other than an agent. Where these rules apply, the third party would account for GST on the underlying supply but would not charge GST to the artist in respect of its third party services.

4. Determining if the Third Party is Acting as an Agent

The determination of whether a person is acting as an agent is a question of fact. It should be noted that the CRA will not typically rule on this important factual issue.

Given that the tax will apply in a very different manner, depending on whether the third party is acting as agent or acting as an independent contractor, it is important this issue be correctly resolved.

The CRA's leading administrative policy with respect to the determination of when an agency relationship exists is contained in Policy Statement P-182R, "Agency" That policy statement describes agency in the following general manner:

> ... is a type of relationship where one person (the principal) uses another person (the agent) to perform certain tasks on its behalf ... In a sense the agent is an extension of a principal, so the actions of the agent are those of the principal ... Agency exists where one person (the principal) authorizes another person (the agent) to represent it and take certain actions on its behalf.

The Policy Statement makes two other important threshold points:

(a) The authority granted by the principal may be express or implied; and

(b) Agency may exist even where there has been no disclosure of the relationship to third parties. For example, agency may exist in circumstances where the third person in conducting business with the agent is not even aware that a principal exists (i.e., the customer assumes that it is purchasing goods directly from the agent).

Policy Statement P-182R provides that, at common law, there are three fundamental indicia of agency, which are as follows:

(a) consent of both the principal and agent;

(b) authority of the agent to affect the principal's legal position; and

(c) the principal's control of the agent's actions.

Each of these three indicia of agency are briefly summarized below.

(a) Consent

The CRA notes that an agency relationship may exist in circumstances where the parties have not formally concluded any type of written arrangement evidencing this relationship. Conversely, a formal agreement which provides that an agency relationship exists will not be conclusive as to whether or not the relationship in fact is one of agency. Although the intention of the parties to form an agency relationship is an important determinant, an agency relationship may exist even where the parties are not aware that they have created this type of relationship. The conduct of the parties is very significant in this respect.

The CRA notes that generally for consent to exist, it should be evident that the purported agent is arranging transactions for the principal and is not transacting business on its own account.

(b) Authority

The most typical situation in which an agent demonstrates that it has the authority to affect the principal's legal position is where the agent is authorized to enter into contracts with third parties on the principal's behalf. The CRA notes that it should be evident that the principal has empowered the agent to act or enter into contracts on its behalf.

Authority may exist even where the agent is not provided with the authority to enter into contracts. For example, the CRA notes that a lawyer may be considered to be an agent when it pays property taxes on behalf of a client.

However, the ability to bind a principal will not in and of itself conclusively determine whether an agency relationship exists. The CRA notes that contracts may become binding on the principal by other mechanisms which include "ratification" or "operation of law".

(c) Control

In an agency relationship, the principal will exert some degree of control over the agent. This control will generally be greater than the control which would be exerted over an independent contractor.

The control could be in the form of a requirement to provide reports or to obtain specific authorization to incur a particular type of expense.

(d) Other Indicators of Agency

Other indicators of agency include the following:

(a) the existence of a fiduciary obligation to another person (i.e., the principal) to disclose secret profits or any additional financial advantage not specifically contemplated by the parties;

(b) the third party does not assume a high degree of risk (typically agents do not assume the bulk of the risk associated with a particular transaction);

(c) accounting practices of the agent should be consistent with an agency relationship;

(d) remuneration of agents is typically in the form of a set fee or commission;

(e) the agent typically agrees to provide best efforts but does not guarantee a particular result;

(f) the agent does not typically alter the property of the principal before it is sold to a customer;

(g) the agent does not typically use the property;

(h) the purchaser's recourse (i.e., with respect to unsatisfactory goods) is against the principal and not the agent; and

(i) the agent does not acquire ownership of the property.

5. Application of These Tests to Third Party Sales

All of the factors set out above should be taken into account in determining whether an agency relationship exists. However, in the context of third party sales, there is one particular criterion which appears to carry far more weight than any of the others. In the rulings, the CRA seems to focus in particular on the issue of whether the third party has been provided with the authority to conclude the contract with the purchaser. This issue relates both to consent and to authority.

In rulings where the third party accepts the offer from the purchaser, and then notifies the vendor that an order has been placed, the CRA has generally concluded that the supply is being made through an agent. However, where the third party merely forwards the order through to the vendor for acceptance, the CRA will generally rule that an agency relationship does not exist.

It should also be noted that in most rulings relating to online sales, the third party will be the person who receives the payment of the consideration from the customer. However, the authority to merely accept payment (without the authority to conclude the contract), will not be sufficient on its own to result in a finding of agency.

C. PLACE OF SUPPLY AND NON-RESIDENT ISSUES

Once the agency issue has been resolved, the application of the place of supply rules will be relatively straightforward.

1. Place of Supply of Goods

The goods which are supplied, either by the vendor or by the agent, will be considered to be supplied in Canada if they are delivered or made available to the customer in Canada. This follows from the application of the ordinary place of supply rules in section 142. Conversely, if the goods are delivered or made available outside Canada, they will be deemed to be supplied outside Canada. The HST rules set out in Part II of Schedule IX will also apply in the ordinary manner. Those rules also relate to the concept of the province where the goods are delivered or made available.

However, where goods are sold through an agent, this method of distribution will have a direct impact on the availability of the non-resident override. The following examples illustrate how the non-resident override will apply depending on the registration status of the agent.

Example 1

A non-resident, non-registrant principal makes a supply of goods to a Canadian customer (with delivery in Canada) through a non-resident, non-registrant agent.

The principal will be the person who is making the supply of the goods. This is because the agent is not a registrant.

The non-resident override will apply and the goods will be considered to be supplied outside Canada.

Example 2

A non-resident, non-registrant principal makes a supply of goods to a Canadian customer (with delivery in Canada) through a Canadian resident, GST registered agent.

The agent will be the person who is making the supply of the goods. This is because the agent is a registrant and is making the supply on behalf of a person who is not required to collect tax.

Because the goods are considered to be supplied by the agent, the non-resident override will not apply and the goods will be subject to tax.

Where goods are supplied by a non-resident through a Canadian agent, a number of other tangential issues should also be considered. The making of supplies through a Canadian agent is one factor which might suggest that the non-resident is in fact carrying on business in Canada. Supplies made by a non-resident in Canada, in the course of a business carried on in Canada, will not be eligible for the override. In addition, a non-resident who makes taxable supplies in Canada in the course of a business carried on in Canada will (unless it is a small supplier) be required to register for GST. The non-resident who makes supplies through a Canadian agent who is not registered should be particularly concerned with this potential exposure.

Where supplies are made through a Canadian dependent agent, the permanent establishment of the agent may be considered to be a permanent establishment of the non-resident. The non-resident would be deemed to be resident in respect of any activities carried on through that permanent establishment. This would typically result in the non-resident being required to register for GST. As a result, the principal would be required to account for tax on the sale of the goods when delivered or made available in Canada. Reliance upon the agent to remit tax would be inappropriate.

2. Place of Supply of the Services (Agency Services and Third Party Services)

Services (including agency services and other third party services) will be considered to be supplied in Canada if the services are performed in whole or in part in Canada. The services will be considered to be performed in Canada where any employee work in connection with the supply is undertaken in Canada. Services may also be considered to be performed in Canada where the supplier's equipment is located in Canada:

... a supply of a service is performed at least in part in Canada if ... the service includes operations performed by a supplier's equipment ... and the equipment is located in Canada.

Accordingly, the services may be considered to be supplied in Canada even where the service provider has no employees in Canada. For example, if the third party or agent hosts its Web site on its server located in Canada, the service will likely be considered to be performed in Canada. The central issue will be whether the operation of a Web site through which third party sales are made or services are provided, will involve "operations performed by the supplier's equipment" when that Web site is hosted on a server in Canada. The CRA seems, thus far, to take a fairly liberal view of this place of performance rule.

TIB 090 also notes that a service will be considered to be performed in Canada where any task relating to the supply is performed in Canada. The CRA has, in a number of rulings, held that Web site or server maintenance, if performed in Canada, will result in the services provided through the Web site (including third party or agency services) being taxable.

Where services are provided in Canada, particularly if those services are provided on a regular and continuous basis or for several clients, this normally suggests that the non-resident service provider is carrying on business in Canada. A non-resident who makes taxable supplies in Canada, in the course of a business carried on in Canada, will be required to register unless it qualifies as a small supplier.

A service provider who delivers its service through a Web site hosted on a server in Canada may also be deemed to be resident in Canada (and to have a permanent establishment in Canada) as a result of the server. This will also involve a registration requirement.

For the purposes of determining whether a permanent establishment exists in connection with a server or Web site, the CRA notes that:

(a) a Web site cannot constitute a place of business because it is not tangible property. This suggests that a Web site also cannot constitute "equipment" (see TIB 090); and

(b) a server is the "supplier's equipment" if it is "at the disposal" of the supplier. The CRA also indicates that it takes the position that a server is not at the disposal of the supplier where the server is hosted in an ISP arrangement (see the discussion relating to permanent establishments in TIB 090).

The suggestion seems to be that the service provider should be concerned where it has at its disposal a server in Canada on which the Web site is hosted.

The resolution of the issues set out above will determine whether the services in issue are performed in Canada. The service provider would then be required to determine whether its services might be subject to HST. The HST rules for services are provided in Part V of Schedule IX.

D. ZERO-RATING ISSUES

1. Tangible Personal Property

Where tangible personal property is considered to be supplied in Canada, zero-rating may be available under Schedule VI, Part V, section 1. The supply must be made to a recipient who is not a consumer and who intends to export the property within a reasonably short period of time. The supplier would need to obtain documentary evidence to support the exportation. A number of other conditions apply, including the condition that the goods not be processed or transformed in Canada prior to export.

Given the requirement for the supplier to obtain documentation in support of the export, and given that the use of this provision may involve exposure for the supplier, it would be preferable for suppliers to arrange for delivery to occur outside Canada.

Zero-rating may also be available under section 12 of Part V. This allows for property to be sent by mail, courier, or common carrier to a destination outside Canada on a zero-rated basis.

2. Services

The services of acting as an agent for a non-resident person, or arranging for procuring or soliciting orders for a person, will not qualify for zero-rating under section 7 of Part V.

However, these services may, when provided to a non-resident person, qualify for zero-rating under section 5. The service will typically qualify where it is provided in respect of a supply made outside Canada by the non-resident person (i.e., the vendor of the goods). The most common situation in which these conditions will be met is as follows:

(a) A Canadian (or non-resident) agent provides agency services (or services related to soliciting sales) to a non-resident, and these services are considered to be supplied in Canada.

(b) The services relate to goods to be sold by the non-resident.

(c) The non-resident supplies the goods to its customers outside Canada (i.e., delivery outside Canada) or is deemed to supply the goods outside Canada because of the non-resident override.

The interaction of the rules in section 177 and the zero-rating ruling in section 5 should be noted. Where the agent is a registrant and is making the supply on behalf of a non-resident who is not registered, the agency services would not be taxable. This is because of the rule in subsection 177(1).

Where the agency services are provided to a non-resident who is registered, zero-rating would apply if the non-resident delivers the goods outside Canada to the purchaser. If the non-resident delivers the goods in Canada, zero-rating would not apply because the supply would not qualify for the override.

E. GST RULINGS

Ruling 1: Third Party is Not an Agent

Ruling 56334[3] considers a third party GST registered person who operates an online auction. Local vendors may sell their goods on the applicant's Web site by way of silent auction. The applicant does not allow for non-resident customers to participate in the auction. Most of the vendors and purchasers are not GST registered.

Potential purchasers bid by sending an email to the applicant. The applicant forwards the email containing a bid to the vendor for acceptance. If the bid is acceptable, the vendor signals its acceptance to the applicant who notifies the purchaser by email. The applicant then takes the payment by way of credit card. The applicant forwards the proceeds, less a commission, to the vendor.

In most cases, the purchaser takes possession of the goods at the vendor's premises, but in some cases the vendor ships the goods to the purchaser. The applicant does not take possession or ownership of the goods.

The Ruling

The CRA did not raise the issue of agency in this ruling. However, it would appear that the CRA reached the conclusion that the third party is not acting as the agent of the local vendors in respect of the sale of the goods. The fact that the online vendor does not have the authority to accept the offers (or bids) appears to be central to this conclusion.

The CRA concluded that the applicant's services (which are independent contractor services) are taxable services. The services would be considered to be supplied in Canada. Zero-rating was not discussed in respect of the services because the vendors are all local Canadian vendors.

The determination of whether the goods are subject to tax when sold by the vendor will turn on the registration status of the particular vendor and the place of delivery of the goods.

---

[3] July 22, 2005.

Conclusions

1. Where the third party does not have the authority to accept offers, the third party will likely not be considered an agent of the underlying supplier in connection with the sale of the goods.

2. The services of the third party will be taxable if performed in Canada.

3. The underlying vendor will be responsible for the collection of GST in respect of the sale of the goods.

Ruling 2: Third Party is Not an Agent

In ruling 40372[4] the applicant, a Canadian GST registered entity, operates a shopping portal through which it provides advertising[5] and third party sales of goods. It represents a number of vendors of goods.

Visitors to the Web site browse the goods offered for sale and place orders online for the purchase of particular items. An email is then sent to the vendor so that the vendor may accept the order. Payment is then accepted by the applicant by way of credit card. The money is forwarded to the vendor less the commission charged for the sale. The vendor accepts and fills the orders. The applicant does not ever take possession or ownership of the products.

Notwithstanding that the applicant accepts the payment from the customer, the applicant is not authorized by the vendor to accept orders. The applicant takes the position that it is not the agent of the vendor.

Where the customer is a Canadian resident, and the vendor is a non-resident, the customer is required to clear the goods through Customs and pay any applicable duties and Division III GST. Vendors who are non-resident individuals and who are not GST registered, are not in Canada at any time in connection with the supply.

The Ruling

The CRA ruled that the applicant is not considered for GST purposes to be the supplier of the goods (i.e., it is not the agent of the vendor). The CRA appears to have concluded that the applicant is not the agent on the basis that it does not have the authority to conclude contracts.

---

[4] March 28, 2003.

[5] See Chapter 12, Advertising Services, for the advertising portion of this ruling.

However, the CRA noted that since the applicant does collect GST from the customers in respect of the sale of the goods, it will be required to report these amounts in its own GST return. Alternatively, if the amounts collected by the applicant on account of GST are passed along to the vendor, the applicant's GST liability is extinguished as soon as the vendor accounts for the tax.

The suggestion seems to be that if GST funds are forwarded by the applicant to a particular vendor who is not registered, the applicant would be responsible for the funds collected. In order to minimize potential exposure on this issue, the CRA has suggested that the applicant speak with each vendor to determine whether they are required to charge GST. This would avoid the exposure which relates to forwarding amounts of GST to a person who does not file returns. However, this would not avoid the exposure which relates to a vendor who, notwithstanding that it is registered, fails to properly account for the GST on the sale of the goods. The better view is that the third party should avoid, where possible, accepting funds on account of GST from the customers.

The CRA indicated that the issue of whether the vendor needs to charge GST will turn on the individual circumstances of each vendor. For example, if the vendor is a small supplier who is not registered, then it would not charge GST.

Conclusions

1. Where the third party is not the agent of the vendor, the third party will not be the person who is required to collect GST in respect of the supply of the goods which is made by the vendor.

2. However, if the third party collects amounts as or on account of GST from the customers, the third party is required to include these amounts in its net tax calculation. Alternatively, the third party may pass along the funds to the vendor to be accounted for by the vendor. However, if the vendor does not properly account for and remit the amounts owing because the vendor is not GST registered or for any other reason, the third party will remain liable for the GST collected.

3. Where the vendor is not GST registered, the third party should never pass along any amounts of GST collected from the customer. The third party may want to seek assurances that amounts of GST forwarded to a particular vendor were in fact properly accounted for and remitted.

Ruling 3: Distinguishing Between Agency and Other Than Agency

Ruling 31695[6] considers a third party (the applicant) who facilitates the sale of art. The applicant is a Canadian GST registered person. It shows works of art on its Web site for the purpose of soliciting sales of the items.

The purchase process proceeds in the following manner. A customer notifies the applicant that it is interested in making a purchase. The applicant concludes the contract and accepts the funds on account of both the art and the shipping and handling fees. The art is owned by the artist and neither possession nor ownership is transferred to the applicant.

The artist ships the art directly to the purchaser. The applicant forwards the funds, including shipping and handling, less commission, to the artist.

Artists are located both in Canada and in the U.S. Many of the artists are not GST registered.

The Ruling

As a threshold issue, the CRA noted that the third party applicant must determine whether it is acting as an agent of the artists. The CRA did not rule on this issue, but strongly suggested that on these facts there was every indication that an agency relationship existed.

Assuming agency, the CRA noted that if the artist is a person who is not required to collect tax (i.e., if the artist is a small supplier), the agent would be the person who is required to account for tax on the sale of the art. However, the agent would not charge GST to the artist on its agency services.

In circumstances where the artist is a person who is required to collect tax (i.e., the artist is registered), the artist would by default be the person who is required to account for tax on the sale of the art. The agent would charge GST on its agency services unless the services are provided outside Canada or the services qualify for zero-rating under section 5 of Part V of Schedule VI.

Where the artist is a person who is required to collect tax, the parties may enter into a subsection 177(1.1) election. Where the election is entered into, the agent would account for the GST on the sale of the art. The agent would still collect GST on its agency services, unless these services were provided outside Canada or zero-rated. Both parties would be jointly and severally liable for any GST not properly accounted for.

---

[6] January 17, 2003.

In connection with all of the above, the determination of whether the art is subject to GST will turn on the issue of who is the person making the supply, where is the place of supply, and what is the person's registration status. For example, if the sale is made by a non-resident, the non-resident override might apply.

The art shipment charges could be considered to be either a component of the sale of the art, in which case they would be taxed at the same rate as the art itself, or they could be viewed as a separate supply. The key to making this distinction lies in the terms of the agreement.

The special art related rules in subsection 177(2) do not apply where the third party is not a listed entity.

Conclusions

1. A third party who assists in the sale of goods should determine, as a threshold matter, whether it is acting as agent for the underlying vendor.

2. The third party, when acting as agent, should then consider whether the principal is a person who is required to collect GST. If the principal is not required to collect tax, the agent will, if acting in the course of a commercial activity, be required to collect and account for the tax. The agent would not charge GST to the principal on its agency services.

3. If the principal is a person who is required to collect tax, the principal would be the person who is making the supply of the goods and would be responsible for remitting the tax collected from the customer. The agent would charge GST on its agency services.

Ruling 4: Third Party is an Agent

Ruling 32977[7] considers a Canadian resident (the applicant) which has developed a Web site to sell the products of third party vendors. The vendor sets the price at which the products will be sold. Persons interested in making a purchase email the applicant to make the purchase. The applicant processes the order and accepts the payment. The product is then shipped directly to the customer by the vendor.

The applicant deducts its sales commission from the price paid by the customer and passes along the remainder of the amount paid to the vendor.

---

[7] May 30, 2003.

The Ruling

The CRA noted that, as a threshold matter, the relationship between the parties must be evaluated. To determine whether an agency relationship exists, the three main *indicia* of agency must be considered:

(a) consent;

(b) control; and

(c) authority.

The CRA did not specifically rule on the issue of agency, but strongly suggested that the relationship was one of agency. This is consistent with the fact that the third party had the authority to accept offers.

The CRA noted that in any case where the supply is not being made through an agent, the vendor would be the person who is making the supply of the goods and would be responsible for collecting and remitting the GST.

Assuming that the supply was in fact made through an agent, the CRA noted that the GST would apply in the following manner:

(a) the default rule is that the principal, if it is a person who is required to collect tax, is the person who is required to account for and collect the tax on any given supply;

(b) if the principal is a person who is not required to collect GST (for example, where the principal is not registered because it is a small supplier) then the agent, if GST registered, is required to collect and remit the tax on the supply (under subsection 177(1)). However, in these circumstances the agency services would not attract any tax;

(c) if the principal is a person who is required to collect the tax, the agent and principal may jointly elect (under subsection 177(1.1)) to have the agent account for the tax on the supply to the recipient. The agency services would remain subject to GST.

Given that the supply could be deemed to be made by either the agent or by the principal, it is critical to determine whether the supply of the goods is considered to be made in Canada. The CRA discusses the following scenarios in its ruling:

Scenario 1: The goods are delivered to the customer outside Canada. The goods will not attract any Division II GST under the place of supply rules. Neither the principal nor the vendor will be responsible for collecting any Division II GST.

Scenario 2: The goods are delivered to the customer in Canada but are to be exported by the purchaser. If the purchaser of the goods is acquiring the goods for export from Canada in circumstances in which section 1 of Part V of Schedule VI would apply, zero-rating would be available regardless of which party has made the supply.

Scenario 3: The goods are delivered in Canada but by a non-resident in circumstances in which the non-resident override applies. If the agent is a non-registrant or is not acting in the course of commercial activities, the supply would never be deemed to be made by the agent under subsection 177(1). The supply would be considered to be made by the principal directly, and may be eligible for the override.

The Services of the Agent

The CRA notes that in all of the possible scenarios, the services of the agent or third party should be considered to see whether they are even supplied in Canada. The CRA made note of the four-part place of performance test to determine whether services are performed in Canada:

(a) Does the service require the person to perform a task (and is that task performed in Canada)?

(b) Is the service performed by way of equipment located in Canada?

(c) Is the service performed by accessing the recipient's equipment by remote location, and the recipient's equipment is in Canada?

(d) Is there any activity undertaken in Canada?

Generally, if the agent has an office or employees in Canada, it will be considered to be providing the service in Canada. However, the service may be performed in Canada where the agent merely has equipment located in Canada, such as a computer server on which the relevant Web site is hosted. If the agency services are performed in Canada, the services may qualify for zero-rating under section 5 of Part V of Schedule VI. For example, if the agency services are provided to a non-resident, and are in respect of a supply made outside Canada by the non-resident, the services will be zero-rated.

The ruling does not discuss any issues relating to whether the person who pays Division III GST will be entitled to recover these amounts as ITCs. However, where goods are to be imported into Canada, the parties should carefully consider who will act as the importer of record of the goods in the context of the rules in section 178.8 and section 180.

Conclusions

1. The manner in which the GST will apply to the sale of the goods and the third party services will turn on whether the third party is an agent of the vendor.

2. The provision by a non-resident person of agency services through a Web site hosted on a server in Canada may be considered the performance of services in Canada because the supply is made through the supplier's equipment located in Canada.

Ruling 5: Resale Situation

Ruling 37297[8] considers a wide range of health related supplies. The applicant is a GST registered Canadian resident company which owns and operates a Web site which is hosted on a server in Canada.

The primary offering of the applicant is health related consulting services. Customers sign up on the Web site for the right to receive consultations in relation to health issues. Third party health care consultants charge the applicant an hourly fee for the time spent on a particular client file. The applicant then charges a marked up hourly fee to the client for the time spent on their particular file. Some of the consultants are located outside Canada.

The consultant will typically recommend a particular herbal remedy for the customer, which may be purchased from the applicant through an order form located on its Web site. Fees for the purchase of the herbal remedy are paid directly from the customer to the applicant.

The purchase by the customer of the particular remedy from the applicant would trigger a corresponding sale of the remedy from the consultant to the applicant. This ensures that the consultant receives the appropriate "credit" for the sale notwithstanding that the sale is not made directly from the consultant to the customer.

However, the consultant is responsible for shipping the remedy to the customer. Delivery of the goods always takes place outside Canada.

The Ruling

The consulting services provided by the applicant to the customer would be considered to be supplied in Canada. However, the service would typically qualify for zero-rating under section 23 of Part V of Schedule VI.

The CRA determined that the applicant was not acting as the agent of the consultants in selling the remedies. This was because the remedies were sold from the consultants to the applicant who in turn sold the remedies to the customer. The fact that possession of the goods was never transferred to the applicant did not impact on the conclusion that a sale had occurred.

---

[8] January 23, 2003.

The goods, when sold by the consultants to the applicant, would not attract GST as they were supplied outside Canada. Similarly, the sale of the goods from the applicant to the customer would not attract GST because the goods were delivered or made available outside Canada.

The ruling does not discuss any issues relating to drop shipments. However, if delivery or possession had been transferred in Canada, the drop shipment avoidance rules might have been applicable.

Conclusions

1. Where a vendor sells goods to a third party who in turn resells the goods to a customer, this is not considered an agency situation. The vendor would be required to collect GST on a taxable sale of goods to the third party. The third party would be responsible for collecting and remitting GST on a taxable sale of the goods to the customer.

2. Services may be considered to be performed in Canada (under the equipment rule) where the supplier provides the supply through a Web site hosted on a server in Canada.

Ruling 6: Online Registration

Ruling 35664[9] considers a person who provides online registration and related supplies through its Web site for its customer's events. The applicant is a GST registered software and Web site hosting company.

The clients are typically associations and event companies which are organizing and hosting conferences, seminars or conventions. The party for whom the applicant acts could be either a resident or non-resident. The attendee of the particular event could be either a resident or a non-resident.

The applicant provides the online registration to the event and characterizes its relationship with the conference organizer as an agency relationship. The applicant collects the fees associated with the event.

The agent also allows the attendee to pre-purchase goods (books or other materials) through its Web site, which will be available at the event. The applicant would collect the fees in respect of these supplies.

The Ruling

The CRA notes that the ruling is premised on the assumption that an agency relation does, in fact, exist. However, it cautions that the parties should verify that this relationship is in fact one involving agency.

---

[9] October 22, 2002.

The CRA noted that the default rule is that the principal is the person who is making the supply to the customer and accordingly it is the principal who is required to account for the GST on the supply. This is the rule which applies where the principal is a person required to collect tax. The agent would charge GST on its agency services, unless the services are provided outside Canada or are zero-rated.

Where the principal is a person who is not required to collect tax, the agent, if a registrant and acting in the course of commercial activities in supplying goods, would be the person who is deemed to make the supply to the customer. The agent would collect and remit GST in respect of the sale of the goods. The agent would not, however, charge any GST to the principal in respect of the agency services.

Conclusions

1. Where an agent who is a registrant supplies goods in the course of commercial activities of the agent on behalf of a principal who is not required to collect tax, the agent will be deemed to make the supply of the goods to the customer. The agent does not charge GST on its agency services.

2. Where the agent makes supplies on behalf of a principal who is required to collect tax, the principal is the person who is required to collect and account for the tax. The agency services will be taxable unless supplied outside Canada or zero-rated.

Chapter 14

Software and Software Related Offerings

A. OVERVIEW

This chapter discusses the manner in which the GST applies to supplies of software where software is the object of the supply.

The manner in which the GST applies where software is merely a *component* of a supply, but the software is not the *object* of the supply, is discussed in Chapter 16, Online Content, Services, and Other General Offerings. This may occur, for example, where a supplier provides the rights to access an information database and allows the customer to use a particular software application to search a database. Issues related to making the distinction between software which is the object of the supply, and software which supports some other supply are discussed in Part 3 of heading C "Current Policies", below.

This chapter will also consider the manner in which GST applies to a number of software related supplies which would typically include technical support, updates, installation support, and software training.

In addition to discussing the manner in which GST applies to the supply of software in electronic format (i.e., by way of the Internet), this chapter will also discuss the manner in which the GST applies to software which is supplied on a physical carrier medium. Although software which is provided on a carrier medium does not qualify as an e-commerce supply, this discussion has been included in order to provide a complete description of the manner in which software is taxed.

B. HISTORIC POLICIES

The manner in which the GST applies to supplies of software has always been, in large part, a matter of administrative policy. It would appear that the leading consideration in the development of the rules has always been to ensure that software consumed in Canada is fully taxable, regardless of the delivery method.

The software rules are contained in a number of different CRA documents. The CRA's historic policies were set out in large part in Technical Information Bulletin B-037 "Imported Computer Software" ("TIB 037"), (dated November 1994), and in Policy Statement P-150, "Tax Treatment of Imported Computer Software" (dated July 1994). Although those documents relate for the most part to software supplied on a carrier medium (the predominant supply methodology at that time), they also briefly discuss software delivered in electronic format.

On the other hand, TIB 090, which was released in 2002, focused almost exclusively upon the manner in which the GST applies to software delivered by way of the Internet.

Given that the historic policies remain in effect even today, and given that the historical policies provide a particular insight into the evolution of the more modern policies, the historic rules are summarized below.

1. Guidance Provided by TIB 037R and P-150

Both administrative documents were developed in connection with what was, at that time, an extremely contentious issue: determining the manner in which GST should apply to software imported into Canada. During the period in which these policies were developed, the electronic transmission of software was rare.[1] Accordingly, the focus of these policy documents related in particular to importations of software on carrier media.

As a general rule, there are very few tax leakage concerns associated with the importation of property into Canada as long as that property is subject to Division III GST. Accordingly, the CRA had good reason, where possible, to characterize software as tangible personal property. In fact, the policies evidence the conceptual difficulties associated with finding a means by which various forms of software could be characterized as tangible personal property and taxed under Division III. The primary difficulty related to the fact that even where software was imported on a carrier medium, the true value of the software was attributable to the programming code, and not to the physical carrier medium.

The CRA's solution involved making the following distinctions with respect to software imported on a carrier medium:

(a) determining whether the software is "custom" or "off the shelf" software; and

(b) if the software is custom, whether the software is sold outright or licensed to the user.[2]

The CRA considered "off the shelf" software to be:

Prepackaged, commercially available software programs which are available to all customers and usable in standard form, such as word processing or spreadsheet applications. Typically off the shelf software is supplied with a standardized license agreement.

---

[1] These policies were released in 1994.

[2] Policy Statement P-150 notes that the reason for the distinction was that advisors had questioned whether the former policy of treating licensed custom software as tangible personal property (and fully taxable based on the value of the carrier medium and programming) made sense. The policy statement notes that many advisors were of the view that the programming component should be considered to be intangible personal property.

"Custom" software on the other hand was defined as "all other types of software, such as software designed and developed to meet a particular customer's specific requirements". The CRA provided the following general description of custom software:

> Custom software is often provided under a specific/signed license agreement between a software licensor (or sublicensor) and a customer (licensee). The software licensor retains extensive rights in the program and the user is granted only a license to use the software, subject to certain conditions.

Given this broad description, it would appear that any reference to "custom software" was in fact a reference to any software other than "off the shelf" (or prepackaged) software. For example, "custom software" could even include software which was not designed to meet a particular customer's specific requirements.

The manner in which the term "custom software" is now interpreted is not nearly as broad. This issue is discussed later in this chapter.

2. The Three Categories of Software

The manner in which the GST applied to software imported into Canada on a carrier medium was resolved primarily by classifying the software into one of the three following categories:

(a) Category 1: Off The Shelf Software

Off the shelf software would be considered to be tangible personal property both for Division II and Division III GST purposes. Where off the shelf software is imported into Canada, the Division III GST would apply based upon the full value of the carrier medium and the value of the instructions (programming) contained on the carrier medium.

The suggestion seemed to be that the place of supply of the software (for Division II GST purposes) would be determined by reference to the same rules which apply to other tangible personal property (i.e., the location where the property is "delivered or made available" to the recipient).

(b) Category 2: Custom Software Sold Outright

Custom software sold outright (i.e., where no rights are retained by the supplier) would be considered to be a supply of tangible personal property both for the purposes of Division II and Division III. The software when imported into Canada would be taxed on the full value of the carrier medium and the value of the instructions (programming) contained on the carrier medium. The following example was provided in TIB 037R to show how the tax would apply:

> A Canadian registrant purchases software outright from a U.S. supplier. The software was designed and developed specifically for the Canadian customer. The Canadian registrant acts as the importer of record of the tapes on which the software is supplied.

The CRA held that in this example the custom software would be considered tangible personal property and would be subject to Division III GST based upon the full value of the carrier medium and the programming code.

It should be noted that a number of recent rulings (see below) have held that a supply of this nature would now be considered a service for Division II GST purposes. Accordingly, notwithstanding that this policy technically remains in effect, it would appear that the characterization of such a supply as tangible personal property is no longer valid.

(c) Category 3: Custom Software Provided by Way of License

Where custom software is provided by way of licence, the Division III GST would apply in a bifurcated manner. The carrier medium would be considered to be tangible personal property and would attract Division III GST at the time of importation. However, the programming code would be considered to be intangible personal property and would not be subject to Division III GST.

The CRA provided the following illustration of the manner in which the tax would apply:

> A Canadian registrant acquires a license to use custom software from a U.S. supplier who is GST registered. Under the agreement the recipient pays a lump sum and an annual license fee for the right to use the software. The Canadian acts as the importer of record and brings the software into Canada on a CD ROM. The software may be used by the recipient anywhere in the world.

The CRA explained that because the custom software was acquired by license, the importer of record would only pay Division III GST on the value of the carrier medium. Where the supplier is GST registered, the recipient would be required to pay Division II GST on the lump sum payment and on the annual license fees. This is because the supply is considered to be intangible personal property which may be used in Canada.

3. Importations of Software without Carrier Medium

Neither TIB 037R nor P-150 focused in particular upon issues relating to the importation of software electronically. This was a reflection of the commercial reality at that time. The CRA did, however, draw the following sweeping conclusions with respect to electronic supplies of software:

(a) Any time software is provided electronically (other than with respect to mere online access), the supply will be considered to be a supply of intangible personal property.

This broad rule seems to suggest, for example, that where custom software is sold outright and delivered electronically, a supply of intangible personal property is being made. However, more recent administrative guidance conflicts squarely with this approach, as evidenced by TIB 090 and many of the rulings.

(b) Where access to an online software program is provided, the supply is considered to be a service.

The CRA explained that there is no transfer of property where online access is provided for only a specified period of time.

More recent administrative policies directly conflict with this approach. TIB 090 specifically provides that the right to use limited duration software is considered to be a supply of intangible personal property.

4. Reconciliation Issues

TIB 090 focused entirely upon issues relating to software delivered in electronic format. This is because the delivery of software on a carrier medium does not qualify as an e-commerce supply. Conversely, the earlier administrative policies focused primarily upon issues relating to software imported on carrier media. Those policies only discussed electronic supplies of software as a tangential matter.

Given the differences in focus, it may be arguable that all three of these government GST documents may each continue to operate with only minimal conflict. Where software is supplied or imported on a carrier medium, the rules in TIB 037 and Policy Statement P-150 should be referenced as the leading authorities. Where software is supplied electronically TIB 090 should be referenced. Conflict between the three policies would be minimal, and would relate only to circumstances where the earlier documents referenced electronic supplies of software.

However, it does not appear that the three policies may be reconciled in such a straightforward manner. This is because attempts to reconcile the policies raise a number of important secondary issues. For example, should software which is imported into Canada on a carrier medium continue to be considered custom software notwithstanding that the software was not specifically designed or developed for a particular person? Unfortunately, there does not appear to be any clear answer to many of these questions.

C. CURRENT POLICIES

As noted above, TIB 037R and Policy Statement P-150 provided only limited guidance with respect to the characterization of software delivered electronically.

Given TIB 090's later release date, and given that it contains a far more detailed analysis of the issues relating to electronic supplies of software, it would appear that the "electronic delivery" rules contained in the earlier policies may now be fully disregarded as inapplicable. The following is a summary of the modern approach established by TIB 090.

1. Intangible Personal Property or a Service

Where a supply is made by electronic means, the supply will be considered either a supply of intangible personal property or a service. Electronic supplies will never be considered to be tangible personal property.

When considering whether a particular supply is a supply of intangible personal property or a service, the following guiding principles should be considered:

(a) *Factors which suggest that intangible personal property is being supplied:*

- a right in a product, or a right to use a product, is provided even if only on a temporary basis;

- a product is provided, which is already in existence;

- a product is created or developed for a specific customer, but the supplier retains ownership of the product; or

- a supply is made of a right to make a copy of a digitized product.

(b) *Factors which suggest that a service is being supplied:*

- the supply does not involve the provision of rights or if rights are supplied they are incidental to the main supply;

- the supply calls for specific work to be performed for a specific person; or

- there is human involvement in the making of the supply.

2. Software Specific Examples Provided in TIB 090

To assist in applying these general guidelines to supplies of software, the CRA in TIB 090 provided 12 software related characterization examples. The 12 examples are reproduced below:

Example 1: Electronic ordering and downloading of digitized products

Customer orders software (or other digitized product) online for downloading to their computer for use. Customer, for a separate fee can order updates and add ons (also delivered electronically).

The software is considered to be supply of intangible personal property. This is because the product is already in existence at the time of ordering and the customer is provided with a copy of the product which is to be downloaded and the right to use the product.

Example 2: Limited duration software

Customer receives the right to use software for a period which is less than the useful life of the software. The software is downloaded onto the purchaser's computer. On termination of the license the product becomes unusable or is deleted.

The software is considered to be a supply of intangible personal property (for the reasons set out in example #1). The limitation placed upon the duration of use does not impact upon this conclusion.

Example 3: Subscription to Web site for downloading of digitized products

The customer pays a fixed periodic fee for the right to download and use existing digitized products (which might include software or other digitized products such as music).

The supply of the right to use digitized products is considered to be supply of intangible personal property. The customer is acquiring the right to use and download (i.e., make a copy of) an existing product.

Example 4: Software maintenance

The customer enters into a software maintenance contract which provides for technical support and software updates for a single annual fee. The customer has the right to copy and use the product (i.e., the updates). The principal object of the contract is the software updates.

The software maintenance is considered to be supply of intangible personal property. This is because the principal object of the supply is the right to receive updates (and not the right to receive technical support).

Example 5: Customer support over computer network

Customer obtains online technical support including installation advice and troubleshooting. This is delivered by means of an online database and online technical information. As a last resort the customer may communicate with a technician by email.

The principal object of the supply must be identified to characterize the supply. If the principal object is the right to access an existing database (and the interaction with technicians is incidental), the supply will be intangible personal property. If the principal object is the right to interact with technicians (and the access to online resources is incidental), then a service is being supplied. This is because the supply would involve specific work done for a specific person.

Example 6: Application hosting

A customer with a perpetual license to use software enters into a contract with a host entity. The host loads a copy of the software on its own server and provides technical support. The customer accesses, executes and operates the software remotely. The software can execute on the host's server (remotely) or can be downloaded to the customer's computer.

This is a supply of a service. The host is not providing any rights in the software because the customer already holds those rights. The host is providing the service of offering space to store and run the application and the service of providing technical support.

Example 7: Application hosting

The customer for a single fee enters into a contract with the host entity (which holds the copyright in the software) to allow access to the application, host the application on a server owned by the host and provide technical support for the hardware and software. The customer accesses and executes the software remotely. The principal object of the contract is the right to use the software application.

This is a supply of intangible personal property because the principal object of the contract is the supply of the right to use software. The services provided (hosting the software and providing technical support) are considered to be incidental.

Example 8: Software related services

A supplier has a license to use software which it hosts on its own server. The supplier enters into an agreement with its customer whereby the supplier will provide back office services of payment processing. The supplier provides the customer with remote access to the software (which resides solely on the supplier's server) so that the customer can enter data with respect to its clients. However, the supplier remains responsible for all other tasks associated with the payment processing (i.e., cheque issuance, bank verification etc.) and uses the software to perform these tasks in an automated manner. The customer is not provided with any rights to use the software other than in the limited manner set out above and is not entitled to download or copy the software.

The supply to the customer is of a service. In making the supply the supplier has a license to use software to assist its personnel in completing the relevant tasks. The customer's access to and rights to use the software are provided in a limited manner and so are considered incidental.

Example 10: Data warehousing

A customer stores its data on servers owned and operated by a supplier. The customer can access, upload, retrieve and manipulate data remotely. The customer is not provided with any software license and no rights in property are transferred to the customer.

This is a supply of a service. This is because there is no provision of rights or property.

Example 13: Online auctions

A Web site operator displays a vendor's items for sale by way of auction. Online shoppers purchase the items from the owner of the goods and not from the operator. The operator is paid a commission by the vendor of the goods. The vendor and the online shopper are able to use software licensed to the operator for limited purposes (i.e. payment processing) but do not have any specific rights to use the software.

The supply is of a service. Although the vendors and the shoppers are able to make the purchase with the use of the software no rights in the software are provided to either of them.

Example 14: Data Retrieval

The supplier has made a repository of online information available to customers which includes industry information and investment reports. The customers pay a fee which enables them to search and extract specific information. The supplier provides both raw data and value added content (such as analysis of data). However, the content is never created for a specific customer and there is no requirement that the customer maintain the secrecy of the information.

This is a supply of intangible personal property. The supplier is providing the right to access and use information already in existence and with the software programs required to search the information. The human involvement (by adding raw data or by providing content) is considered to be an input to the supply.

Example 15: Access to interactive Web site

A supplier makes a Web site available to subscribers with digital content. The digital content is not necessarily owned by the supplier. Subscribers interact with the content only while online.

The supply is intangible personal property. The subscribers acquire the right to access content (including software) while online. Although a copy of the software or digitized product is not made available to the subscriber there is a right to view, access or use the product while online. Any human involvement is considered an input to the supply.

3. Summary of Guidance Provided by the Examples

The software examples suggest that the four following guiding principles should be considered in characterizing any supply of software delivered electronically:

(a) A threshold distinction must be made between software which is being supplied to the customer as the principal object of the supply and software which is provided to the customer as a means of enhancing the use or enjoyment of some other supply.

Many supplies involve a software component where software either is not supplied to the customer (i.e., the software is an input to the supply) or the software is not the principal object of the supply. Where software is merely an input or is not the object of the supply, the software will not be the determinant in characterizing the supply.

The following are examples of situations (from above) where the customer benefited from the software, but the software was not the principal object of the supply.

Example	Issue	Relevant Supply
8	Payment processing whereby supplier allows customer access to software for data entry	Payment processing service
10	Data storage whereby supplier allows customer to link in to supplier's software online	Data storage service
13	Online sales whereby supplier allows customer to access its software	Service of selling the goods
14	Online information which may be searched by customer using supplier's software	Supply of online information (intangible personal property)

Where it has been determined that some other supply (i.e., a supply other than software) is being provided, the manner in which the tax will apply is discussed in Chapter 16, Online Content, Services, and Other General Offerings.

(b) Where as a result of the application of the threshold test described in (a) above, it is determined that rights to access or use software are the object of the supply, the rights to use the software will be considered a supply of intangible personal property. This will include situations where:

  (i) a licence is provided to download and use software. See examples 1 and 3;

  (ii) the software is not fully licensed to the user (i.e., the user is provided with more limited rights to use the software). See example 15;

  (iii) the rights to use the software are provided only for a temporary period of time. See examples 2 and 15; or

  (iv) the software is only accessed remotely (i..e., application hosting). See example 7.

As noted previously, this conclusion is in direct conflict with the guidance provided in TIB 037R. For example, TIB 037R provided that online access to software is a service. The position set out in TIB 037R appears to be unsupportable given the results provided in TIB 090 examples 2 (temporary download and use of software), 7 (application hosting) and 15 (online use of software).

(c) Where software is specifically designed and developed for a particular customer and is sold outright to the customer, the supply will be considered to be a supply of "custom software". The supply of custom software is considered to be a service. Although none of the TIB 090 examples consider this issue, this position is reflected in several rulings (discussed below) released subsequent to TIB 090.

(d) Where software is bundled with other products or services to form a single supply, the characterization of the supply will require that the "principal object of the supply" be determined. If the principal object of a software maintenance contract is access to one-on-one technical support (and any upgrades or access to existing resources are incidental), the supply will be a service. However, where the principal object of the supply is access to an existing database (or other online resource) or upgrades, the supply will be intangible personal property. See, TIB 090 examples 4 (updates are the principal object) and 5 (online technical support is the principal object).

D. PLACE OF SUPPLY ISSUES RELATING TO SOFTWARE

The following summarizes the current position of the CRA with respect to the identification of the place of supply of software.

1. Intangible Personal Property — GST Issues

Where a supply of software is considered to be intangible personal property, the supply is considered to be made in Canada if the software may be used in Canada. This rule is contained in paragraph 142(1)(c) of the ETA. The CRA interprets the term "may be used" as being equivalent to "allowed to be used". The CRA explains this important concept in the following terms:

> In determining whether intangible personal property may be used in Canada reference may be made to any written agreement for the supply that contains terms governing the place of use of the intangible personal property. This is common practice in a business to business transaction. In a consumer transaction there may be a general restriction as to the use of the intangible personal property, to which the recipient agrees either expressly or implicitly upon acquisition of the supply. The restriction may be explained on the website through which a product is supplied.[3]

The "allowed to be used" test is particularly important because it seems to limit the scope of responsibility of the supplier to monitor the location where intangible property is actually used. While a supplier may contractually preclude a recipient from using property in a particular location, as a practical matter the supplier may not be in a position to enforce this type of restriction. Further, even where the supplier is able to determine that software is being used (in breach of the contract) in a particular location, the consideration owing in respect of the supply will typically already have been paid.

In determining the place of supply of software which is intangible personal property, the location where the software executes will be only one of a number of relevant factors to be taken into account. "Use" for GST purposes will regularly occur in locations in which the software does not execute. The broad concept of "use" relates to any location where the recipient is allowed to obtain the benefit of the software. This should be contrasted with the position of many provincial tax regimes which rely much more heavily upon the concept of place of execution for determining the place of supply of software.

---

[3] TIB 090.

2. Intangible Personal Property — HST Issues

A supply of intangible personal property which does not relate to real property, tangible personal property, or services to be performed, is considered to be supplied in a particular province where all or substantially all of the Canadian rights in respect of the property can be used only in that province. This rule is contained in subparagraph 2(*d*)(i) of Part III of Schedule IX. The reference to "Canadian rights" is a reference to only those rights which can be used in Canada.

It should be noted that for the province of supply rules, the ETA uses the term "can be used", whereas in connection with issues relating to the general place of supply, it uses the term "may be used". One suggestion might be that there was an intention to create two separate standards. However, it would appear that the CRA has not in fact made any such distinction.

The rule in subparagraph 2(*d*)(i) applies where the Canadian rights to use the intangible personal property are restricted to a single province. The CRA in TIB 090 provides the example of an application service supplier located in Newfoundland which provides licences to use software through its Web site. The recipient in this example is a Nova Scotia company. The contract restricts the use of the software to the customer's offices in Nova Scotia. This is considered to be a supply which is made in Nova Scotia because the rights may only be exercised by the customer in Nova Scotia.

Where the test in subparagraph 2(*d*)(i) does not apply, the test in subparagraph 2(*d*)(ii) provides that a supply of intangible personal property which does not relate to real property, tangible personal property, or services to be performed is considered to be supplied in a province where the following two tests are met:

(a) the place of negotiation of the supply is in the province; and

(b) the property may be used otherwise than exclusively outside that province.

The CRA notes that where there are no restrictions as to the place where the software may be used the intangible property will always meet the "may be used otherwise than exclusively outside the province" test. The "place of negotiation" is the location of the supplier's permanent establishment which is associated with the individual principally involved in the negotiation. The practical impact of this rule is that the supply which is unrestricted as to use will be considered to be supplied in the province of negotiation.

The CRA in TIB 090 provided the following example of the application of this rule. The supplier of the software in issue is Canadian and operates from a permanent establishment in Ontario. The software is downloaded by the purchaser from the supplier's Web site, which is hosted on servers located in the supplier's Ontario offices. The software agreement does not restrict the location where the software may be used. This supply would be considered to be made in Ontario because the place of negotiation is in Ontario (the location of the supplier's permanent establishment), and the software may be used otherwise than exclusively outside Ontario.

This province of supply rule, where applicable, may result in unintended consequences. For example, where a supplier which operates from a location in one of the harmonized provinces makes a supply to a resident of an other than harmonized province (and without the suitable restrictions as to use), the supply will be considered to be made in the participating province from which the supplier operates and accordingly will be taxed at the 14% rate.

In circumstances where the rules set out above do not establish a place of supply then the rule in section 3 will apply. This rule will deem the supply to be made in a participating province where:

(a) The place of negotiation is in Canada and the Canadian rights can only be used primarily in the participating provinces; or

(b) The place of negotiation is outside Canada, the property can only be used exclusively in Canada and the Canadian rights can only be used primarily in the participating provinces.

3. Services — GST Issues

A service is deemed to be supplied in Canada under the general place of supply rules where the service is performed in whole or in part in Canada. It is only where the service is wholly performed outside Canada that it will be considered to be supplied outside Canada.

(a) Human Element

To determine whether services are performed in part in Canada, the traditional approach (i.e., the approach which relates to the human element) to locating services should be the first consideration:

The place where a service is performed is traditionally the place where the person physically doing the work is situated. For example, if a non-resident sends a technician to Canada to provide programming services, the place of performance is in Canada as the service is physically performed in Canada.

That the scope of activities which may constitute performance of a service in Canada is extremely broad is demonstrated by the following example:

... a supplier may prepare a report in Canada in respect of programming services carried on outside Canada. As the report is a component of the services supplied, the place where the report is prepared must be considered when determining the place of supply.[4]

Extended employee activities which do not form a component of the service being supplied, but which do "relate to the performance of the service" should also be taken into account. TIB 090 place of performance rule 4 establishes that a service will be deemed to be performed in Canada where:

> ... any activity related to the performance of the service is undertaken in Canada.

This may include employee activities which relate to establishing means to allow for services to be subsequently provided, such as maintaining or upgrading Web sites or servers.

(b) Equipment Element

In addition to the requirement to take into account employee activities, equipment related functions must also be considered in order to locate the place of performance of services. A service will be considered to be performed in Canada where:

(a) the service includes operations performed by the supplier's computer equipment and that equipment is located in Canada; or

(b) the service involves doing something to or with the recipient's computer equipment by accessing it from a remote location and the recipient's computer is located in Canada;

Non-residents should carefully take into account these extended place of supply rules when providing services to Canadian customers.

4. Services — HST Issues

The general province of supply rules for services are contained in Part V of Schedule IX. These rules are analogous to the rules described above for intangible personal property.

The first rule (the rule in paragraph 2(a) of Part V) provides that a service is considered to be supplied in a particular province if all or substantially all of the Canadian element of the service is performed in that province. The "Canadian element" of a service is the portion of that service which is performed in Canada. This rule could apply to locate a supply in any province in Canada.

---

[4] This example was provided in TIB 090.

The CRA in TIB 090 provided the following example of the application of this rule:

> A transportation company contracts with an ISP in Manitoba to host a financial management software application which is licensed to the company. The software is hosted on servers at the ISP's facilities in Winnipeg. The ISP maintains the servers and provides technical support to the company's employees, who access and use the software remotely. All of the services supplied by the ISP are performed in Manitoba.
>
> The supply of the hosting service is made in the province of Manitoba as all or substantially all of the Canadian element of the service is performed in that province.

The second rule (the rule in paragraph 2(*b*) of Part V) provides that a service is considered to be supplied in a particular province if the place of negotiation for the supply is in the province and all or substantially all of the service is not performed outside that province. The CRA in TIB 090 provided the following example of the application of this rule:

> A supplier in Ontario enters into a contract with a retail company in Quebec to design the retailer's Web site. The supplier does not retain any rights to the design or the site. The contract is negotiated by the ISP's sales representative, who works out of the ISP's permanent establishment in Ottawa. Approximately half of the Web site design work is performed in Ottawa, and the other half is performed in Quebec.
>
> The supply of the service is made in Ontario, as the place of negotiation for the supply is in Ontario, and all or substantially all of the service is not performed outside that province.

The third rule provides that where the rules in paragraphs 2(*a*) and 2(*b*) do not locate a supply, the supply will be deemed to be made in a participating province under section 3 in the following circumstances:

(a) the place of negotiation of the supply is in Canada and the Canadian element of the service is performed primarily in the participating provinces; or

(b) the place of negotiation of the supply is outside Canada, all or substantially all of the service is performed in Canada, and the Canadian element of the service is performed primarily in the participating provinces.

Each of the rules set out above requires that the place (or places) of performance of the service be identified. The identification of the place of performance will require that the extended performance rules relating to computer equipment be taken into account.

(a) Special Province of Supply Override

The Place of Supply (GST/HST) Regulations provide for special override rules in connection with certain services. Among the services which are subject to special province of supply rules are a "technical support service provided by means of telecommunications and which relate to the operation or use of computer hardware or software". Many software related technical support services and training services, will fall into these special province of supply rules. These rules, where applicable, override the general province of supply rules set out above.

The operation of these complex rules is described in detail in Chapter 5, Place of Supply. Any person who supplies a computer related service to a person who will in turn re-supply that service to a third party, should be particularly careful to ensure that they have fully considered these override rules. This is because where the service is to be re-supplied, the identification of the province of supply of the service will often require that issues relating to the location of the third party be taken into account. The operation of these rules is commonly misunderstood.

E. NON-RESIDENT ISSUES

Many supplies made by non-residents of software or software-related services (including programming services and technical support services), will be deemed to be made in Canada under the ordinary place of supply rules (the section 142 rules). It is also not uncommon for software and software related supplies made by non-residents to be deemed to be made in a participating province under the rules in Part V of Schedule IX or under the Place of Supply (GST/HST) Regulations.

Where the supplier is GST registered, there will be a requirement to collect GST (or in some cases HST). However, many non-resident suppliers will be entitled to rely upon the non-resident override contained in section 143 which provides that where a non-resident, non-registered person makes supplies in Canada (i.e., under the rules in section 142) other than in the course of a business carried on in Canada, the supply will be considered to be made outside Canada.

1. General Considerations

Generally, the factors which lead to the conclusion (particularly with respect to services) that the supply was made in Canada, are factors which will be taken into account in determining whether the non-resident person is carrying on business in Canada. These same factors may also be taken into account in determining whether supplies are being made through a permanent establishment in Canada.

For example, a person who provides services through its server in Canada will typically be considered to have performed the service in Canada. This is because the service includes operations performed by the supplier's equipment in Canada. This issue is very closely linked to the issue of whether the person is making supplies through a permanent establishment in Canada. Where a non-resident makes supplies (which are significant and essential) through a server which is at its disposal in Canada, the non-resident will be deemed to have a permanent establishment in Canada (i.e., the server). The non-resident will also be deemed to be resident in Canada in respect of any activities carried on through a permanent establishment in Canada. Accordingly, making supplies of services through a server in Canada may result in the service being performed in Canada, and may also result in a finding that the non-resident is deemed to be a Canadian resident.

The connection between the performance of service rules and the tests for carrying on business in Canada are slightly less direct. In the example set out above, where a person provides services through a server located in Canada, a very proximate connection to Canada will already have been established.

However, in any circumstances where it is determined that a particular service is performed in Canada, an essential component of the carrying on business in Canada test, and the permanent establishment in Canada test, will also be met.

2. Specific Issues

(a) Web site in Canada

Operating a Web site in Canada will not result in a finding that the non-resident person has a permanent establishment in Canada. The CRA takes the administrative position that a Web site is not tangible personal property (because it consists only of software and electronic data) and so cannot be considered to be a fixed place of business. The CRA has noted that:

> At a minimum a "place of business" of a person requires that a certain amount of physical space be at the disposal of the person.

As a result, a non-resident who provides software (or services) through a Web site which is available to be accessed from Canada will not be considered to have a permanent establishment in Canada as a result of the Web site. The provision of software (or services) through a Web site however would be a factor to be taken into account in determining whether the person is carrying on business in Canada.

Servers, however, are more problematic, and are discussed below.

(b) Server in Canada

A server may, in the CRA's opinion, constitute a "fixed place of business" and so can in some circumstances be considered a permanent establishment. The CRA notes that:

> A server on which a Web site is stored is tangible personal property having a physical location. The server may constitute a fixed place of business of a non-resident person, if it is at the disposal of the person (i.e., operated and owned or leased by the person).

The CRA makes an important distinction between Web sites hosted in typical ISP arrangements (when the Web site owner pays a periodic fee for the right to have its Web site hosted by the ISP) and Web sites hosted on servers located in Canada which are owned or leased by (or otherwise at the disposal of) the non-resident person.

As a result of this distinction the following conclusions may be drawn:

(a) if a non-resident were to have a Web site hosted on a server located in Canada by way of a typical hosting arrangement (i.e., Web site hosted by an ISP) then the non-resident would not be considered to have a permanent establishment in Canada as a result of these activities. This is because the server is not "at the disposal" of the non-resident;

(b) if a non-resident were to have a server at its disposal in Canada (i.e., owned or leased by the non-resident) then the server might constitute a permanent establishment of the non-resident.

The server which is at the disposal of the non-resident will only be considered a permanent establishment of the non-resident if the activities carried out through the server are considered an "essential and significant" part of the overall business activities of the enterprise. However, significant and essential activities can be carried on at a server even where no personnel are required to be present at the location of the server.

The CRA also notes that ISP arrangements will not typically be sufficient to meet the second branch of the permanent establishment test. The ISP will not be the agent of the non-resident because it does not have the authority to conclude contracts in the name of the non-resident person. Secondly, the ISP, even if it were an agent, would not meet the dependent agent test in that it hosts the Web sites of many different businesses.

The provision of software or services through a server in Canada would also be a factor to be taken into account in determining whether the non-resident person is carrying on business in Canada. The following example from TIB 090 (Example 2) demonstrates how a non-resident person may be found to be carrying on business in Canada in circumstances where there is no permanent establishment in Canada.

Example #2: Software applications

A non-resident supplies the right to use various software applications to customers in Canada. The software is provided through the non-resident's Web site which is stored on a server in Canada. The server is not at the disposal of the non-resident (web hosting is provided by an ISP). The software applications are stored on the same server as part of the Web site. Canadian customers order the software online and their approval is provided automatically. The customer is then provided with access to the selected software. Customers are invoiced electronically according to the number of hours they have used the application in issue. The Canadian ISP processes the payments for the vendor. After sales support is provided by a Canadian independent contractor. The non-resident advertises through its Web site and through Canadian newspapers.

The CRA concluded that the non-resident is in fact carrying on business in Canada. This is because of the advertising in Canadian newspapers, the use of an independent contractor in Canada for after sales support, the provision of payment processing by independent ISPs located in Canada, and the presence of the automated interactive Web site stored on a server in Canada.

F. SUPPLIES TO NON-RESIDENTS (ZERO-RATING)

1. Services

Where software related services are supplied to a non-resident person there are a number of zero-rating provisions which may be applicable to provide relief. These include section 7 (general services), section 8 (advertising services) and section 23 (consulting, advisory or professional services). Generally, the application of these provisions is not contentious because the relief provided is quite broad.

This is to be contrasted with the narrow manner in which the zero-rating relief provision for intangible personal property has been interpreted. For this reason it is typically preferable that a particular supply be characterized as a supply of a service when zero-rating relief is sought.

2. Intangible Personal Property

Where intangible personal property is supplied to a non-resident there is only one zero-rating provision which may potentially apply. The rule in section 10 of Part V of Schedule VI provides that zero-rating is available in respect of:

> A supply of an invention, patent, trade secret, trade-mark, trade-name, copyright, industrial design or other intellectual property or any right, license or privilege to use any such property, where the recipient is a non-resident person who is not registered at the time the supply is made.

Although this provision may appear to be extremely broad in nature, it has been consistently interpreted by the CRA in a manner which does not allow for zero-rating for a number of software related supplies. TIB 090 provides the following example of a software supply which will qualify for zero-rating:

Example #1: Software provided electronically to non-resident

A non-resident, non-registrant customer purchases software which is downloaded from the supplier's Web site.

The CRA ruled that this is a supply of intangible personal property which qualifies for zero-rating under section 10.

TIB 090 provides a second example of a software supply which does not qualify for relief:

Example #2: Interactive digitized product Web site

The supplier sells subscriptions to access a Web site which features digitized content including music, videos, games and other activities. The subscribers are not permitted to download copies of the products but can interact while online from any location.

This is a supply of intangible personal property which does not qualify for zero-rating. The CRA explained that there is no supply of intellectual property in this example.

It would appear that where software is allowed to be downloaded by the recipient of the supply then intellectual property will be considered to be supplied and zero-rating will be available. However, where mere online access is provided to software (or to other digitized content) then intellectual property is not being supplied and zero-rating would not be available. Given that downloading of software appears to be critical, it would seem to follow that software provided by way of application hosting will not qualify for relief.

(a) Other Guidance

TIB 090 does not discuss whether software which may be downloaded and used but only on a temporary basis might qualify for zero-rating.

However, given that temporary use software which may be downloaded is treated for place of supply purposes in the same manner as software which may be used indefinitely, it would appear that the zero-rating rules would also apply in the same manner (i.e., the temporary use software should qualify for zero-rating).

(b) Concerns With This Position

Given that the place of supply rules which relate to intangible personal property are very broad in nature, and given that the zero-rating relief is quite narrow, many supplies of intangible personal property made to non-residents will be subject to tax. This narrow position has been criticized by many in the industry as being too restrictive.

A recent decision of the Tax Court of Canada however has cast significant doubts on the correctness of the CRA's narrow position with respect to the scope of section 10. In *Dawn's Place Ltd. v. Her Majesty the Queen*, 2006 GTC 70 (T.C.C.) (currently under appeal), the Tax Court was asked to consider whether memberships provided to non-resident individuals qualified for zero-rating relief under section 10. Each of the non-resident members was provided with a non-exclusive, limited, and revocable license to download and view the content of an adult Web site. The corresponding content included images, text, logos, graphics, information, software, computer code and applications, animations, video, and other multimedia.

The Minister took the position that the supply of the membership did not qualify for zero-rating. The Minister acknowledged that the materials contained on the Web site were copyright protected. However, the Minister appears to have adopted the position that the mere license to access and use the copyrighted materials was not sufficient to meet the section 10 requirements.

The Tax Court of Canada rejected the Minister's argument and held that zero-rating was in fact available for the memberships. The Court made particular note of the broad wording of section 10 which established that zero-rating is available for any "... right, licence, or privilege to use ..." intellectual property. This decision is currently being appealed by the Minister.

G. RULINGS

1. Custom Software

(a) What is Custom Software?

The CRA in the 1990's seemed to adopt a fairly liberal interpretation of the term "custom software". For example, the CRA, in TIB 037 and in Policy Statement P-150 (both of which were released in 1994), discussed the manner in which the tax would apply to custom software which was either sold outright or which was licensed to a particular customer .

(b) CRA Retraction From Earlier Position

The CRA now seems to have adopted a narrower view of what constitutes custom software. It would appear that software will only be considered custom in nature where the customer is provided with full ownership of the software. The CRA now describes custom software in the following manner:

> The CCRA considers "custom designed software" to be software that is specially designed, developed or modified for a particular customer and that the customer has ownership at the end of the process. Generally this means that the customer owns all of the rights to the software.[5]

Although the use of the word "generally" leaves open the possibility that software may be considered to be custom in nature in circumstances where ownership is not transferred to the customer, in practical terms it would appear that the CRA no longer characterizes the term "custom software" this broadly.

Accordingly, it would appear that when specially designed or modified software (or any other form of unique software) is merely licensed to a recipient, the supply would not qualify as a supply of custom software. The suggestion is that the determination of the manner in which the tax will apply to licensed software will require the application of the rules for other than custom software. Those rules are described under heading 2, below.

(c) How is Custom Software Characterized?

The CRA's current position is that where custom software is provided to the customer, and the customer obtains all rights to the software code upon completion, the supply will always be considered a service. The explanation for this apparent shift in position (away from the position that custom software could be intangible personal property or tangible personal

---

[5] Ruling 6277 dated November 6, 2001.

property depending on whether it was delivered on a medium), is explained below:

> Since the supplier of the design or development services does not retain any rights to the software, the supply of the design of the software is not a supply of intangible personal property, but rather a supply of a service of designing the software.

A supply of a custom software service may also be provided where a supplier modifies existing customer owned software for the purpose of meeting the client's specific needs.

The rulings set out below describe the CRA's administrative position with respect to the taxation of programming developed from scratch, and with respect to custom modifications.

(i) Programming from Scratch

Ruling 1: Programming from Scratch

Ruling 6277[6] considered the supply of software which had been specifically designed and developed for the particular customer. The supplier specializes in custom programming software for the home consumer.

The programming is done from a location in Canada.

The Ruling

The CRA ruled that the software will be considered custom if it is specifically designed, developed or modified for a particular person, and the recipient acquires ownership at the end of the process.

> The CCRA considers "custom designed software" to be software that is specially designed, developed or modified for a particular customer and that the customer has ownership at the end of the process. Generally this means that the customer owns all of the rights to the software. Since the supplier of the design or development services does not retain any rights to the software, the supply of the design of the software is not a supply of IPP, but rather a supply of a service of designing the software.

The ruling did not discuss whether the presence of a carrier medium would have any impact on this characterization as a service. The suggestion seems to be that the existence of a medium would be irrelevant.

This supply was considered to be made in Canada because the programming was performed in Canada.

---

[6] November 6, 2001.

Conclusions

1. The development of custom software from scratch for a customer will be a supply of a service where the customer is provided with the ownership of the software at the end of the process

2. The service will be supplied in any place where the service is performed. This will typically be the offices from which the programmer operates.

Ruling 2: Software Development

Ruling 34132[7] also considers a supply of the development of software. The custom software, once developed becomes the sole property of the customer. The software is delivered to the customer in electronic format.

The Ruling

The CRA ruled as follows:

> Programming from scratch a custom solution where the client owns the software upon completion, is considered to be a supply of a service ...

The ruling also notes that this service, when provided to a non-resident, would typically be zero-rated under section 7.

Conclusions

1. The development of custom software from scratch for a customer will be a supply of a service where the customer is provided with the ownership of the software at the end of the process.

2. Zero-rating will typically be available in respect of this supply when provided to a non-resident.

Ruling 3: Software for Use in Equipment

Ruling 37480[8] considers supplies relating to software development. An individual resident in Canada provides software design and implementation services for a customer in the U.S. The services relate to computer products which are owned by the non-resident customer. It would appear that the software developed by the individual would be incorporated into existing software owned by the customer. The Canadian is paid $9,000 per month for these development services.

---

[7] July 4, 2001.

[8] December 19, 2001.

The non-resident, who is not registered and does not have a permanent establishment in Canada, sells the finished software throughout the world. However, the Canadian does not ever have any contact with the non-resident's customers in Canada (i.e., he is not an agent or sales representative).

The Ruling

The CRA concluded that the development and implementation of custom software which will be owned by the customer following completion, is a supply of a service.

> Developing and implementing custom software where the client owns the software upon completion is considered to be a supply of a service for GST/HST purposes.

The service is performed in Canada, and so is subject to GST. However, the service should qualify for zero-rating under section 7.

Although extensive information was provided as to the location where the recipient will use the programming code, and as to the manner in which it will sell or license the software (to its customers), this information did not appear to be relevant.

Conclusions

1. The development of custom software for a recipient will be considered a supply of a service where the recipient acquires ownership rights to the code upon completion.

2. This service will typically qualify for zero-rating when provided to a non-resident.

Ruling 4: Software Development

Software development is also considered in ruling 35353[9]. The applicant is a GST registered computer programmer in Canada who designs software for non-residents.

The applicant works on the existing software by linking in over the Internet to the non-resident's servers in the U.S. where the software resides. The program once completed will reside on the non-resident's server in the U.S.

---

[9] September 13, 2002.

The Ruling

The CRA ruled that as long as the supplier does not retain any property rights in the software upon completion the supply will be characterized as a service. The supply will be taxable because it is made in Canada (i.e., the service is performed from the applicant's home in Canada).

The CRA also noted that the HST might apply. Where all or substantially all of the Canadian element of a service is performed in a particular province, the supply will be considered to be made in that province. This rule is set out in Part V of Schedule IX.

The service would qualify for zero-rating under section 7. The reference to section 7 as the relevant zero-rating provision suggests that the CRA does not view software development as a consulting service.

Although not discussed in the ruling, if the non-resident customer had visited Canada to discuss the programming with the supplier, zero-rating likely would not have been available. Section 7 provides that zero-rating is not available under that section where:

(a) a service is made to an individual who is in Canada at any time when the individual has contact with the supplier in relation to the supply; or

(b) a service rendered to an individual while that individual is in Canada.

It may be arguable that if the recipient visited Canada to discuss the project before the programming commenced (i.e., to make arrangements with the supplier) then the supply might still qualify for zero-rating. However, if the recipient were to visit Canada while the service was being performed, the supply likely would not qualify for zero-rating.

For this reason a non-resident who is not registered would be best served to arrange for meetings to occur in the U.S. If the recipient is an individual, the recipient should not visit Canada at any time in connection with the supply (including initial consultations).

Conclusions

1. Software development is a service where the recipient is provided with ownership of the software upon completion of the programming.

2. If all or substantially all of the Canadian element of the service is performed in a single province, the supply will be made in that particular province.

3. The service will generally qualify for zero-rating when provided to a non-resident.

(ii) Software Modifications

Ruling 5: Modifications

In ruling 25957[10], the supplier modifies existing client owned software to meet the client's specific needs. The supplier also programs custom software solutions for the client from scratch.

The Ruling

The CRA ruled that each of the two supplies would be considered to be a supply of a service.

The ruling does not discuss whether the conclusion turns on issues relating to the presence of a carrier medium. This silence seems to suggest that the supply would be considered a service regardless of whether it is provided on a medium or delivered electronically.

Conclusions

1. Modifying client owned software is considered to be a service.

2. This conclusion appears to follow regardless of whether the modifications are delivered on a carrier medium or are provided electronically.

2. Software Which is not Custom Software

The supply of a license to use software which is not custom software will be characterized according to whether a medium is used to deliver the software. Where there is no medium (i.e., the software is delivered electronically), the supply will be considered intangible personal property. Where there is a medium, the supply will be characterized as tangible personal property.[11] This long standing distinction was first made in TIB 037.

(a) Software Supplied on A Carrier Medium

As noted above, software supplied on a carrier medium which is not custom software, is considered to be a supply of tangible personal property. This will include both software which is shrink wrapped, and other software which is available in physical format.

---

[10] October 9, 2001.

[11] See for example ruling 6277 dated November 6, 2001.

(i) Shrink Wrapped Software

Two rulings which consider software sold in a shrink wrapped (or "off the shelf") format confirm the principle established in TIB 037 that software sold in this format remains a supply of tangible personal property notwithstanding that the value of the product lies in the programming code (and not in the carrier medium). The place of supply and zero-rating rules which apply to the supply of the software will be the same as those which apply to any other type of tangible personal property.

Ruling 6: Shrink Wrapped Software

Ruling 33694[12] considers a shrink wrapped product which is licensed by a Canadian GST registered supplier to non-resident customers. The customer pays a one time license fee up front for the right to use the software. In return the customer obtains a non-exclusive and non-transferable right to use the software. The applicant mails the software to the customer.

The Ruling

The CRA concluded that the supply was of tangible personal property.

The supply of the right to use software which is not custom software may be a supply of tangible personal property or intangible personal property depending on the medium by which it is supplied. Specifically if the software is supplied on a physical medium it is considered to be a supply of TPP while if it is supplied electronically it is considered to be a supply of IPP.

The place of delivery of the product would be the determining factor for locating the place of supply. Similarly, zero-rating might be available in the same manner as with other goods (see for example, sections 1 and 2 of Part V of Schedule VI).

The CRA did note that if the software had been considered to be intangible personal property (i.e., delivered electronically), the zero-rating rule to be considered would be section 10:

A supply of software that is a supply of IPP ... may qualify for zero-rating under section 10 ...

Conclusions

1. The supply of a license to use shrink wrapped software will be considered to be a supply of tangible personal property.

---

[12] January 14, 2003.

2. The software will be supplied in Canada if it is delivered or made available to the recipient in Canada. The location where the software may be used is irrelevant.

3. The zero-rating provisions which should be considered are those which relate to ordinary supplies of tangible personal property.

(ii) Other than shrink wrapped software on a carrier medium

There is no requirement that the software be supplied in a shrink wrapped format to be characterized as tangible personal property. Software (other than custom software) when supplied on a disk by way of license will also be considered to be tangible personal property. For example, the CRA in ruling 6277[13] notes as follows:

> The supply of the right to use software that is not custom software may be a supply of intangible personal property (IPP) or tangible personal property (TPP) depending on the medium by which it is supplied. Considering your client supplies and delivers the software electronically over the Internet, the supply is treated as a supply of IPP.

> Where the supply is deemed to be made in Canada the supply of intellectual property ... is zero-rated under section 10 ...

(b) Other than Custom Software Supplied Electronically

Electronically supplied software, which is not custom software, is a supply of intangible personal property. This will include software which is licensed to the user for download to the customer's computer, software which is licensed for only a limited duration of time, and software which is merely allowed to be accessed and used by the customer (i.e., it does not execute on the customer's computer). This category also includes software specifically designed for a particular user, but in circumstances where the user does not obtain ownership of the programming (i.e., it does not qualify as custom software because of the rights retained by the supplier).

To determine if zero-rating is available under section 10 for the supplies described above, a distinction must be made between supplies where intellectual property is being provided and supplies where intellectual property is not being provided. However, the circumstances in which zero-rating will be available under section 10 in respect of software delivered electronically is difficult to ascertain. This difficulty is attributable, in large part, to the fact that the rulings issued to date have not provided a comprehensive description of the section 10 qualification criteria. However, the CRA seems to be suggesting (in the rulings below) that section 10 relief will only be available where a licence to use software is being provided, and the software

[13] November 6, 2001.

downloads to the recipient's computer. Other more limited rights to access or use software will not qualify for zero-rating relief.

(i) Rights to Download *and* Use Software for Indefinite Period

The CRA has consistently held that the electronic supply of software which is not custom software is a supply of intangible personal property. The electronic delivery of software is typically achieved through email or by downloading from a Web site. These customers are typically provided with a substantial bundle of rights. However, customers are increasingly being provided with the right to access and use software by way of remote access (i.e., without download). This latter format, which is growing very rapidly in popularity, typically involves the provision of a more limited bundle of rights to the customer.

As a result of the application of the section 142 place of supply rules for intangible personal property, the software, when supplied under any of these arrangements, will be taxable in the location where it may be used. Similar use-based rules are also provided for determining the province of supply. The concept of the place where software may be used may be far more broad than the place where software may be downloaded.

In a number of rulings, the CRA has made seemingly broad statements which, if interpreted literally, might suggest that all supplies of software which are considered to be intangible personal property will qualify for zero-rating when supplied to a non-resident who is not registered. For example, in ruling 6277 the CRA noted that:

> The CCRA considers the supply of software that is a supply of IPP to be intellectual property. Where the supply is deemed to be made in Canada, the supply of intellectual property or any right, license or privilege to use any such property is zero-rated ... under section 10 of Part V of Schedule VI ...

However, broad statements like the one set out above do not appear to accurately reflect the position of the CRA. The CRA seems to have made a distinction between supplies of software which involve a full download, and supplies of software which involve only online access. Only the former will qualify as intellectual property for the purposes of applying the zero-rating rules in section 10. The CRA's position may however, be open to challenge on the grounds that it is too restrictive. For example, in *Dawn's Place Ltd. v. Her Majesty the Queen*, 2006 GTC 70 (T.C.C.) (currently under appeal), it was successfully argued that the sale of memberships qualified for zero-rating relief under section 10.

Ruling 7: Electronic Delivery of Software

Ruling 41030[14] considers the electronic provision of software which is not custom software. The applicant licenses software through its Web site. The customer enters into a non-exclusive and non transferable license agreement with the applicant which allows the customer to download a copy of the software onto its own computer. The software is designed to be used by the customer to assess and evaluate the skills of its salespeople.

Where the software is licensed to a non-resident, the license agreement entered into with the customer specifically provides that the software is not allowed to be used in Canada.

The Ruling

The CRA held that the supply is of intangible personal property because the software is other than custom software and is delivered by electronic means. The CRA explained that:

> Depending on the medium by which it is supplied, the supply of software that is not custom designed software may be a supply of tangible personal property (TPP) or intangible personal property (IPP). As the software supplied by XXX by way of license is not customized for a particular client and is supplied and delivered by electronic means via the internet, the supply is considered ... to be a supply of IPP.

In this case, given that the software cannot be used in Canada, the GST would not apply. However, even if the supply were considered to be made in Canada, the CRA confirmed that zero-rating would have been available under section 10:

> ... the CCRA considers the supply of software by way of license that is a supply of IPP to be a supply of intellectual property.

Conclusions

1. The supply of other than custom software by electronic means is considered a supply of intangible personal property.

2. The software is considered to be supplied in Canada if it may be used in Canada.

3. The supply of a license to download and use software is considered to be a supply of intellectual property which qualifies for zero-rating under section 10.

---

[14] February 17, 2003.

Ruling 8: Electronically Delivered Software

Ruling 30860[15] considers a similar factual situation. The supplier licenses software (which is not in any way customized) to its clients. The software is to be downloaded from the supplier's Web site.

The Ruling

The CRA concluded that the license to the software was intangible personal property. The supply was made in Canada because there were no restrictions as to the location where the software may be used.

However, the CRA ruled that this supply qualifies as intellectual property. As a result zero-rating is available under section 10:

> A supply of software made by way of license, such as the supply of software made by XXXXX by way of license is a supply that qualifies for zero-rating under this provision ...

Conclusions

1. The licensing of software through the supplier's Web site is considered a supply of intangible personal property.

2. Where the software is provided by way of license the supply will be considered intellectual property and will qualify for zero-rating.

Ruling 9: Software Licensed for Re-supply Purposes

In ruling 32644[16] the supplier provides software by way of license to non-resident entities with the understanding that the non-resident entities will re-supply the software by way of license to their own customers. The software is not custom software.

The supplier allows for downloading of the software from its Web site. However, if the customer would like to be provided with a hard copy the supplier will send the master copy on a CD.

The Ruling

The CRA ruled that the software when downloaded from the Internet will be a supply of intangible property. The software will also qualify for zero-rating under section 10 when it is supplied in intangible format. However, when the software is supplied on a CD, it will be considered to be tangible personal property.

---

[15] May 27, 2003.

[16] June 24, 2003.

The ruling alludes to, but does not discuss, a number of important issues. One issue is how the tax applies where the supplier provides a particular customer with the software in both the electronic and the hard copy format but for a single consideration. The application of the two sets of rules could easily lead to different results.

The second issue is whether the "use" which must be considered in connection with the supply of intangible personal property (i.e., for the purposes of determining place of supply) is limited to the use by the immediate customer, or whether it should also include any subsequent "use" of the product (i.e., by customers of the customer). The better view is that the subsequent use would not be required to be taken into account.

Conclusions

1. The electronic supply of other than custom software is considered to be a supply of intangible personal property.

2. The supply of other than custom software on a carrier medium is a supply of tangible personal property.

3. Where the software is licensed to a user who intends to re-supply the software, it is not clear whether the "use" which must be taken into account in locating the supply is the use only by the customer of the supplier, or whether subsequent uses must also be taken into account. The better view seems to be that subsequent use is not required to be taken into account.

Ruling 10: Software Licensed to Indian Bands

Ruling 51795[17] considers software which is supplied by way of license to Indian bands and band empowered entities. The software in issue which is not custom software could be provided in either a physical format or in an electronic format.

The Ruling

The CRA ruled that the software is a supply of intangible personal property when supplied electronically (i.e., downloaded from the Internet) and it is a supply of tangible personal property when delivered on a CD.

This ruling (including the circumstances in which the supply may be made on an exempt basis in connection with the reserve) is discussed in Chapter 18, Indians and Band Councils.

---

[17] March 14, 2005.

Conclusions

1. Software which is not custom software and which is downloaded from the supplier's Web site, is considered to be a supply of intangible personal property.

2. Software delivered on a CD is a supply of tangible personal property.

Ruling 11: Software in Various Formats

Ruling 25957[18] considers the supply of software in various formats. The supplier designs Web sites and in connection with this design work the supplier offers to:

(a) purchase off the shelf software for use on a client's Web site;

(b) modify existing software to meet the client's needs; and

(c) program from scratch for the client.

The Ruling

The CRA ruled that software delivered electronically is considered to be a supply of intangible personal property unless the software qualifies as custom software (i.e., ownership rights provided to the recipient):

> ... where the product is "off the shelf" software delivered on a tangible medium, it is characterized as a supply of tangible personal property. Where the software is supplied electronically (downloaded as a digitized product) it is considered to be a supply of intangible personal property. Programming which involves modifying existing software (client owned software) or programming from scratch a customized solution where the client owns the software upon completion is characterized as a service.

It would appear from the above that any software purchased for use on the Web site was in fact re-supplied to the customer (and not used merely an input to some other supply).

Conclusion

The electronic delivery of software will be considered a supply of intangible personal property unless the software is custom software.

(ii) Rights to Download and Use Software on a Temporary Basis

It is not uncommon for software to be available for download and use for only a limited period of time. Unless a renewal payment is made the

---

[18] October 9, 2001.

software will typically become unusable after the contract period has expired.

There are no rulings which specifically consider the issue of software which may be downloaded and used for only a limited period of time. However, this issue was considered in TIB 090 (example 2). In that example, the customer was provided with the right to download and use software for a period of time which was less than the useful life of the product. Upon termination of the license, the copies of the software became unusable or were deleted. The example merely noted that this is considered to be a supply of intangible personal property.

The example did not discuss whether this offering would qualify for zero-rating under section 10. However, given that for place of supply purposes the CRA treats temporary downloads of software in the same manner as unlimited duration software, it would appear that zero-rating would be available for both forms of software.

The manner in which the CRA now characterizes the supply of the right to use software on a temporary basis should be contrasted with its earlier position as set out in TIB 037. In that earlier administrative document, the CRA had stated that the provision of the right to use software for a limited period of time was a supply of a service. The CRA explained at that time, that no rights were being supplied when the recipient receives a limited duration right to use software. It would appear, given example 2 in TIB 090, that this position is no longer valid.

(iii) Mere Rights to Use Software While Online (No Downloading of Software)

The CRA has consistently held that the right to access software while online (i.e., software which does not download to the user's computer and which is not provided by way of license) is a supply of intangible personal property.

This type of supply does not, according to the CRA constitute a supply of intellectual property. As a result, the CRA has taken the position that zero-rating under section 10 is not available. However, this position may be open to challenge in light of the Tax Court's decision in *Dawn's Place Ltd.*, which is described above.

Ruling 12: Right to Use Software While Online

Ruling 33383[19] considers the situation where the supplier provides rights to its customer to access and use software which resides and executes

---

[19] December 18, 2002.

on the supplier's server. The contract also allows for the clients of the customer to access and use the software when they visit the customer's Web site. The software provides currency conversions.

The software appears on the customer's Web site as if it actually is a part of the Web site. However, the use by the customer (and by its clients) of the software, always involves an interaction with the supplier's servers on which the software resides. The customers of the supplier are all over the world (as are their clients).

The supplier retains all intellectual property rights in the software.

The Ruling

The CRA concluded that the right to access and use the software was a supply of intangible personal property. This supply was deemed to be made in Canada because it was not limited to use outside Canada.

The CRA also concluded that zero-rating is not available under section 10. In reaching this conclusion the CRA noted that the principal object of the supply was the right provided to end users to access and use the software.

The CRA seems to be making the distinction between the right to download software under a full software license (where zero-rating is available), and more limited rights to use software (where zero-rating is not available).

Conclusions

1. Where rights to use software are provided and the access to the software is provided electronically the supply will be considered intangible personal property.

2. The supply will not qualify for zero-rating. This appears to be because the software does not download to the recipient's computer or because all intellectual property rights are reserved by the supplier.

Ruling 13: Software Which does not Download

Ruling 34397[20] also considers software which does not download to the recipient's computer. The GST registered Canadian supplier provides access to its online interactive keyboard program for a fee. The employees of the applicant regularly develop and maintain the program. The employees also provide training, technical support, and other related services.

---

[20] September 23, 2002.

The access is sold to government agencies, schools, individuals, and music training centres. The software application is hosted on a server which is owned by the company and which is located in its offices in Canada. Clients are provided with individual codes to access the program. The clients are not allowed to download any permanent file to their computer.

The Ruling

The CRA noted that the application of the principal object test would likely result in the conclusion that a single supply of access to an online interactive music program was provided (with technical support and systems for administration, evaluation, and monitoring of student progress). Given this characterization, the supply would be considered to be intangible personal property (i.e., the right to use and interact with software while on line).

In terms of the place of supply, the CRA noted that absent restrictions as to use outside Canada, the supply would be considered to be made in Canada. The CRA also went on to suggest that to qualify as a supply outside Canada, however, the contract would need to restrict the use both to a specific school and to the computers located in that school.

The CRA ruled that zero-rating would not be available because the software does not qualify as a supply of intellectual property.

> ... in this situation there are no provisions in Schedule VI to the ETA that would zero rate the supply by the Company of access and interaction with its software application while online.

Conclusions

1. The provision of online access to a software program is considered a supply of intangible personal property.

2. Online access to software is not considered a supply of intellectual property and does not qualify for zero-rating.

Ruling 14: Software and Data Processing

Ruling 30957[21] considers the provision of software along with a number of related supplies. The supplier provides data processing services which involves the use of software which resides on the supplier's mainframe in the U.S. Canadian customers access this software remotely from Canada.

There is a separate software agreement relating to the "use" of the software. It is not clear whether any separate fee is charged for the right to

---

[21] November 21, 2002.

use the software apart from the monthly access fee which is charged to the customer for the right to access the mainframe.

The software is used by the customers for inventory control, accounting, sales documentation and other business purposes. The supplier notes that its system allows customers to avoid the requirement to purchase expensive computer hardware.

The Ruling

The CRA ruled that a single supply is being made of a right to use software. This is a supply of intangible personal property.

> ... it appears that the supply being made ... is a single supply of the right to use software, which is a supply of intangible personal property. Although X co. is also hosting the software and undertaking the necessary steps in order to allow the client to access that software, the supply is essentially the provision of the right to use software.

In reaching this conclusion, the CRA noted that if the clients were to receive any one of the elements alone (e.g., connection to mainframe, installation of hardware at customer's site, needs analysis and systems design) they would not serve any useful purpose.

In terms of place of supply the CRA ruled that if the right to use software may be exercised from Canada, the supply will be made in Canada.

In order to determine the province of supply, the rules in Part III of Schedule IX should be considered. The rule in subparagraph $2(d)(i)$ would apply only if all or substantially all of the Canadian rights in respect of the supply of the software may be used in only one province. Where the rights are not restricted in this manner, the rule in subparagraph $2(d)(ii)$ provides that the supply is made in the province of negotiation as long as the rights may be used otherwise than exclusively outside that province. Where the place of negotiation is outside Canada, the supply will be made in a participating province if the property can only be used exclusively in Canada, and the Canadian rights can only be used primarily in the participating provinces. Otherwise, the supply will be considered to be made in an other than participating province.

The ruling did not consider the issue of whether zero-rating might be available. The suggestion appears to be that zero-rating would not be available.

Conclusions

1. The supply of the right to access and use software supported by the right to remotely access the supplier's hardware for the purposes of data

processing may be considered a single supply of intangible personal property (i.e., the right to access software).

2. The supply will be considered to be made in Canada where the software may be accessed or used from a location in Canada.

3. Where there are no restrictions as to locations where the software may be used and the place of negotiation is outside Canada, the supply will not be subject to HST.

4. It does not appear that zero-rating is available in respect of this supply of software access.

Ruling 15: Right to Access Information and Use Search Software

In ruling 36605[22] the supplier provides subscribers who are engaged in a particular industry with the right to access its Web site for news stories, articles, legislation, forms, surveys and reference materials. The supplier describes the supply as a supply of an information service.

Subscribers are also provided with the right to use software programs owned by the supplier to perform search functions. The subscribers do not acquire any ownership rights in respect of the software programs which are stored on the supplier's Web site but which are used to access the information. The subscribers also do not acquire any ownership rights in respect of the information provided. However, they may print and make copies of the materials, subject to certain restrictions.

The Ruling

The CRA ruled that the supply of the right to access and use information and the right to access and use the software which is required to search and retrieve the information is considered to be a supply of intangible personal property.

The place of supply will be determined by reference to the location where the user may access and use the information. The province of supply considerations are the same as those set out in ruling 14 above.

The CRA noted that "the supply of the right to access information" is not a supply which would qualify for zero-rating.

Conclusions

1. The supply of the right to access online information which is supported by the right to access and use software (to perform search functions)

---

[22] October 28, 2002.

is considered a single supply of intangible personal property (i.e., the right to receive information).

2. The supply will be made in Canada if the information may be accessed or used in Canada.

3. The supply will not qualify for zero-rating.

(iv) Application Hosting

Ruling 16: Application Hosting

Ruling 42607[23] considers an application hosting arrangement. The software resides and executes on the supplier's server. The customer is not entitled to copy or download the software. The customer accesses the software remotely from the Internet or from a dedicated telecommunications line.

The software relates to financial services and management accounting functions. Where a telecommunications line is used to access the software the telecommunication services are provided by a third party Internet service provider. Unlike the situation in ruling 33820 (below) the rights to the software are held by the supplier.

The customer is entitled however to download secondary software which facilitates access to the non-resident's server and which helps the customer to input data. The non-resident supplier will also provide the customer with access to information produced by using the software (either electronically or by way of hard copy report).

The Ruling

The CRA ruled that this is a supply of intangible personal property. The supply will be considered to be made in Canada (even though the software resides on the non-resident's server in the U.S.) if the software may be used in Canada. If there are no restrictions as to the place of use then it is assumed that the software may be used in Canada. The CRA noted that:

> ... in the above situation we would look at whether or not there are any restrictions with respect to where Corporation A may obtain access to, execute and operate the software application.

> Where there are no restrictions with respect to where the recipient may obtain access and use of the supplier's software application that is hosted on the supplier's server, the supply of access to and use of the software application is considered to be made in Canada regardless of where the server which hosts the software application is located. However, if an

---

[23] February 24, 2003.

agreement for the supply states that the recipient may only access and use the software application from its computers located outside Canada, the supply would be considered to be made outside Canada even in the case where the software application is hosted on a server in Canada.

The supplier in this case was GST registered and accordingly was not entitled to take advantage of the non-resident override.

The ruling does not discuss zero-rating. However, it would appear given the results in other similar rulings, that the supply would not be considered to be intellectual property (because a full licence is not provided or because the software does not download to the recipient's computer). Accordingly, it would not qualify for zero-rating under section 10.

Conclusions

1. The supply of software by means of an application hosting arrangement is considered a supply of intangible personal property.

2. The supply will be made in Canada if the recipient may obtain access to, execute or operate the software from a location in Canada.

3. It is not clear whether zero-rating might be available in respect of application hosting.

Ruling 17: Application Hosting (Software Owned by Recipient)

In ruling 33820[24] the supplier, a Canadian GST registered person, provides application hosting. However, the supplier does not supply the software (either by license or otherwise) because the software which is hosted was developed by and owned by the customers.

The customer has entered into the application hosting arrangement to provide a means by which its own clients may access the software. The clients are not provided with a license to the software.

The Ruling

The CRA considers the supplier to be providing a service to the customer (i.e., the person who owns the software). This service would be considered to be supplied in Canada because of the equipment based place of performance rule or because of the "any activity" rule:

> Where the supply of the service including operations performed by a supplier's equipment that is located in Canada or where any activity related to the performance of the service supplied is undertaken in Canada, the

---

[24] March 17, 2003.

service is performed at least in part in Canada and consequently deemed to be made in Canada.

The tasks which should be taken into account in applying the activity based rule include tasks relating to maintaining the server (and which strictly speaking would not appear to be activities relating to the performance of the service). This conclusion follows from ruling 37297 (briefed in Chapter 16).

The CRA noted that this service should be expected to qualify for zero-rating under section 7.

Conclusions

1. The supply of application hosting, where the recipient of the supply holds pre-existing software rights is considered a supply of a service.

2. The service will be supplied in Canada where any activity related to the performance of the service is undertaken in Canada or where the supplier's equipment is located in Canada.

3. Zero-rating is typically available in respect of this service under section 7.

3. Software Which is Incidental to Some Other Supply

The two rulings described below discuss the provision of rights to use software in connection with the delivery of some other supply. This important issue is also discussed in greater detail in Chapter 15, Telecommunication Services and Related Supplies. Rulings 14 and 15 (above) should also be considered in connection with this issue.

Ruling 18: Software Which is a Component of Another Supply

Ruling 31642[25] considered issues relating to the provision of the rights to customers to use software. The supplier provided investment related data through its Web site. The data could be used to make charts, graphs or other displays to assist in evaluating investment opportunities and performance. The software was used to allow access to this data.

The customer was charged a monthly subscription fee for the right to access the data. The supplier did not levy any separate charge for the right to use the software.

---

[25] December 9, 2002.

The Ruling

The CRA ruled that the supply which was provided was of the right to access and use data. This is a supply of intangible personal property.

In concluding that the supply related to the data (and not to the software) the CRA seemed to be taking into account the fact that the software was provided for no charge and so was not the principal object of the supply.

The CRA also ruled that the supply of the right to access data would not qualify as a supply of intellectual property and so would not qualify for zero-rating.

Conclusions

1. Where the right to access information is supplied and in connection with that supply the customer is allowed to use software the supply will not be a supply of software.

2. The supply of the right to access data is a supply of intangible personal property but is not a supply of intellectual property.

Ruling 19: Package with Software

Ruling 38697[26] considered a supply of a business solutions package which appears to be investment related. The applicant supplier charges a monthly subscription fee to its customers for access to the following:

1. Access to a software program which allows the customer to create and edit portfolios for each of its clients. The customer is also allowed to store data on the applicant's server. The customer's clients are each provided with a password to access their own portfolios.

2. Access to software which allows the customer of the applicant to post information created by the customer on a server owned by the applicant. The customer would provide passwords to its clients to allow them to access the information.

3. Online marketing. The customer is provided with template software to create its own Web site. The customer then uses this Web site to advertise. The applicant hosts the customer's Web site.

The Ruling

The CRA seemed to take the position that the applicant was supplying intangible personal property in connection with items #1 and #2 but that

---

[26] March 7, 2003.

this was not a supply of software. This supply would not be considered to be intellectual property for zero-rating purposes.

The third item was a supply of an advertising service. This is because the principal object of the supply related to the advertising. Zero-rating could be available under sections 7 or 8.

Conclusions

1. A package which allows the customer to create portfolios and store data on the supplier's Web site may be considered to be a supply which is other than a supply of software notwithstanding that software is essential to the delivery of this supply.

2. The supply of the package will be considered to be intangible personal property where the entire process is automated and does not involve any human interaction.

4. Software Training, Technical Support, Updates and Related Issues

It is common for a wide variety of service and product offerings to be provided in connection with supplies of software. The more common offerings include:

(a) maintenance support;

(b) upgrades;

(c) technical support;

(d) installation support; and

(e) training.

The threshold issue to be considered where software is supported by another offering is whether the second offering constitutes a separate supply or whether a single supply of multiple elements is being provided. Where the second offering constitutes a separate supply the incidental supply rule should be considered. Where applicable the incidental supply rule will deem the second supply to be a component of the first supply.

Where it is determined that a single supply is being made then the principal object of the supply must be identified. As a general rule, where any of the offerings noted above are considered to form part of a single software related supply the principal object of the supply will usually be the right to access or use the software.

Where it is determined that the software related offering is a supply which is separate from the software (i.e., the offering is provided by a person other than the software supplier or where the offering seems to be independent from the software), the offering will be characterized as either a supply of a service or intangible personal property.

Where access to existing resources is provided to the user, the supply will be considered to be a supply of intangible personal property. This would typically include, for example, the provision of the rights to download updates from the supplier's Web site or the provision of support in the form of access to existing databases or other online resources. Where more personalized offerings are supplied, the supply will be considered a service. This may include, for example, one on one training, installation support, or technical support.

Where a package is provided which includes both access to existing resources and access to personalized services, the principal object of the supply is required to be identified.

Unfortunately, as demonstrated in many of the rulings set out below, the CRA will generally avoid discussing this distinction. The CRA has explained that this particular question of fact is to be resolved by the supplier.

Ruling 20: Installation, Technical Support and Upgrades

In ruling 33694[27], the applicant (a GST registered Canadian resident) licensed generic commercial software to its customers. A one time fee was paid for the license which included the right to have the software installed on the customer's computers, in the event that they required this assistance. Otherwise the software was mailed to the customer on a disk.

The applicant also offered customers the option of subscribing for technical support and updates under a separate agreement (the support and update agreement). This involved a separate annual fee. The technical support would be provided on-site, by telephone or by way of modem depending on the particular customer need. The updates would be delivered by mail or would be delivered by employees in person on visits to the customer's offices.

The Ruling

The CRA concluded that the shrink wrapped software would be considered a supply of tangible personal property. However, it did not discuss the characterization of the installation services included in the price of the

---

[27] January 14, 2003.

software. It would appear that the CRA, from its silence, regarded the services as forming a component of the single supply of the software.

The CRA explained that the technical support and updates would be characterized as separate supplies (apart from the software) and that they could be either services or a supply of intangible personal property.

If the principal object of the supply under the support and update agreement was the updates, then the supply would be intangible personal property. If the principal object was the technical support, the supply would be a service. It appears that a single supply of software was not considered as a possibility because of the existence of the separate agreement, and because of the separate consideration in respect of the support option.

Assuming that the principal object of the support supply is the right to receive updates, and assuming that the updates are delivered on a carrier medium (which was contemplated in the facts provided with the ruling), it is not clear why this supply would not be characterized as a supply of tangible personal property. For example, where the initial supply of software is provided on a carrier medium it is beyond dispute that tangible personal property is being supplied. It is not clear whether the CRA has administratively adopted the position that updates must never be tangible personal property or whether this result is merely anomalous.

The CRA specifically cautioned that if the supply was considered to be a service, it would qualify as a "computer related service" when provided by way of telecommunications. This would involve the application of the special province of supply rules contained in the Place of Supply (GST/HST) Regulations. The CRA did not discuss the manner in which these special province of supply rules would apply on the facts.

Conclusions

1. Where the service of installing software is provided to a customer for no additional charge (apart from the software fee) the installation service may be considered a component of a single supply of software.

2. Where a support agreement is entered into separately from the software licensing agreement the offerings provided under the support agreement will typically be considered to be a supply which is separate from the supply of the software.

3. Where the principal object of the support agreement is the provision of updates or access to an online database the supply will be considered intangible personal property. Where the principal object is the right to receive personalized services then the supply will be a service.

4. Technical support services are considered to be a "computer related service" and may be subject to special province of supply considerations which are set out in the Place of Supply (GST/HST) Regulations.

Ruling 21: Maintenance Included With Price of Software

In ruling 32644[28], the Canadian GST registered supplier provides software by way of license to non-residents. The customers will re-supply the software to their own customers.

The software (and supporting manuals) are all delivered electronically via the Internet. However, at the customer's request the software will be mailed on a carrier medium and a manual will be printed and mailed to the customer.

The license of the software includes the right to receive upgrades for no additional charge for a limited period of time. The supplier also offers an optional maintenance agreement which will allow for upgrades and technical support beyond the period provided for in the baseline agreement. A separate fee is charged for the optional agreement.

The Ruling

The CRA ruled that where the maintenance offerings are included with the cost of the software, a single supply will be considered to be made of the licensed software.

However, if the maintenance services involved a separate charge, a separate supply would be considered to be made. If the principal object of the supply of the maintenance contract is the upgrades, the supply is intangible personal property. However, if the principal object is the supply of technical support then the supply is a service.

Where a service is being provided the CRA noted that the four-part place of performance test should be considered to locate the supply.

In terms of zero-rating the CRA concluded that the services should be considered to be in the nature of advisory or consulting services and would typically qualify for zero-rating under section 23. The CRA also noted that if training services are provided, section 7 should be considered as the relevant zero-rating provision.

The CRA did not discuss the special province of supply rules contained in the Place of Supply (GST/HST) Regulations.

---

[28] June 24, 2003.

Conclusions

1. Maintenance offerings which are provided with the software for no additional fee will not be considered to be separate supplies apart from the software.

2. Maintenance offerings for which a separate charge is levied will be considered a separate supply. The principal object of the supply test will be used to determine whether the supply is intangible personal property or a service.

Ruling 22: Training and Technical Support

In ruling 34397[29], the supplier provided the right to access keyboard training programs. The supplier also offered training support to its licensees with respect to the appropriate use of the software.

The Ruling

The CRA concluded that where a single charge is levied for access and technical and curriculum support, and administration and evaluation systems, a single supply of intangible personal property would be supplied which is in the nature of the right to access the program.

However, if the training is considered to be a separate supply then the training would be considered a service. The suggestion was that the training would only be a separate supply where a separate training related charge was levied. If the training were considered to form part of the single supply of the right to use software then the single supply would be considered a supply of intangible personal property.

The CRA noted that a separate supply of training would ordinarily qualify for zero-rating under section 7. However, the right to access the program would not qualify for zero-rating.

Conclusions

1. Where a single charge is levied for the right to access a software program, and included in that charge are rights to receive technical support and other related offerings the presumption is that a single supply is being made. The single supply is in the nature of the right to receive access to the software.

2. Where a separate charge is levied for any of the secondary offerings then the presumption seems to be that they will be considered a separate supply.

---

[29] September 23, 2002.

3. The supply of training is a service which will typically qualify for zero-rating under section 7.

Ruling 23: Technical Support

Ruling 51795[30] considers the supply of software and a software support plan. Purchasers of the software are entitled to receive services related to troubleshooting and related to general operation of the software. The principal object of the supply is the technician's services.

The Ruling

The software was considered to be a supply of intangible personal property because it was other than custom software and it was delivered electronically.

The CRA held that if the cost of the software support plan was included in the software license fees, a single supply of software would have been made.

However, if there is a separate charge for the support plan then the CRA will consider that a separate supply has been made. The separate supply will be considered to be a service if it relates to access to the work of technicians, interaction with technicians or specific work performed by technicians. However, if the support relates to the provision of a right to use existing technical information (for example online documents or access to a troubleshooting database) and the interaction with the technicians is incidental then the supply will be intangible personal property.

Conclusions

1. Where a support plan is provided for no additional charge with software, a single supply of software will be made.

2. A separate supply will be considered to be made where there is a separate charge for the support plan.

Ruling 24: Software and Hardware Maintenance

Ruling 36218[31] considers the provision of hardware and software maintenance services. The supplier is a non-resident who provides the services to Canadian customers. In most cases the problems are resolved by way of the telephone or by way of email with instructions provided by the supplier from

---

[30] March 14, 2005.

[31] February 5, 2004.

its offices in the U.S. However, remote diagnostics are also used to solve problems. The package also allows for the customer to download updates.

The Ruling

The CRA concluded that if the principal object of the supply is the provision of technical support provided by interaction with technicians, a service is being provided. This would be considered specific work done for a specific customer. If, however, the principal object of the supply is the right to obtain software (and that software is bundled with interactive technical support or with the right to access a technical database), a supply of intangible personal property is being provided.

Where a service is being provided, the four-part place of performance test should be considered. In particular the third branch of the test (which relates to remote access) suggests that the service would be performed in Canada where the supplier logs on to the customer's computer in Canada.

It is not clear how the remote diagnostic (or remote access) test will apply where the supplier *might* be required to log on to the customer's computer to repair a particular issue, but it is not known at the time the contract is entered into whether this access will be required. For example, it is not clear whether a GST registered, non-resident supplier who repairs 95% of all problems without employing the remote access option should charge GST to all of its Canadian customers (on the basis that it might be required to obtain remote access).

Conclusions

1. Where a separate supply of technical support is provided (apart from software), the principal object of the supply must be determined in order to characterize the supply as either intangible personal property or a service.

2. Where a service is provided, the four-part place of performance rules should be considered to locate the supply.

3. Where the supplier remotely logs in to the customer's computer in Canada to provide the service, the service will be performed in Canada.

4. It is not clear how this test should be applied where the supplier does not know, at the time the supply is made to a particular customer, whether it will be required to obtain remote access to that customer's computer.

Ruling 25: Other Software Related Offerings

In ruling 30860[32], the software supplier provides secondary offerings which relate more to the content than to the functionality of the software.

The applicant is a GST registered person who provides software (which relates to managing retail operations) by way of license. The customer downloads the software from the Internet. The supplier also offers what it refers to as "online services" which relate to managing retail operations. A separate charge is levied for this optional offering.

The Ruling

The CRA held that the software is intangible personal property and that the "online services" are also a supply of intangible personal property. Each of the supplies will be considered to be made in Canada if the property may be accessed or used in Canada.

In reaching the conclusion that the online services are intangible personal property (and not a service) the CRA seemed to take into account that there is no personalized component to the offering. Instead the subscribers are allowed to access various pre-existing content including calculation applications, data and reports.

The CRA concluded that the software will qualify as intellectual property as it is provided by way of license agreement. Accordingly, the software would qualify for zero-rating under section 10. However, the "online services" (which are in fact intangible property) do not qualify as intellectual property and so are not zero-rated.

Conclusions

1. The right to access secondary offerings which are in the nature of existing content will be considered to be a supply of intangible personal property notwithstanding that the supplier has characterized the offering as being in the nature of a service.

2. The right to access digitized information is not a supply which is eligible for zero-rating under section 10.

---

[32] May 27, 2003.

Chapter 15

Telecommunication Services and Related Supplies

A. OVERVIEW

One of the most important threshold issues to be resolved with respect to any e-commerce supply is whether the supply is a telecommunication service. As every e-commerce supply involves an element of telecommunications, this distinction may be very difficult to draw.

The identification of supplies which are in the nature of telecommunication services is particularly important because telecommunication services are subject to a number of special considerations. These include special telecommunication specific place of supply and province of supply rules. Telecommunications are also subject to special zero-rating rules which are far more restrictive than the rules which apply to ordinary services.

This chapter focuses in particular on making the distinction between telecommunication services and other than telecommunication services. The manner in which the GST applies to telecommunication services will be discussed. This chapter will also focus upon the application of the GST to a number of services which are not telecommunication services but which rely heavily upon telecommunications for the delivery of the particular supply.

Among the supplies considered in this chapter are:

(a) supplies made by ISPs;

(b) security related supplies;

(c) teleconferencing supplies;

(d) long distance supplies;

(e) wide area network supplies;

(f) the supply of bandwidth;

(g) data processing; and

(h) data backup.

B. CHARACTERIZATION OF THE SUPPLIES

1. Distinction Between Telecommunication Services and Other Services

Where a supply is being made which involves a telecommunications element, a threshold determination must be made as to whether:

(a) the supply is a supply of a telecommunication service; or

(b) telecommunications are used as a means by which other property and services are supplied.

The CRA, in TIB 090, underscores the importance of this critical issue in the following manner:

> The characterization of supplies made by electronic means extends beyond determining whether a supply is intangible personal property or a service, to determining whether a supply may be a telecommunication service. The definition of a telecommunication service in the Act is broad, and because of the nature of electronic commerce, a number of typical supplies made by electronic means are also telecommunication services.
>
> If a supply is characterized as a telecommunication service it is subject to special place of supply and zero-rating rules for telecommunication services.

Where it has been determined that a particular supply is a supply of intangible personal property, it follows that the supply cannot be a supply of a telecommunication service. The telecommunications will be considered to be a means by which the intangible personal property is supplied. However, where it is determined that a service is being supplied, consideration should be given as to whether that supply is a telecommunication service.

2. Predominant Purpose Test

To determine whether a telecommunication service is being supplied, the CRA has developed a "predominant purpose" test. TIB 090 states that generally a telecommunication service is being supplied where the predominant purpose of the supply relates to any of the following:

(a) providing for the emission, transmission or reception of signs, signals, etc. (e.g., voice or data) through a telecommunications network or similar technical system;

(b) making available a telecommunications facility for the emission, transmission or reception of signs, signals, etc., through a telecommunications network or similar technical system; or

(c) providing a means through which other services or intangible personal property (e.g., content in a digitized format) are delivered, rather than to provide the services or intangible personal property.

Conversely, the CRA provides that a supply will likely not be considered a telecommunication service where:

(d) a telecommunication service is used or consumed by the supplier in making a supply of a service or property (other than the supply of a telecommunication service);

(e) the supply includes the provision of a telecommunication service, but only as a means of delivering another service or property; or

(f) the telecommunication service supply is incidental to the supply of another service or property.

The test in part (d) requires that the supplier distinguish between "inputs" to the supply (which are not to be taken into account in characterizing the supply), and the elements of the supply itself. Although in theory it may appear that drawing this distinction would be relatively straightforward, in practice this is typically a very difficult issue to resolve. This same difficult distinction with respect to inputs is also required to be made in resolving the single versus multiple supply issue. Accordingly, the administrative guidance which has been provided with respect to bundled supplies on that issue may also be of assistance with respect to telecommunication services.[1]

Where the telecommunication service is a component of what is being provided to the customer (i.e., the telecommunication service is not an input), it does not necessarily follow that a telecommunication service is being supplied. This is as a result of the part (e) and (f) tests. Each time a supply is made, which comprises a telecommunication service component and an other than telecommunication service component, rules (e) and (f) must be reconciled against rule (c).

In fact, many of the rulings described below relate to situations where a telecommunication service was provided to the customer as a component of a supply but the supply was characterized as other than a telecommunication service. It should be noted that the "predominant purpose" test appears to be very similar to the "principal object" test which the CRA uses to characterize a single supply which is comprised of multiple elements. In effect, under either test, the CRA will draw a conclusion as to which of the various components of the supply represents the essence (or true value) of the supply.[2]

3. TIB 090 Examples

The following are summaries of examples provided in TIB 090 which demonstrate the manner in which the CRA distinguishes between telecommunication services and other than telecommunication services. The full version of the examples are set out in Chapter 3, Characterization of Supplies.

---

[1] Single versus multiple supplies are discussed in Chapter 4, Single versus Multiple Supplies.

[2] The "principal object" test is described in detail in Chapter 4.

Supply	Telecommunication Service?	Rationale
An ISP provides consumers with access to the Internet by providing the user with a modem.	Yes	The predominant purpose of the service is to provide the recipient with a connection to the Internet.
A supplier provides email services to a corporate customer. Incoming and outgoing mail is routed through the server which is connected to a network.	Yes	The predominant purpose of the service is to allow the customer to send and receive emails.
An ISP provides Web site hosting. The ISP houses the website of the customer on its servers, provides security for the website and ensures that the Web site is accessible over the Internet.	No	The predominant purpose of the supply is the storage and maintenance of the Web site. The ISP consumes a telecommunication service in providing the service.
An ISP provides a customer with Internet access, an email account and space on the ISPs server to host a Web page.	Yes	The predominant purpose of this single supply is allowing the customer to connect to the Internet.
A supplier provides consumers with a service which allows the consumer to make calls over the Internet through its own computer.	Yes	The predominant purpose is to provide the transmission of voice communication.
A supplier is retained by a tax preparer to efile income tax returns which have been prepared by the tax preparer. The supplier validates the data before sending.	Yes	The predominant purpose of the service is to electronically transmit data.
A supplier is retained by an individual to prepare and electronically file its tax return with the CRA.	No	The predominant purpose of the single supply is the preparation of the tax return (and not the electronic filing of the return).

Supply	Telecommunication Service?	Rationale
The supplier provides consumers with the right to access and download digitized products.	No	The supply is of the right to access and use intangible personal property. The supplier uses a telecommunication service to provide the supply.
The supplier provides consumers with the right to receive audio or visual content over the Internet (which is broadcast in real time).	Yes	The predominant purpose of the service is to provide broadcast content. This supply is analogous to that which is provided by a traditional television or radio broadcaster.

4. Guiding Principles

The examples set out above suggest that the following guiding principles should be considered in determining whether a supply is a telecommunication service.

(a) The provision by an ISP of:

(i) access to the Internet is a telecommunication service;

(ii) access to the Internet with other bundled services such as email accounts or the right to host a Web page is usually a telecommunication service;

(iii) Web site hosting is a service, but it is not a telecommunication service; and

(iv) Web site design is not a telecommunication service.

(b) The provision of a service which allows for the consumer to make telephone calls (or transmit data) over the Internet is a telecommunication service.

(c) The provision of a service of transmitting data for a customer is a telecommunication service. However, where the service requires that the supplier perform substantial functions related to creating or manipulating the data prior to sending the data, then the supply may be other than a telecommunication service.

(d) For some supply offerings, the CRA will take into account whether the service in issue is analogous to that which is provided by suppliers who do not make supplies through the Internet. For example, where the service in issue is analogous to a traditional broadcasting service, the service will more likely be considered a telecommunication service. The application of this special principle may lead to seemingly anomalous or inconsistent results. For example, the CRA's current position appears to be that:

(i) where consumers are provided with the right to access digitized content over the Internet, this will be a supply of intangible personal property; but

(ii) where consumers are provided with the right to access live streaming over the Internet, this will be considered a supply of a telecommunication service.

C. PLACE OF SUPPLY ISSUES

1. Intangible Personal Property and Services Which are Other Than Telecommunications Services

Where it has been determined that a particular supply is other than the supply of a telecommunication service, the ordinary place of supply rules will apply. A full description of these place of supply rules is contained in Chapter 5, Place of Supply. Specific rulings on these issues are provided in Chapter 16, Online Content, Services, and Other General Offerings.

2. Telecommunication Services

(a) GST

Where it has been determined that a telecommunication service is being supplied, the place of supply rules which will apply are contained in section 142.1 of the ETA. However, to apply those rules, the nature of the telecommunication service must first be determined. The service may be either:

(a) the service of emitting, transmitting or receiving signs, signals, writing, images or sounds or intelligence of any nature by wire, cable, radio, optical or other electromagnetic system or by any similar system; or

(b) making available for such emission, transmission, or reception telecommunications facilities of a person who carries on the business of supplying services referred to in paragraph (a).

This distinction is important because different place of supply rules will apply to each of the types of supplies. The supply will be deemed to be made in Canada if:

(a) in the case of a telecommunication service of making telecommunications facilities available, the facilities or any part thereof are located in Canada; and

(b) in any other case,

(i) the telecommunication is emitted and received in Canada; or

(ii) the telecommunication is emitted or received in Canada, and the billing location for the service is in Canada.

The term "telecommunications facility" is defined in the following manner:

... any facility, apparatus or other thing (including any wire, cable, radio, optical or other electromagnetic system or any similar technical system, or any part thereof) that is used or is capable of being used for telecommunications.

The broad manner in which the facilities based place of supply rule operates is demonstrated by the following TIB 090 example:

An ISP located in Canada provides Internet access to customers. Internet access is a telecommunication service which involves making available telecommunications facilities.

The supply of the Internet access is deemed to be made in Canada as the facilities or part thereof which enables connection to the Internet are located in Canada.

The rulings described later in this chapter further emphasize the broad nature of these rules.

(b) HST

It is only where a supply is deemed to be made in Canada that the province of supply rules must be considered. A telecommunication service which is supplied outside Canada, either because of the application of the place of supply rules contained in section 142.1 or because of the non-resident override in section 143, cannot be supplied in a participating province.

Where a telecommunication service is supplied in Canada, the province of supply rules which may be applicable are located in the following sections:

(a) **Part VIII of Schedule IX:** This part contains the general province of supply rules relating to telecommunication services.

(b) **Place of Supply (GST/HST) Regulations:** Section 10 of the regulations establishes special province of supply rules which where applicable will override the province of supply rules contained in Part VIII of Schedule IX. These rules apply to:

(i) a computer related service

A "computer related service" includes a technical support service provided by means of telecommunications. However, a technical support service would not likely be considered to be a telecommunication service because the telecommunications element is merely the means by which the service is delivered. A "computer related service" also includes a service involving the electronic storage of information and computer-to-computer transfers of information. These would both typically be considered to be telecommunication services.

(ii) Internet access

As noted in the TIB 090 examples described above, the supply of Internet access is considered to be a telecommunication service.

(c) **Section 9 of the Place of Supply (GST/HST) Regulations:** This section provides special rules relating to a service accessed by dialing 1-900 or 1-976 numbers. However, as these supplies are not considered to be in the nature of e-commerce, these rules are not considered in this book.

(d) **Section 136.4:** The granting of sole access to a recipient of a communications channel which is to be used to transmit telecommunications between a place in a participating province and a place in another province is considered to be two separate supplies, each of which will be taxed according to the proportion of the channel which is located in the respective province.

A detailed description of the manner in which the province of supply rules listed above operate is contained in Chapter 5, Place of Supply.

D. NON-RESIDENT ISSUES

Non-residents who provide telecommunication services in Canada should be particularly aware of the circumstances in which they may be required to be registered. Telecommunication service providers, in addition to relying upon servers to provide the service, may also rely upon other equipment including routers, network equipment and switches. The ownership of or use of equipment which is located in Canada will always be taken into account in applying the carrying on business in Canada test and the permanent establishment test.

1. Permanent Establishment Issue

A non-resident will be deemed to be resident in Canada in respect of supplies made through a permanent establishment of the supplier which is located in Canada. The CRA has emphasized throughout TIB 090 that equipment, including equipment which operates automatically, may be considered to constitute a permanent establishment.

Although the CRA in TIB 090 has focused upon explaining how servers may meet the equipment requirements, there is every reason to believe that other equipment will also be required to be taken into account. This should be expected to include any of the equipment listed in the definition of "telecommunications facility".

Where a non-resident telecommunication service provider relies upon equipment located in Canada to deliver any supply which is significant in relation to the business of the supplier, it should be expected that the equipment will constitute a permanent establishment of the non-resident. The equipment need not necessarily be owned by the non-resident. The equipment will meet the requisite test if it is at the disposal of the non-resident (i.e., the non-resident has access to the equipment). Conversely, if the equipment in issue is not at the disposal of the non-resident, the equipment will not constitute a permanent establishment of the non-resident under part (a) of the permanent establishment definition.

Where supplies are made by a non-resident telecommunication service provider through a dependent agent, any permanent establishment of the agent may also be considered to be a permanent establishment of a non-resident. This is a rule provided for in part (b) of the definition of permanent establishment.

To the extent that the non-resident is making supplies through a permanent establishment in Canada, the non-resident will be deemed to be resident in Canada and the non-resident override will not be available.

2. Carrying on Business Issue

The CRA has noted in TIB 090 that a non-resident would be expected to have a substantial presence in Canada before being considered to be carrying on business in Canada. The CRA has also emphasized that the determination of whether a person is carrying on business in the e-commerce environment will involve special considerations which take into account the particular supply being provided. It is difficult to ascertain with any certainty what these special considerations might be.

However, it is clear from Policy Statement P-051R2, "Carrying on Business in Canada", that where services are provided in Canada, there will always be an enhanced risk that the non-resident will be found to be carrying on business in Canada. This risk is even further exacerbated where the service involves a greater number of Canadian customers, where the services are provided over a prolonged duration, or where the services involve increased presence in Canada.

In applying the carrying on business test, issues relating to tax leakage and other tax policy considerations should also be taken into account. For example, if the non-resident were allowed to provide the services in Canada with the benefit of the override, would the CRA suffer tax leakage? Further, if the non-resident were allowed to provide the services in Canada with the benefit of the override, would this place Canadian suppliers or non-resident registered suppliers at a competitive disadvantage?

E. ZERO-RATING ISSUES

The circumstances in which zero-rating is available for supplies of telecommunication services are extremely narrow. Section 22.1 of Part V of Schedule VI provides that zero-rating will only be available in the following circumstances:

> A supply of a telecommunication service where the supply is made by a registrant who carries on the business of supplying telecommunication services, to a non-resident person who is not a registrant and who carries on such a business, but not including a supply of a telecommunication service where the telecommunication is emitted and received in Canada.

This zero-rating provision is highly unusual in a number of respects because it requires that:

(a) the supplier be a registrant (registered or required to be registered);

(b) the non-resident be engaged in the business of supplying telecommunication services; and

(c) the non-resident not be a registrant.

The second and third tests described above place a high level of responsibility upon the supplier to obtain assurances from the recipient. For example, a Canadian telecommunication service provider may provide services to a non-resident who is not GST registered. However, if the non-resident in fact makes supplies in Canada in the course of a business carried on in Canada, and is not a small supplier, then it will be a registrant (i.e., it is required to register). As discussed in the section above, it may be very difficult to accurately determine whether a non-resident is carrying on business in Canada.

F. RULINGS

The rulings are organized into the following categories:

(a) Internet service providers.

(b) Web site design, maintenance and hosting.

(c) Internet Security.

(d) Teleconferencing, long distance, bandwidth and networks.

(e) Data processing and access to mainframe.

1. Internet Service Providers

Ruling 1: Internet Access

Ruling 42342[3] considers issues relating to the supply of Internet access to a non-resident corporation. The Canadian GST registered ISP invoices the Canadian parent company of the non-resident for the supply of Internet access, the benefit of which is enjoyed by the non-resident. The server which provides the connection to the Internet is located in the U.S.

The Ruling

The CRA ruled that providing access to the Internet is a telecommunication service of making a telecommunications facility available. This is the service which is described in part (b) of the definition of "telecommunication service".

The CRA concluded that pursuant to section 142.1, the supply is deemed to be made outside Canada:

> Based on the information provided and assuming that, as well as the server, all other facilities, or any part thereof, that are used or are capable of being used to enable connection to the Internet are located outside Canada, the

---

[3] September 23, 2002.

Internet access supplied by the ISP to the Canadian company's subsidiary is not deemed to be a supply made in Canada.

It is interesting to note, from the passage referred to above, that the CRA seems to have suggested that the supply was made to the non-resident. However, this position does not seem to be correct. This is because the Canadian parent company was the person who agreed to be legally responsible for the payment of the ISP services. Fortunately, the conclusion reached by the CRA as to the manner in which the tax applies does not turn on this particular issue.

Conclusions

1. The provision of Internet access is a telecommunication service of making telecommunications facilities available.

2. The supply is made in Canada if any of the facilities (i.e., servers or other hardware) which allow for connection to the Internet, are located in Canada.

3. Where all of the facilities are located outside Canada, the supply is made outside Canada.

Ruling 2: Internet Access

In ruling 33056[4] the applicant, a GST registered Canadian company, describes its business as a "global Internet service provider". The ruling sets out three different scenarios for consideration.

Issue 1

In the first scenario, the Internet access is provided to a non-resident in circumstances where there is no telecommunications facility in Canada which would allow for connection to the Internet. The server and all other facilities used by the supplier to provide the service are located outside Canada.

Ruling on Issue 1

The CRA held that the service in issue is to be characterized as a telecommunication service under part (*b*) of the definition of "telecommunication service" (the service of making telecommunications facilities available).

Pursuant to paragraph 142.1(2)(*a*), a supply of making telecommunications facilities available is deemed to be a supply made in Canada where any of the telecommunications facilities are located in Canada. Where the facili-

---

[4] September 12, 2002.

ties are located outside Canada, as is the case here, the supply is deemed to be made outside Canada. Given that the supply is deemed to be made outside Canada, there is no need to consider the rules relating to the province of supply.

The CRA, however, cautioned that the definition of "telecommunications facility" is extremely broad and includes:

> ... any facility, apparatus or other thing (including any wire, cable, radio, optical or other electromagnetic system, or any similar technical system, or any part thereof) that is used or is capable of being used for telecommunications.

The suggestion seemed to be that the supplier should carefully consider whether any facility might be located in Canada.

Issue 2

In this scenario, the supply is also made to a non-resident but some of the facilities which allow for connection to the Internet are located in Canada.

Ruling on Issue 2

The CRA ruled that this supply of a telecommunication service is deemed to be made in Canada under the rule set out in paragraph 142.1(2)(a). This is because some of the facilities which allow for connection to the Internet are located in Canada.

The CRA noted that zero-rating might be available under section 22.1 of Part V of Schedule VI. The CRA noted that where zero-rating is not available (and it would appear that this particular supply would not qualify because the recipient is not in the business of re-supplying telecommunication services), the province of supply rules must be considered.

Section 3 of Part IX of Schedule IX references special province of supply override rules which are contained in the Place of Supply (GST/HST) Regulations. Where applicable these rules override the general province of supply rules contained in Schedule IX.

The supply of access to the Internet is a supply contemplated by the override rules. Section 10 of the Place of Supply (GST/HST) Regulations provides two separate rules for services relating to Internet access depending on whether there is to be a single final recipient of the service or multiple final recipients of the service. The term "final recipient" is defined as follows:

> "final recipient" in respect of a computer related service or access to the Internet, means a person who is the recipient of a supply of the service or

access and who acquires it otherwise than for the purpose of supplying it to another person.

The CRA summarized the operation of the subsection 10(1) rules as follows:

> ... when there is to be a single final recipient of a supply of Internet access made by a particular supplier, and the recipient acquires the supply under an agreement either with the particular supplier or another supplier, the supply is made in a particular province if the final recipient avails itself of the access at a single ordinary location in that province and:
>
> - the particular supplier maintains information sufficient to determine that location; or
>
> - it is the normal business practice of the particular supplier to obtain information sufficient to determine that location.

In any other case involving a single final recipient, the supply of Internet access will be made in a particular province if the mailing address of the recipient of the supply is in that province.

The CRA summarized the rules with respect to multiple final recipients as follows:

> ... Where in the case of each final recipient, there is a single location at which the final recipient avails itself of the access and:
>
> - either the particular supplier maintains information sufficient to determine that location; or
>
> - it is the normal business practice of the particular supplier to obtain information sufficient to determine that location;
>
> the supply is made in the province, if any, that would be determined under the place of supply rules for intangible personal property under Part III of Schedule IX to the Act ... to be the province in which the particular supply is made if the Internet access were attainable in each province in which, and to the same extent to which, the final recipients avail themselves of the access. In other words, the place of supply rules in this Schedule are to be applied to the supply of Internet access as a supply of intangible personal property.
>
> In any other case involving multiple final recipients, the supply of Internet access will be made in a particular province if the mailing address of the recipient is in that province.

Applying all of the above, the CRA concluded that this scenario involved a single final recipient (the recipient corporation) who availed itself of the Internet access at a single ordinary location in the U.S.

The first part of the "single final recipient" rule would not apply because the recipient, as a non-resident, did not avail itself of the service at a single ordinary location in a province. The second part of the "single final recipient" rule did not apply because the mailing address of the recipient is not in a province (the mailing address is in the U.S.).

Given that the rules in subsection 10(1) could not be applied to the particular supply, the general telecommunications province of supply rules contained in Part VIII of Schedule IX were to be considered. However, the application of those rules did not result in the supply being considered to be made in a participating province because the facilities were not located in a participating province and the invoice for the service was not sent to an address in a participating province. Accordingly, the supply was subject to GST at the rate of 6%.

Issue 3

In this scenario, a single supply of Internet access is provided to a non-resident company which has offices both in Canada and the U.S.

Ruling on Issue 3

The CRA noted at the outset that it assumed that the applicant is making a single supply of Internet access to a single final recipient. The CRA noted that this supply would be deemed to be made in Canada if any of the telecommunications facilities are located in Canada.

The CRA made an interesting point with respect to the availability of zero-rating under section 22.1. Given that zero-rating is not available where the supply is made to a person who is a resident of Canada, the CRA warned that the supplier should ensure that the recipient is not deemed to be resident in Canada under the rules contained in section 132. In this case, the recipient may not qualify as a non-resident because it has offices in Canada. Further, if, in fact zero-rating is not available, the CRA noted that the province of supply rules would need to be considered.

The CRA noted that the non-resident customer would be a single final recipient who avails itself of the services at more than one location (i.e., at its offices in Canada and in the U.S.). Accordingly, the first branch of the single final recipient rule would not apply (i.e., because of the multiple locations). The second branch of the single final recipient rule also would not apply because the mailing address of the recipient is outside Canada.

The CRA concluded that the supply would be subject to GST (but not HST). In reaching this conclusion, the CRA seems to have determined that the general telecommunications rule contained in section 2 of Part VIII does not apply. This rule provides that a telecommunication service of making telecommunications facilities available, is deemed to be supplied in a province where all of the telecommunications facilities are ordinarily located in that province. Alternatively, if all of the telecommunications facilities are not located in a single province, the supply will be deemed to be made in a particular province if the invoice for the supply of the service is sent to an address in that province. The invoice in this particular case was sent to an address outside Canada.

The CRA, however, warned that if the non-resident had qualified as a single final recipient who availed itself of the Internet access at a single ordinary location in a participating province, and the supplier maintained sufficient information to determine that location (or would be able to determine this location using ordinary business practices), the supply would be made in that province and would be subject to HST.

Secondary Issue

The CRA was also asked to comment on whether its conclusions would be different if the Internet access was provided by the applicant's U.S. affiliate on behalf of the applicant. The applicant noted that this would involve the U.S. affiliate making its facilities available to the applicant.

Ruling on Secondary Issue

The CRA noted very generally that this would be considered a substantial change in facts which would require a distinct analysis. For example, in Situation 2 (supply of access provided to non-resident by supplier with some facilities in Canada), the facilities would now be located in the U.S. and accordingly the supply would be deemed to be made outside Canada when supplied by the applicant. The CRA explained that:

> In this case the U.S. affiliate is supplying its facilities to the Company who is in turn making these facilities available to the non-resident and none of the Company's facilities in Canada are used or may be used to enable connection to the Internet. If in providing the non-resident's Internet access the Company's telecommunications facilities in Canada are made available to enable connection to the Internet in certain situations, for example, in circumstances where the U.S. affiliate's facilities cannot accommodate the connection, the supply of Internet access will be deemed to be made in Canada.

Conclusions

1. The provision of Internet access is a telecommunication service of making telecommunications facilities available.

2. The supply is made in Canada if any of the facilities (servers or other hardware) which allow for connection to the Internet are located in Canada.

3. If the supply is made in Canada, the province of supply override rules must be considered.

4. If there is a single final recipient of the Internet access service, the supply is made in a particular province if the recipient avails itself of the access at a single ordinary location in the province, and that location is known to the supplier or should be known to the supplier. If the recipient does not avail itself of the service at a single ordinary location, or if that location is not known and would not normally be known, then the supply will be made in the province in which the recipient has its mailing address.

5. If there are multiple final recipients of the Internet access service, and the final recipients avail themselves of the access at a single ordinary location in the province and that location is known to, or should be known by the supplier, the province of supply is determined in accordance with the rules in Part III of Schedule IX as if the supply were a supply of intangible personal property. In any other case, the province of supply will be the province in which the recipient has its mailing address.

6. Where the supply cannot be located by applying the override rules in the Place of Supply (GST/HST) Regulations, the Part VIII province of supply rules will apply.

7. A telecommunication service of making telecommunications facilities available is deemed to be supplied in a province where all of the telecommunications facilities are ordinarily located in that province. If all of the telecommunications facilities are not located in a single province, the supply will be deemed to be made in a particular province if the invoice for the supply of the service is sent to an address in that province.

2. Web site Design, Maintenance, and Hosting

Ruling 3: Design and Maintenance

Ruling 25769[5] considers the supply of Web site design and maintenance. In this ruling a Canadian GST registered person was retained to design a Web site for a non-resident. The Web site (and all of its pages) once completed, are sent electronically to the customer's server in the U.S.

The Web site is to be hosted by the customer. However, the Canadian does access the Web site from time to time from Canada in order to update and perform maintenance.

---

[5] June 28, 2001.

The Ruling

The CRA concluded that the design and maintenance were supplies of services. This is because the designer does not retain any ownership or property rights in the Web site once completed (in which case the supply would be intangible personal property).

The service is considered to be supplied in Canada because the individuals who worked on the Web site operated from a location in Canada. The services were considered to be supplied other than in a participating province because the individuals operated exclusively from an office located outside the participating provinces. The relevant rule is contained in paragraph 2(*a*) of Part V:

> Considering that the Web site design and maintenance services supplied by xxxxxx to the non-resident client are performed entirely in the province of xxxxx, the supply is deemed to be made in that non-participating province and subject to GST at 7% unless it is zero-rated.

The CRA also noted that the Web site related services should qualify for zero-rating under section 7.

> ... it appears that none of the exclusions in section 7 ... are relevant and the supply of the service by xxxx to the non-resident client is zero-rated.

As a result of the above, the Canadian supplier of the Web site design and maintenance services may provide its services to non-residents without any GST applying to the supply. In this regard, see also ruling 35167.[6]

Conclusions

1. When performed in Canada, the service of designing and maintaining a Web site will be a service which is supplied in Canada.

2. The service will typically qualify for zero-rating under section 7 when supplied to a non-resident.

Ruling 4: Web site Design

Ruling 34134[7] also considers a Canadian who provides Web site design but does not provide Web site hosting. The Canadian GST registered person designs the Web site for U.S. customers and then emails the Web sites to the customers. The client is responsible for arranging its own hosting solutions. The applicant does not retain any rights in the Web site once completed.

---

[6] March 28, 2002.

[7] September 23, 2002.

The Ruling

The CRA ruled that this is a taxable service which is considered to be supplied in Canada as a result of the tasks performed in Canada.

In terms of locating the province of supply, the CRA noted that pursuant to paragraph 2(a) of Part V of Schedule IX, a service is considered to be supplied in a particular province if all or substantially all (i.e., 90% or more) of the Canadian element of the service is performed in that province.

The CRA also notes that the service may be considered to be supplied in a particular province under paragraph 2(b) where the place of negotiation is in that province, and all or substantially all of the service is not performed outside that province. The CRA reached the conclusion that this particular supply was made outside of the HST provinces for the following reasons:

> ... the supply is deemed to be made in a non-participating province because the supply of the Web site design to the non-resident company is performed entirely in the province of xxxxxx. Therefore, where a client is resident in Canada the supply is subject to GST at 7%.

The CRA also concluded that zero-rating would be available under section 7 when the service is provided to a non-resident.

In this case the applicant charged GST to the client in error in the past. The CRA notes that this error may be corrected by refunding the GST paid and by issuing a credit note to the client. The applicant would then claim a deduction (in its next GST return) for the amount of GST refunded back to the client.

Conclusions

1. When performed in Canada, the service of designing a Web site will be a service supplied in Canada.

2. Where all or substantially all of the service is performed in a non-participating province, the supply will be considered to be made in that non-participating province and the GST will only apply at the rate of 6%.

3. The service will typically qualify for zero-rating under section 7 when supplied to a non-resident.

Ruling 5: Design with Hosting Provided In-house

Ruling 34141[8] considers a Canadian GST registered person who provides Web site design and hosting to both residents and non-residents. The server used by the Canadian to provide the hosting is owned by the supplier and is located in Canada.

---

[8] July 14, 2003.

The Ruling

The CRA concluded that the Web site design and hosting are both services and are separate supplies. In order to determine the location where those services are performed, the Canadian is required to consider the four-part performance of services test. The service will be considered performed in Canada if:

1. The service requires a person to perform a task and the person performing the task is in Canada;

2. The service involves computer equipment operations and the supplier's equipment is in Canada;

3. The service involves doing something to or with a customer's equipment by accessing it from a remote location and the customer's equipment is in Canada; or

4. Any activity related to the performance of the service is undertaken in Canada.

The CRA, without explanation, reached the conclusion that the hosting and design services were performed in Canada. These conclusions seem to follow from the fact that the design work was done in Canada and the hosting was provided from a server located in Canada with work performed by employees in Canada.

The CRA noted that zero-rating should be available in respect of both services under section 7. To the extent that zero-rating is not available, the identification of the province of supply would involve different rules for the two different supplies. The design services would be considered to be supplied in a particular province if all or substantially of the Canadian element of the services are performed in that particular province. This rule is contained in paragraph 2(*a*) of Part V of Schedule IX.

The hosting services would, however, be subject to the prescribed override rules in section 3 of Part IX of Schedule IX. The rule provides that, notwithstanding any other rule in Schedule IX, a supply will be made in a province if it is prescribed as supplied in that province.

Pursuant to section 10(1) of the Place of Supply (GST/HST) Regulations, where a supplier makes a supply of a "computer related service" (which includes Web site hosting), and there is to be a single final recipient of the service, the supply will be made in a particular province if there is a single ordinary location in the province at which the final recipient avails itself of the service and either:

(a) the supplier maintains information sufficient to determine that location; or

(b) under normal business practice the supplier would obtain that information.

In any other case, where a computer related service is supplied, the supply is made in a particular province if the mailing address of the recipient is in that particular province.

The CRA explained that where a single final recipient of a hosting service does not avail itself of the service at a single ordinary location, or where the information requirements are not met, the province of supply will be determined by reference to the mailing address of the recipient. The CRA provided the following example:

> ... if the mailing address of the recipient of a taxable (other than zero-rated) supply of Web site hosting is in one of the participating provinces (e.g. New Brunswick) the supply by XXXX is made in New Brunswick and subject to HST at the rate of 15%. If the mailing address of the recipient ... is in a non-participating province, the supply is subject to GST at a rate of 7%, unless the supply is zero-rated.

The CRA also noted that a separate set of special rules would apply where there are multiple final recipients. In terms of the final recipient requirement, the CRA explained that:

> A "final recipient" means a person who is the recipient of a supply of the service who acquires it otherwise than for the purpose of supplying it to another person.

The CRA did not explain what would constitute "availing oneself" of a computer related service in the context of Web site hosting. It would appear that in applying the "availing oneself" test, the person who should be taken into account is the corporation which is the recipient of the service (and not the general public which uses the Internet and who could access the Web site).

Conclusions

1. A hosting service is considered to be supplied in Canada where the person supplying the hosting operates from Canada or uses a server located in Canada to provide the hosting service.

2. Web site hosting is considered to be a "computer related service" for the purposes of applying the HST rules.

3. A hosting service, other than one which is zero-rated, is considered to be made in a particular province if there is a single final recipient of the service, the final recipient avails itself of the service at a single ordinary location in that province, and the supplier maintains (or would normally maintain) information sufficient to determine that location. Otherwise, the

supply will be made in a particular province where the mailing address of the single final recipient is in that particular province.

4. Hosting services are typically zero-rated pursuant to section 7 when supplied to a non-resident.

5. Web site design is considered to be provided in a particular province if all or substantially all of the services are performed in that particular province.

Ruling 6: Design and Hosting with Third Party

In related ruling 32573[9], the Canadian GST registered person provides Web site design and hosting.

The Canadian supplier rents a block of space on an ISP's server to host its own Web site. It also re-supplies portions of this space to its Canadian resident and non-resident customers for the hosting of their own Web sites.

The Ruling

The CRA concluded that the design and hosting are services which are performed in Canada. This seems to be because the supplier operates from Canada. The CRA again noted, as in previous rulings, that zero-rating should be available under section 7 for the services when provided to a non-resident.

The ruling suggests that where a person provides hosting and operates from offices in Canada, the location where the server is located will not be relevant. Further, there does not seem to be any distinction drawn between the supplier hosting Web sites on its own server or making arrangements for the hosting to be provided by the server of a third party.

The province of supply of the design services will be determined in the same manner as described in ruling 5 above. The province of supply of the hosting services, when provided by the Canadian applicant, would be determined by reference to the override rules. It should be expected that there would be a single final recipient of the service (i.e., the customer of the applicant). If that recipient were to avail itself of the service at a single ordinary location in a province, and that location is known (or should be known) by the supplier, the supply would be made in that location. In all other cases involving a single final recipient, the supply would be made in a particular province if the mailing address of the recipient is in that province.

The ruling does not discuss the application of these rules from the perspective of the ISP who supplies Web site hosting to the applicant for

---

[9] April 4, 2003.

re-supply purposes. The application of the override rules from the perspective of the ISP are particularly complex because the rules require that the ISP take into account facts which relate both to its own customer (i.e., the Canadian applicant) and the Canadian applicant's customer. For example, the override provides that where there is to be one final recipient of the hosting service, the supplier must consider whether that recipient avails itself of the service at a single ordinary location in a province and whether it knows of this location. This rule would require that the ISP make the determination with respect to the final user, and not with respect to the Canadian applicant. It is only where there is no single ordinary location for the ultimate user, or where the ISP is not able to determine this location, that it may rely upon the fall-back rule. The fall-back rule requires that the ISP consider the mailing address of the recipient of the supply (the Canadian applicant) and not the mailing address of the single final recipient.

Conclusions

1. The CRA does not distinguish between web hosting provided directly by the supplier on its own servers and Web hosting provided with the use of servers of a third party (such as an ISP).

2. Where Web site hosting is provided through a chain of suppliers, each of the suppliers in the chain must, for the purpose of locating the province of supply, consider the "ordinary location" of the end user of the service (as opposed to the ordinary location of the immediate recipient of the service). It is only where the supplier cannot make this determination, or where there is no one ordinary location in a province, that the supplier may rely upon the province of supply rule which relates to the mailing address of the recipient of its supply.

Ruling 7: Design and Hosting

In ruling 2743[10], the applicant is a Canadian entity which provides web design and hosting but strictly for residents of the U.S. The ruling does not describe how the hosting service is provided.

The Ruling

The CRA again confirmed that these services are provided in Canada and that zero-rating would be available under section 7.

The absence of any discussion relating to the location of the hosting server suggests that this is not a particularly important element in circumstances where the Canadian supplier operates from Canada. The fact that

---

[10] September 14, 2001.

the supplier operates from Canada results in the conclusion that the services are performed in Canada.

Conclusions

1. Web site design and hosting are considered to be services and are performed in Canada where the supplier operates from a location in Canada.

2. These services will typically qualify for zero-rating pursuant to section 7.

Ruling 8: Design and Hosting

Ruling 34150[11] deals more specifically with the issues relating to cross border hosting.

The applicant is a Canadian GST registered individual who provides web design and hosting for her Canadian resident customers. The applicant rents space on servers located in the U.S. in order to provide the hosting service.

A U.S. company supplies the use of the servers to the Canadian and does not charge GST on these fees. The applicant passes along the Web site hosting cost to her clients without markup.

The Ruling

The design services and the hosting services are considered to be supplies of services which are supplied in Canada. This appears to be because the supplier operates from Canada. The fact that the supplier merely passes through the hosting cost without markup does not change the manner in which this supply is characterized:

> The fact that the server is located outside Canada does not by itself change the tax status of the supply. The tax status of the supply is not affected if the client (i.e., the applicant) decides to add a markup prior to billing her customers.

The CRA concluded that the services when provided to non-residents would qualify for zero-rating under section 7. However, when the services are provided to Canadian residents the supply would be taxable at 6% or 14%.

This ruling demonstrates that the minimal activities of the Canadian in providing the hosting services (i.e., merely arranging for the hosting), will result in the supply being made in Canada. In this ruling, it is apparent that

---

[11] September 28, 2001.

the Canadian is performing no tasks relating to the operation or maintenance of the server, or relating to ensuring that there is an appropriate connection to the Internet.

It should also be noted that if the hosting had been provided directly to the Canadian customer by the U.S. entity (the entity which owns the servers), then the supply would have been considered to be made outside Canada. However, the Canadian customer would, in those circumstances, have been obligated to self-assess under Division IV except if registered and making supplies in the course of a commercial activity.

Where hosting is provided to non-residents, the two alternate methods of delivery of the hosting service would result in the same tax consequences. Where the Canadian re-supplies the hosting service, the supply is zero-rated under section 7. Where the U.S. entity provides the hosting service directly to the customer, the supply would be considered to be made outside Canada.

Conclusions

1. A Canadian who re-supplies a hosting service, which has been supplied to the Canadian by a non-resident hosting entity, will be considered to be providing a service in Canada if the Canadian operates from Canada.

2. Zero-rating will typically be available when the supply is provided to a non-resident.

3. These results will follow regardless of whether a mark up is added by the Canadian or whether the costs are merely flowed through to the customer.

Ruling 9: Design and Hosting

Ruling 37260[12] considers a Canadian GST registrant who provides Web site design and hosting for both Canadian and U.S. clients.

In some cases, the Web sites will be hosted on servers located outside Canada. The ruling does not describe the nature of the relationship between the person providing the hosting and the Canadian applicant.

The Ruling

The CRA ruled that the hosting services will be considered to be supplied in Canada, including where the servers used are located outside Canada:

---

[12] November 25, 2002.

... a supplier located in Canada may host web sites on servers located outside of Canada, but may perform certain tasks (e.g. programming, maintenance) from its office in Canada. As a result of the performance of these tasks in Canada, the supply is deemed to be made in Canada.

The rationale provided for locating the supply in Canada suggests that there might be circumstances where a Canadian could provide hosting through a server outside Canada which would not be considered to be a service performed in Canada. Where the Canadian merely provides a copy of the Web site to the hosting party, and does not engage in maintenance or programming, the suggestion seems to be that services might not be performed in Canada. It should be expected that the CRA would actively resist such an interpretation.

The services would typically qualify for zero-rating when supplied to non-residents. However, where the services do not so qualify, the province of supply must be considered. The identification of the province of supply would be determined in the same manner as in ruling 6 above.

Conclusions

1. Web site design and hosting are considered to be services. Either of the services will be supplied in Canada if the person making the supply operates from Canada.

2. It may be arguable that if the Canadian supplier provides the hosting through a server located outside Canada, and the Canadian does not perform any programming or maintenance functions on the server, the service might not be considered to be performed in Canada. However, this argument would likely meet with substantial resistance from the CRA.

3. The services will typically qualify for zero-rating when supplied to non-residents.

4. The province of supply override rules should be considered to locate the province of supply of the hosting service.

Ruling 10: Hosting Provided Alone

The provision of Web site hosting as a standalone supply is considered in ruling 31968.[13] The Canadian GST registered applicant leases a server in the U.S. to host its customer's Web sites. The Canadian is not charged any GST by the U.S. company which provides the server space. The applicant charges its customers a monthly hosting fee.

---

[13] June 25, 2002.

The Ruling

The CRA confirmed that the hosting of Web sites is a service. The CRA noted that the supply is considered to be made in Canada for the following reason:

> Whether the server hosting the Web site is situated outside Canada, where any activity related to the performance of the service supplied by xxxx is undertaken in Canada, the service is considered to be performed at least in part in Canada and consequently deemed to be made in Canada.

The "any activity related to the performance of the service" test is a reference to the fourth place of performance test. Given that any task performed in Canada will result in the conclusion that the service is supplied in Canada, it would appear that there is no tax advantage to be gained by making use of a non-resident hosting service.

The CRA concluded that when hosting is supplied to non-resident customers zero-rating would be available under section 7.

The ruling also discusses the application of the HST where supplies are made to Canadian residents. The ruling notes that if the single final recipient of the hosting service avails itself of the service at a single ordinary location in a particular province, then the hosting will be provided in that province as long as this location is known to the supplier (or would ordinarily be known to the supplier). Otherwise, assuming a single final recipient of the hosting service, the province of supply will be the province of the mailing address of the recipient.

Conclusions

1. A hosting service will be considered to be supplied in Canada where the person supplying the hosting operates from Canada. This will include situations where the server in issue is located outside Canada.

2. The service will typically qualify for zero-rating.

3. The province of supply rules which would apply are contained in the Place of Supply (GST/HST) Regulations.

Ruling 11: Hosting Provided with Own Servers

Similarly, ruling 32706[14] considers a hosting service provided to non-residents as a stand alone supply. The Canadian applicant uses its own server in Canada to provide the hosting.

---

[14] July 9, 2002.

The Ruling

The CRA ruled that this service is provided in Canada. This conclusion appears to be based on the fact that the server and the offices of the supplier are located in Canada. The CRA also noted that this supply would qualify for zero-rating when provided to non-residents.

The issues relating to the identification of the province of supply are the same as those set out in ruling 5 above.

Conclusions

See rulings above.

Ruling 12: Virtual Hosting

In ruling 36209[15], the applicant characterized the service which it provides as "virtual hosting". The applicant is a Canadian resident and GST registered. The Web sites are hosted on a server located in Canada.

The Ruling

The CRA concluded that what has been referred to as "virtual hosting" is really just Web site hosting.

The CRA ruled that this is a service which is performed, and accordingly, supplied in Canada. The HST could apply if the single final recipient of the Web site hosting service avails itself of the service at a single ordinary location in a participating province which is known (or should be known) to the supplier. Otherwise the mailing address of the recipient will be the critical determinant.

> ... generally where the final recipient of a web site hosting service is located in one of the participating provinces the supply is subject to HST ...

The CRA noted that zero-rating would be available when the service is provided to a non-resident.

Conclusions

See rulings above.

Ruling 13: Design, Hosting and Domain Name Registration

Ruling 37937[16] considers supplies in the nature of design, hosting and domain name registration. The Canadian GST registered individual in this

---

[15] October 22, 2002.

[16] December 30, 2002.

case provides web design, hosting and domain name registration for clients located in the U.S. The Canadian does not retain ownership of the Web sites once developed.

The server which hosts the Web sites is located in the U.S. The ruling does not indicate whether the server is leased to or owned by the applicant.

With respect to domain name registrations, the Canadian pays an amount to the registrar (who could be either an American or Canadian registrar) and this cost is passed along to the customer.

The Ruling — Design and Hosting

The CRA concluded that the three supplies are each considered to be separate supplies of services. Web site design and hosting are considered to be supplies made in Canada because these services are performed by the Canadian in Canada.

> Given that all of the activities carried out in designing a Web site or hosting a Web site (e.g., programming and maintenance activities) are carried out in Canada, the ... services are deemed to be made in Canada.

The ruling notes that the services should be zero-rated under section 7.

With respect to the application of the HST to hosting, the CRA applied the same tests as are considered in the rulings above.

> ... where a single final recipient of a web site hosting service provided by you does not avail itself of the service at a single ordinary location or where the conditions above with respect to information are not met, the determination of the place of supply is based on the mailing address of the recipient.

The Ruling — Domain Name Registration

At the outset the CRA noted that the application of the GST to domain name registration (which is considered a service) will turn on two issues:

(a) whether the applicant is acting as agent for its customer;[17] and

(b) whether the registrar is required to charge GST in respect of the registration of the domain name.

Where not acting as agent

Where the Canadian applicant is not acting as the agent for the customer when incurring the domain name expense, the services provided to the customer by the applicant relating to arranging for the domain name

---

[17] The ruling notes that Policy Statement P-182 "Agency", [The current version is P-182R] will assist in making the determination whether the cost was incurred as agent of the customer.

registration would be subject to tax. This is because the applicant operates from Canada and would be considered to perform these services in Canada. However, those services would qualify for zero-rating under section 7 if the customer is a non-resident.

To the extent that GST is charged to the Canadian applicant by the registrar, the Canadian applicant would claim an ITC.

Where acting as agent

Where the applicant is acting as agent for the customer in incurring the domain name expense, the applicant would not charge any additional GST to the customer when passing along the charge. The applicant would pass along to the customer any GST charge levied by the registrar. Given the agency relationship, these charges, including the GST expense, would be considered expenses of the principal (the customer) and accordingly, the customer would be the only person who could claim an ITC in respect of the GST expense.

The CRA explained the operation of these common law agency rules as follows:

> If you are an agent, we consider the registrar to have supplied the registration of the domain name to your customer, and you, as the agent, to have made a supply of services ... to your customer. Therefore the registrar is responsible for charging and remitting any GST/HST that may apply to the registration of the domain name. You have to charge and account for GST/HST on your service of acting as an agent ... unless the supply of your service is zero-rated.

Any charge levied in respect of the agency services (i.e., any charge which is in addition to the fees levied by the registrar) would be subject to GST unless the charge qualifies for zero-rating pursuant to section 5:

> The service of acting as an agent of a non-resident person is excluded from zero-rating under the provisions of section 7 ... However, section 5 ... zero rates the supply made to a non-resident person of a service of acting as agent of the person in certain circumstances. Specifically, the service is zero-rated if it is in respect of either a supply to the non-resident that is zero-rated elsewhere in Part V of Schedule VI to the ETA or a supply made outside Canada by or to the non-resident. Therefore, if the domain name registration supplied by the registrar to the non-resident customer is zero-rated or deemed to be made outside Canada, then your service of acting as agent on behalf of your non-resident customer will be zero-rated.

Given that registering a domain name is considered to be a service, the suggestion is that the registrar would charge GST to the applicant if the registrar is a GST registered person who operates from Canada. However, if the registrar is a Canadian who is not registered (i.e., a small supplier), it would not charge the GST to the applicant. If the registrar is a non-resident person then the registrar would not charge GST to the applicant because the service is performed outside Canada.

Conclusions

1. A supply of registering a domain name is a service. Where the registrar operates from a location in Canada the registrar will typically be considered to be supplying the service in Canada.

2. Where the registrar provides the domain name service to a person who is incurring the expense on its own account, the recipient will be required to pay the GST. Where this recipient is acting on behalf of another person in securing the service (but is not their agent), it would charge the GST to the person on the services which it provides in Canada. The services may qualify for zero-rating under section 7.

3. Where the registrar provides the domain name service to a person who is incurring the expense as agent for another person, the agent would not claim any ITC in respect of the service. The agent would pass through the costs to the principal including any GST charged by the registrar. The agent would collect GST on its agency services if provided in Canada, unless zero-rating is available pursuant to section 5.

Ruling 14: Design, Hosting, and Domain Name Registration

Related ruling 35795[18] considers a Canadian GST registered applicant who provides web design, hosting and domain name registration. The Canadian charges a single, all inclusive fee for all of the above. The customers are both residents and non-residents.

The Ruling

The CRA again confirmed that all of the above are considered to be supplies of services. With respect to domain name registration, the CRA noted that:

> The supply of domain name registration consists of registering the requested domain names of the company's customers on their behalf with an accredited domain name registrar. There is no transfer of property rights by the company to its customers with respect to this supply.

Given that the supplies are all considered to be services, the four-part services place of performance test would need to be considered to determine if the supplies are made in Canada.

---

[18] January 27, 2003.

The CRA concluded that all of the services are provided in Canada. This appears to follow from the fact that the employees of the applicant operate from Canada.

With respect to the registration of domain names, the CRA again confirmed that the agency issue would need to be considered. The analysis is the same as described in ruling 13 above.

Conclusions

1. The registering of domain names is a service. This is because there is no transfer of property rights associated with this supply.

2. Determination of the place of supply requires that the four-part place of performance test be considered. Where the person offering the service (including on a re-supply basis) operates from Canada, the service will be considered to be performed in Canada.

Ruling 15: Hosting and Domain Name Registration

In ruling 33447[19], the applicant provides Web site hosting and domain name registration for its customers both in and outside Canada.

The applicant charges its clients a monthly fee for the provision of web hosting. A one time fee is charged for registering the domain name with a central registry. The registration of the domain name does not ever involve any transfer of rights from the customer to the applicant. To provide hosting the applicant leases a server which is located in the U.S.

The Ruling

The CRA ruled that domain name registration and hosting are each services and that in this case they are performed in Canada. The ruling again confirms that, where employees of the supplier operate from Canada, the location of a server outside Canada will not result in the supply being made outside Canada.

This ruling did not discuss the possibility that the fees paid to the central registry were paid as agent for the customer. It would appear, given the commentary provided in the rulings described above, that this silence was attributable to an oversight.

---

[19] September 21, 2001.

Conclusions

1. Where a Canadian service provider supplies Web site hosting, the delivery of the service through a server outside Canada will not result in the supply being made outside Canada.

2. There will be a sufficient connection to Canada to locate the supply in Canada where the supplier operates from offices in Canada.

Ruling 16: Hosting, Web Design and Advertising

In ruling 38637[20], the supplier is a newly formed entity which provides Web site hosting, Web site design and advertising. The customers are located both in Canada and in the U.S.

The applicant has requested a ruling on the issue of whether it is required to register for GST purposes and whether it must charge GST on the various supplies.

The Ruling

The CRA concluded that pursuant to subsection 240(1), the applicant is required to be registered unless it qualifies as a small supplier.

The supplies of hosting, Web site design, and advertising are each considered to be supplies of services which are performed in Canada. This appears to be because the applicant operates from offices located in Canada.

The Web design and advertising services will be considered to be supplied in a particular province if all or substantially all of the Canadian element of the service is performed in that province. The CRA also discussed the province of supply override rules. With respect to hosting, the CRA suggested that in most cases the mailing address of the recipient would be used to locate the province of supply.

Zero-rating for Web site design, hosting, and advertising would be available under section 7. Advertising services, to the extent that they do not qualify under section 7 (for example, when provided to an individual who is in Canada at the time the service is performed), would be eligible for zero-rating under section 8 when provided to a non-resident who is not registered.

Conclusions

1. When advertising is provided with Web hosting and Web design, the CRA will typically consider each of the supplies to be separate supplies.

---

[20] November 18, 2002.

2. The place of supply of advertising, web hosting and Web design will be in Canada when the supplier operates from offices in Canada.

Ruling 17: Bundle of Supplies Related to Hosting

Ruling 6277[21] considers an applicant who in addition to hosting and design provides a number of other related supplies. The GST registered Canadian applicant offers Canadian and U.S. clients all of the following (although not necessarily bundled together for a single fee):

(a) Intranet design and hosting;

(b) Web site design and hosting;

(c) Web site programming and maintenance;

(d) Web site technical support;

(e) hardware and software sales;

(f) on site consulting and training; and

(g) arranging third party contracts.

The server which hosts the sites is located in the U.S. but all development work is done in Canada. The Web site programming is done in one of three ways:

(a) Applicant purchases off the shelf software to use on a client's site;

(b) Applicant modifies existing software to meet a client's needs; or

(c) Applicant programs from scratch.

The Ruling

The CRA treated each of the offerings as separate supplies. This seems to be because the supplier did not typically offer the bundle of supplies together.

The CRA ruled that the Web hosting, on site consulting and training, arranging third party contracts, and site maintenance are properly characterized as services. The technical support could be characterized as a service (advising clients on specific issues) or intangible personal property (access to pre-existing technical documentation). The hardware sales are a supply of tangible personal property. The application of the GST to the programming and software supplies are discussed in Chapter 14, Software and Software Related Offerings.

---

[21] November 6, 2001.

Zero-rating could be available under section 7 (general), section 8 (advertising services), or section 23 (advisory and consulting services) for the various supplies. Intangible personal property which is intellectual property may qualify for zero-rating under section 10.

Conclusion

Where a supplier offers a number of different Internet based offerings on a standalone basis, each of the supplies will be considered separately.

Ruling 18: Web Design with Data Backup

Ruling 39421[22] considers Web design along with data backup and general consulting. The applicant is GST registered. Where Web design is provided, the supplier does not retain any rights in the Web site materials.

Data backup is provided to customers electronically. The customer orders the data backup through the supplier's Web site. Once the customer has provided its credit card information, it may download its files to the supplier's server without any assistance on the part of the supplier. Technical support with respect to backup or recovery is only provided where specifically requested by the customer. Generally, it is expected that the customer will not require assistance.

Consulting services relating to installing hardware and software are also offered.

The Ruling

The CRA ruled that all of the above are to be characterized as services and are considered to be supplied in Canada. This seems to be because the supplier operates from Canada.

In terms of the application of the HST the CRA broke down the supplies between design and general consulting (category 1 services) and data backup and recovery (category 2 services).

Category 1 Services

Pursuant to paragraph 2(*a*) of Part V of Schedule IX, the category 1 services are performed in a particular province where all or substantially all of the Canadian element of the services are performed within that province. Where the services are performed in more than one province, and if the place of negotiation is in a particular province and not all or substantially all of the service is performed outside that province, the supply will be in the province where the negotiation occurred. Failing the application of

---

[22] December 3, 2002.

either of the above two rules, the rule in section 3 will apply. This rule provides that the supply will be made in a participating province (and subject to 14% tax) where:

(a) the place of negotiation is in Canada and the Canadian element of the service is performed primarily (50% or more) in the participating provinces; or

(b) the place of negotiation is outside Canada, all or substantially all of the service is performed in Canada and the Canadian element of the service is performed primarily in the participating provinces.

Category 2 Services

Data backup is considered to be a "computer related service" and is subject to the regulatory override rules. This is because a computer related service includes the electronic storage of information and/or computer to computer transfers of information. Where there is a single final recipient of a data back-up service, the supply is made in a particular province if the recipient avails itself of the service at a single ordinary location within that province and the supplier:

(a) maintains information sufficient to determine that location; or

(b) has a normal business practice that would involve obtaining this information.

If any of the above tests are not met, and there is a single final recipient, the supply will be made in a particular province where the mailing address of the recipient is in that province.

It would appear that in most cases the supplier would not normally be aware of the location where the recipient avails itself of this service. Accordingly, it should be expected that the mailing address of the customer would be determinative of the province of supply.

The CRA concluded that all of the services should qualify for zero-rating when provided to non-residents.

Conclusions

1. Data backup and recovery is considered a service, including where the data backup and recovery is performed on an automatic basis.

2. Data backup and recovery is considered to be a "computer related service".

3. If there is a single final recipient of the data backup service and the recipient avails itself of the service at a single ordinary location in a particular province and the supplier is aware of this location (or should be aware of this location under normal business practices), the supply will be considered to be made in that province. Otherwise the mailing address of the recipient will determine the province of supply.

4. The zero-rating rules in section 7 would determine the application of zero-rating to data back up services provided to non-residents.

Ruling 19: Subcontracting Arrangements

Ruling 7787[23] considers a Web site design and hosting supplier who subcontracts this work out to a third party. The supplier is a Canadian entity.

Situation 1

The applicant (A) has entered into an agreement with its customer to design, maintain, and host the customer's Web site. The applicant performs the design work itself but subcontracts the maintenance and hosting to B. B is a Canadian resident corporation.

B maintains the Web site in house but further subcontracts the hosting to corporation C. C is a company resident in the U.S. The Web site will reside on a server owned by C which is located in the U.S.

Each of A and B can access the Web site (to perform maintenance functions) from their computers in Canada.

B invoices the applicant on an hourly basis for maintenance services and on a monthly basis for hosting services.

The applicant has asked how the tax applies with respect to supplies from B to A.

Situation 2

The applicant (A) has entered into an agreement with its customer to construct, maintain and host the customer's Web site.

A subcontracts everything (construction, maintenance and hosting) to corporation B.

B hosts the Web site on its own servers.

A invoices the customers on an hourly basis for work performed and a monthly fee for hosting.

---

[23] November 8, 2001.

The applicant has asked how the tax applies with respect to supplies from B to A and on supplies from A to its customer.

The Ruling

The CRA ruled that all of the following are services:

(a) constructing a Web site (where the customer owns the site on completion);

(b) providing a customized software solution to fix a Web site where the client owns the Web site on completion;

(c) Web site maintenance (upgrading software, fixing bugs, updating data, etc.) all in connection with a Web site owned by the client; and

(d) Web site hosting.

These services are all supplied in Canada if performed even partially in Canada. The CRA seemed to take the position that each of the services supplied by A to its customer would be considered to be supplied in Canada (because of the fact that A operates from offices in Canada) regardless of whether the work was actually performed by A, or was subcontracted out to third party suppliers.

Web site construction or maintenance would be supplied in a particular province under the rule in paragraph 2(*a*) if all or substantially all of the service is performed in the particular province. Where this rule does not apply, the rule in paragraph 2(*b*) should be considered. This rule holds that the supply will be made in the province of negotiation except if all or substantially all of the service is performed outside that province.

With respect to Web site hosting, the province of supply rules are contained in the override regulations. Where a hosting service is supplied and there is a single final recipient of the supply (who is not necessarily the person to whom the supply is made) who avails itself of the service at a single ordinary location in a province (which is known or should be known to the supplier), the supply is made in that province. Otherwise, in circumstances where there is a single final recipient of the service, the supply will be made in a particular province if the mailing address of the recipient (i.e., the direct recipient) of the supply is in that province.

Similarly, where a hosting service is supplied and there are multiple final recipients of the supply, and each of those final recipients avail themselves of the service at a particular single location (which is known or should be known to the supplier), the supply will be made in a particular province to the extent that the final recipients avail themselves of the service in that province.

These rules place an enormous responsibility upon any person who supplies Web site hosting to a recipient for re-supply purposes. The "final recipient" who must be taken into account in locating the supply is not the person who is the recipient of the service. Rather, it is the person (or persons) who will be the final beneficiary (or beneficiaries) of the Web site hosting service. Where the supplier provides Web site hosting (as here) through a chain of re-suppliers, each of the suppliers in the chain is required to consider with respect to the ultimate user (or with respect to each of the ultimate users), whether that user will avail itself of the service at a single ordinary location and whether the supplier has been provided with sufficient information to determine that location (or would normally be provided with sufficient information to determine that location).

It is only where the supplier is not able to "look through" the chain (to the end user or end users) to make this determination, that the particular supplier may rely upon the default rule which locates the supply by reference to the recipient of the supply.

Conclusions

1. Where a person supplies Web site design, hosting and repair services from a location in Canada the supply will be considered to be made in Canada including where the supplier subcontracts the functions out to non-resident third parties.

2. The province of supply of Web site hosting will be determined by reference to the regulatory override rules.

3. Where hosting is provided by a supplier to a recipient who intends to re-supply the service (either to another supplier or to an end user or multiple end users) the supplier must consider the "single ordinary location/single location" rule by reference to the end user(s) (and not to the recipient of the supply).

4. The supplier would only be entitled to rely upon the fall back rule where there is no single location (or single ordinary location) or where that location cannot be ascertained. The fall back rule allows for the province of supply to be determined by reference to the mailing address of the recipient (i.e., the direct recipient) of the supply.

3. Internet Security

Ruling 20: Extranet Security

Ruling 41980[24] considered secure access provided by a GST registered Canadian company. The applicant company is an Extranet virtual private network provider. The secure access is provided by using a software application and other components bundled together under a single contract. The applicant's protocol (secure sockets layer provider) allows for private documents to be sent via the Internet. Employees and key contacts outside of the company (primarily customers) can access the secure documents by way of the secure access system (SAS). Authentication is achieved through user name and password, digital certificates or security tokens. The security package may be used from any location in the world where users have access to the Internet.

To provide this security, the applicant provides its customers with the following:

(a) hardware which remains owned by the applicant (routers, servers and controllers). The hardware is installed in the customer's premises by the applicant; and

(b) a non-exclusive and non-transferable license to use the supplier's encryption software.

The applicant does not allow the customer access to the hardware notwithstanding that the hardware is physically located on the customer's premises (along with a copy of the encryption software). The software performs the primary function of copying the customer's data and other software applications to the applicant's servers on site at the customer's premises. The software also allows for the verification of the users identity and security clearance.

Two distinct packages are offered:

Package 1: Virtual private network with installation and repair, technical support, and digital certificates.

Package 2: Package 1, plus a directory and service of enrolling and deleting users, control of the security protocol (i.e., limiting access broken down by user) and remote customization of software to meet customer's specific needs.

All services (other than installation, repair and maintenance which are carried out at the customer's premises) are carried out remotely from the

---

[24] April 4, 2003.

applicant's office. These services are provided via remote Internet connection.

A separate consulting service is also offered under a separate agreement. Where this option is triggered, the applicant will provide an on site visit to determine the security needs of the customer.

The applicant will also supply the customer with basic Internet access if this is not already in place. The applicant purchases the Internet access from an Internet service provider and then resells this access to the customer.

The Ruling — Security Packages

The CRA noted at the outset that the two packages involve the bundling of a number of different services and intangible property. In applying the single versus multiple supply guidelines, the CRA reached the conclusion that a single supply was in fact being provided under each of the two packages, except to the extent that software customization was provided in the second package. The software customization was considered to be a separate supply. The software customization issues are considered below.

The CRA also concluded that, notwithstanding the substantial service component (technical support, installation, repair and services re: access of various users) of each of the two packages, the single supply was a supply of intangible personal property (and not a telecommunication service). The CRA reasoned that the principal object of the supply was the right to use software which enables employees and customers to obtain secure access to the company's computerized resources. This supply is deemed to be made in Canada because there are no restrictions as to the place where the intangible property may be used.

The CRA also concluded that the supply was made in a non-participating province, and accordingly subject only to GST:

> [applicant] is required to collect the GST at the rate of 7% on the supply of the IPP, even in cases where the recipient or the end user (employee, client or business partner) is located in a participating province.

The identification of the province of supply seems to have been based upon the application of the rule contained in subparagraph 2(*d*)(ii) of Part III of Schedule IX. This rule holds that a supply will be deemed to be made in a particular province if the place of negotiation is in the province and the property can be used otherwise than exclusively outside the province. It would appear that the applicant negotiates the contracts from an office located in one of the non-participating provinces.

The CRA did not discuss zero-rating in connection with this supply.

The Ruling — Customization of Package

The CRA concluded that insufficient information had been provided to allow for a ruling on the issue of customization of the package. The CRA noted that the characterization of the supply would turn on the degree of human involvement in the making of the supply of the customized software.

If the degree of human involvement in the customization of the software was minimal, the supply might be considered to be a part of the single supply of intangible personal property (i.e., part of the packages). However, if the degree of human involvement in customizing the software was more extensive, the supply would likely be a separate supply of a service. The suggestion from the ruling, including the fact that the CRA declined to rule on the issue, is that this test would be very difficult to apply with any certainty.

The Ruling — Consulting Services

The consulting services (i.e., security needs analysis) would always be characterized as a separate supply of a service. Where this service is provided to a Canadian customer, the service is deemed to be supplied in Canada. This is because the service always involves a visit to the customer's facilities in order to assess the required level of security. The CRA did not discuss whether the services might be considered to be performed in Canada where the customer is located in the U.S. The issue to be considered is whether work performed in Canada (from the supplier's office) in connection with the supply of the service would be sufficient to constitute performance in Canada.

In terms of the province of supply, the CRA considered the rules contained in Part V of Schedule IX. Applying the rule in paragraph 2(*a*) of Part V, the CRA held that where all or substantially all of the Canadian element of the service is performed in a particular province, the supply will be made in that province. Where this rule does not apply, the CRA noted that the rule in section 3 should be considered. It summarized that rule as follows:

> ... a supply is made in a participating province where the place of negotiation is outside Canada and all or substantially all of the service is performed in Canada, and the Canadian element of the service is performed primarily (more than 50%) in the participating provinces. For example, if 90% or more of ... consulting service is performed in Canada and the portion of the service that is performed in Canada is performed primarily in Nova Scotia and New Brunswick, the supply of the service is deemed to be made in the participating provinces and subject to HST at the rate of 15%.

The CRA noted that where neither of the above rules apply the supply will be deemed to be made in a non-participating province pursuant to section 144.1 of the ETA.

It is not clear why the CRA did not refer to the alternate province of supply rule contained in paragraph 2(*b*) of Part V. That rule provides that a supply will be made in a province where the place of negotiation is in the province, and it is not the case that all or substantially all of the service is performed outside the province. It would appear that this silence may have been attributable to an oversight.

Although the ruling does not discuss zero-rating in connection with the consulting services, the services should qualify for zero-rating under section 23 when provided to a non-resident.

The Ruling — Internet Access

The CRA concluded that the separate supply of Internet access was a telecommunication service of making telecommunications facilities available. This service will be considered to be supplied in Canada if any of the facilities used to provide the connection to the Internet are located in Canada.

In terms of the province of supply, the CRA considered the rule contained in section 3 of Part IX of Schedule IX, which cross references the Place of Supply (GST/HST) Regulations.

Pursuant to section 10 of the Regulations, where there is a single final recipient of a supply of Internet access, the supply will be made in a particular province if there is a single ordinary location within the province at which the final recipient avails itself of the access and this location is either known to the supplier or would ordinarily be known by the supplier. In any other case, the supply of access is made in a province if the mailing address of the recipient is in that province.

> ... where a single final recipient of Internet access provided by [applicant] does not avail itself of the access at a single ordinary location or where the conditions set out above with respect to the information are not met, the determination of the place of supply is based on the mailing address of the recipient. For example, if the mailing address of the recipient ... is in one of the participating provinces, such as New Brunswick, the supply is made in New Brunswick and subject to the HST at the rate of 15%.

Conclusions

1. Electronic security packages may be characterized as a single supply of intangible personal property notwithstanding that the package includes hardware, right to use software, and various service elements. This is

because the principal object of the supply is the right to use the security software.

2. The supply of the intangible personal property will be deemed to be made in Canada where there are no restrictions with respect to the place where the property may be used.

3. The property will be considered to be supplied in the province of negotiation if it is not the case that all or substantially all of the property can be used outside the province of negotiation.

4. If other supplies are provided separately from the package, they may be carved off and considered as separate supplies. This will include for example, security needs consulting services.

5. Where a client is being provided with the right to use software, and the software is being customized for the customer, the characterization of the customization will be a function of the "degree of human involvement" in performing the customization. If the human involvement is minimal, the customization may be considered to form part of the single supply of the intangible personal property. However, where the human involvement is more extensive, the customization will be considered to be a separate supply of a service.

This ruling raises a number of complicated issues which include the following:

(a) How would a supplier determine with any certainty the principal object of a security related supply which is comprised of various elements? In this case, it was concluded by the CRA that the principal object was the right to access the software. However, it would appear that the principal object could easily have been characterized as a security service.

(b) Even after the principal object of the supply has been identified, how and when should a supplier "carve off" specific discrete elements from the package? In this ruling, only the customization of the software was carved off as a separate supply.

(c) It is not clear whether zero-rating would be available in respect of the packages which were provided. Given that the principal object of the supply was the right to use the software, and the software was licensed to the recipient and downloaded to its office (albeit onto hardware owned by the supplier), it appears arguable that zero-rating would be available under section 10. Unfortunately, the CRA did not in the ruling discuss zero-rating. Further, in ruling 21 below, the CRA ruled on related facts that zero-rating relief would not be available. However, ruling 21 may be distinguishable in that the CRA characterized the supply as being in the nature of security certificates (and not specifically software).

Ruling 21: Registration Authority

Ruling 39061[25] considers a security package provided to clients who are located both inside and outside Canada. The applicant is a GST registered Canadian corporation which is a "registration authority". As a registration authority, it provides security certificates to its customers which are used to guarantee a person's identity for the purpose of accessing information electronically.

The certificate is in the form of an electronic message which identifies the certificate holder. When a person is issued a certificate the applicant guarantees the client's identity. Any person making a secure sockets connection to the client's computers can then have their identity verified by means of the certificate. The authorized user is provided with a "private key" which allows them to log on from any computer in the world in order to gain computer access to private information. A public key can also be provided by the client to a person anywhere in the world to decrypt a message sent from the client.

The applicant does not restrict the location where the certificates may be used. Annual fees are typically charged to the clients which includes hardware, driver software and connection cables at no extra charge.

The Ruling

The CRA ruled that the supply of the certificate is a supply of intangible personal property. Although the CRA did not specifically discuss the single versus multiple supply issue, it is evident that it concluded that the supply (including the provision of hardware) was in fact a single supply. Unfortunately, it was not clear from the ruling whether the principal object of the supply was the right to use the software or the right to use the certificates which verify a person's identity.

The CRA held that the supply is considered to be made in Canada because there are no restrictions as to the location where the certificate may be used.

In terms of the province of supply, the CRA concluded that the GST would always apply at the rate of 6%. This conclusion was based on the application of the rules contained in paragraph 2(*d*)(ii) of Part III of Schedule IX. Those rules provide that the supply will be made in a particular province if the place of negotiation is in the province (in this case it

---

[25] March 28, 2003.

appears that the supplier operates from premises located outside of the participating provinces) and the intangible personal property may be used otherwise than exclusively outside that province.

> Where there are no restrictions regarding the province in which the IPP may be used it will always be the case that the IPP may be used otherwise than exclusively (90% or more) outside the province where the place of negotiation occurred. Therefore, as a GST/HST registrant with a permanent establishment in [a non-participating province] that is a place of negotiation, the supplies of the certificates by [the applicant] are deemed to be made in ... a non-participating province.

The CRA also concluded that this supply of intangible personal property is not one which would qualify for zero-rating.

Conclusions

1. Security package bundles which relate to authenticating users may be characterized as a single supply of intangible personal property (including those which include hardware and other tangible personal property).

2. Where there are no restrictions as to the location where the security related property may be used, the supply will be deemed to be made in Canada.

3. Zero-rating does not apply to this type of supply.

4. Where there are no restrictions as to the location where the property may be used, the supply will typically be deemed to be made in the province of negotiation.

4. Teleconferencing, Long Distance, Bandwidth and Network Services

Ruling 22: Teleconferencing

In ruling 36061[26], the applicant is a GST registered Canadian company which provides teleconferencing to individuals and businesses both in Canada and the U.S. The applicant refers to this as a bridging service.

The applicant uses computer hardware and software which allows the customer to call a 1-800 number to obtain access to the teleconferencing service. The equipment used to provide the service and the applicant's offices are located in Canada but outside of the participating provinces.

The applicant has asked whether it is required to charge GST when the moderator who initiates the teleconference call (and the person who is

---

[26] March 26, 2002.

billed) is located in the U.S. Where the moderator is in the U.S. the other call participants may be in Canada or outside Canada.

The Ruling

The CRA ruled that the service falls within paragraph (*a*) of the definition of "telecommunication service" (i.e., it is the service of emitting, receiving or transmitting sounds ...). Under the place of supply rules contained in section 142.1, the supply is made in Canada where the telecommunication is emitted and received in Canada or the billing location is in Canada and the telecommunication is either transmitted or received in Canada. The billing location is considered to be in Canada where the telecommunication facility used to initiate the service is located in Canada.

The CRA ruled that the bridging equipment used by the applicant, and which is located in Canada, is a telecommunications facility which is used to initiate the service. Further, this bridging equipment is used to emit the telecommunications (i.e., to initiate the service). As a result, the supply is deemed to be made in Canada, including where the supply is made to a non-resident.

The CRA held that this supply would be subject to the GST at the rate of 6%. This conclusion appears to be based on the rules contained in section 2 of Part VIII of Schedule IX. The HST would not apply because the telecommunication is not emitted and received in an HST province and is not emitted or received in an HST province in circumstances where the billing location is in the province.

The CRA ruled that there were no zero-rating provisions which would apply to this supply. It should be noted that the zero-rating provision for telecommunications services (section 22.1 of Part V of Schedule VI) only applies where the recipient is engaged in the telecommunications business.

Conclusions

1. The provision of teleconferencing services is a supply of a telecommunication service under the part (*a*) definition.

2. The supply will be made in Canada where the telecommunication is emitted and received in Canada or where the telecommunication is emitted or received in Canada and the billing location is in Canada. The billing location will be in Canada where the telecommunication facility (i.e., hardware) used to provide the service is in Canada.

3. Where the telecommunication is not emitted and received in a participating province, and the telecommunications facilities are located outside of the participating provinces, the supply will not be subject to HST.

4. Zero-rating is not available in respect of this service.

Ruling 23: Long Distance Minutes

Ruling 8404[27] considers the issues surrounding the supply of long distance minutes over the Internet. The applicant purchases long distance minutes from a third party which is a traditional telecommunication service provider. The applicant will allow for customers to purchase blocks of minutes through its Web site in return for payments of between $5 and $100. All payments will be by way of credit card and the approval and processing portion of the credit card payment will be handled by a third party clearing house.

Once payment has been processed, a PIN is issued through the Internet to the customer. To make a long distance call, the customer calls a toll free number, enters the PIN and the long distance number. The amount deducted from the account will be a function of the origin of the call, the destination of the call and the duration of the call.

The third party long distance minutes supplier does not provide the applicant with detailed information relating to specific calls made. It merely provides an invoice for the cost of the call to the applicant.

The Ruling

The CRA held that this is a supply of a telecommunication service under part (*a*) of the definition. The CRA made note of the ordinary place of supply rules for telecommunications services (where emitted and received and where the billing location is located) but seemed to acknowledge that the application of these rules would be untenable in the circumstances (given that the applicant was not provided with access to this information at any time).

The CRA concluded that a practical solution was in order. The place of supply would be determined in the same manner as with long distance telephone cards. The CRA noted that with long distance cards, the supply is considered to be made in the location where the card is sold to the recipient both for GST and HST purposes:

> ... if the card is provided to a recipient in a retail establishment that is located in a participating province, HST at the rate of 15% will apply to the value of the consideration.

---

[27] March 28, 2002.

This analogous approach resulted in the establishment of the following rule:

> In the case of minutes supplied over the Internet, it is the CRA's position that the supply of the telecommunication service is made where the PIN is provided to the recipient, i.e., the recipient's address.

The CRA's ruling suggests that the supplier should obtain from the customer, at the time of ordering the minutes, the customer's personal address (given that the cards would be sold predominantly to individuals). This address would dictate whether the minutes are subject to GST and if so at which rate.

It would be easy to see how this rule could result in considerable abuse. For example, purchasers might be able to avoid, or minimize their GST obligations by providing misleading information as to their home address.

Conclusions

1. The supply of long distance minutes over the Internet is a supply of a telecommunication service.

2. The service will be considered to be supplied (both with respect to country of supply and with respect to province of supply) in the province of the recipient's mailing address.

Ruling 24: Routed Wide Area Network

In ruling 34340[28], the applicant provides a routed wide area network. The network is used primarily to transport customer data but could also be used for other unspecified purposes.

The network is not considered to be a "point to point" network because there are network switches between the point of emission and the point of reception. Further, this network is capable of servicing several customers.

The Ruling

The CRA ruled that the supply was a telecommunication service under part (*b*) of the definition (i.e., a service of making telecommunication facilities available). In reaching this conclusion, the CRA noted that the predominant purpose of the supply is to provide the customer with access to the equipment to allow for transmission of data:

> It appears that the predominant purpose of ... network service is to provide the customer with the equipment and technology that connects its

---

[28] October 31, 2002.

computers to a network that allows for the speedy transmission and reception of data with a high level of security.

The CRA ruled that this supply would be made in Canada if any of the facilities used in providing the service are located in Canada. The CRA noted that in applying this facilities test, it would also take into account less significant items of hardware regardless of value including, for example, LAN jacks.

In terms of the province of supply, the CRA noted that this is not a supply which would be subject to the special place of supply rules in section 136.4. Those rules apply only to the granting of sole access to a telecommunications channel for the purpose of transmitting telecommunications. The CRA reached this conclusion on the basis that the supplier was not granting sole access to a single client:

> ... customer is not granted sole access as many customers may be sharing a part of the frame relay network that forms part of the xxxxx network service.

Similarly, the special rules contained in the Place of Supply (GST/HST) Regulations would not apply because this is not a "computer related service". A computer related service includes the electronic storage of information and computer to computer transfers of information.

Given that the regulatory rules would not apply, the province of supply is to be determined in accordance with the rule in section 2 of Part VIII. Under that rule, a supply of making available telecommunications facilities will be made in a province if:

(a) All of the facilities are ordinarily located in that province; or

(b) All of the facilities are not located in that province but the invoice is sent to an address in that province.

The CRA provided the following examples of the operation of these rules:

> ... if a ... network service only involves a customer's locations in the province of New Brunswick such that all of the facilities that form part of the ... network service supplied to the customer, and that are made available to the customer are located in New Brunswick, the supply of the service is deemed to be made in New Brunswick ...

> ... where the facilities that are made available to the customer are located in more than one province, the supply will be made in the province where the invoice is sent. For example, if the ... network service involves a customer's locations in Ontario and Nova Scotia the supply will be deemed to be made in Ontario if the invoice is sent to an address in Ontario ... if

the invoice is sent to an address in a participating province [the supply would be subject to 15% HST]

... if there were [network facilities] located in the U.S. the charge ... would also be subject to GST at the rate of 7% ... if the invoice is sent to an address in the U.S. the charge would remain subject to GST at the rate of 7% as the supply is made in Canada since part of the facilities that are made available are located in Canada and pursuant to section 144.1 ... the supply of the ... network service would be deemed to be made in a non-participating province.

The CRA ruled that zero-rating would not be available because the recipient is not in the business of providing telecommunication services.

Conclusions

1. The supply of the right to transmit data over a secure network, which is not dedicated to the use of a single customer, is a supply of a telecommunication service of making telecommunication facilities available.

2. Where any of those facilities are located in Canada, the supply will be deemed to be made in Canada.

3. This supply is not considered to be the granting of sole access to a telecommunications channel (as provided for in section 136.4).

4. This supply is not a "computer related service" (i.e., it is not the computer-to-computer transfer of information) and so the province of supply rules contained in the Place of Supply (GST/HST) Regulations do not apply.

5. Under the Part VIII province of supply rules, the supply will be deemed to be made in a particular province where: (a) all of the facilities are ordinarily located in that province or, (b) all of the facilities are not located in that province but the invoice is sent to an address in that province.

Ruling 25: Bandwidth

Ruling 34339[29] considers the supply of bandwidth. The applicant is a Canadian GST registered entity and refers to itself as a "web based managed solutions provider".

It offers its clients a basic package which includes Web site hosting, a fixed amount of electronic storage space, a fixed number of email accounts and support all for a single monthly fee. Customers also have the option of paying for extra online or offline storage space, monthly or daily backup services, domain management, statistical tracking and added bandwidth.

---

[29] March 21, 2003.

The invoices for bandwidth reflect a charge which is a function of the amount of bandwidth actually used by the client.

The applicant has asked only about how the GST applies to bandwidth when supplied to non-residents.

The Ruling

The CRA noted that the bandwidth could be considered either a separate supply or part of a single supply of the managed solution package. Assuming that the bandwidth is a separate supply, the CRA concluded that the supply would be a telecommunication service under part (*b*) of that definition. This is because it involves making telecommunication facilities available. The CRA noted that this supply would not qualify for zero-rating where the recipient is not in the telecommunication business.

The CRA explained that the application of the place of supply rules would turn on whether this supply was considered to be access to a "telecommunication channel" as defined in subsection 136.4(1). A telecommunications channel is defined as:

> A telecommunications circuit, line, frequency, channel, partial channel or other means of sending or receiving a telecommunication but does not include a satellite channel.

However, the CRA did not offer an opinion as to whether the supply was in fact the provision of access to a telecommunications channel. Instead it described the rules which would be applicable for either outcome of this threshold issue.

Assuming it is a telecommunications channel

Pursuant to subsection 136.4(2), the supply of a telecommunication service of granting to the recipient sole access to a telecommunications channel for transmitting telecommunications between a place in a particular province and a place in another province is considered to be the making of separate supplies in each province.

The rules for determining the province of supply are contained in section 3 of Schedule VIII. Those rules relate back to section 136.4, which provides that the supply will be made in a particular province based upon a distance calculation. This would mean that if one supply is deemed to be made in a non-participating province, and the other supply is deemed to be made in a participating province, the supplier would charge the non-resident GST at two different rates in connection with the two supplies. The allocation would be done on a distance basis.

The CRA also noted that it follows a similar allocation approach where a telecommunications channel spans Canada and another country. The supplier would only charge GST to the extent (based on distance) that the channel spans Canada.

Assuming it is not a telecommunications channel

The place of supply rules which would apply are contained in paragraph 142.1(2)(*a*). Under those rules the supply is deemed to be made in Canada if any part of the facilities are located in Canada.

In terms of the province of supply, the relevant rules are contained in section 2 of Part VIII. The supply would be made in a particular province if all of the facilities are located in that particular province or in any other case if the invoice for the supply is sent to an address in that province.

The CRA summarized the application of these rules where supplies are made to non-residents as follows:

> ... where ... supplies are made of a telecommunication service of making telecommunications facilities available to a non-resident and the supply is not zero-rated, and all of the telecommunications facilities are located in a non-participating province the supply is subject to GST at a rate of 7%. Where the telecommunications facilities are not all located in [a participating province] and the invoice is not sent to an address in a province (e.g., the address is in the state of Maine) the supply will be considered to be made in a non-participating province ... and subject to GST at a rate of 7%.

Conclusions

1. Where a supply of bandwidth is a separate supply, the supply will be considered a supply of a "telecommunication service" of making telecommunication facilities available.

2. A determination must be made as to whether the supply is the granting of sole access to a telecommunication channel or other than granting of sole access to a telecommunication channel.

3. If the supply is of sole access to a telecommunication channel and that channel spans Canada and another country, the supply will be taxed only in proportion to the extent that it spans Canada. If the channel spans provinces which are subject to tax at different rates, the channel will be taxed at the rate which corresponds with the proportion of the channel which spans the particular province.

4. If the supply is not the provision of sole access to a telecommunications channel, the supply will be considered to be made in Canada if any of the facilities are located in Canada.

5. The supply will be deemed to be made in a particular province if all of the facilities are located in that province. The supply will also be deemed to be made in a particular province if all the facilities are not contained in a single province, but the invoice is sent to an address in that province.

5. Data Processing and Access to Mainframe

Ruling 26: Access to Mainframe

Ruling 30957[30] considers issues relating to the provision of access to a mainframe which is located in the U.S. The supplier is a GST registered non-resident which provides its clients with an elaborate software package intended to handle all of their daily business needs, including inventory control, accounting, sales documentation and other business functions.

The software package resides on the supplier's mainframe in the U.S. which allows the customer to use the mainframe to perform data processing (the client is saved from the cost of purchasing an expensive mainframe computer). As a result, the supplier also provides secure access to its mainframe.

The customer pays four separate fees:

(a) Software licensing fee;

(b) Fee for installation of networking equipment at customer's office (to allow for connection to the mainframe);

(c) Fee for consulting service (customer needs analysis and setting up the mainframe to allow for customer connection); and

(d) Monthly access fee (which is the fee for the use of the mainframe).

The Ruling

The CRA concluded that a single supply of the right to use software was being provided and that this is considered to be a supply of intangible personal property. The CRA noted that any one of the elements if supplied alone, would be of no use, and that each element supplied appeared to be contingent on the other elements.

The CRA concluded that the supply would be made in Canada if the recipient could use the property in Canada. The province of supply would be determined in accordance with the rules contained in paragraph 2(d) of Part III. If all or substantially all of the Canadian rights in respect of the

---

[30] November 21, 2002.

property may only be exercised in a single province, the supply is made in that province.

The supply will be considered to be made in the province of negotiation if the property may be used otherwise than exclusively outside that province. Otherwise (i.e., place of negotiation outside Canada and no restrictions as to use) the supply may be deemed to be made in a participating province under the rule contained in section 3 of Part III. That rule provides that if the place of negotiation is outside Canada, the property may be used exclusively in Canada and the Canadian rights may be used primarily in the participating provinces, the supply will be subject to HST. Otherwise, the supply will be subject to GST.

The CRA does not discuss zero-rating. The suggestion is that zero-rating would not be available.

Conclusions

1. The provision of mainframe access to software (including where data processing is be done on the mainframe) may be considered to be a single supply of software.

2. The rules which apply are those which apply to application hosting of software (discussed in more detail in Chapter 14, Software and Software Related Offerings).

Ruling 27: Data Backup and Recovery

In ruling 39421[31] the applicant, a GST registered corporation, provides data backup and recovery as well as a number of other related services. The customer signs on for the service through the applicant's Web site where the applicable credit card payment is made. Once the payment has been processed, the customer's account is activated.

The customer then downloads its files to the applicant's data server. Customers can typically download and recover their files unassisted through the applicant's Web site. However, technical support is available if needed.

The Ruling

The CRA ruled that the data download and recovery supply is a supply of a service. It is interesting to note that this service would typically involve absolutely no human interaction.

The CRA indicated that the service would be supplied in Canada if any part of the service was performed in Canada. The suggestion seemed to be

---

[31] December 3, 2002.

that since the applicant's offices were located in Canada, the service would be considered to be performed in Canada.

In terms of the province of supply, the CRA noted that as a threshold matter, the ordinary "services" place of supply rules would not apply (i.e., those contained in Part V of Schedule IX). This is because the supply of data backup and recovery services are considered to be "computer related services" as that term is defined in the Place of Supply (GST/HST) Regulations. A computer related service includes "a service involving the electronic storage of information and computer to computer transfers of information".

Pursuant to section 10 of the Regulations, where there is to be a single final recipient of a supply of a computer-related service, the supply is made in a particular province if:

(a) the final recipient avails itself of the service at a single ordinary location in that province, and

(b) this location is either known to the supplier or

(c) it is the ordinary business practice of the supplier to know this information.

Where there is to be a single final recipient of the supply, and *any* of these conditions are not met, the supply will be made in a province if the mailing address of the recipient is in that province.

It should be expected that in most cases there will be a single final recipient of the service and that the recipient will avail itself of the service at a single ordinary location in a province. However, it should also be expected that the supplier would not normally know the location where the recipient will avail itself of the service (the supplier may not know where the recipient's computers are located) and the supplier may not know the mailing address of the recipient (because the payment is made by credit card over the Internet).

The suggestion seems to be that the supplier must specifically ask the customer to provide either the ordinary location at which they will use the service or their mailing address in order to locate the province of supply.

Conclusions

1. Data backup and recovery is a service including where it is performed automatically without human interaction.

2. The service is considered to be supplied in the location where the service is performed. This would likely include the location where any employees of the supplier are situated and the location of the automatic equipment (such as data servers).

3. The service is considered to be a "computer related service". When it is supplied to a single final recipient, it is supplied in a particular province if the recipient avails itself of the service in that province and the supplier knows this location (or would normally know this location). Otherwise, it is supplied in a particular province if the mailing address of the recipient is in that province.

Chapter 16

Online Content, Services, and Other General Offerings

A. OVERVIEW

This chapter considers the manner in which the GST applies to a wide range of general offerings. The supplies considered in this chapter relate to memberships, images and graphic design, music and points programs, and access to information in the form of online magazines and databases. The chapter will also consider a number of different service offerings which support the content offerings noted above.

This chapter has been designed to be particularly broad in scope so that issues relating to the characterization of a wide range of supplies may be considered in detail. In particular, this direct comparison of different offerings is intended to provide a greater insight into the leading characterization indicators.

Notwithstanding the broad nature of this chapter, certain types of supplies will not be considered. Where a supply is in the nature of the right to access or use software, the manner in which the GST will apply to the software supply is discussed in Chapter 14, Software and Software Related Offerings (which also discusses issues relating to the provision of software related services). This chapter will, however, discuss software related supplies where the object of the supply is something other than the right to access or use software (i.e., where software is relied upon for the purpose of delivering some other supply).

A similar distinction has been made with respect to telecommunication related supplies. Every one of the supplies discussed in this chapter, relies upon telecommunications for its delivery. However, the object of the supplies which are discussed in this chapter will be something other than various telecommunication services. Supplies which relate specifically to telecommunications (for example, the provision of the rights to use a telecommunications channel), are discussed in Chapter 15, Telecommunication Services and Related Supplies.

This chapter does not consider third party sales, advertising services, or educational offerings. Each of these subjects is discussed in their own distinct chapters.

B. CHARACTERIZATION OF SUPPLY

Many of the supplies considered in this chapter will have characteristics which will make it difficult to determine whether services or intangible personal property is being supplied. Making this distinction will require a careful consideration of the CRA's characterization guidelines. The CRA explains in TIB 090 that, in making the distinction, the following guidelines should be considered:

If the supply is of an existing product or a product created for a group of customers who receive rights to the product (eg subscriptions for data delivered on a periodic basis), it is characterized as a supply of intangible personal property.

If there is human involvement in the making of the supply or specific work is performed by a person for a specific customer, and the supply does not involve the transfer of rights, it is characterized as a supply of a service.

In some cases, particularly where both intangible personal property and services are being supplied, the "principal object of the supply" test will be required to be applied to resolve the characterization issue.

1. Factors Which Suggest That Intangible Personal Property is Being Supplied

TIB 090 establishes that the presence of any of the following will suggest that a supply provided electronically is a supply of intangible personal property:

(a) a right in a product or a right to use a product for personal or commercial purposes is provided such as:

— intellectual property or a right to use intellectual property (e.g., a copyright); or

— rights of a temporary nature (e.g., a right to view, access or use a product while online);

(b) A product is provided that has already been created or developed, or is already in existence;

(c) A product is created or developed for a specific customer, but the supplier retains ownership of the product; or

(d) A right to make a copy of a digitized product is provided.

2. Factors Which Suggest That a Service is Being Supplied

TIB 090 establishes that the presence of any of the following will suggest that a supply provided electronically is a supply of a service:

(a) the supply does not include the provision of rights (e.g. technical know how) or if there is a provision of rights, the rights are incidental to the supply;

(b) the supply involves specific work that is performed by a person for a specific customer; or

(c) there is human involvement in making the supply.

TIB 090 provides a number of examples of situations which are intended to illustrate the distinction between services and intangible personal property. Those examples are reproduced in Chapter 3, Characterization of Supply.

3. Practical Approach to Making the Distinction

To distinguish between services and intangible personal property, it may be more appropriate to view all electronic offerings as occupying a particular position along a continuum. This approach is premised on the idea that virtually every electronic offering will involve at least some element of a service, and some element of intangible personal property.

At one end of the spectrum would be "pure" service offerings such as one-on-one online consulting. This type of pure offering would not involve the provision of any rights to use or access existing materials or any other form of intangible personal property.

At the other end of the spectrum would be "pure" intangible personal property offerings. For example, this would include the right to access and use a database containing pre-existing information. The content would not be tailored in any way to the specific customer.

Most offerings, however, would fall somewhere closer to the centre of the spectrum. This may include situations where a customer is provided with the right to access existing information but in certain cases that information is specifically tailored for the customer. Alternatively, a customer is provided with the right to access a digitized product but the use of that product is supported by some other, more personalized, offering.

The rulings and examples provided in TIB 090 seem to suggest that the following trends have emerged in connection with the characterization requirement:

Right to use existing content

(a) the right to access existing information (including copyrighted materials) will be considered to be a supply of intangible personal property. Typical informational Web sites include access to industry specific information, access to sports information (for example, detailed statistics and commentary to be used by persons in fantasy sports pools), medical information databases, legal issues databases, fitness and health related databases, and general interest Web sites. The information may take on any one of a number of forms:

(i) at one end of the spectrum would be raw information, statistics or other similar digitized content. For example, an automotive industry Web site may provide raw data as to the dollar value of vehicles imported into Canada during a particular time period; or

(ii) at the other end of the spectrum would be highly refined subjective commentary. This type of material would typically be subject to copyright protection. For example, a human resources Web site may provide articles setting out suggestions for identifying good candidates. However, the human element involved in compiling this type of information or creating the commentary would generally be considered an input to the supply.

(b) the customer may be provided with the right to use a particular software application to search an informational database. Given that the object of the supply is the right to access or use the content (and not the right to access or use the software), the supply will not be considered a supply of software. It should be expected that the supply will be considered to be intangible personal property.

(c) when information is provided to the customer in circumstances where the supplier assumes a slightly more active role in personalizing the offering, the supply will still be considered to be intangible personal property. For example, the customer may establish preferences as to the type of information which it would like to receive. The supplier would then "push" the relevant information (for example, news clippings or stock quotes) to the user by means of emails or other forms of alerts. Generally, this type of offering will still be considered to be a supply of intangible personal property even though the offering has to some extent been personalized for the particular customer. However, a threshold will eventually be crossed. As the personalized element of the offering becomes more prominent, the offering could be considered to be in the nature of a service.

(d) the provision to customers of the right to use more elaborate, but existing online offerings would be considered to be a supply of intangible personal property. For example, supplying the right to access music, videos and games, would be a supply of intangible personal property. The human element associated with adding the products to the Web site or in maintaining the Web site occurs "behind the scenes" and would be considered an input to the supply.

Right to access or use other than existing content

(e) where specific content is provided to the customer (which is not pre-existing content), the distinction between services and intangible personal property becomes more difficult to draw:

(i) where the supplier provides the customer with the right to use copyrighted materials, the supply will be intangible personal property. Even where the copyrighted materials are specifically developed for the customer, the supply will be characterized as intangible personal property (see in particular ruling 42608 below); and

(ii) where the supplier develops materials specifically for the customer in which the supplier does not retain any copyright (i.e., full ownership passes to the customer), the supply is a service.

(f) similarly, where technical information (which is not pre-existing) is supplied to a customer, it may be very difficult to draw the distinction between services and intangible personal property:

(i) where the supplier undertakes to compile information for the specific customer (for example, the supplier performs a research function) and provides the customer with a license to use that information, the supply will be intangible personal property. The fact that the materials were specifically compiled for that customer would not result in a finding that a service has been provided (as long as the information is licensed to the customer); and

(ii) where the supplier undertakes to compile information for the specific customer and provides the customer with outright ownership of that information, the supply will be a service.

More general services

(g) where a supplier provides personalized information to a customer in connection with the offering of a consulting service, this will be considered to be a supply of a service. However, if the supply involves only the provision of materials which are subject to copyright, or if it merely licenses the information to the customer, the supply will be subject to the exception set out above and will be considered to be a supply of intangible personal property.

(h) where a consultant provides a hybrid combination of offerings (i.e., information provided outright to the customer along with materials which are protected by copyright or licensed to the customer), then assuming that a single supply is made the "principal object of the supply" will need to be ascertained. For example, consider an IT consultant who has been retained to advise a customer on how to set up a computer network. The consultant may provide the right to view copyrighted materials which relate to general network issues. However, to the extent that the customer encounters specific issues not covered by the existing materials, the consultant would provide specific advice.

(a) Special Characterization of Memberships

A wide range of offerings may be provided under the heading of "memberships". These underlying offerings may be in the nature of services, or in the nature of intangible personal property. For example, a particular membership may provide the user with the right to access a database of existing information relating to a particular subject matter (in which case the underlying supply would be considered to be intangible personal property). Alternatively, a membership may involve providing the user with the right to interact on a one-on-one basis with consultants (in which case the underlying supply would be considered to be a service).

The term "membership" is defined in subsection 123(1) in a manner which explicitly recognizes that the member is being provided with certain rights which may include the right to receive services:

> "Membership" includes a right granted by a particular person that entitles another person to services that are provided by, or to the use of the facilities that are operated by, the particular person and that are not available, or are not available to the same extent or for the same fee or charge to persons to whom such a right has not been granted, and also includes such a right that is conditional on the acquisition of ownership of a share, bond, debenture or other security.

Notwithstanding that by definition, a membership may include the right to receive services administratively, the CRA takes the position that where a membership is provided, the recipient is always being provided with a supply of intangible personal property.

(b) Timeshares and Loyalty Points Programs

With respect to timeshares, the CRA has thus far taken the position that intangible personal property is in fact being provided when the timeshare points are purchased.

With respect to loyalty points, the CRA has taken the position that the characterization of supply tests should be applied only at the time when the points are redeemed. The nature of the supply will be determined by reference to the particular property or service which has been purchased with the points. For example, in ruling 26 below the loyalty points were redeemed to purchase an airline ticket. Accordingly, the supply was considered to be a supply of a transportation service.

C. PLACE OF SUPPLY ISSUES

1. Services

(a) GST

Once it has been determined that a particular supply is a supply of a service, then locating the place of supply will be a function of the place of performance of the service. There will be two factors to consider in locating the place of performance:

(a) the location(s) from which employees operate in connection with the making of the supply; and

(b) the location of any equipment through which the supply is made.

(b) Employees

The rules which provide that performance is occurring in Canada in connection with employee activities are as follows:

(a) the service requires a person to perform a task (i.e., the supplier acts through one or more of its employees), and the person performing or physically carrying out the task is situated in Canada at the time the activity is done; or

(b) any activity related to the performance of the service is undertaken in Canada.

The challenge in applying these rules is to identify any person who is performing any task relating to the supply, or who is performing any activity related to the performance of the service. It would appear that the second of these two tests is intended to be far broader in scope and may include employees who, for example, provide secondary or support functions in connection with the supply.

As a starting point, the supply will be considered to be made in the location of the supplier's office from which the employees operate in connection with the making of the supply. So, if the supply is a consulting service delivered electronically, and the employees providing the consulting service operate from the supplier's head office, the supply will be considered to be made in the location of the head office.

Alternatively, if consulting services are provided mainly from the supplier's head office, but employees also visit the customer's office to perform any task which is a component of the service, the service will be performed at both the head office and at the client's offices. It would not appear to matter that only a small portion of the tasks were performed at the client's offices.

The second rule suggests that the location from which support or secondary services are provided (if those services relate to the performance of the supply) should also be considered. The rule also seems to suggest that activities should be taken into account even where the activities do not form a component of the service provided to the recipient. The activities are merely required to "relate" to the performance of the service.

The scope of activities which should be taken into account in locating the place of supply of a service is an issue which is considered in more detail in Chapter 5, Place of Supply.

(c) Equipment

Given that many services may easily be provided from remote locations, it is not surprising that the CRA has also broadened its rules relating to the place of performance of services provided through equipment. These broad rules take into account, for example, the location of equipment (both supplier's and recipient's) which is used directly in connection with the service. Administratively, the CRA notes that services will be considered to be performed in Canada where:

(a) the service includes operations performed by a supplier's equipment (e.g., computer equipment), and the equipment is located in Canada;

(b) the supply involves doing something to or with a recipient's equipment by accessing it from a remote location, and the recipient's equipment is located in Canada (however, this does not apply to a service wholly performed outside Canada, where the results are subsequently delivered electronically to a recipient's computers in Canada, e.g., a programming service carried out at the supplier's location outside Canada and e-mailed to a recipient in Canada).

The rule in part (b) relates in large part to programming, repair or diagnostic services provided from a remote location, and will not typically be applicable to the supplies which are considered in this chapter.

The rule in part (a) however, should be considered far more carefully. Very little guidance has been provided to date with respect to the meaning and scope of this rule. However, the limited guidance which has been provided suggests that the CRA takes a broad view of this rule, which position may be summarized as follows:

(a) a "supplier's equipment" will include servers but will not include Web sites which are hosted on those servers;

(b) the equipment will likely be considered to be "a supplier's equipment" if it is owned or leased by the supplier or is otherwise at the disposal of the supplier. The conclusion that any equipment which is at the disposal of the supplier will be considered "supplier's equipment" is derived from the commentary provided by the CRA with respect to the meaning of "permanent establishment". Specifically, the CRA has held that a server may be considered to be "at the disposal" of the non-resident (and thus qualifies as the non-resident's server) in circumstances where it is not owned or even leased by the non-resident;

(c) a server which is hosted in a typical ISP arrangement is not likely to be considered a "supplier's equipment". Again, this conclusion has been reached on the basis of the CRA's interpretation of the meaning of "permanent establishment" and relates to the fact that the server would not ordinarily be considered to be "at the disposal" of the supplier; and

(d) operations carried out through the server which may constitute performance of a service through the server include:

(i) communicating with the customer (or with third parties) through the server (i.e., by email or by way of online forums such as chat rooms);[1]

(ii) the provision of information through the server (i.e., information contained on the Web site);

(iii) accepting information through the Web site;

(iv) accepting orders or accepting payment for the orders through the server (either from the customer or from third parties).

(d) HST

The identification of the places where performance occurs will also be critical for identifying the province of supply of a service. For example, a service will be supplied in a province if all or substantially all of the service is performed in that province. A service will be considered to be supplied in the province of negotiation for the supply where it is not the case that all or substantially all of the service is performed outside that province. Where the two rules described above do not locate the province of supply, a third rule may also apply which requires that a determination be made as to whether the Canadian element of the service is performed primarily in the participating provinces.

---

[1] For example, in ruling 37297, the CRA ruled that when a server and Web site in Canada were used to disseminate information (i.e., a service), the service was performed in Canada.

2. Intangible Personal Property

(a) GST

The general rule with respect to intangible personal property is that it is considered to be supplied in Canada if the property may be used in whole or in part in Canada. Intangible personal property may also be considered to be supplied in Canada where it relates to real property situated in Canada, to tangible personal property ordinarily situated in Canada, or to a service to be performed in Canada.

The general rule requires that consideration be given to whether the property may be used in Canada. The fact that, as a practical matter, the recipient would never be expected to use the particular property in Canada is irrelevant including in situations where the property would serve no useful purpose in Canada. For example, consider a supplier which provides the right to access a database which lists restaurants located in Florida. If the recipient is not precluded from accessing this database while in Canada, the supply will be considered to be made in Canada even though as a practical matter the recipient would not typically be expected to access material of this nature from outside Florida.

(b) HST

The province of supply rules for intangible personal property all relate to the place where the property may be used. For example, a supply of intangible personal property will be supplied in a province where all or substantially all of the Canadian rights in respect of the property can be used only in that province. A supply of intangible personal property will be supplied in the province of negotiation for the supply if the property can be used otherwise than exclusively outside that province. Otherwise, the supply will be made in a participating province if:

(a) the Canadian rights in respect of the property cannot be used otherwise than primarily in the participating provinces, and

(b) the place of negotiation is outside Canada and the property cannot be used otherwise than exclusively in Canada.

(c) Memberships

Special province of supply rules may apply to supplies of memberships. These rules are contained in the Place of Supply (GST/HST) Regulations.

Where a membership is supplied to an individual, and the Canadian rights in respect of the membership may be exercised otherwise than exclusively in one province, the supply will be made in a particular province if the mailing address of the individual is in that province. In all other cases, the province of supply rules which relate to memberships are the general rules which are contained in Part III of Schedule IX.

D. NON-RESIDENT ISSUES

Where a non-resident is supplying intangible personal property in Canada (i.e., a supply which may be used in Canada) the non-resident will, if GST registered, be required to collect the GST and possibly the HST in respect of the supply. The non-resident who is not registered will typically be entitled to take advantage of the non-resident override. To ensure that the override is available the non-resident will want to consider:

(a) whether the non-resident is deemed to be resident in Canada:

(i) The non-resident will want to ensure that it is not making any supplies through a permanent establishment (i.e., a fixed place of business including a server) which is at the disposal of the non-resident and located in Canada.

Although the location of the server is not relevant in determining whether the supply of intangible personal property is made in Canada, the location of the server will be relevant for locating a possible permanent establishment;

(ii) The non-resident will also want to ensure that it is not making supplies through a dependent agent located in Canada. The permanent establishment of the dependent agent could be considered to be the permanent establishment of the non-resident (i.e., if the supplies made through the agent are significant in relation to the overall business activities of the non-resident).

(b) whether the supply is made in the course of a business carried on in Canada. The non-resident who provides only intangible personal property from a location outside Canada, would ordinarily be required to have established some other more substantial presence in Canada before the "carrying on business" threshold would be met.

Where the non-resident is providing services in Canada, the permanent establishment and carrying on business issues should be even more carefully considered. Generally, there appears to be a strong presumption that where core services are performed in Canada (either as a result of employee activities or as a result of equipment), the non-resident is in fact carrying on business in Canada.

The main exception seems to relate to "one-off" services of a limited duration, which involve minimal (or no) employee presence in Canada, and which are made other than through a permanent establishment in Canada. This strict standard is reflected in the "Carrying on Business in Canada" and "Meaning of Permanent Establishment" Policy Statements, which are discussed in Chapters 8 and 9, respectively.

E. ZERO-RATING ISSUES

1. Services

Numerous zero-rating provisions are available in respect of the supply of services. The broadest provision is found in section 7 and allows for zero-rating even where the non-resident recipient is GST registered. The section 7 relief, however, is not available where the service is rendered to an individual (including an individual employee of a corporation) while that individual is in Canada. The relief is also not available where the service is made to an individual who is in Canada at any time and has contact with the supplier in relation to the supply.

A number of other carve-outs may also apply. For example, a service in respect of tangible personal property which is situated in Canada at the time that the service is performed, will not qualify for relief. Ruling 48298 (discussed below), in particular, demonstrates how broadly this carve-out will be interpreted. In that ruling, a service provided in respect of rebate applications was disqualified from zero-rating relief. It was held that the document itself was the tangible personal property in respect of which the service was provided.

Many of the services described in this chapter will be considered to be advisory, professional, or consulting services. Those services are zero-rated pursuant to section 23.

2. Intangible Personal Property

The only zero-rating provision that may apply to supplies of intangible personal property is contained in section 10. The relief applies where the supply is made of intellectual property or any right, license or privilege to use such property to a non-resident who is not registered. Intellectual property for the purposes of this provision includes an invention, patent, trade secret, trade mark, trade name, copyright or industrial design.

Administratively, the CRA does not interpret this provision in a particularly broad manner. It appears to be the view of the CRA that a very substantial bundle of rights would be required to be provided to the recipient before relief would be available. For example, the mere right to access information, or a database, will never qualify for this relief. Similarly, the

CRA takes the position that memberships do not ever qualify for zero-rating under this section.

This narrow interpretation of section 10 is a substantial problem for suppliers of intangible personal property who are deemed to be making supplies in Canada (i.e., where the supplier cannot as a practical matter limit access to the property to locations outside Canada). Among the techniques commonly employed to minimize the harsh application of these rules is the entering into of separate parallel agreements with a single recipient.

It is not clear whether the CRA's narrow interpretation of section 10 will endure. One recent court case in particular, has suggested that the CRA has to date interpreted section 10 in a manner which is far too restrictive.

At issue in *Dawn's Place Ltd. v. Her Majesty the Queen*, 2006 GTC 70 (T.C.C.) (currently under appeal), was whether memberships provided to non-resident individuals qualified for zero-rating under section 10. A non-resident who purchased a membership would be granted a licence to access the supplier's adult content Web site. The contact entered into between each non-resident and the supplier specified that the non-resident was being provided with a non-exclusive, limited and revocable licence to download and view the contents of the Web site. The corresponding content was defined to include "images, text, logos, graphics, information, software, computer code and applications, animations, video and any and all types of multimedia".

The Minister of Revenue appears to have conceded that the Web site materials were copyright protected. However, the Minister's primary argument was that section 10 relief should not be available because the supplier was only providing the recipients with limited rights to access and view the copyrighted materials (i.e., the supplier was not relinquishing its copyright to the recipients).

The Tax Court of Canada rejected the Minister's narrow interpretation of section 10 and concluded that relief was, in fact, available where memberships were provided to non-residents. In reaching this conclusion, the Court noted that section 10 specifically provided that "... any right, license, or privilege to use any such [i.e., copyrighted] property ..." qualifies for relief.

The CRA has since appealed this decision to the Federal Court. If in fact the broad interpretation of section 10 which was adopted by the Tax Court of Canada prevails, then it should be expected that many other e-commerce copyright supplies will similarly qualify for zero-rating.

F. SPECIFIC RULINGS

The rulings below have been organized into the following categories:

1. General offerings

2. Databases, memberships and online magazines

3. Graphic design

4. Music

5. Timeshares and loyalty points programs

1. General Offerings

Ruling 1: Electronic Exercises

At issue in ruling 42608[2] were two separate packages which related to psychological testing. The supplier operates a Web site (which seems to be hosted in Canada) that contains the exercises. The supplier owns the patents, maintains the Web site and administers the business in every way.

The first package allows the customer to go online and sort cards in a certain way. The manner in which the cards are sorted provides a particular insight into the individual's behaviour patterns. The computer program automatically analyzes the results and sends the results to the customer by email with patented information describing the meaning attributed to the results. There is no human involvement in this package.

The second package provides all of the above plus the customer is also entitled to discuss the results over the phone with a consultant for up to one hour. For higher fees the customer can discuss the results with more senior employees of the supplier.

The Ruling

The first package

The CRA concluded that the first program is a supply of intangible personal property. This result flows from the fact that there is no human involvement in either the testing (which is performed automatically) or the delivery of the results (which are delivered automatically to the customer). The customer is also being provided with the right to use digitized patented materials relating to their particular test results but does not acquire ownership of the patented materials.

---

[2] February 19, 2003.

The supply will be considered to be made in Canada if the Web site can be accessed or used by a person in Canada. The CRA concluded that zero-rating would not be available in respect of this supply. This seems anomalous given that the customer is being provided with the right to interact with (i.e., use) patented materials.

The second package

The CRA concluded that the second package is a single supply of a service. The CRA did not explain how it reached the conclusion that a single supply was delivered or why this supply was a supply of a service.

Given the conclusion reached with respect to supply #1, it is beyond dispute that there was an intangible personal property element to the supply. However, it appears that the CRA reached the conclusion that a single supply of a service was provided because either:

(a) the principal object of the contract was the right to receive the consulting services (and not the right to take the automatic test or the right to receive the standardized content); or

(b) a multiple supply was made but the intangible personal property supplies were incidental to the supply of the service.

The CRA ruled that this service is performed in Canada because all of the service components are performed in Canada (i.e., the employees of the supplier operate from Canada).

Zero-rating would not be available under section 7 because "consulting, professional and advisory services" are carved out of that provision. However, the ruling notes that the services might be zero-rated under section 23.

Conclusions

1. Where the supply is of the right to interact with electronic content (but ownership of the content does not pass) and there is no human involvement in the delivery, the supply will be intangible personal property.

2. The right to interact with digitized content (including patented content), and the right to receive and use patented materials, does not qualify for zero-rating under section 10. This conclusion may not be correct in light of the Tax Court decision in *Dawn's Place*, referenced above.

3. Where intangible personal property is supplied along with a substantial service offering, the supply may be characterized as a single supply of a service.

4. The consulting service may qualify for zero-rating under section 23.

Ruling 2: Training Courses

Ruling 36218[3] considers the supply of training courses provided over the Internet. In this ruling the applicant is a GST registered charity (and a public institution) which is the recipient of a number of training services provided by non-residents. At issue is the application of the GST to various training courses provided to employees of the applicant.

The first supply

The first training course is provided by a non-resident who is not registered. The courses relate to various basic business skills including management and learning how to use software. The courses are taken automatically over the Internet without the assistance of any instructor. There is however a minimal amount of live support provided as required.

Ruling on the first supply

The CRA concluded that this type of electronic supply could potentially be characterized as either a service or intangible personal property. To make this distinction the applicant would be required to determine whether the electronic courses and support constitute a single supply or multiple supplies.

The CRA suggested that a single supply was likely being provided in the circumstances. The next stage of the test is to identify the principal object of the supply. If the principal object of the supply is the access to the software (i.e., to access and interact with the software while online), the supply is of intangible personal property. If the principal object is the provision of support services, the supply is a service.

The CRA suggested that the principal object would likely be the right to access the training software and so the supply would be a single supply of intangible personal property. In reaching this conclusion the CRA seems to have determined that the support services provided would be minimal.

This supply would be considered to be supplied in Canada because the property was allowed to be used in Canada. However, the non-resident override would likely apply to deem the supply to be made outside Canada. The CRA cautioned that if the override were not available for any reason, the applicant would need to consider whether it should be paying HST as well. Although not discussed in the ruling, the applicant would likely be obligated to self-assess under Division IV in the event that the non-resident override was not available.

---

[3] February 5, 2004.

The second supply

The second vendor is also a non-resident and non registered person. It provided the applicant with consulting services in the form of written reports and recommendations (by way of email) on specific technology issues.

Ruling on the second supply

The CRA held that this supply would be considered to be a service. In reaching this conclusion the CRA noted that the consulting services involved specific work provided for a specific person and did not involve the provision of rights to existing products. In reaching this conclusion, the CRA did not seem to consider whether those same reports were also provided to other customers.

Although not specifically discussed, it would appear that if the supplier had provided the customer with the right to view and use copyright or patent protected reports, the supply would likely have been considered to be a supply of intangible personal property. However, when existing reports are provided to a customer which are not copyright or patent protected (even if not specifically designed for the customer), the supply will be a service.

The CRA indicated that this service was supplied outside of Canada. This appears to be because the supplier's employees do not enter Canada and because the server used to provide the reports was located outside Canada.

The third supply

The third supply is of software and hardware maintenance services. Those supplies are discussed in Chapter 14, Software and Software Related Offerings.

Conclusions

1. The right to interact while online with digitized content (including training courses) is typically considered to be a supply of intangible personal property.

2. However, where the content is provided along with customer support, a single or multiple supplies could be considered to be made. If the supply is a single supply, the principal object of the supply must be identified. Where the support provided is minimal, the CRA may conclude that a single supply of intangible property has been supplied.

3. The provision to a customer of specific electronic reports is considered to be a supply of a service. This conclusion will follow even where the reports are not customized or created for the particular customer. However,

if the reports are patent or copyright protected, and the customer is merely provided with the right or license to use the reports, the supply may be intangible personal property.

Ruling 3: Electronic Consulting

At issue in ruling 37297[4] were consulting services provided to customers. The applicant was a Canadian GST registered entity which owned and operated a Web site which was hosted on a Canadian server. Through this Web site the applicant provided health related consulting. However, the consultation services were actually delivered by third party consultants who were paid a fee by the applicant for their services. Many of the consultants were non-residents of Canada.

The basic package allows for customers to log onto the applicant's Web site and receive consultations in respect of particular health issues. The questions are typically asked and answered by way of email. For an enhanced fee the customer can purchase 30 minute blocks of time in a chat room to discuss health related issues with a consultant.

The customers always paid their fees to the applicant who would in turn pay an hourly fee to the consultant who worked on the client file. The fee charged by the applicant to the customer would be higher than the fee charged by the consultant to the applicant. This difference related to the applicant's overhead costs and profit margin.

This ruling also considered issues relating to the sale of goods. These issues are discussed in Chapter 13, Third Party Sales of Goods.

The Ruling

The CRA considered the consulting services to have been supplied by the applicant. This is because the applicant provided the customers with the right to interact with third-party health consultants.

The CRA also concluded that the services are considered to be supplied in Canada including in circumstances where the consultant who communicates with the customer is a non-resident operating solely from a location outside Canada. In reaching the conclusion that the services are performed in Canada, the CRA noted that both the Web site and the server on which the applicant's Web site resides, are located in Canada. With respect to zero-rating, the CRA did note that the services should qualify under section 23 of Part V of Schedule IX when provided to a non-resident.

This conclusion as to the place of performance of the services is important because it may possibly demonstrate the broad scope of the

---

[4] January 23, 2003.

equipment based place of performance rules. The relevant administrative rule provides that a service is generally considered to be performed in Canada where:

> ... the service includes operations performed by a supplier's equipment (e.g., computer equipment), and the equipment is located in Canada ...

It is interesting to note, however, that in its ruling, the CRA did not specifically reference the equipment based performance rule set out above. Instead, the CRA seemed to rely upon considerations which took into account both the human element associated with the supply, and the equipment element. The CRA explained that:

> The Company [i.e., the applicant] is carrying out activities (i.e., maintenance of the Web site and platform for online consultations) in Canada that are part of the provision of its consultation services. The fact that these activities are carried out in Canada means that consultation services provided by the Company are performed in whole or in part in Canada.

At first blush, the CRA's conclusion may appear to be based more upon considerations relating to location of employee activities than to the place where the equipment performs operations. However, the deficiency with this line of reasoning is that the employee activities referred to do not appear to be components of the supply. For example, the customer is not purchasing services which relate to maintaining a Web site. Rather, the customer is purchasing the right to receive health related consultations (i.e., the Web site is merely a means by which this service is provided).

An alternative view may be that the CRA has reached its place of performance conclusion on the basis of performance rule 4. That rule provides that a supply will be performed in Canada where "any activity related to the performance of the service is undertaken in Canada". However it is not clear whether the maintaining of a Web site should be considered to be "the performance of the service". The better view is that the maintenance of the Web site is merely an input to the supply of the consulting service.

Regardless of which of the views described above is correct, the inescapable conclusion is that where a service is delivered through the supplier's equipment located in Canada, the supply will generally be considered to be performed in Canada.

Conclusions

1. The provision of personalized consulting through an electronic forum is considered to be a supply of a service.

2. Consulting services may be considered to be performed in Canada when they are delivered through a supplier's Web site hosted on a server in Canada.

3. The server does not necessarily need to be owned or leased by the supplier to constitute "the supplier's server".

4. Delivering emails and providing access to chat rooms through a server appears to constitute services which are "operations performed by a supplier's equipment". Alternatively, the maintenance in Canada of equipment which allows for customers to access chat rooms or email services, may be services which are considered to be "a part of the supply" of services which are performed in Canada.

Ruling 4: Agent Providing Electronic Enrolment in Courses

In ruling 35664[5], the supplier provides its customers with assistance in enrolling individuals in the customer's events. The supplier is a GST registered software and Web site hosting company which provides online registration. The supplier also collects on behalf of its customers, through the Web site, the fees associated with attending the particular event.

The supplier also sells books and materials to individuals which are associated with the particular event. The books are sold by the supplier as an agent of the conference organizer. The agent collects the fees associated with the books.

The Ruling

The CRA ruled that the supplier was providing a service to its customers (the conference organizers).

It would appear that the software used by the supplier to provide this service was not considered to be part of the supply (i.e., the software was in the nature of an input to the supply). These services were performed in Canada because the supplier operated from a location in Canada.

Conclusions

1. Where a supplier relies upon an electronic resource (i.e., software) to provide a service the supply will be a service.

2. The supplier should, as a threshold matter consider whether the software is being supplied to the customer or whether it is merely an input to the supply.

---

[5] October 22, 2002.

Ruling 5: Call Centre Services

Ruling 38169[6] considers a number of threshold GST issues in connection with a supply provided by a Canadian corporation to its parent corporation in the U.S. The applicant is a U.S. resident corporation which provides call centre services for its customers located both in Canada and the U.S. The applicant operates strictly from its own premises in the U.S.

However, a Canadian subsidiary of the applicant provides call centre services to the applicant on a subcontract basis. In an overflow situation, some of the phone calls made to the applicant are re-routed to the Canadian subsidiary's offices in Canada. The Canadian company invoices the applicant for its services on a cost plus basis.

The parent corporation has asked whether the Canadian subsidiary might be considered the agent of the parent corporation and whether the subsidiary's offices might be considered to be a permanent establishment of the non-resident.

The Ruling

The CRA first considered whether the Canadian subsidiary would be considered an agent of the parent corporation. To make this determination it applied the factors established in Policy Statement P-182R, "Agency". The CRA concluded that the relationship is not likely one of agency because the subsidiary did not seem to be subject to a high level of control from the parent corporation and because the subsidiary was not provided with a great deal of authority (i.e., to enter into contracts or otherwise). The suggestion was that this relationship would be better characterized as an independent contractor relationship.

The CRA also noted that even if it were determined that an agency relationship exists, the subsidiary would not constitute a permanent establishment of the applicant. This is because the subsidiary would not be considered to be a "dependent agent". The CRA noted that to distinguish between a dependent and an independent agent the following factors should be considered:

(a) Is the agent subject to detailed instructions or control?

(b) Does the entrepreneurial risk lie with the agent or with the principal?

(c) Does the agent sell the goods in its own name or in the name of the principal? and

(d) Does the agent act for other people?

---

[6] October 22, 2004.

Even assuming that the agent was a dependent agent, the CRA concluded that the offices of the subsidiary would not constitute a permanent establishment of the parent corporation. This is because the parent corporation was not making supplies through the subsidiary.

Conclusions

1. The permanent establishment of an agent in Canada will only be considered to be a permanent establishment of a non-resident if the agent is a dependent agent and the principal makes supplies through the agent.

2. The making of supplies by the agent to the principal will not be relevant in determining whether supplies are made through the agent.

Ruling 6: Fulfillment and Data Backup

Ruling 48298[7] considers a similar relationship to that discussed in the ruling above. The applicant is a U.S. resident corporation which is not GST registered and which provides administrative services to its clients in connection with consumer rebates. The applicant receives rebate applications, processes the applications, and then mails out cheques to its client's customers. It then invoices its customers for the services provided.

To the extent that the customers of it clients are located in Canada, the service is subcontracted to the Canadian subsidiary of the applicant. The Canadian subsidiary is GST registered.

The rebate application forms received by the applicant are forwarded in bulk to the Canadian subsidiary. In order for the Canadian subsidiary to process the applications, it is required to access the applicant's customer database which is stored on its mainframe in the U.S. The subsidiary accesses the mainframe by trunk line and is able to pull files and enter information directly into the database.

The Canadian subsidiary invoices its parent company for the services provided in Canada.

The Ruling

The CRA concluded that services were being provided to the applicant by the subsidiary. Given that the services were performed from the subsidiary's offices in Canada, the place of supply of the services is in Canada.

However, the CRA reached the conclusion that the services did not qualify for zero-rating under section 7. This was because paragraph 7(e) carves out services which are provided in respect of tangible personal

---

[7] September 3, 2004.

property which is situated in Canada at the time the services are performed. The tangible personal property in issue was the rebate forms which had been filed by the consumers and which had been shipped in bulk to the subsidiary.

The CRA concluded that, applying the policies established in Policy Statement P-169, "Meaning of in Respect of Real Property Situated in Canada and in Respect of Tangible Personal Property that is Situated in Canada at the Time the Service is Performed, for Purposes of Schedule VI, Part V, Sections 7 and 23 to the *Excise Tax Act*", there was sufficient nexus between the services and the forms to disqualify the services from zero-rating. The focus of the service was the verification of the data contained in the documents (and not merely the entering of data as proposed by the applicant).

This nexus between the tangible personal property and the service also meant that the services would not qualify for zero-rating under section 23.

This restrictive approach to the interpretation of section 7 is very damaging for outsourcing arrangements involving Canadian service providers. To avoid this harsh result, the parties to such a transaction might want to consider having the non-resident scan the applications into an electronic format for the use of the Canadian service provider. This approach would seem to satisfy the zero-rating requirements of section 7.

Conclusions

1. Services will not be eligible for zero-rating under sections 7 or 23 where they are "in respect of" tangible personal property situated in Canada when the service is performed. This rule applies even where the property in issue is of inconsequential value.

2. To determine if the services are "in respect of" tangible personal property, the parties should consider the nexus between the service and the property.

3. Canadian persons providing outsourced data processing services to non-residents should consider obtaining documentation in electronic format to avoid this zero-rating carve out.

2. Access to Information, Memberships, and Online Magazines

Ruling 7: Sporting Subscription

Ruling 13454[8] considers subscriptions to a sports Web site which are provided by a GST registered non-resident. Subscribers to the Web site pay a monthly fee for access to sports related raw data, statistics and commentary. This information is typically used by the subscriber to assist in making decisions in connection with sports pools or gambling. Subscribers sign on through the Web site where they are provided with a user name and password. The subscribers are typically individuals and may be resident in Canada, the U.S., or anywhere in the world.

The information is stored on a Web site which is hosted on a server located outside Canada.

The Ruling

The CRA concluded that the supply was the right to access and use existing information which constitutes a supply of intangible personal property. The place of supply of the property would be any location from which the information could be accessed and used. Given that non-residents were not restricted in terms of the location from which they could access the Web site, the supplies to non-residents would be subject to tax.

This supply would not be subject to HST, however, because the place of negotiation is outside Canada, and the rights were not restricted to use in the participating provinces.

The CRA noted that the only potentially applicable zero-rating provision would be the section 10 provision. The CRA suggested (but did not specifically rule on the issue) that zero-rating would not be available on these facts. On this issue, also see, for example, ruling 25959 below.

Conclusions

1. The right to access and use existing information contained on a Web site is a supply of intangible personal property.

2. The supply is made in Canada when the Web site may be accessed from a location in Canada.

3. It appears that the CRA has taken the position that zero-rating would not be available under section 10.

---

[8] March 26, 2001.

Ruling 8: Industry Specific Information

Ruling 25959[9] considers the provision of a license to access a wide range of industry specific information. The applicant is a GST registered entity. For an annual fee it provides a license to customers for the right to access information contained on its Web site. Customers are provided with a unique user name and password. The rights provided are limited, non-exclusive and non-transferable. For example, the customer has limited rights to reproduce the materials.

The information provided includes a number of reports, studies, and databases all of which relate to the industry in which the customer operates. The applicant's marketing materials indicate that its expert reports deliver reliable and unbiased information.

The rights, title and interest (including copyright and other intellectual property rights) in the material belong to and will remain at all times with the applicant (or where provided by a third party supplier the rights will remain with the third-party suppliers). The customer does not acquire any property rights in the intellectual property.

The Ruling

The CRA held that the right to access information is a supply of intangible personal property. The supply will be considered to be made in Canada as there are no contractual restrictions which limit the access rights to locations outside Canada.

With respect to zero-rating, the CRA concluded that "the supply under consideration does not appear to qualify for zero-rating under section 10". The CRA did not elaborate on the reasons why it reached this conclusion. However, the facts portion of the ruling noted that "The client expressly acknowledges and agrees that it will acquire no proprietary interests in ... the material". It would appear that the CRA may be drawing a distinction between the transfer of ownership of patented or copyrighted materials and the mere provision of a license to use such materials.

As noted above, many practitioners have openly criticized the narrowness of the section 10 zero-rating provision. Further, the decision of the Tax Court in *Dawn's Place*, referenced above, suggests that the CRA's position may no longer be correct.

Conclusions

1. The right to access and use patented or copyrighted materials contained within a Web site is a supply of intangible personal property.

---

[9] March 26, 2001.

2. The supply will be considered to be made in any location from which the Web site can be accessed or where the information may be used.

3. Zero-rating may not be available in respect of this type of information supply.

Ruling 9: Web Site Containing Information

Ruling 6211[10] also deals with a subscription which relates to the provision of information. In this case the applicant, a Canadian resident who is not GST registered, provides the subscriptions from its Web site. The Web site is located on a server in the U.S. The subscription gives the person unlimited access to information for a period of 90 days.

In order to interest potential customers, the applicant has set up a corresponding Canadian Web site with limited content for free. The Canadian Web site encourages visitors to visit (and sign on for) the U.S. subscriptions site.

Customers who pay to access the Web site are entitled to download files containing information to their own computer to use and print. However, the customer is not entitled to resell or distribute the information and does not ever acquire ownership of the material.

It would appear that the supplier specifically set up the Web site through which the taxable supplies are delivered outside Canada for tax planning purposes.

The Ruling

The CRA concluded that the right to access a Web site (where downloading of digitized products can occur) is a supply of intangible personal property. Subscribers are being provided with the right to use and copy products for personal use.

If there is no restriction as to where the products may be used, the supply will be considered to be made in Canada. The CRA notes that to determine the province of supply, the place of negotiation of the supply would be required to be identified.

The CRA concluded that zero-rating would not be available under section 10 as this is not a supply of intellectual property:

> The supply of IPP made by your client is not considered to be a supply of intellectual property nor a right to use such property . . .

---

[10] June 25, 2002.

However, the CRA's position may no longer be correct in light of the *Dawn's Place* decision of the Tax Court.

In terms of the HST, the CRA noted that where there are no restrictions as to the location where the property may be used the rule in paragraph 2(*d*)(i) of Part III will not apply. However, the rule in paragraph 2(*d*)(ii) will apply where the place of negotiation is in Canada and the rights may be exercised otherwise than exclusively outside that province.

As noted above, the Canadian applicant structured its affairs in an unusual manner which appears to be related to the registration requirement. It delivered taxable subscriptions through its U.S. hosted Web site but did not charge any fees to access its Canadian hosted Web site. Although the ruling did not discuss any registration issues, it would appear that this tax planning technique was ineffective. The applicant would be considered resident in Canada regardless of the location of the server and would be required to be registered if it made supplies in Canada in either the course of a business carried on in Canada, or while engaged in an adventure or concern in the nature of trade in Canada. The one exception would be where the applicant qualifies as a small supplier.

Conclusions

1. The right to access a database from which digital products may be downloaded is a supply of intangible personal property.

2. The supply will be considered to be made in any place in which the products may be accessed or used.

3. Where there are no restrictions as to the place where the rights may be exercised and the place of negotiation is in Canada, the province of supply will be determined with reference to the place of negotiation.

4. A Canadian entity will be required to collect the GST in respect of the supply of intangible property including in situations where the Web site and server are located outside Canada.

5. The CRA takes the position that zero-rating is not available in respect of the right to access and download informational products.

Ruling 10: Medical and Scientific Databases

In ruling 36506[11], the applicant is a GST registered U.S. company which is primarily engaged in the business of selling hardcopy books which it mails to customers in Canada and the U.S.

---

[11] November 21, 2002.

The applicant has also established a number of databases which are available to subscribers while online. The databases contain scientific, medical and educational content. Customers sign on for the databases and are assigned a username and password.

The parent company of the applicant is located in Canada and is responsible for providing limited services to the applicant. These services include payment processing (with respect to Canadian orders) and performing tax and accounting functions.

The Ruling

The CRA ruled that the supply of a right to access a database is a supply of intangible personal property. Where there is no restriction on where the database may be used, the supply is considered to be made in Canada (including where the customer is located in the U.S.). The CRA held that the supply is not made in an HST province as there is no specific connection to the participating provinces.

The CRA held that zero-rating is not available for this type of product.

This ruling provides an example of a situation where registration for one purpose (i.e., the sale of the hardcopy books) resulted in a completely different supply (the electronic offering) losing the benefit of the non-resident override. In this case the suggestion was that the applicant was required to register as a result of the sale of the books in Canada. However, the applicant likely would not have been required to register if it had only supplied electronic products to Canadians.

For this reason the applicant should have considered establishing a new non-resident corporate entity to supply the electronic products. This entity would be entitled to make supplies in Canada without any obligation to register or collect the tax, as long as it is not carrying on business in Canada and does not have a permanent establishment in Canada. It would appear that if this alternative arrangement had been followed, the non-resident would not have been considered to have a permanent establishment in Canada as supplies are not made through the Canadian parent company. Further, even assuming that supplies are made through the parent corporation, it would not likely constitute a dependent agent. However, the applicant may have been required to be registered in any event because of the carrying on business in Canada test. The CRA has indicated that among the factors to be considered are:

(a) the place where a non-resident solicits business;

(b) the place where agents of the non-resident are located; and

(c) the place where payments are processed.

Conclusions

1. The supply of access to an electronic database is a supply of intangible personal property and is considered to be supplied in any place where it may be accessed.

2. The CRA takes the position that this supply is not one which qualifies for zero-rating under section 10.

Ruling 11: Online Magazine

Ruling 34390[12] considers the dangers associated with operating from an HST province. In that ruling the applicant is a Canadian GST registered person which operates from offices located in an HST province. The applicant makes an online magazine available to subscribers across Canada. All magazine revenue comes from subscriptions (no advertising is provided in the magazine).

The magazine is in the form of a file which subscribers can download from the Internet. Subscriptions are available on a monthly or annual basis.

The Ruling

The CRA ruled that this is a supply of intangible personal property because the magazine is in electronic format and provides users with the right to view existing information. The CRA noted that if the same magazine were to be offered in a paper format, it would be considered a supply of tangible personal property.

Because the subscription does not restrict the location where the user can access the magazine the supply is considered to be made in Canada. The CRA also reached the conclusion that the magazine subscription fees are subject to HST regardless of whether the customers are located outside of the HST provinces. This is because the place of negotiation of the supply is in a participating province, and there are no restrictions as to where the property may be used. The HST would also apply to subscribers located outside Canada.

The CRA also confirmed that the property is not intellectual property, and so zero-rating is not available where supplies are made to non-residents.

This is an example of the extremely harsh rules associated with the application of the HST in circumstances where zero-rating is not available. As this is a consumer product, very few (if any) subscribers will be eligible to claim ITCs.

---

[12] November 21, 2002.

Given that the zero-rating rules are extremely limited with respect to intangible personal property, it is critical that when subscriptions are supplied to non-residents the supply be considered to be made outside Canada. This approach, however, would not eliminate the 14% charge levied against Canadian subscribers who are outside of the HST provinces (unless specific restrictions are implemented as to the location where they may access or use the products). Where the supplier is not prepared to limit access in this manner it may wish to consider whether it would be advantageous to operate from a location outside of the HST provinces.

Conclusions

1. Suppliers of intangible personal property who operate from an HST province will be required to charge 14% tax to subscribers located in Canada including those subscribers who are located outside of the HST provinces. This harsh result may be avoided by restricting the use of the product.

2. Given that zero-rating is unavailable for many supplies of intangible personal property, the tax will also apply to non-residents unless the contract restricts their use of the property to a location outside Canada.

Ruling 12: Fitness Web Site Membership

Ruling 33627[13] considers the supply of a membership to a Web site through which various offerings are made available. The supplier is a GST registered Canadian entity which sells memberships to Canadian and non-resident customers to access its fitness based Web site.

The customers are provided with access to fitness related chat rooms, editorials, photo galleries, and profiles. Members also receive discounts on purchases of merchandise from the supplier and on purchases of fitness instruction.

The Ruling

The CRA ruled that the supply is a "membership" as that term is defined in subsection 123(1). This is because for a fee people are being provided with rights which are not available to the general public.

The membership is a supply of intangible personal property notwithstanding that services appear to be provided as a component of the offering (for example, access to chat rooms).

The supply is considered to be made in any location where the membership may be used.

---

[13] September 9, 2002.

Where the membership is provided to an individual, and the Canadian rights in respect of the membership may be exercised otherwise than exclusively in a single province, the supply will be made in a particular province if the mailing address of the individual is in that province. In all other cases the province of supply rules contained in Part III of Schedule IX should be considered. For example, where there are no restrictions as to the location where the membership rights may be exercised, and the place of negotiation for the supply is in Canada, the province of supply will be the province of negotiation.

The CRA also ruled that zero-rating is not available in respect of supplies of memberships. Accordingly, to avoid the incidence of tax to non-residents, the subscriptions provided to non-residents should be restricted in such a way that the non-resident cannot exercise any of the rights in connection with the membership from a location in Canada.

Conclusions

1. A membership, including an electronic membership, is considered a supply of intangible personal property. The membership will be considered to be supplied in any location where membership rights can be exercised.

2. The CRA takes the position that memberships do not qualify for zero-rating. However, in light of the Tax Court's decision in *Dawn's Place* (referenced above), this position may be open to challenge.

3. A membership which is provided to an individual will be made in the province of the mailing address of the individual where the rights may be exercised otherwise than exclusively in a single province.

4. Where the special membership province of supply rule does not apply, the province of supply (i.e., the override rule) will be determined by reference to the general rules for intangible personal property.

Ruling 13: Job Search Videos

Ruling 33017[14] considers the supply of electronic job search videos. The applicant provides the videos to subscribers through its Web site. The videos can be viewed while the subscriber is online but cannot be downloaded.

Customers pay by credit card for a pre-determined number of viewing hours. Customers also have the option of ordering a binder which contains CD ROMs of the videos along with a workbook. The binders are only available to Canadian customers and are typically mailed to the customer.

---

[14] August 16, 2002.

The Ruling

The CRA ruled that the supply of the right to view a video over the Internet is a supply of intangible personal property. This supply will be considered to be made in Canada if the user is permitted to access the videos from a location in Canada.

The supply might also be considered to be subject to HST. Absent any restrictions as to the place of use the province of supply will be the province of negotiation for the supply.

The CRA concluded that the right to view the videos does not qualify for zero-rating under section 10.

The binders are treated as a separate supply of tangible personal property and are supplied in the location where they are delivered to the customer.

Conclusions

1. The right to view videos while online is a supply of intangible personal property and is supplied in the location where the user may access the videos.

2. Absent any restrictions as to the place of use, the province of supply will be the province of negotiation for the supply.

3. The CRA has adopted the position that zero-rating is not available in respect of this product. However, this position may be open to challenge in light of the Tax Court's decision in *Dawn's Place*, referenced above.

Ruling 14: Live Interactive Web Site

Ruling 13555[15] deals with membership to a live interactive Web site. The applicant is a Canadian GST registered person but the Web site in issue is hosted on a server located in the U.S. All maintenance is performed from the applicant's offices in Canada.

Customers who sign up online are provided with access to various Web site features including live online chats, interactive contact, and tools to build their own personal Web page. Individuals have the option of signing on for no charge to receive the right to view limited content.

Customers also have the option of paying an additional fee to post materials on the supplier's Web site.

---

[15] March 30, 2001.

The Ruling

The CRA ruled that the supply is considered to be a "membership" as that term is defined in subsection 123(1). The membership is considered to be intangible personal property and is supplied in the location where it can be accessed. Accordingly, if the agreement does not limit access to locations outside Canada, the GST must be charged both to Canadian residents and to non-residents.

The supply could also be subject to HST. The regulatory override rules could apply to this supply if the membership is supplied to an individual. Where the supply is made to an individual, the supply will be made in the province of the mailing address of the recipient unless the membership rights may be accessed in only one province. In all other cases the ordinary province of supply rules will apply. As a result, if all or substantially all of the rights may only be exercised in a single province, the supply will be considered to be made in that province. The supply will also be considered to be supplied in the province of the place of negotiation if the property may be used otherwise than exclusively outside that province.

The right to post materials on the supplier's Web site is a separate supply of an advertising service. This is because the supply is the creation and communication of a message for the purpose of soliciting business. This service is supplied in Canada because it is partially performed in Canada. Although the CRA does not explain how it reached the conclusion that the service was performed in Canada, it appears that this conclusion flows from the fact the supplier is based out of Canada.

The CRA noted however that the advertising service should be zero-rated under section 8. The supply of the membership would not qualify for zero-rating.

Conclusions

1. The supply of a membership which provides the right to access a live interactive Web site (including where the Web site offers personalized interactive content) will be considered to be a supply of intangible personal property. The supply will be made in any location where the user may interact with or use the Web site.

2. The CRA has adopted the position that zero-rating is not available in respect of the supply of a membership. This position may be open to challenge.

3. Allowing a user to post materials on the Web site is considered to be a separate supply of an advertising service and will normally qualify for zero-rating under section 8.

Ruling 15: Membership with Online Chats

Ruling 41917[16] relates to an online membership which is supported by online chats. The applicant is a GST registered person which has Web sites hosted on servers located in the U.S. Customers sign up to obtain access to Web sites for their specific content and features which includes online chat rooms where subjects of interest to customers can be discussed. The subject matter of the Web sites appears to be the creation of personal web pages.

Customers are provided with three options. First, they can sign on for no fee and have limited access to informational resources and can post comments. For an additional fee the customers can post an advertisement. For a second additional fee customers receive full membership access which includes access to live chat rooms, interactive content and specific tools to build their own personal web page.

The Ruling

The CRA ruled that allowing a customer to post an advertisement is the provision of an advertising service (the creation and communication of a message). The service would be supplied in Canada because it is partially performed in Canada (presumably because the applicant's employees are located in Canada). These services would be eligible for zero-rating under section 8.

The membership would be considered to be a supply of intangible personal property notwithstanding that the membership involves personalized services. If the intangible property is not restricted to use outside Canada, the supply will be considered to be made in Canada. Where the membership is supplied to an individual, the special province of supply override would apply if the mailing address of the recipient is in Canada and the rights are not limited to a particular province. Otherwise, the province of supply rules would be those contained in Part III relating to intangible personal property.

The supplier should consider limiting access for non-residents to computers located outside of Canada in order to avoid the incidence of GST.

Conclusions

1. A membership is a supply of intangible personal property, including where the supply involves interactive content.

2. The supply is made in any location where the Web site is permitted to be accessed.

---

[16] January 29, 2003.

3. Where the membership is provided to an individual, the special province of supply rules should be considered.

Ruling 16: Third Party Subscriptions to Web sites

Ruling 34703[17] considers a GST registered person who sells subscriptions to a Web site. However, the Web site and materials on the Web site are not owned by the applicant. The applicant merely bills and collects the payment from the subscriber by credit card and provides the user name and password required to enter the target site.

Subscribers sign up with the applicant online for the right to visit and access the target site. Subscribers are not allowed to download anything from the site (the rights are limited to viewing privileges). There are no restrictions placed on the subscribers as to the locations from which they may exercise these viewing privileges.

The Web site owner operates from a location outside Canada. The applicant pays a commission to the Web site owner each time that the applicant signs on a new subscriber (or renews a subscriber).

The Ruling

The CRA concluded that the supply of access to a Web site provided by the applicant is a supply of intangible personal property. The content is considered to be intangible property because the Web sites contain existing information and information is never developed for a specific user.

The supply is made in Canada because the Web sites may be accessed from Canada. The CRA also confirmed that the supply of access to a Web site would not qualify for zero-rating under section 10. In terms of potential application of the HST the CRA noted that the place of negotiation for the supply should be considered (i.e., the rule in subparagraph 2(*d*)(ii)) because there are no restrictions placed on the access rights.

The CRA in this ruling did not discuss the issue of agency. This silence suggests that the CRA did not view this as an agency arrangement.

Conclusions

1. The sale of the right to access a Web site (including a Web site which is not owned by the supplier) is a supply of intangible personal property.

2. The supply of a right to access a Web site will not be a supply which qualifies for zero-rating. This position may be open to challenge in light of the Tax Court decision in *Dawn's Place*, referenced above.

---

[17] June 4, 2002.

Ruling 17: Web Site Membership Involving Data and Software

In ruling 31642[18], a non-resident who is GST registered supplies data to subscribers. The data is used by the subscriber to make investment decisions. The subscriber is entitled to log in and access the data from anywhere in the world.

The subscriber also receives access to software which is to be installed on the subscriber's computer. The software, once installed, allows the customer to plot out graphs and perform other functions for the purpose of monitoring various investment vehicles. There is no separate charge for the access to the software.

The primary method of delivery of the software is by way of download from the supplier's Web site. However, a disk containing the software may be mailed to the subscriber at their request.

The data which the subscriber is tracking does not download to the customer's computer. Instead the subscriber merely accesses the data which resides on the supplier's server.

The Ruling

The CRA concluded that a single supply is being provided on the facts. The supply is considered to be intangible personal property because it is the provision of the right to access and use data. The supply is considered to be made in Canada because access rights are not restricted to locations outside Canada.

The CRA did not consider that software was being supplied because there was no separate charge for the software, and because the software performs the function of facilitating access to the data. It would appear that the conclusion would be the same where the software is delivered in physical format.

Zero-rating is not available in respect of this supply under section 10 because there is no right supplied to access intellectual property.

Conclusions

1. The provision of the right to access data will be considered to be a single supply of intangible property relating to the access to the data, including where software is provided to the customer to facilitate access to the data.

2. The right to access data does not qualify for zero-rating.

---

[18] December 9, 2002.

Ruling 18: Adult Entertainment

Ruling 25287[19] considers supplies relating to the provision of adult entertainment. The applicant is a GST registered person. It describes its primary offering in a more general manner as a "subscription to an online magazine". The offering is provided through the applicant's Web site, which is hosted on its own server in Canada.

The applicant also designs Web sites for its customers. The Web sites once completed are sold to the customer.

The applicant notes that most of its clients are located in the U.S.

The Ruling

The CRA rules that designing a Web site will be considered a supply of a service if the customer owns the Web site once the work has been completed. The service would typically qualify for zero-rating under section 7 when provided to a non-resident.

The provision of a subscription to the online magazine would be considered a supply of intangible personal property. The property would be supplied in Canada if access were allowed to be exercised in Canada. The ruling notes that the provision of rights in intangible personal property might be subject to HST. In particular, if all or substantially all of the Canadian rights may be exercised only in a participating province, the supply would be subject to HST. Further, if the place of negotiation is in one of the participating provinces, and there are no restrictions as to the place where the property may be accessed, the supply will be subject to HST.

The ruling did not discuss the availability of zero-rating in connection with the supply of intangible personal property. However, it would appear that the CRA would take the position that zero-rating is not available because intellectual property rights are not being provided.

Conclusions

1. The supply of the right to access an online magazine is a supply of intangible personal property.

2. The supply is considered to be made in Canada if the magazine may be accessed from Canada.

3. Where there are no restrictions as to the location where access may be exercised, then if the place of negotiation is in Canada the province of supply will be in that particular province.

---

[19] June 13, 2002.

3. Images and Graphic Design

Ruling 19: Photo Images

Ruling 33574[20] considers a Canadian GST registered entity which purchases photo images from a non-resident supplier. The recipient downloads the images from the supplier's Web site and uses the images in developing print advertisements for its customers.

The Canadian's concern relates to the fact that it was not charged GST by the non-resident supplier.

The Ruling

The CRA ruled that making images available to be downloaded from the Internet is a supply of intangible personal property. The supply is considered to be made in Canada because there is no restriction as to the place where the images may be downloaded or used. The CRA noted that even where the images are of real property, they will not be considered to be intangible personal property which relates to real property.

The CRA noted that the supplier was likely correct not to have charged the GST to the recipient because of the non-resident override. However, the CRA also noted that if it should ultimately turn out that the supplier was required to charge Division II GST, the recipient will be entitled to make its ITC claim at that time.

The CRA surprisingly did not in this ruling mention the potential application of Division IV GST. It would appear that the recipient would not be required to self-assess under Division IV as the images are used exclusively in making taxable supplies (of advertising services) in the course of a commercial activity. Had the recipient been using the images for some exempt purpose or for personal use there would have been a self-assessment requirement.

Conclusions

1. When photo images are provided electronically, this is a supply of intangible personal property.

2. The supply is considered to be made in the place where the images may be downloaded or used.

---

[20] August 30, 2002.

Ruling 20: Digitized Artwork

Ruling 32742[21] deals with the sale of digitized artwork. The supplier, a GST registered Canadian, sells digitized artwork to both residents and non-residents of Canada. The purchasers are typically newspapers and magazines which will use the artwork in their publications.

In return for a fee, the client receives a non-exclusive, non-transferable license to use a single item of artwork on a one-time only basis in the client's online or print publications. Clients are only entitled to access the artwork if they have previously registered online with the supplier. While online, the client can browse, purchase and download artwork. The artwork may be accessed online for a period of 24 hours from the time of the first download.

Under the license agreement the client agrees to print with the artwork a credit line and a trademark/copyright notice. The supplier reserves the right to revoke the license at any time. The license agreement does not restrict where the artwork may be used.

The supplier operates from a permanent establishment which is not located in a participating province. It is from this location that it negotiates its contracts.

The Ruling

The CRA ruled that the supply of the artwork is a supply of intangible personal property which is intellectual property. Because the artwork is not restricted as to place of use the supply will always be deemed to be made in Canada under the section 142 place of supply rules. Accordingly, the supply will be taxed in the following manner:

(a) supply to Canadian resident (including in HST province):   6%

(b) supply to non-resident who is registered: 6%

(c) supply to non-resident who is not registered: 0%

The CRA specifically concluded that zero-rating would be available under section 10. The conclusion relating to the province of supply followed from the fact that the place of negotiation was not in the participating provinces and the rights were not limited to any particular province.

Conclusions

1. Digitized artwork is considered to be a supply of intangible personal property.

---

[21] July 12, 2002.

2. The supply is made in the place where the artwork may be downloaded or used.

3. Digitized artwork which is protected by copyright or patent protection will qualify for zero-rating under section 10 when licensed to a non-resident customer who is not registered.

Ruling 21: Photography and Graphic Design Packages

Ruling 42434[22] deals with a print manager which provides a number of different supplies, many of which are provided on an outsourced basis. The ruling is particularly important in that is considers a number of complicated characterization issues in connection with digital media. The ruling also demonstrates how changes in the media may result in changes in the characterization of the supply.

A typical supply in connection with photography would arise in the following manner:

(a) Customer will approach the supplier to provide a certain type of digital picture (some particular event, scene or object).

(b) The supplier will hire a photographer to take the picture either in a traditional or digital format. Where the picture is taken in a traditional film format, the negative will be provided to the customer.

(c) The supplier will invoice the customer for the photographer's work which is charged on a hourly basis. The supplier will also charge for image scanning and emailing of the picture to the customer. If the customer wants the picture on a CD, the supplier also charges for copying the image to the CD and for the CD itself.

Customers may also ask for graphic design work (logos, etc. which will be used in brochures or other print materials). The supplier would provide the design work by way of a third party supplier and would then integrate the design into a printed material.

This work is charged out at an hourly rate. The design work is sent to the customer by email or by CD. If the design is sent on a CD, a charge is made for putting the design onto the CD.

The Ruling — Photography related supplies

With respect to the photography related supplies, the CRA noted that the first issue to be considered is whether single or multiple supplies are being made (i.e., creating images, scanning, emailing and copying to CD). The CRA noted that a single supply is typically made (applying P-077R2)

---

[22] September 24, 2004.

where two or more elements are supplied, and one of those elements is so dominated by the other element that the first element has lost its identity for fiscal purposes.

In this case it appears that multiple supplies are being made. In support of this conclusion the CRA noted that:

(a) there are at least two distinct elements to the transaction (the creation of digital images and the scanning of the image to a CD);

(b) the two elements separately satisfy the customer's needs;

(c) the customer is aware of the different elements;

(d) although the second element is contingent on the first the first is not contingent on the second; and

(e) the customer has the option of acquiring either of the two elements separately.

The second issue to be considered is the characterization of the nature of the various supplies. The CRA noted that the property or services guidelines contained in TIB 090 should be consulted to make this determination. The guidelines provide that a service is likely provided where:

(a) the supply does not include the provision of rights or if there are rights they are incidental to the supply;

(b) the supply involves specific work that is performed by a person for a specific customer; and

(c) there is a human element involved.

Applying these three tests, the CRA reached the conclusion that a service is in fact being provided when a digital image is created by the photographer. However, the copies provided of the digital images on CD will be considered to be a supply of tangible personal property. This conclusion is consistent with the software rule which holds that where software is provided on a physical carrier medium, it will be considered to be tangible property.

The Ruling — Design work

The CRA reached the conclusion that the graphic design work (when supplied alone) is a supply of a service (and not a supply of intangible personal property). This characterization of the graphic design work as a service does not change if the design is placed on a CD.

In reaching this conclusion the CRA noted that the graphic design work requires a high level of expertise and skill. As a result of this work new property is produced but that property has no use in and of itself. It is only useful when it is used to produce an item such as a brochure.

The Ruling — Design work and brochures

Where a customer contracts to purchase both graphic design and a brochure, there may be either a single supply or two separate supplies. The two elements are the finished brochure and the printing plate (the prepress used to make the brochure) which is provided to the customer.

In this case, the CRA ruled that the client is receiving a single supply of the brochures. Although the client receives the printing press the product which the client is interested in receiving is the finished brochure. The suggestion seems to be that the graphic design work becomes an input to the creation of the brochure when the object of the supply is the brochure itself. As this supply is predominantly property related, a single supply of property is being made.

Conclusions

1. The manner in which the GST will apply to design work will involve a number of complex considerations including differentiating between single and multiple supplies.

2. The application of the GST will be very fact specific given the nature of the supplies and given the alternative methodologies for structuring the delivery.

Ruling 22: Reproduction of CDs

Ruling 35021[23] considers issues relating to the reproduction of CDs. The applicant reproduces CDs from a master CD and then prints a label onto the CD, assembles the CD into a case and poly wraps the CD. The CDs are then shipped to the customer in an HST province.

The ruling does not discuss ownership of the master CD or of the information contained on the master CD.

The Ruling

The CRA ruled that this supply would likely be characterized as a supply of tangible personal property. However, the ruling evidences a particular reluctance on the part of the CRA to be definitive on this issue:

> Based on the information provided, XXXXX appears to be producing tangible personal property (TPP) in the form of the XXXXX for supply by

---

[23] October 8, 2003.

way of sale to XXXXX. However, to make a conclusive determination in this regard would require consideration of the terms of the agreement for the supply between XXXX and XXXX and all relevant facts.

Conclusions

1. Generally, where a CD is produced for sale to a customer the supply will be considered a supply of tangible personal property including where the CD contains an intangible personal property component.

2. However, there may be circumstances where the supply will be characterized as something other than tangible personal property (i.e., a service). This issue will typically be resolved by examining the agreement between the supplier and recipient.

4. Music Related Supplies

Ruling 23: Individual Music Tracks

In ruling 31560[24], a U.S. corporation which is not GST registered sells individual music tracks over the Internet to customers located in Canada and the U.S. The customer acquires the right to download and use the data file for personal use only. The consumer is not entitled to resell the track or to use the track for commercial purposes.

The data files are downloaded by the consumer from a server located in the U.S.

The Ruling

The CRA characterizes the supply as a supply of intangible personal property.

The purchasers are provided with a copy of the product and the right to use the product.

Given that the supply may be acquired and used in Canada (there are no restrictions as to the place where the download may occur) the supply will be considered to be made in Canada. This will be the same result whether the consumer is a person located in Canada or a person located in some other country.

The CRA suggested however that the non-resident would likely be eligible for the non-resident override and so would not be required to collect Division II GST on the supply.

---

[24] September 10, 2002.

The ruling does not discuss whether zero-rating might be available in respect of this product.

Although not specifically noted in the ruling there would be a requirement on the part of the consumers in Canada to self assess under Division IV. As a practical matter most Canadians will not even be aware of this obligation. Given the relatively low value of each particular supply, and the tremendous difficulties associated with identifying the purchasers, enforcement of this provision would be virtually impossible.

The CRA seemed to acknowledge this practical difficulty. It suggested that the supplier may want to consider becoming GST registered so that it may begin collecting the GST from Canadian customers. However, the suggested approach could result in other difficulties. For example, if the supplier were to become GST registered then supplies made to non-residents may become taxable. If the supplier is not able to restrict the access and use of the data file to locations outside Canada then the supplier would also be required to collect Division II GST from the non-resident customers.

Given the considerable potential for revenue loss in connection with this type of supply the non-resident should be particularly careful to ensure that it does not undertake any activity which would jeopardize its use of the override.

Conclusions

1. The right to download and access music is considered to be a supply of intangible personal property.

2. The property will be supplied in Canada if the property may be downloaded or used in Canada.

Ruling 24: Internet Radio Station

Ruling 32713[25] considers supplies of music provided through an Internet radio station. The applicant is not GST registered.

Among the primary goals of the radio station is the promotion of independent musicians from around the world. The applicant provides three different types of supplies in connection with its Web site:

> (a) a fee may be charged to a musician in return for the musician being allowed to have his/her biography and photo posted on the Web site along with their music;

---

[25] August 16, 2002.

(b) the applicant provides banner and audio advertising for a fee; and

(c) the applicant assists the musician in promoting and selling its CDs.

The Ruling

The CRA concluded that each of the first two supplies are the provision of advertising services. This is consistent with the broad manner in which the CRA has characterized advertising (and which is discussed in more detail in Chapter 12, Advertising Services).

In terms of zero-rating, the CRA suggests that sections 7 or 8 might provide relief. Although section 8 relates specifically to advertising services, the relief is not available where the non-resident is registered. Section 7 on the other hand relates generally to all services but does not contain any similar restriction based on registration status. The carve outs in section 7 (for example, services rendered to individual while in Canada) will not typically apply in an e-commerce setting.

With respect to the sale of the CD, the CRA concluded that this would be a supply of tangible personal property. The place of supply would turn on the location where the CD is delivered or made available to the customer. Zero-rating would likely be available under either of section 1 or section 12.

Conclusions

1. The promotion of musicians through an online radio station is considered to be an advertising service which is provided to the musician.

2. The service will be considered to be supplied in Canada when the supplier operates from a location in Canada.

3. Zero-rating in respect of an advertising service may be available under either of section 7 or section 8.

5. Timeshares and Loyalty Points Programs

Ruling 25: Rights to use Resort Properties

The leading ruling on this issue is contained in ruling 7613.[26] It is worth noting at the outset that this has been a difficult issue for the CRA. The ruling formally revoked an earlier ruling relating to the same facts. In the previous ruling the supply had been determined to be made outside Canada and not subject to GST.

---

[26] May 8, 2003.

The applicant company is GST registered and owns resort properties located both inside and outside Canada. The applicant sells timeshare interests in the properties by way of a points system. Non-resident customers purchase a number of points which can be redeemed in the future to stay at various properties. Each unit of property is assigned a nightly point value, with more luxurious rooms and better locations being assigned a higher point value than other corresponding rooms.

When the points are purchased the customer is not asked to select which property they might be interested in staying in. It is only after the stay occurs that the appropriate number of points are deducted from the customer's account.

The Ruling

The CRA held first of all that the supply is a supply of intangible personal property which relates to real property. More specifically the supply is of a non-specific right to use an interest in real property by way of lease, license or similar right. However, the exercise of the non-specific right will eventually result in the acquisition of a specific right to use real property in Canada. Because some of the properties are located in Canada, and some are located outside of Canada, the supply is considered to be made partly in Canada and partly outside Canada.

Generally, a supply of intangible personal property will be considered to be supplied in Canada if the property may be used in whole or in part in Canada. If this place of supply rule were to have applied, the entire supply would be subject to GST. However, because the intangible property related to real property, the CRA relied upon the second intangible personal property place of supply rule. The CRA applied this rule in a flexible and equitable manner which allowed the supplier to allocate the potential use between properties in Canada and properties outside Canada.

Accordingly, the CRA concluded that the GST would apply at the time of purchase of the points but only to the extent that properties owned at that time by the supplier were located in Canada. The CRA suggested that a fair and reasonable methodology for allocating between Canada and the rest of the world would likely involve counting the number of rooms available in Canada as a proportion of rooms available worldwide. Presumably, the same system would be used to determine the manner in which the HST would apply.

It is not clear whether the same result would have followed had the points also been made available to Canadian residents.

It is interesting to note that the CRA has not adopted this type of approach with respect to other supplies of intangible personal property. The more typical approach has involved an "all or nothing" determination (i.e., the first rule for intangible personal property). For example, if intangible personal property were to be licensed to 75 users of a company but in circumstances where only 25 of those users are physically located in offices in Canada, the rulings issued to date suggest that the CRA would apply the GST to the full value of the supply. However, ordinarily the parties would avoid such a harsh result by restricting the access rights of the non-resident employees to locations outside of Canada.

It would appear that if this particular supply had been taxable when provided to non-residents zero-rating would not have been available. This is because intellectual property was not being supplied.

It is not clear whether any of the rebates normally available under the visitor rebate program would be available to non-residents who stay in Canada. It is arguable that the rebates would not be available because the supply relates to points and not to room nights.

Conclusions

1. The supply of intangible personal property which relates to real property may be eligible for special place of supply allocation rules where the real property is located partially in and partially outside Canada.

2. This type of allocation is not available for intangible personal property which does not relate to real property.

Ruling 26: Air Miles Points Redemptions

Ruling 34565[27] considers the redemption of air mile reward points. The applicant is an individual who has accumulated points under a travel loyalty program and who has recently redeemed the points for a trip.

In this case, the applicant booked a trip (using points as the consideration) from Montreal to Denver via Chicago and return. The points program administrator charged GST to the applicant in respect of the trip.

The Ruling

The CRA concluded that the trip itself (a supply of a passenger transportation service) was a supply which was made in Canada. This is because a supply of a passenger transportation service is considered to be made in Canada if the service is performed in part in Canada.

Zero-rating is only available pursuant to section 3 of Part VII of Schedule VI if a continuous journey is provided and either the origin or

---

[27] March 28, 2002.

destination of the continuous journey is a location outside of Canada and the U.S. In this case a single ticket was issued with origin and destination in Canada and so zero-rating was not available.

However, notwithstanding that the supply was made in Canada and zero-rating was not available the CRA concluded that GST should not have been charged to the applicant. This was because the applicant did not pay any consideration for the ticket.

The CRA explained that anything which may be exchanged for property or a service qualifies as a "coupon" as that term is defined in section 181. In this particular case, the customer redeemed a coupon to pay for the full value of the flight and so, pursuant to section 181 there was no consideration to which the GST could apply. If the coupon had not been sufficient to fully pay for the air travel, the GST would only have applied to the price paid net of the coupon.

The CRA suggested that the customer request a refund of the amount of GST paid under subsection 232(2).

The ruling underscores how the underlying supply must be carefully considered when determining the application of tax to points programs.

Conclusions

1. Rights provided under points programs to purchase goods or services may be considered to be coupons.

2. The GST does not apply to the value of the coupon. The GST only applies to any consideration paid which is in excess of the value of the coupon.

Chapter 17

Internet Courses, Electronic Books, and other Educational Offerings

A. OVERVIEW

This chapter considers supplies which are educational in nature. While many of the supplies discussed in this chapter are delivered in a purely electronic format, this chapter also considers educational offerings which are in the nature of in-person services and hard copy textbooks. These more traditional educational offerings are discussed because they are often provided together as a package along with advanced e-commerce offerings.

Although the focus of this chapter is upon educational offerings, this chapter will also consider electronic books which are being provided for other than educational purposes (i.e., for general use and enjoyment). Accordingly, the subject matter of this chapter includes:

(a) hard copy textbooks with electronic "add ons";

(b) electronic books; and

(c) e-commerce courses and education.

Given that educational offerings are typically bundled, this chapter focuses in particular upon distinguishing between single and multiple supplies and upon the characterization of more complex supplies.

B. CHARACTERIZATION OF SUPPLIES

1. Hard Copy Textbooks with Electronic Add Ons

This category describes offerings which centre around the sale of a textbook but are supported by one or more forms of electronic offerings. The electronic offering is typically in the form of either a CD ROM which is included with the textbooks (i.e., shrink wrapped with the book), or by the provision of rights to access an online resource which is not available to the general public.

The electronic offerings would ordinarily relate to and support the information provided in the textbook, and may include up-to-date information (i.e., information which has been compiled subsequent to the release of the textbook), additional resources, exercises, or other learning aids. Where electronic access is provided to a Web site, this access is typically restricted to purchasers of the textbook by means of a password and user name. Because the electronic offerings assist in promoting the sale of the package, their inclusion is typically noted prominently in the textbook packaging and marketing materials.

TIB 090 does not specifically deal with issues relating to the sale of hardcopy text books which are supported by electronic offerings. This is likely because the provision of a textbook or CD ROM is not, strictly speaking, considered to be an e-commerce supply. The provision of online access to information is a subject which is discussed in TIB 090. However, that chapter focuses upon electronic access provided as a standalone supply.

Where a textbook is sold alone (i.e., unsupported by electronic offerings) the characterization of the supply is straightforward. The textbook will always be considered to be tangible personal property.

Where a textbook is provided with a CD ROM, tangible personal property will also be considered to be supplied. However, the supply may be considered to be either a single supply of tangible personal property or multiple supplies of tangible personal property.

Similarly, when access to an online resource (i.e., the supplier's Web site) is provided along with a supply of tangible personal property a determination must also be made as to whether the access forms part of a single supply or whether multiple supplies are being made. Where multiple supplies are made, the incidental supply rule must also be considered. The incidental supply rule, where applicable, deems a single supply to be made because of the incidental nature of one or more of the supplies.

In the rulings issued to date, the CRA has consistently leaned towards characterizing the supply of a textbook supported by electronic offerings (either a CD ROM or online access) to be a single supply of a "new product". There seems to be a particular reluctance on the part of the CRA to carve off the electronic elements as separate supplies.

This is not to say that the electronic offerings could not ever be carved off from the supply of the textbook. For example, where the electronic offerings are also available to be supplied separately from the textbook, or where the textbook may be purchased (for a lower price) without the electronic offerings, a finding of separate supplies may follow. However, this distinction may be largely academic because most publishers who support textbooks with electronic offerings will only offer the complete package.

Although it would appear that the CRA does treat the supply of a "new product" as a supply of tangible personal property, the CRA has made clear that this educational product is something distinct from the sale of a textbook sold alone. As discussed below, this distinction is important when considering the application of the HST point-of-sale printed book rebate.

2. Electronic Books

Electronic books are by their very nature available strictly on line and contain no tangible elements. The supplier may choose to either make the books available for viewing only while the customer is online, or may allow for the books to be downloaded to the customer's computer. The download would, for example, allow the user to print a copy of the book or save it to a hard drive.

The supply of an electronic book will not typically involve any form of personalized service (any service component would relate strictly to creating or posting the book) and so the supply will be characterized as intangible personal property.

It should be noted that, in addition to the discussion contained in this chapter, many of the issues raised in connection with electronic books are similar to those raised in connection with the provision of access to online magazines and raw informational resources. Where issues of ambiguity are encountered on a particular set of facts the rulings referenced in Chapter 16, Online Content, Services, and Other General Offerings, should also be consulted.

3. E-Commerce Courses and Training

E-Commerce courses and training may be provided in a wide variety of formats. At one end of the spectrum are courses which do not involve any element of human interaction. Materials, testing, and evaluations are all provided or performed automatically by existing programs to which the users are provided access.

At the other end of the spectrum are courses which offer the user a high degree of personalized services. For example, employees of the supplier may in some cases visit the customer's premises to provide additional onsite training, technical support, testing or evaluations. This is particularly common with respect to educational offerings provided to commercial entities or educational institutions. Between these two extremes are suppliers who provide only minimal personalized services. These services are typically provided from the supplier's premises which may or may not be located in Canada.

Where the offering does not involve any personalized services, the supply will be characterized as a supply of intangible personal property. Where the supply involves some element of human services, the supply might be considered to be a single supply of a service, a single supply of intangible personal property or multiple supplies comprised of a service and intangible personal property. The rulings demonstrate the factors which the CRA will consider in making this difficult distinction.

C. GST AND HST PLACE OF SUPPLY ISSUES

As noted above the appropriate characterization of a particular supply (or bundle of supplies) will be critical for ensuring that the correct place of supply rules are applied.

1. Textbooks

Where textbooks are sold with electronic offerings, including CD ROMs or online access, the rulings issued to date have concluded that a single supply of a new product has been provided. The CRA characterizes this new product as a supply of tangible personal property. Accordingly, under the section 142 place of supply rules, the supply will made in the place where the product is delivered or made available to the recipient of the supply.

The rules relating to the province of supply of tangible personal property are contained in Part II of Schedule IX. Section 1 of Part II provides that a sale of tangible personal property will be considered to be supplied in an HST province (and subject to 14% tax) where the property is delivered or made available in the province to the recipient.

It should also be noted that under section 3 of Part II, property will be deemed to be delivered in a province if the property is shipped to a destination in the province specified in the contract for carriage, or possession of the property is transferred to a common carrier or consignee that the supplier has retained on behalf of the recipient to ship the property. The property is also deemed to be delivered in a particular province if the property is sent by mail or courier to an address in that province. This rule is particularly important for suppliers located outside of the HST provinces (including suppliers located outside Canada) who ship their goods into the HST provinces.

2. Electronic Books

Electronic books are considered to be a supply of intangible personal property and are considered to be supplied in Canada if they may be accessed or used at a location in Canada. Where a supplier does not contractually limit the use and access to locations outside Canada, the supply will always be considered to be made in Canada even if, as a practical matter, the recipient is not likely to exercise this right from within Canada (for example, if the supply is made to a resident of Greece).

The non-resident override, in many cases, will operate to temper these harsh results. Where the non-resident override does not apply (for example, where the supplier is registered) contractual restrictions relating to place of use should be implemented to ensure that the supply is made outside Canada.

The starting point for determining the province of supply is the rule contained in subparagraph 2(*d*)(i) of Part III of Schedule IX. This rule provides that intangible personal property will be considered to be supplied in a particular province if all or substantially all of the Canadian rights in respect of the property can be used only in that province. "Canadian rights" are defined in section 1 of Part III to mean that part of the intangible personal property that can be used in Canada.

This rule will only apply where the supplier restricts the use of the Canadian rights in respect of the property to a particular province. For example, the supplier may contractually provide that where a resident of Ontario acquires access to an e-book, the customer may only access and use the book from locations within Ontario.

Where there are no restrictions as to the place where property can be used, this test will never be met. The next test to be considered is the one in subparagraph 2(*d*)(ii). That test provides that a supply will be considered to be made in a particular province where the place of negotiation of the supply is in that province, and the property can be used otherwise than exclusively outside of that province.

The place of negotiation is defined in section 1 of Part I of Schedule IX as the location of the supplier's permanent establishment at which the individual principally involved in negotiating for the supplier the agreement for the supply ordinarily works, or to which that individual ordinarily reports. It also includes the location where offers are made or accepted. Because the sale of an e-book would not ordinarily involve any negotiation (at least not in the traditional sense), it should be expected that the location of the supplier's office where the offer is made or accepted, will be the relevant location.

In most cases where the supplier operates from a location in Canada, this rule will locate the province of supply as being the province in which the supplier's offices are located. One exception relates to situations where the recipient is only entitled to use the property outside the province. It should be noted, for greater clarity, that if the recipient may only use the property outside Canada, the supply would not be considered to be made in Canada.

Where the recipient may use the property in Canada (and the supply is made in Canada), the use is not restricted to only one province (i.e., the rule in subparagraph 2(*d*)(i)), and it is the case that the property can be used exclusively outside the province of negotiation (the rule in subparagraph 2(*d*)(ii)), then the rule in Section 3 of Part III of Schedule IX should be considered. This rule provides that the supply will be deemed to be made in a participating province where:

(a) the Canadian rights in respect of the property cannot be used otherwise than primarily in the participating provinces; and

(b) where the place of negotiation is outside Canada, the property cannot be used otherwise than exclusively in Canada.

These rules will result in non-resident supplies (where the supply is not restricted to use outside Canada) being deemed to be made in a participating province if the Canadian rights in respect of the property are available to be exercised primarily in the participating provinces. Otherwise, the supply will be subject to GST at the rate of 6%.

(a) E-Commerce Courses and Training

As noted above, e-commerce courses and training are provided in a wide variety of formats and as a result may, if considered to be a single supply, be characterized either as intangible personal property or a service. Where multiple supplies are considered to be made, each supply will be subject to its own place of supply considerations.

Where a single supply (comprised of multiple elements) is made, the "principal object of the supply" test must be applied to determine whether a service or intangible personal property is being supplied. Generally, where electronic educational offerings are supplied and are supported by only minimal technical support, the supply will be characterized as a single supply of intangible personal property.

However, where more extensive service offerings are provided (i.e., beyond technical support) and the service offerings are particularly valuable, the supply will be considered a service. Some of the more extensive service offerings might include training (particularly if onsite at the recipient's office), testing, evaluation services, and consulting services.

It would appear that the relative value of these service offerings (and accordingly the principal object of the supply), will be determined at least in part, by comparing the fees charged in connection with learning packages which involve a no-service component to those offered with a service component. Where there are no alternative packages to be referenced for comparison purposes, it would appear that the CRA is prepared to compare and evaluate the relative value (or relative importance) of the various offerings to determine which offering represents the "principal object".

Where a training program is considered to be a supply of intangible personal property, the supply will be made in Canada if the training program may be used or accessed from Canada. In terms of the application of the HST, the considerations will be the same as those set out under the heading "Electronic Books" above.

Where the supply is considered to be a service, the supply will be made in Canada where any portion of the services are performed in Canada. In most cases, the identification of where the services are performed will be relatively straightforward because the services will be performed in locations referenced by the activities of the supplier's employees. Where the employees travel to the customer's location to provide the services (for example, on-site training services), the customer's office will constitute one of the locations where the services are performed. The supplier's own office will also typically be considered to be a place where services are performed.

However, the extended place of performance rules relating to supplies made through the supplier's equipment should also be considered. For example, if training (or any service which supports the training) is provided through a Web site hosted on a server in Canada, the service will likely be considered to be supplied in Canada. As discussed in ruling 37297 (see Chapter 16), allowing a customer to interact with external consultants (e.g., by chat room and by email) through a supplier's server in Canada constitutes the performance of the service through the server. This suggests that, for example, if a non-resident delivered training related services through a Web site which is hosted on its server in Canada, then the services would be considered to be performed in Canada.

The extended "performance of supply" rules should also be considered where the supplier remotely accesses the customer's computers in connection with the provision of the service. If the supply involves doing something to or with the recipient's computers, the service will be considered to be performed in Canada if the recipient's computers which are accessed are located in Canada. This may include a supplier who accesses a customer's computers to troubleshoot problems with the training software which resides on the customer's computer.

Under paragraph 2(*a*) of Part V of Schedule IX, a service is considered to be supplied in a particular province if all or substantially all of the Canadian element of the service is performed in that particular province. Where this rule does not apply, the service will be performed in the province of negotiation for the supply as long as all or substantially all of the services are not performed outside that province. This rule is contained in paragraph 2(*b*) of Part V.

The third province of supply rule is contained in section 3. This rule provides that if the Canadian element of a service is performed primarily in a participating province (including through equipment located in that province), the province of supply will be that participating province in which the greatest proportion of the services are performed unless the place of negotiation is outside Canada, and not all or substantially all of the service is performed in Canada.

Further, if the supply is considered to be a technical support service relating to the operation or use of computer hardware of software, the special province of supply rules contained in the Place of Supply (GST/HST) Regulations should be considered. These rules, where applicable, override the ordinary province of supply rules described above.

In applying each of the province of supply rules described above, the extended place of performance rules described in TIB 090 should be carefully considered.

D. NON-RESIDENT ISSUES

1. The Non-resident Override

The non-resident override is important with respect to educational supplies because the place of supply rules are extremely broad. The override relief is particularly important with respect to intangible personal property as demonstrated by the following example:

Example

Corporation A operates from offices located in Seoul, Korea and provides the right to its customers to download an electronic book for a fee.

The customers of Corporation A may be located anywhere in the world but for the most part they are individuals residing in Korea.

There are no restrictions placed on the customers as to the location where they may download or use the book.

Given that the book may be downloaded or used anywhere in the world, including Canada, the product will be considered to be supplied in Canada under the section 142 place of supply rules. Applying the province of supply rule in paragraph 3(*d*) of Part III of Schedule IX, the supply would be considered to be made outside the participating provinces.

If the non-resident override were not available this supply (including when made to a customer in Korea who will never actually use the book in Canada) would be subject to GST at the rate of 6%.

Similarly, the place of supply rules relating to a service are quite broad. A non-resident who sends employees into Canada to perform any function or task in connection with the supply will be considered to be making a supply of services in Canada. A service may also be considered, for the reasons set out above, to be supplied in Canada in connection with the equipment of the supplier.

Fortunately, the broad place of supply rules are tempered by the application of the non-resident override. The override will deem the supply to be made outside Canada if the following three conditions are met:

(a) the supplier is a non-resident (and does not make supplies through a permanent establishment in Canada);

(b) the supply is not made in the course of a business carried on in Canada; and

(c) the supplier is not GST registered.

(a) Permanent Establishment Issues

A non-resident will be deemed to be resident in Canada in respect of activities carried on through a permanent establishment in Canada. A permanent establishment is a reference to a fixed place of business of the particular person through which the person makes supplies. It is also a reference to a fixed place of business of another person, other than an independent agent, who is acting in Canada on behalf of the particular person and through whom that person makes supplies in the ordinary course of business.

Most non-residents providing e-books, educational offerings, or other related supplies will not typically encounter problems under the permanent establishment rules. This is because a Web site is not considered by the CRA to constitute a permanent establishment. Accordingly, for example, making supplies through a Web site which is hosted on an ISP server in Canada should not result in a finding that the non-resident has a permanent establishment in Canada. However, where the Web site is hosted on a server which is at the disposal of the non-resident (i.e., leased, owned or otherwise available to the non-resident), the server may be considered a permanent establishment if the activities carried out through the server are significant in relation to the overall business of the person.

Similarly, if the non-resident makes use of the services of a dependent agent to provide supplies, any permanent establishment of the dependent agent may be deemed to be a permanent establishment of the non-resident. In either case, the non-resident would lose the benefit of the non-resident override.

(b) Carrying on Business Issue

A non-resident who makes a supply, including the supply of an e-book or educational supply, in the course of a business carried on in Canada, will not be eligible for the non-resident override. A typical non-resident supplier would easily be able to control and minimize its presence in Canada in order to ensure that it does not encounter difficulties under this rule.

Among the issues to be considered in limiting this exposure are whether the non-resident would have sales representatives in Canada, accept contracts in Canada, process payments in Canada, maintain a bank account in Canada, send employees to Canada to provide services in connection with the supply, or solicit orders by other means in Canada (for example, through Canadian newspapers). The CRA has emphasized that it will take into account a wide range of factors in determining whether a non-resident is carrying on a business in connection with e-commerce supplies. It should be expected that these rules will be applied aggressively where there is a significant potential for revenue loss to the CRA (i.e., where sales are made to Canadian consumers).

(c) Registration Issue

The non-resident who is registered for any reason, including in relation to unrelated supplies. will not be able to operate under the non-resident override.

The non-resident who is not registered, but is required to be registered, will also be unable to avail itself of the override. This is because the non-resident registration requirement is tied to the concepts of making supplies through a permanent establishment (a non-resident who makes supplies through a permanent establishment in Canada is generally required to be registered) and to the concept of carrying on business in Canada (a non-resident who makes supplies in the course of a business carried on in Canada is generally required to be registered).

(d) Planning Issues

Non-residents who make supplies in Canada as a result of the application of the place of supply rules should ensure that they are not deemed to be residents in Canada (i.e., by making supplies through a permanent establishment in Canada), and that they are not considered to be carrying on business in Canada.

Particularly where intangible personal property is being supplied without an appropriate place of use restriction, the risks associated with failing to qualify for the non-resident override are substantial. Consider the following example:

Example

Corporation A is a corporation which operates from offices located in Pasadena, California. It is not GST registered.

It supplies e-books to customers all over the world.

The corporation does not restrict the location where the books may be accessed or used.

To encourage sales in Canada, Corporation A advertises extensively in Canada. It also processes payments in Canada, in respect of Canadian customers, and posts the payments to a Canadian bank account.

Corporation A takes the position that the non-resident override is applicable to its supplies made in Canada.

If the CRA were to determine that Corporation A is in fact carrying on business in Canada, the non-resident override would not apply and Corporation A would be required to be registered unless it is a small supplier.

All of the supplies made by Corporation A, from the time that it is first required to be registered, would be subject to GST including those supplies which are made to non-residents.

Given the substantial risks associated with any failure to meet the requirements of the non-resident override, the non-resident should, when supplying intangible personal property to non-residents, consider contractually limiting their use of the products to locations outside Canada. This will limit the non-resident's exposure in the event that the override fails.

Alternatively, the non-resident may wish to consider registering for GST purposes so that it would charge the GST to the Canadian purchasers of the products. The non-resident would still be free to offer supplies to non-residents which are not subject to GST as long as the appropriate contractual limitations are implemented.

E. ZERO-RATING ISSUES

Where the services considered in this chapter are provided to non-residents, zero-rating will typically be available under either section 7 (general services), section 18 (training services) or section 23 (consulting, professional or advisory services).

Unfortunately, supplies discussed in this chapter which are considered to be intangible personal property will not typically qualify for zero-rating when provided to a non-resident. The CRA seems to take the position that educational products, or e-books delivered electronically, will not in most cases qualify for zero-rating under section 10 of Part V of Schedule VI. Similarly, the CRA seems to take the position that the requirements of section 10 are not met when the right is provided to interact and use an online program or instruction. This shortcoming is exacerbated by the fact that supplies of intangible personal property, when provided by suppliers in an HST province, may be subject to tax at the rate of 14% under the place of negotiation rule. For this reason it is critical that Canadian suppliers ensure that when supplies are made to non-residents the use of the product by the non-resident is limited to a location outside Canada.

F. RULINGS

1. Hard Copy Textbooks with Electronic Offerings

The two rulings described below involve textbooks which are supplemented by one or more electronic offerings.

Ruling 1: Textbooks with CD ROMs

Ruling 53919[1] considers the application of the GST where hardcopy textbooks are sold with a CD ROM in the sleeve of the book. The supplier offers three different textbooks each supported by a CD ROM. The books, which are offered for sale across Canada, are educational in nature.

The CD ROM is a free inclusion with each of the three books the applicant markets. The CD ROM which accompanies the first textbook includes additional self-tests, grammar modules, exercises and case studies. The textbook also provides the Internet address for the applicant's Web site which may be visited for more content. There is no password provided for this Web site as access is available for free to the general public. The second CD ROM contains self-directed activities (aimed at assisting the customer in finding employment) and also contains software to assist in creating cover letters and resumes. The third CD ROM contains audio lectures, practice questions, and tools to track the student's progress.

The two main issues which the applicant has raised are as follows:

(a) How do you characterize the supply when there is a hardcopy book and a CD ROM?

(b) Is the textbook point of sale rebate set out in section 259.1 available in respect of this supply?

The Ruling

The CRA noted, as a threshold issue, that the conclusions contained in this ruling are fact specific and that the same results should not necessarily

---

[1] December 8, 2004.

be expected to apply to other textbook offerings. The CRA further noted that with any supply of a textbook and a CD ROM, there are three potential characterization outcomes:

(a) a single supply is being made;

(b) two distinct supplies are being made and no one supply is incidental to the other; or

(c) two distinct supplies are being made but one supply is incidental to the other.

In determining whether a single supply or multiple supplies were being made, the CRA noted that it would take into account the method of packaging, the labeling of the product, availability of other products, and pricing methodologies. With respect to the three textbook offerings in issue, the CRA ruled that a single supply was in fact being provided.

In reaching this conclusion (that it is a single supply), the CRA acknowledged that the student was made aware prior to purchase that the package included both a CD ROM and a textbook (which would ordinarily suggest multiple supplies). However, because the two items could not be purchased separately, a single supply was considered to be made.

Notwithstanding that a single supply was considered to be made, this supply was not characterized as a textbook or a CD ROM. Instead the CRA concluded that what was being supplied may be referred to as a "new product". According to the CRA, this new product could best be described as "a learning resource which has been packaged together in an integrated format to meet the student's needs".

> In some cases an item that consists of a book and another product packaged together and sold for a single price will be considered to be a single supply of a new product that does not fall within the definition of a printed book.

The CRA concluded that this "new product" is a supply of tangible personal property. Accordingly, the identification of the place of supply of this new product would take into account the location where it was delivered or made available to the purchaser.

The characterization of the product as "a new product" is important in the context of the section 259.1 point of sale HST rebate. That section allows for vendors of "printed books" which are subject to the 14% HST to offer an 8% point of sale rebate to any person purchasing the printed book. However, the CRA concluded that this "new product" is not a "printed book" and accordingly does not qualify for the point of sale rebate. The ruling also suggests that any retailer who erroneously rebates the 8% tax to customers will be held liable for the amount of tax rebated to customers in error.

To ensure that the point of sale rebate is available, the supplier may wish to consider restructuring the offering so that the textbook is considered to be a separate supply of a "printed book". The CRA suggested that if the two offerings could be acquired separately, or if one or more of the elements could be substituted, multiple supplies might be considered to be made. However, it is not clear whether the point of sale rebate would be available if the CD ROM is considered to be part of the single supply as a result of the incidental supply rule.

Conclusions

1. The sale of a textbook with a CD ROM may be considered to be a single supply, or each may be considered to be a separate supply.

2. Where multiple supplies are made, one of the supplies (the CD ROM) might be considered to be incidental to the other supply (the textbook).

3. Where a single supply is made, other than in connection with the incidental supply rule, the supply will be characterized as a "new product" which is not a "printed book".

4. The new product appears to be considered to be a supply of tangible personal property for the purpose of applying the place of supply rules.

5. The point of sale HST rebate provided in section 259.1 will not be available in respect of this new product.

6. Where a single supply is considered to be made as a result of the application of the incidental supply rule, it is not clear whether the single supply would be characterized as "a new product" or a "printed book".

Ruling 2: Textbook with CD ROMs and Internet Access

Ruling 45733[2] also considers the sale of textbooks which are supported by CD ROMs and by access to the supplier's Web site. The purchasers of the textbooks are educational institutions which purchase the books for the purpose of reselling them to students who attend courses provided by the institution.

The supplier sells all of the textbook related supplies, which are in issue in the ruling, for a single price. The marketing materials provided with the textbook indicate that the end user is being provided with Web site access and a CD ROM. The end user (who opens the shrink wrapped package) is provided with a passcode which allows access to a protected Web site which

---

[2] December 8, 2004.

contain additional information and, in some cases, provides access to chat rooms, online journals etc.

The Ruling

The CRA again concluded that the package (which included a textbook, a CD ROM and the right to access a protected Web site) would be considered to be a single supply of a "new product" (i.e., an "extensive learning resource in several formats integrated to meet the recipient's needs"). This new product would not be considered to be a "printed book" for the purpose of the point of sale rebate.

In support of the conclusion that a single supply was provided, the CRA noted that the customer may be aware of the separate elements which are provided (which would suggest multiple supplies), but the distinct elements cannot be purchased separately and there is no opportunity to substitute any of the elements.

The CRA acknowledged that there may be circumstances where a second product may be packaged with a book and the book will be considered to be a "printed book" for the purposes of the rebate. However, it would appear that as long as the items cannot be purchased separately, this test will likely never be met.

It is important to note that the CRA did not characterize this new product for place of supply purposes. Given that the supplies involve an electronic access component, it may be arguable that the supply should be considered to be intangible personal property. However, given that the sale always involves a physical component (the textbook and CD ROM), and given that the CRA has in a long line of rulings held that shrink wrapped products are tangible personal property (including, for example, software), it would appear likely that this product will be characterized as tangible personal property.

Conclusions

1. Where a CD ROM and online access is provided with a text book for a single price, and the three elements cannot be substituted or obtained separately, a single supply will be considered to be made.

2. The single supply will be considered to be a "new product".

3. This new product is not a "printed book" and is not eligible for the HST point of sale rebate.

4. This new product appears to be a supply of tangible personal property (although the CRA did not specifically rule on this issue).

Supplementary Notes

The CRA was asked subsequent to the issuance of this ruling to reconsider its position. In ruling 45733R[3], the CRA again concluded that the printed book point of sale rebate would not be available in respect of the products in issue in this ruling. On this issue, see also ruling 60367[4], which also resulted in a finding that the point of sale rebate is not available for the packaged supply.

Fortunately, notwithstanding the position of the CRA, point of sale rebate relief is now being provided directly by the provinces of Nova Scotia, New Brunswick, and Newfoundland. Those provinces announced on August 18, 2006 that they would provide the point of sale rebate to purchasers in respect of the following:

(a) printed books packaged with a CD ROM if the material on the CD ROM supplements, and is integrated with, the book; and

(b) products specially designed for students enrolled in a qualifying course, consisting of a printed book packaged with a CD ROM, and/or access to a Web site, containing related materials.

Given that the rebate in the circumstances described above is being offered by the provinces (and not by the CRA), issues relating to the scope of the rebate should be resolved by reference to materials issued by the respective provinces.

2. Electronic Books

Ruling 3: Electronic Book Available through Supplier's Web Site

In ruling 41194[5], the electronic book in issue was provided through the supplier's Web site. Once the online sale has been completed, the supplier sends an email to the customer containing a password and a link to the Web site from which the book may be downloaded. The purchaser downloads the book, and is free to read the book from their computer or may even print the book. The supplier also encourages the customers to share the downloaded book with family members.

The purchaser operates from offices located in one of the non-participating provinces.

---

[3] February 13, 2006.

[4] June 3, 2005.

[5] February 25, 2003.

The Ruling

The CRA ruled that this is a supply of intangible personal property. Because the supplier does not contractually restrict the location where the book may be downloaded and used, the supply is considered to be made in Canada including where it is sold to a non-resident customer. Although the supplier provided details of the location of its server, it appears that the CRA regarded this element as being irrelevant.

The CRA also concluded that zero-rating would not be available under section 10 in respect of this supply. It appears that the CRA has taken the position that the supply is not a supply of intellectual property as required by section 10.

Given that the supply is considered to be made in Canada, the CRA also cautioned that this supply could be considered to be one which is subject to HST (including when supplied to non-residents). The starting point for the HST analysis on these facts is the rule in subparagraph 2(d)(ii) of Part III of Schedule IX. This is because the books do not relate to real or tangible personal property or to services, and there are no restrictions as to the province or group of provinces in which the property may be used. If there had been restrictions as to place of use, the rule in subparagraph 2(d)(i) may have applied.

Under subparagraph 2(d)(ii), the supply will be considered to be made in the province of negotiation unless the property may be used exclusively (i.e., 90% or more) outside that province. Given that there are no restrictions as to the province of use, the supply will be deemed to be made in the province of negotiation, regardless of the location of the customer. This rule will also apply to customers located outside of Canada.

As a result, if the supplier's office from which the negotiations occurred is located in one of the participating provinces, the supply when made to Canadian residents (regardless of their province of residence) or when made to non-residents will always be subject to 14% HST.

It should be noted that the delivery of the product through a server located in one of the HST provinces (in circumstances where the supplier does not have an office in the province through which negotiations occur) would not appear to result in the supply being subject to HST. This is because the definition of the "place of negotiation" refers to the location of the supplier's permanent establishment at which the individual principally involved in negotiating for the supplier ordinarily works, or to which the individual normally reports.

An employee would not ordinarily work at, or report to a location, which merely houses a server. As a result, the server will not typically be sufficient to locate the supply in a particular province.

Conclusions

1. The supply of an electronic book will be considered to be a supply of intangible personal property.

2. Where there are no restrictions as to the place where the book may be used, the supply will be considered to be made in Canada.

3. This supply will not be eligible for zero-rating under section 10 when supplied to a non-resident.

4. Where there are no restrictions as to the province in which the book may be used, the supply will be considered to be made in the province of the supplier's office to which the individual responsible for negotiating the contract reports.

Ruling 4: Electronic Book

Ruling 36992[6] considers the supply of electronic books by a Canadian resident supplier. The supplier provides the books both to residents and to non-residents.

The supplier did not previously charge GST when supplies were made to U.S. customers because the sales were concluded in U.S. dollars. The supplier is questioning whether that position is correct.

The Ruling

The CRA ruled that the supply was of intangible personal property:

> Customers who order the e-books are being provided with a copy of the product as well as the right to use the product.

This supply is considered to be made in Canada because there are no contractual restrictions as to the place of use of the property.

The CRA also ruled that the supply would not qualify for zero-rating. This is consistent with the CRA's narrow view of section 10. This narrow approach seems anomalous given that the right which is provided undoubtedly relates to a copyrighted work.

With respect to the HST, the CRA again adopted the approach described in ruling 3, above. This supply is considered to be made in a non-participating province because:

---

[6] October 25, 2002.

(a) there are no restrictions as to the province of use (which precludes the operation of the rule in subparagraph 2(*d*)(i)); and

(b) the supplier's office of negotiation is located in a non-participating province.

Conclusion

See ruling 3 above.

Although neither of rulings 3 or 4 discuss e-books supplied by a non-resident, it should be expected that where e-books are provided by non-residents and there are no restrictions as to the place of use of the property, the book will be considered to be supplied in Canada. This will include situations where the customer is a non-resident person. However, in most cases the non-resident override will provide the necessary tax relief.

Where the supply is made by a non-resident person, the place of negotiation will typically be outside Canada. Accordingly, the province of supply (where there are no restrictions as to use) will be determined by reference to the rules in subsection paragraph 3(*d*) of Part III of Schedule IX. Those rules provide that the supply is deemed to be made in a participating province if the following two conditions are satisfied:

(a) the Canadian rights in respect of the intangible property cannot be used otherwise than primarily in the participating provinces; and

(b) where the place of negotiation is outside Canada, the property cannot be used otherwise than exclusively in Canada.

In the situation involving a non-resident supplier as outlined above, neither of these conditions would be satisfied, and the supply would not be subject to the HST. Again, the non-resident override will in most cases provide the necessary relief from all forms of Division II GST.

In circumstances where the non-resident does not collect the GST from a Canadian purchaser who acquires the rights to download and use the book, the purchaser will be required to self-assess the GST owing under Division IV. The applicable rate of tax would be 14% where the recipient is a resident of a participating province.[7]

3. E-Commerce Courses and Education

The rulings set out below demonstrate how the level of human involvement in the supply directly affects the characterization of the supply.

---

[7] See section 218.1 of the ETA.

Ruling 5: Distant Learning

Ruling 32573[8] considers a distant learning package which is provided by a Canadian GST registered person to customers located both in and outside of Canada. The learning package resides on a server in Canada. It is not clear whether the program will download to the customer's computer or whether it will execute on the supplier's server.

The Ruling

The CRA ruled that the distant learning education package is a supply of intangible personal property:

> ... the supply of the right to access the XXXX, the principal object of which is to allow the recipient to access, use and retrieve information or to interact with the site while on-line, would be considered to be a supply of intangible personal property.

In reaching this conclusion the CRA undoubtedly took into consideration that the only human involvement associated with this supply was the development of the learning package. This type of human involvement is considered to be an input to the supply.

Given that there were no restrictions as to place of use of the learning package, the supply is considered to be made in Canada.

The CRA specifically noted that this supply would not qualify for zero-rating under section 10 or under any other section.

In terms of the HST, the CRA noted that the primary province of supply rule is contained in subparagraph 2(d)(i) of Part III of Schedule IX. That rule provides that a supply of intangible personal property will be made in a particular province where all or substantially all of the Canadian rights in respect of the property may be used only in that province. Where there are no restrictions regarding the province in which the property may be used, the rule in subparagraph 2(d)(i) will not apply.

The rule in subparagraph 2(d)(ii) provides that a supply of intangible personal property will be considered to be made in a province if the place of negotiation is in the province, and the property may be used otherwise than exclusively outside the province. Where there are no restrictions (as is the case here) regarding the province in which the property may be used, it will always be the case that the property may be used otherwise than exclusively outside the province of negotiation. Accordingly, where the place of negotiation is outside of the HST provinces, then under subparagraph 2(d)(ii) the supply will be deemed to be made in that province and subject to GST at 6%.

---

[8] April 4, 2003.

Conclusions

1. The supply of online educational tools which does not involve any human interaction will be considered a supply of intangible personal property.

2. The supply will be considered to be made in Canada where there are no restrictions as to the place where the property may be used.

3. Where there are no restrictions as to the province in which the supply may be used, the supply will be considered to be made in the province of the supplier's office of negotiation.

Ruling 6: Education Supported by Some Human Involvement

Ruling 36218[9] considered the application of the GST to distant learning supplies from the perspective of the person who is the recipient of the supply. The Canadian resident recipient has enquired as to the tax status of three different offerings which it had purchased from suppliers. The first two offerings are educational in nature and are summarized below. The third offering which relates to software maintenance contracts is discussed briefly in Chapter 14, Software and Software Related Offerings.

Offering #1

The CRA ruled that although an interactive learning program could be either intangible personal property or a service (or multiple supplies), based on these facts, and given the minimal service component, the supply would be a single supply of intangible property.

Ruling on Offering #1

The CRA ruled that although an interactive learning program could be either intangible personal property or a service (or could be multiple supplies), based on these facts, and given the minimal service component, the supply would be a single supply of intangible property.

> Where there is a single supply, and the principal object of the supply is access to a software application that is maintained on the supplier's Web site, to interact with the software while online (i.e., the right to access and interact with the software program while online), it is the CRA's position that the supply is characterized as intangible personal property . . .

On the facts the CRA concluded that the supply would likely be considered a single supply of intangible property because the primary object is the access to the program:

---

[9] February 5, 2004.

... it appears that the access to the on-line training programs on the non-resident's Web site, where together with the access the non-resident may provide support services, is a supply of intangible personal property where the primary object of the supply is the right to access and interact with the program.

The suggestion seems to be that where some minimal technical support is provided in respect of the educational program, this will not typically result in the conclusion that multiple supplies are being made or that the supply is a service.

The CRA also noted that the property would be considered to be supplied in Canada because of the rights provided to access the program from Canada. However, the CRA also noted that the non-resident override would likely apply to deem the supply to be made outside Canada. Where the supply is deemed to be made outside Canada, the recipient would typically be required to self-assess the tax owing under Division IV.

The CRA also commented on the potential application of the HST in circumstances where the non-resident supplier is registered and cannot avail itself of the non-resident override. The rules to be applied, according to the CRA, are those contained in subparagraphs 2(d)(i) and (ii) of Part III of Schedule IX. The CRA concluded that by applying the rule in subparagraph 2(d)(ii), the supply would be deemed to be made in a non-participating province (and subject to GST at the rate of 6%) because the place of negotiation is outside of the participating provinces. Unfortunately, this conclusion seems to be anomalous.

In particular, the rule in subparagraph 2(d)(ii) establishes place of supply rules which only apply where the place of negotiation is in "a province". However, where the supplier operates from offices located in another country, the place of negotiation will never be in a Canadian province. It would appear that the HST rules which should have been considered are those contained in subparagraphs 3(d)(i) and (ii) of Part III of Schedule IX.

Offering #2

The second offering was in the nature of educational consulting services. The supplier provided written reports and recommendations to the applicant by way of email. Typical subjects covered included how to design a computer network. The parties intended that the customer would use the information provided to design and implement its own systems.

Ruling on Offering #2

The CRA ruled that if this supply involved specific work done for a specific person, and did not involve a right to use an existing product, the supply would be a supply of a service.

In practice, this determination can be very difficult to make because the two elements are not typically mutually exclusive. Specific work can be done for a specific person which involves the right to use existing products. Those existing products may be tailored for the particular customer or the existing products may be supplemented by specific work done for the customer (i.e., the supplier provides general information but also answers questions relating to the interpretation of the general information).

Unfortunately, the CRA did not offer guidance on the manner in which this test should be applied where both specific work is performed and the right to use existing materials is provided. However, it would appear that if the supplier prepares customized reports which have been researched and written in response to specific customer questions, this would be a supply of a service.

Conversely, if the supplier merely provided a bundle of generic reports (and these same reports are also provided to other customers), this would appear to be a supply of intangible personal property. However, what is not clear is how the distinction is to be made where a minimal degree of customization is provided. Another difficult distinction issue relates to circumstances where the supplier customizes the supply, but only by deleting existing information or reports which are not relevant to the particular purchaser.

The suggestion seems to be that the supplier will be required on the particular facts to make a judgment call as to the principal object of the supply.

On the facts of this ruling, the distinction does not appear to be relevant. Although the supply, if considered to be intangible personal property, would be supplied in Canada under the place of supply rules, the non-resident override would likely apply since the non-resident is not GST registered. If the supply were considered to be a service, it would be considered to be supplied outside Canada because employees of the supplier operate from premises outside Canada and merely email the reports to the customer in Canada.

Conclusions

1. The provision of the right to use and interact with an online educational software program will be considered a supply of intangible personal property.

2. The right to use and interact with an online educational software program will also be a single supply of intangible personal property where a minimal amount of technical support is provided for the customer, as long as the technical support does not alter the principal object of the supply.

3. The supply will be considered to be made in Canada where the rights to use the program may be exercised from a location in Canada.

4. Where the supplier is a non-resident who is registered, and there are no restrictions as to the province of use, the province of supply might be determined in accordance with the rules contained in subparagraph 2(*d*)(ii) of Part III of Schedule IX. However, this conclusion appears to be anomalous given that the non-resident supplier would not negotiate the contract from a Canadian province.

5. With respect to an educational consulting supply, if the supply involves specific work done for a specific person and does not involve a right to use an existing product, a service will be supplied.

Ruling 7: Education with Some Human Involvement

Ruling 42608[10] considers the supply of various packages of electronic exercises.

The psychological exercises were previously offered by the supplier only in person. The client would historically attend at the supplier's office where they would sort cards which were presented to them. The manner in which they sorted the cards allowed for conclusions to be drawn by the test administrator.

The applicant now offers the tests in an online format. The applicant owns the patents to the tests and maintains the Web site and administers the business.

The customer selects a package through the Web site. The basic package does not provide for any human involvement. The customer sorts the cards online and is provided with a computer generated analysis of the results.

The more expensive packages involve live consultations (by way of telephone) with progressively more senior consultants (for higher fees) to discuss the results of the tests.

---

[10] February 19, 2003.

The Ruling

The CRA ruled that the basic package is a supply of intangible personal property because there is no human involvement in the making of the supply.

As long as the Web site contract provides that the test cannot be undertaken by a person from a location in Canada, the supply will be considered to be made outside Canada.

Where the supply is made in Canada (i.e., the test is available to be taken by a person while in Canada), zero-rating will not be available. This is consistent with the CRA's narrow view of the section 10 zero-rating provision.

The CRA determined that the identification of the province of supply will turn on the application of the rules contained in subparagraph 2(d)(ii) of Part III of Schedule IX. This is because there are no restrictions as to the province where the property may be used (the rule in subparagraph 2(d)(i)). Under the rule in subparagraph 2(d)(ii), the supply is considered to be made in the province of the supplier's place of negotiation. Since the supplier's office is located in other than a participating province, the supply is only subject to GST including when supplied to non-residents.

The more advanced packages are considered to be a single supply of a service. This conclusion seems to have involved the application of the principal object test. The application of that test seems to have resulted in the conclusion that the intangible property component of the supply is of relatively inconsequential value as compared to the services component. The ruling does not, however, describe the fees which were charged for the various packages.

This service is performed in Canada because the consultants who provide the service are located in Canada. However, the service would ordinarily qualify for zero-rating under section 23 when supplied to a non-resident. When the services are supplied to a Canadian resident, the rule in paragraph 2(a) of Part V of Schedule IX establishes that the services are performed in other than a participating province and are taxable at 6%. This is because all or substantially all of the portion of the services performed in Canada, are performed in a non-participating province (i.e., at the supplier's office).

The ruling notes that the services might qualify as exempt. However, the ruling does not describe the provision under which this exemption might be granted. The grounds for exemption which the CRA seems to have considered are found in Part II of Schedule V which relates to certain medical services. Among the exemptions is a supply made by a practitioner relating to psychological services (see section 7 of Part II of Schedule V).

This ruling demonstrates how the characterization of the supply as a service provides for substantially greater opportunities for zero-rating where non-resident customers are involved.

Conclusions

1. The supply of testing of individuals through an online evaluation program and the provision of automatic evaluation results is a supply of intangible personal property.

2. The supply will be considered to be made in Canada if the test may be accessed from Canada.

3. The supply when provided to a non-resident will not qualify for zero-rating.

4. When the supply is made to a Canadian resident, and there are no restrictions as to the province of use, the province of supply will turn on the place of negotiation. If the place of negotiation is in a participating province, the supply will be taxed at 14%. Otherwise the supply will be taxed at 6%.

5. Where the online testing of individuals is supported by one on one interactive consultations with respect to the results, and the principal object of the supply is the service component, the supply will be considered to be a single supply of a service.

6. The service will be considered to be supplied in Canada where the supplier operates from premises in Canada.

7. The services when supplied to a non-resident will be zero-rated under section 23. Where the services are supplied to Canadian residents and the supplier operates from a single Canadian province the province of supply will be that single Canadian province.

Ruling 8: Education with More Human Involvement

Ruling 34397[11] considers the supply of an educational program which relates to learning to play keyboard instruments. The supplier is an Ontario corporation which is GST registered. The customers of the supplier are government agencies, schools, private and commercial music training centres, and individuals.

---

[11] September 23, 2002.

The program resides on a server which is owned by the supplier and which is located in the supplier's offices. The supplier's employees regularly maintain and upgrade the program. The users are not (with one exception) entitled to download any permanent file to their computer. Each individual user is provided with an access code to enable access to the supplier's Web site and program.

Technical support is not provided with the basic package. However, an enhanced package includes the right to receive technical support relating to both the curriculum and relating to technical issues associated with the use of the program.

For larger institutional clients, the supplier will provide training for the customer's instructor. This training is provided either at the supplier's office or at the customer's office. In some cases the customer's office is located outside of Canada.

The Ruling

The basic package (which involves no technical support) is considered to be a supply of intangible personal property. With respect to supplies involving access to the program and technical support, the CRA held that this may be either a single supply or multiple supplies. Where a single supply is made, and the principal object of the supply is the access to a software application, the supply will be intangible personal property:

> ... it appears that the access to the online interactive music program supplied to a school, where together with the access, the Company provides technical and curriculum support, and systems that assist in the administration, evaluation and monitoring of the student's progress, is a single supply where the primary object of the supply is the right to access and interact with the program and, as such, a supply of intangible personal property.

Although the CRA concluded on these facts that a single supply was provided (and that this supply should be considered to be intangible personal property), the CRA did not rule out the possibility that multiple supplies could in similar circumstances be considered to be made.

The training services were considered separately. The CRA noted that if the training is considered to be a separate supply from the single supply set out above, the training will be considered to be a service. However, where the training is provided with the access, and is considered to be part of the single supply of access, the supply will be considered to be a supply of intangible personal property if the principal object of the single supply is the right to access and interact with the software application. The CRA made no suggestion as to which of these two interpretations should be adopted.

Intangible Personal Property

The place of supply of the single supply of the intangible personal property will turn on whether there are any contractual restrictions relating to the place where the program may be used. The supply will be made in Canada where there are no such restrictions:

> ... where the agreement for the supply does not specifically restrict the client's access to the program to the location of the school, or otherwise, the supply will be considered to be made in Canada. However, if the agreement for the supply states that the client may only access the program from computers located in a specified school and that school is located outside Canada, the supply is considered to be made outside Canada.

Where the supply is made to a non-resident person zero-rating will not be available:

> ... there are no provisions in Schedule VI to the ETA that would zero rate the supply by the company of access and interaction with its software application while on line.

The determination of the rate of tax which will apply to the supply will turn on the application of the rules in subparagraphs 2(*d*)(i) and (ii) of Part III of Schedule IX. Under subparagraph 2(*d*)(i), the supply will be considered to be made in a particular province if all or substantially all of the Canadian rights in respect of the property may only be used in that province. The CRA provided the following example of the manner in which this result may come about:

> ... if the agreement for the supply of the access stated that the program could only be accessed from computers that are located in a specified school and that school was located in Ontario, the supply of the access would be considered to be made in Ontario.

However, where there are no restrictions as to the province in which the supply may be used, the rule in subparagraph 2(*d*)(i) cannot apply. The rule in subparagraph 2(*d*)(ii) may then apply by default. As a result of this rule, the supply will be deemed to be made in the province of negotiation. If neither of these rules results in the application of any of the deeming rules, the rule in section 3 of Part III of Schedule IX must be considered. This will include situations where the supply is made by a non-resident.

The Services

Assuming that the training services are considered to be a separate supply, these services will be considered to be supplied in Canada if any element of the training is provided in Canada.

The CRA did, however, suggest that the training could be provided outside of Canada "if no part of the activities carried out by the company in performing the training service are carried out in Canada ...". This raises the difficult issue of identifying the scope of the training services. For example, an employee, prior to traveling to the U.S. to provide training would no doubt do background work in the home office to prepare. Would these background tasks constitute the performance of training services or does the performance of the service only begin once the supplier begins to interact with the customer?

In circumstances where the service is not zero-rated, the service will be supplied in a particular province where all or substantially all of the Canadian element of the service is performed in that province. The CRA noted that in most cases this rule would be sufficient to locate the province of supply, because the training for a particular customer would ordinarily be provided in one location (which could be either the supplier's offices or the customers offices).

Training services provided to non-residents would typically qualify for zero rating pursuant to section 7.

Conclusions

1. The right to access an online educational software program will be considered to be a supply of intangible personal property.

2. The right to access an online educational program supported by technical support, may be considered to be either a single supply or multiple supplies. If multiple supplies are made, the access is intangible personal property, and the technical support (if it involves human interaction) will be a supply of a service. If a single supply is made, and the principal object of the supply is the right to access the online program, the supply will be intangible personal property.

3. The right to access an online program is considered to be supplied in Canada where the program may be accessed from Canada.

4. Where there are no restrictions as to the province in which the program may be accessed, the program will be considered to be supplied in the province of negotiation.

5. Zero-rating is not available in respect of the supply of the right to access an online program.

6. If the training services provided by the supplier are considered to be a separate supply, the services will be supplied in the location where any activity relating to the performance of the service occurs.

7. The training will normally qualify for zero rating under section 7 when supplied to a non-resident.

8. Where the training is provided to a customer in a single location, the service will be considered to be supplied in that particular province.

Chapter 18

Indians and Band Councils

A. OVERVIEW

This chapter outlines some of the special tax considerations associated with making e-commerce related supplies to Indians and to related entities.[1] The primary issue relates to section 87 of the *Indian Act* (Canada), which provides that:

(1) Notwithstanding any other Act of Parliament or any Act of the legislature of a province, but subject to section 83 and section 5 of the *First Nations Fiscal and Statistical Management Act*, the following property is exempt from taxation:

(a) the interest of an Indian or a band in reserve lands or surrendered lands; and

(b) the personal property of an Indian or a band situated on a reserve.

(2) No Indian or band is subject to taxation in respect of the ownership, occupation, possession or use of any property mentioned in paragraph (1)(a) or (b) or is otherwise subject to taxation in respect of any such property.

In addition to the *Indian Act* the determination of whether a particular transaction is subject to GST may also require the examination of any treaties or other agreements entered into by the particular Indian Band. Further, to determine whether GST applies, Remission Orders issued by the Governor General in Council should also be considered. The interpretation of all of the above may also require an examination of the Canadian Constitution and corresponding common law.

Given this complex background, suppliers of e-commerce offerings will, when making such supplies to Indians or related entities, bear a considerable responsibility to ensure that the supply is subject to appropriate tax treatment.

B. ISSUES

1. Characterization Issues

At the outset it should be noted that the characterization of e-commerce supplies provided to Indians or related entities will involve the same considerations as where e-commerce supplies are provided to other than Indian recipients. There are no special characterization rules to be applied.

---

[1] Throughout this chapter the term "Indian" is referenced because this is the term used in the legislation (such as the *Indian Act*), and in CRA publications.

2. Exemptions

The fundamental issue relates to the identification of the circumstances in which GST should be charged on a particular supply. The CRA has administratively created a series of guiding principles to be used to determine whether a particular supply will qualify for exempt status. This guidance is intended to give effect to the direction provided in section 87 of the *Indian Act*.

Generally, those rules require that there be a particular connection between the reserve (or reserve activities), and the supply in order for the supply to be tax exempt. The complete guidance is contained in TIB B-039R3, "Application of GST to Indians" ("TIB 039R3").

3. TIB 039R3 Guidance

TIB 039R3 provides guidance which is broken down in relation to supplies of tangible personal property, intangible personal property, and services. Where services are supplied, a separate set of special rules are set out for Band Empowered Entities ("BEEs") and Indian Bands. Most of the exemptions, which are set out below, require that the vendor obtain supporting documentation from the purchaser.

(a) Tangible Personal Property

With respect to tangible personal property an exemption will be available when the property is acquired on the reserve by either an Indian, an Indian Band, or an unincorporated BEE. The reference to "on reserve" appears to be a reference both to the location from which the supplier operates, and to the place where the goods are delivered.

Incorporated BEEs may purchase goods on an exempt basis where the goods are delivered to the reserve, and the property is purchased for band management activities. The term "band management activities" is an administratively defined term. The activities will only qualify where they are not ones in respect of which an input tax credit may be claimed. The CRA defines the term "band management activities" in part as follows:

> "band management activities" are activities or programs undertaken by a band or band empowered entity that are not commercial activities for which they would otherwise be entitled to an input tax credit.

Where the tangible personal property is acquired off-reserve (i.e., from a vendor located off the reserve), the property may be purchased on an exempt basis by an Indian, an Indian Band, or an unincorporated BEE, if the property is delivered by the supplier or its agent to the reserve. With respect to incorporated BEEs, all the conditions set out above must be met, and in addition, the property must be purchased for band management activities.

The CRA takes a strict view of the delivery requirement. For example, GST will apply if an Indian uses his or her own vehicle to bring the property to the reserve.

(b) Intangible Personal Property

The CRA notes that relief will be provided in respect of intangible personal property where the property "is situated on the reserve". The CRA explains that intangible personal property will meet this test where there are sufficient factors to connect it to the reserve. One of the examples provided in TIB 039R3 relates to a golf membership which will qualify for relief because the membership rights can only be exercised on the reserve (i.e., the golf course is located on the reserve).

The CRA notes that software supplied over the Internet will be exempt where the Indian lives on the reserve, and the supplier can demonstrate that the software was downloaded to a computer on the reserve. There is no discussion of the manner in which the tax might apply to software which does not download to the user's computer (i.e., remote access), or to other supplies of digitized content (for example, music, video games, information sites etc).

(c) Services Provided to Individual Indians

The services rules for individual Indians are broken down by type of service. The category of services referred to in TIB 039R3 as "services for property" (for example, repair services in respect of vehicles) will be exempt where the service is performed totally on the reserve, and the property is located on the reserve. The category of services referred to as "services for individuals" (which appears to be a reference to services which do not relate to property and might include a service such as a haircut), will be exempt where the service is performed totally on the reserve, and the recipient of the service is located on the reserve at the time the service is performed. The CRA explains in TIB 039R3 that where services are not totally performed on the reserve, the services will be taxable unless the services are "for real property interests on a reserve". The suggestion seems to be that services which are performed even in part off-reserve will be taxable unless the requisite connection can be made to real property interests on-reserve.

The use of the term "for real property" is unusual. The ETA contains numerous references to tests which are based on the concept of an "in respect of" or "in relation to" connection. However, the ETA does not for any purpose reference a "for" connection test. It is not known whether the "for real property" test (or the corresponding "services for property" test), is intended to be a narrow or broad test, or how it might compare to the "in respect of" or "in relation to" tests. As a result, it should be expected that there will be difficulties in interpreting the portions of TIB 039R3 which rely upon this connection concept.

(d) Services Provided to BEEs or Indian Bands

Services are exempt when acquired by BEEs (incorporated or unincorporated) or by an Indian Band for band management activities or "for real property" on a reserve. These services will qualify even where they are performed off-reserve.

It would appear that most e-commerce supplies will not be capable of meeting the "for real property" test. However, if in fact the "for real property" test is broader than the "in respect of" test, it may be possible that some software may be sufficiently connected. For example, software which relates to land management activities or to the construction of buildings might qualify. Given that the scope of the "for real property" is an unknown variable, there is, at this time, no way of predicting with any certainty how the GST might apply in the circumstances.

The "purpose" test (i.e., services acquired for the purpose of band management activities), however, appears to be far more broad and perhaps may be relied upon to find relief.

4. Planning Opportunities

The administrative exempting guidelines described above are notoriously broad and appear capable of supporting a multitude of different interpretations. Further, the guidelines are extremely general and provide only limited guidance with respect to e-commerce related issues.

Persons seeking exemption in respect of e-commerce supplies made to Indians, BEEs, or Indian Bands should consider the connecting factors tests set out in TIB 039R3. The challenge will then be to attempt to relate those administrative tests to the specific e-commerce guidance provided in TIB 090 and in the e-commerce rulings.

There may be opportunities to use the more general e-commerce guidance (in TIB 090) to argue by analogy, that a particular supply is sufficiently connected to the reserve that it should not be subject to tax. For example, the TIB 090 administrative place of performance rules for services might be used to support the position that there is a strong connection between a particular service and the reserve.

It should also be noted that the administrative guidelines in TIB 039R3 remain largely untested. It may be possible to develop alternative positions based upon the direction provided in the *Indian Act* or by reference to constitutional documents.

C. RULINGS

Ruling 1: Software with Support Plan

Ruling 51795[2] considers the supply to a BEE of software which is supported by a support plan. The support plan provides the BEE with access to technical support in the form of troubleshooting. Technical support is also provided for issues relating to the general operation of the software.

The software was downloaded at the BEE's office and was intended to be used within that office. The BEE office is not located on the reserve.

The supplier invoiced the BEE for an amount of GST in connection with the license of the software and in connection with the supply of the support plan. The BEE has questioned whether the supplier's position is correct.

The Ruling

The CRA noted that under section 87 of the *Indian Act*, property must be consumed on a reserve in order to qualify for GST relief.

The Software

The CRA further explained that where intangible personal property is supplied (in this case the software), the property will be considered to have been consumed on the reserve where the rights in respect of the property may only be exercised on the reserve. This test would not be met on the facts of this ruling because the rights were allowed to be exercised at the BEE's office which is located off reserve.

The CRA also provided a second more lenient test which, if met, would result in the property being considered to be consumed on reserve. This test considers whether the software is "connected" to the reserve. The software will be considered to be "connected to the reserve" where both of the following tests are met:

---

[2] March 14, 2005.

(a) the software is provided to an Indian that lives on a reserve, to an Indian Band on a reserve or to a BEE that maintains a physical presence on a reserve; and

(b) the software provider can establish that the software is downloaded onto a computer on the reserve at the time of acquisition.

On the facts this second test also would not be met. This is because the software was downloaded to a computer which is located off reserve.

It should be noted that the CRA did not apply its "purpose" test (i.e., the test which allows for exemption where a supply is acquired by a BEE off reserve but for band management activities) to this particular supply. It would appear that the purpose test is only available in respect of services, and not intangible personal property. It follows that for software there must be a restriction of use to the reserve (test #1) or a download to a computer on the reserve (test #2).

The Support Plan

The CRA explained that the threshold issue with respect to the support plan relates to whether the plan is considered to be a separate supply or whether it is a component of the single supply of the software. The CRA suggested that if there were no separate charge for the plan, a single supply of software would be provided.

If the plan is a separate supply, a determination would be required to be made as to whether it is in the nature of intangible personal property (i.e., the right to receive updates, right to use online documentation etc.) or a service (i.e., interactive technical support). The resolution of this issue would involve the same considerations as where the supply is provided to any other person.

If it is determined that the support plan is a separate supply of a service, the CRA noted that the service would not be taxable if it was acquired by the BEE for band management activities or "for real property on a reserve". The CRA concluded the issue by merely referencing TIB 039R2. It would appear arguable that the support plan, if considered a service, would be eligible for exemption under the purpose test.

If it is determined that the support plan is a separate supply of intangible personal property, the second test would be applied. This test would require download to a computer on reserve and a supply made to a BEE which maintains a presence on reserve. Because the supply is not in the nature of a service, the purpose test relief would not be available.

Alternative Factual Situations

The applicant asked that the CRA consider the manner in which the GST would apply where the software and support plan are acquired at an office located on the reserve but for use at the off-site location.

The CRA ruled with respect to the software license that the first test would not be met. This is because the software could be used other than exclusively on the reserve. The second, more liberal test might provide relief, however, if the software is downloaded to a computer on the reserve.

The CRA was less specific with respect to the support plan. It suggested that if the support plan is a service, the tests in TIB 039R2 should be consulted to see if there would be sufficient connection to the reserve (as the service is acquired for qualifying band management activities). If however, the support plan is intangible personal property, the connecting factors test would be required to be considered (i.e., where does the software download).

The applicant also questioned whether the tax treatment would be preferable where the software is provided on a physical carrier medium. The CRA noted that generally where tangible personal property is delivered to a reserve, the supply will be exempt. However, where the recipient is an incorporated BEE, the property must in addition be acquired for band management activities.

Conclusions

1. Where intangible personal property is supplied, an exemption will be available if the property may only be used on the reserve.

2. Where intangible personal property is supplied which may be used other than on the reserve, an exemption will be available if the software is downloaded to a computer on the reserve and the software is provided to an Indian that lives on a reserve, to an Indian Band on a reserve, or to a BEE that maintains a physical presence on a reserve.

3. Where a software related service is provided, the service will be exempt if it is performed entirely on the reserve. However, an exemption would also be available if the service is acquired by a BEE for band management activities or "for real property on a reserve".

4. Computer software supplied on a disk will be exempt if the disk is delivered to the reserve, except that, if the recipient is an incorporated BEE, the property must also be acquired for band management activities.

Ruling 2: Web Site Hosting

Ruling 31085[3] considered the provision of Web site hosting to Indians. In scenario A, Web site hosting is provided alone (i.e., the package does not include Internet access). In scenario B, the Web site hosting is provided as a package along with Internet access.

The Ruling

Scenario A

The CRA ruled that this is a service which is other than a telecommunication service. If the service is performed exclusively on the reserve, GST would not apply. The service will be considered to be performed at least partially off-reserve if:

(a) the service requires a person to perform a task, and that task is performed off reserve; or

(b) the service includes operations performed by the supplier's computer equipment and any of that equipment is located off-reserve.

It would appear that this test could never be met where the supplier operates from a location off reserve. While there may not be any specific tasks performed by individuals off reserve (i.e., the test in paragraph (a) above), there will always be tasks performed off reserve in connection with the supplier's computer equipment. In this case it was held that the hosting service would not meet the test for relief because Web site hosting is carried out at the supplier's head office.

The second test which might provide relief is the purpose test. That test provides that where an Indian band, tribal council or BEE purchases the Web site hosting for band management activities or for real property interests on the reserve, the GST does not apply. The purchaser would need to provide the certificate described in TIB 039R3 in support of this exemption.

Scenario B

The CRA considers this to be a supply of a telecommunication service. The supply by the ISP is typically a single supply of:

(a) a connection to the Internet;

(b) an email account; and

(c) space on the ISP's server.

---

[3] February 26, 2002.

Administratively, the CRA takes the position that the predominant purpose of this combined supply is the connection to the Internet. As a result it is a single supply of a telecommunication service.

When this service is provided to an individual Indian it will be tax exempt only if provided on a reserve. Administratively, the CRA takes the position that the supply is exempt where:

(a) the recipient is a resident of the reserve; and

(b) the invoice is sent to the reserve address.

The supplier of the service is required to maintain documentation to support that the supply was made to an Indian who is registered under the *Indian Act*. The CRA will accept a notation on the invoice/sales document of the registry number of the band number and family number.

Where the supply is made to an Indian band, tribal council, or BEE, it is not subject to tax when acquired (either on or off the reserve) for band management activities. The supplier is required to obtain a certificate from the recipient attesting to the intended use.

Conclusions

1. The supply of Web site hosting alone is considered to be a supply of a service which is not a telecommunication service.

2. If the service is performed using the supplier's equipment which is located off-reserve, the service will be considered to be performed off-reserve and will not qualify for relief under the primary test. However, where an Indian band, tribal council, or BEE is the recipient of the supply of Web site hosting, the supply will be exempt as long as the service is acquired for band management activities or for real property interests on the reserve.

3. The supply of an Internet access package alone but which includes Web site hosting, is considered to be a supply of a telecommunication service. When the service is supplied to an individual Indian, it will be exempt if the recipient is a resident of the reserve and the invoice is sent to a reserve address.

4. Where the package is provided to an Indian band, tribal council or BEE, either on or off the reserve, GST will not apply if the package is acquired for qualifying band management activities.

Ruling 3: Tangible Personal Property Sold over the Internet

Ruling 61756[4] considers the sale to an Indian of tangible personal property over the Internet. The customer is an Indian who sent digital images to the applicant for processing. The applicant is a GST registered entity which operates from a location which is off the reserve.

The applicant delivers the prints to the customer on the reserve. The ruling suggests that the payment for the processing is made by credit card over the Internet and the prints are mailed out to the customer.

The Ruling

The CRA ruled that tangible personal property was being supplied. It also ruled that this supply would be GST exempt as long as the applicant delivered the prints to the reserve and the applicant obtained proof of the customer's registration under the *Indian Act*. The CRA suggested that in order to satisfy this evidentiary requirement the customer should send in to the applicant a copy of their Indian status card.

Conclusions

Tangible personal property may be sold over the Internet to an Indian on an exempt basis, but the vendor must deliver the property to the reserve and must obtain a copy of the customer's status card.

---

[4] November 16, 2005

Topical Index